Civil Society in British History

Civil Society in British History

Ideas, Identities, Institutions

EDITED BY
JOSE HARRIS

OXFORD
UNIVERSITY PRESS

OXFORD
UNIVERSITY PRESS

Great Clarendon Street, Oxford OX2 6DP

Oxford University Press is a department of the University of Oxford.
It furthers the University's objective of excellence in research, scholarship,
and education by publishing worldwide in

Oxford New York

Auckland Cape Town Dar es Salaam Hong Kong Karachi
Kuala Lumpur Madrid Melbourne Mexico City Nairobi
New Delhi Shanghai Taipei Toronto

With offices in

Argentina Austria Brazil Chile Czech Republic France Greece
Guatemala Hungary Italy Japan South Korea Poland Portugal
Singapore Switzerland Thailand Turkey Ukraine Vietnam

Oxford is a registered trade mark of Oxford University Press
in the UK and in certain other countries

Published in the United States
by Oxford University Press Inc., New York

First published 2003
First published in paperback 2005

British Library Cataloguing in Publication Data
Data available

Library of Congress Cataloging in Publication Data
Data available

Typeset by Hope Services (Abingdon) Ltd.
Printed in Great Britain
on acid-free paper by
Biddles Ltd
King's Lynn, Norfolk

ISBN 0-19-926020-6   978-0-19-926020-1
ISBN 0-19-927910-1 (Pbk.)   978-0-19-927910-4 (Pbk.)

1 3 5 7 9 10 8 6 4 2

Preface and Acknowledgements

THIS BOOK, WHICH draws upon the very disparate specialist research interests of its contributors, stemmed from a series of informal meetings, workshops, and seminars held in 1999–2001 by a group of historians working in Oxford. The common theme of these meetings was to investigate the various uses of the ubiquitous but ill-defined term 'civil society', and its applicability (if any) to the understanding of British ideas, institutions, and relations with other cultures, over the past several hundred years. Participants in those meetings included a number of friends and colleagues who do not appear in the final volume, but whose thoughts contributed substantially to its final shape. The authors would particularly like to thank Ewen Green, Janet Howarth, Ross Mckibbin, and John Robertson for their input at various stages. Our late colleague, Colin Matthew, was also an active participant in early discussions, and it will be a matter of regret to many that his projected contribution on 'Civil Society and the Union of England and Wales, Scotland, and Ireland' was never written. Another person who deserves mention is Asa Briggs, who for many years fostered conviviality and argument among Oxford historians of modern Britain. With Asa's retirement conviviality declined, but the legacy of argument fortunately remains. Ruth Parr and Anne Gelling gave helpful advice about the final shape of the project and its conversion into a book. After the project was complete, the contributors had the good fortune to be invited to share their ideas with a number of Japanese historians at two international research seminars, held at the Kobe Institute, and at the International Research Center for Japanese Studies attached to the University of Kyoto. Although these two seminars came too late to affect the text of the completed work, their very lively discussions strongly confirmed what had become a central theme of an otherwise very diverse project—that conceptions of 'civil society', both in theory and in institutional practice, varied widely according to historical and cultural context. The authors would especially like to acknowledge the help of Professor Kumie Inose, Professor Haita Kawakatsu, and Professor Minoru Takada in arranging these seminars. The editor of the volume, Jose Harris, would personally like to thank the Leverhulme Foundation, whose generous support while she was a research professor opened up the possibility of thinking about long-term perspectives that often get obscured by the pressures of research specialization. Grateful thanks also to St Catherine's College, the Queen's College, and the Oxford Modern History faculty, for the occasional 'beer and sandwiches' lunches that kept the project going.

Contents

List of Contributors

John Davis is a fellow of the Queen's College, Oxford, and author of *Reforming London: The London Government Problem 1855–1900* (1988). His current research is on town planning and urban problems in Britain and Germany during the 1950s, 1960s, and 1970s.

Michael Freeden is a professor of Politics in the University of Oxford, and director of the Centre for the Study of Political Ideologies. His books include *The New Liberalism: An Ideology of Social Reform* (1978) and *Ideologies and Political Theory: A Conceptual Approach* (1996).

Kathryn Gleadle is a fellow of University College, Oxford. She is the author of *The Early Feminists: Radical Unitarians and the Emergence of the Women's Rights Movement, 1831–1851*, and editor of several studies of women in eighteenth- and nineteenth-century British society.

Lawrence Goldman is a fellow of St Peter's College, Oxford. His books include *Science, Reform and Politics in Victorian Britain: The Social Science Association 1857–1886* (2002).

Adrian Gregory is a fellow of Pembroke College, Oxford, author of *The Silence of Memory: Armistice Day, 1919–1946* (1994), and co-editor (with Senia Paseta) of *Ireland and the Great War* (2002).

Matthew Grimley is a fellow of Lincoln College, Oxford. His book, *Citizenship, Community and the Church of England: Anglican Theories of the State 1926–1939*, is forthcoming (2003).

Jose Harris is a professor of Modern History in the University of Oxford. Her books include *William Beveridge: A Biography* (2nd edn., 1997), and *Ferdinand Tönnies: Community and Civil Society* (2001).

Brian Harrison was formerly a professor of Politics in the University of Oxford, and author of numerous works on nineteenth- and twentieth-century social and political history. He is currently editor of the *New Dictionary of National Biography* (forthcoming, 2004).

Joanna Innes is a fellow of Somerville College, Oxford, and co-editor (with Hugh Cunningham) of *Charity, Philanthropy and Reform: From the 1660s to 1850* (1998). She researches on many aspects of government and social policy in the eighteenth and early nineteenth centuries.

Nicholas Owen is a fellow of the Queen's College, Oxford, and author of *The Labour Party and the Indian Question* (forthcoming).

Senia Paseta is a fellow of St Hugh's College, Oxford. She is the author of *Before the Revolution: Nationalism, Social Change and Ireland's Catholic Elite, 1879–1922* (1999), and co-editor (with Adrian Gregory) of *Ireland and the Great War*.

Tim Rowse is a senior research fellow in the School of Social Sciences at the Australian National University. His books include *White Flour, White Power: From Rations to Citizenship in Central Australia* (1998) and *Nugget Coombs: A Reforming Life* (2002).

Raphael Schapiro is a D.Phil. student at Nuffield College, Oxford, and works on the application of economic theory to the history of public utilities.

John Stevenson is a fellow of Worcester College, Oxford. He is the author or editor of more than thirty books, and currently works on the culture and politics of the countryside in twentieth-century Britain.

Philip Waller is a fellow of Merton College, Oxford. His books include *Democracy and Sectarianism: A Political and Social History of Liverpool, 1868–1939* (1981). He is currently writing a history of late-Victorian and Edwardian 'best-sellers'.

'The more one reads of man's notions about the meaning and method of civil society, the more often is one inclined in despair to say that truth has as little to do with politics as it has with most politicians'.
(J. N. Figgis, *Studies of Political Thought from Gerson to Grotius* 1907)

Introduction:
Civil Society in British History:
Paradigm or Peculiarity?

The ancient concept of 'civil society' largely disappeared from Anglo-American and European political discourse for much of the twentieth century.[1] It resurfaced in two seminal German works of the 1960s, Habermas's *The Structural Transformation of the Public Sphere* (1962) and Dahrendorf's *Society and Democracy in Germany* (1965), each of which slowly percolated into English-language discussion of social and political history over subsequent decades.[2] Both these authors, otherwise very unalike in their political and philosophical views, portrayed 'civil society'—by which they meant autonomous social and economic institutions outside the sphere of government—as a central arena of the historical transition to 'modernity'. For Dahrendorf a flourishing civil society was the practical embodiment of the legal, economic, political, and personal freedoms set out in F. A. Hayek's 'constitution of liberty'; while for Habermas civil society had been the 'precondition' for the emergence of a new kind of 'bourgeois public sphere', which since the late-seventeenth century had increasingly replaced the cultural, sociable, normative, and taste-creating roles once performed by royal courts and kingly governments. Both accounts portrayed the evolution of civil society as closely linked to the growth of markets and cities, the rise of 'public opinion', the genesis of new forms of privacy and self-awareness, and the burgeoning of a multitude of self-generating free associations that performed a 'public' function but operated largely without reference to the realm of the state.[3]

Place of publication is London, unless otherwise specified, throughout the notes.

[1] It was wholly unmentioned, for example, in such major reference works as Gould and Kolb (eds.), *A Dictionary of the Social Sciences* (1964); *The Encyclopaedia of the Social Sciences* (New York, 1968 edn.); *The Encyclopaedia of Philosophy* (1968 edn.); and David Walker (ed.), *The Oxford Companion to Law* (Oxford, 1980). By contrast, the *New Palgrave Dictionary of Economics and the Law* (1998) devoted no less than fourteen columns to 'civil society'.

[2] Jürgen Habermas, *Strukturwandel der Öffentlichkeit. Untersuchungen zu einer Kategorie der Bürgerlichen Gesellschaft* (Berlin, 1962); Ralf Dahrendorf, *Gesellschaft und Demokratie in Deutschland* (Munich, 1965). Whereas Dahrendorf's study rapidly appeared in English, Habermas's book was not translated until 1989; but both works were highly influential in the wider debate that took shape in the 1970s (see Ch. 4, below).

[3] Ralf Dahrendorf, *Society and Democracy in Germany* (English edn., 1968), 128–9, 200–10; Jürgen Habermas, *The Structural Transformation of the Public Sphere* (English edn., 1989), 19–20, 23, 30–43, 51–6.

Use of the term 'civil society' gathered momentum in the 1970s and early 1980s in the German *Sonderweg* debates, where the imperfect formation of 'civil society' in nineteenth-century Germany was widely portrayed (along lines suggested by Dahrendorf) as a major cause of subsequent 'pathological' developments in that country's national history.[4] Not until the end of the cold war in the late-1980s, however, did the term 'civil society' burst into the public arena as a commanding theme in contemporary political debate.[5] Since 1989 it has enjoyed a remarkable renaissance, not just in academic political thought but in the language of popular politics, moral persuasion, markets, and the mass media. Over the past two decades, literally thousands of titles on 'civil society' have been published in Eastern and Western Europe, Britain and North America—some of them detached and analytical, some actively critical, but many more extolling the benefits of civil society, and urging its promotion and extension. Portrayed initially as a societal counterweight to excessive state power (in both authoritarian regimes and 'over-governed' democratic ones), it has more recently come to be seen in a rather different light as a means of reconstituting civic peace in places where state authority seems to have lost general legitimacy (as in Ulster, Kosova, Afghanistan, southern Africa, and other areas of multi-ethnic conflict).[6] And, concurrently with these hoped-for practical applications in the present, 'civil society' has been increasingly invoked in scholarly reinterpretations of the past, where it has supplemented and in some contexts even displaced the more familiar categories of state, party, nation, mass movement, and social class. In much recent historical writing 'civil society' has been identified as present or latent in many earlier historical structures, even where the human participants in those structures had rarely if ever made explicit use of the term.[7]

In much of this discussion, the social and institutional history of Britain has frequently been cited as a paradigm example. Both Habermas and Dahrendorf, in their rather different accounts of the growth of liberal institutions and a 'bourgeois public sphere', portrayed developments in Britain from the early eighteenth century as the pattern and pioneer of an ever-expanding civil society (its citizens linked together by contract, choice, 'civility', and self-interest, rather than by the organic, sacramental, and interpersonal ties typical of more

[4] Ch. 4, below.

[5] John Keane (ed.), *Civil Society and the State: New European Perspectives* (1988), both recorded and helped to shape the international revival of the term. Other influential works included Jean L. Cohen and Andrew Arato, *Civil Society and Political Theory* (Cambridge, Mass., 1992); Ernest Gellner, *Conditions of Liberty: Civil Society and its Rivals* (1994); and Michael Walzer (ed.), *Towards a Global Civil Society* (Oxford, 1995).

[6] e.g. J. W. de Gruchy and S. Martin (eds.), *Religion and the Reconstruction of Civil Society* (University of South Africa, 1995); Commonwealth Foundation, *Democratic Government in Zimbabwe: Citizen Power* (Harare, Zimbabwe, 2000).

[7] e.g., *Urban History*, 25: 3, Dec. 1998, Special Issue on 'Civil Society in Britain'; John Garrard, *Democratisation in Britain: Elites, Civil Society and Reform since 1800* (2002); Nancy Bermeo and Philip Nord, *Civil Society before Democracy: Lessons from Nineteenth-century Europe* (2000): Kathleen D. McCarthy (ed.), *Women, Philanthropy, and Civil Society* (Bloomington, Ind., 2001).

traditional polities).[8] Similarly in the *Sonderweg* debates Britain was frequently cited as an exemplar of a 'free and civil country' which had steered its way from 'feudalism' to 'modernity', without the excesses of civil violence, ethnic and class antagonisms, and overweening concentrations of state power, often experienced by its continental neighbours and by Germany in particular.[9] And to many other commentators it appeared that, despite the stresses of industrialization, mass urbanization, empire, and two world wars, British political and legal institutions had been markedly more successful than those elsewhere in Europe at containing and 'including' the new interest groups, classes, and potentially disintegrative social forces generated by capitalism and economic change. Moreover, even when accompanied by large-scale expansion of state power, the processes of containment and absorption in Britain seemed to have occurred in tandem with continuous expansion of personal freedom and of civil and constitutional rights. Above all, Britain was perceived as being (along with the United States) one of the classic heartlands of 'civil association'. It was seen as a society where social relations largely took the form of partnerships, fraternities, groups, and congregations freely entered into by entrepreneurs, workmates, neighbours, and fellow-citizens, and which were regulated only very lightly by parliament and common law—in marked contrast to the much more 'corporatist' or 'holistic' traditions of nineteenth- and early twentieth-century Germany, or the heavy-handed state *dirigisme* of post-revolutionary France.[10]

All of this is in many ways a very familiar, long-established, even conventional, narrative to students of the last three centuries of British history. It has much in common with the understanding of Britain's national character and identity generated by the Second World War (a time when very few people used the actual language of 'civil society').[11] But for the historian who wants to go beyond the level of grand generalization, the picture of Britain as an archetypal civil society poses a number of questions and difficulties. The most obvious of these is: how far is the story true? Was the path of social and institutional growth in Britain quite so gradualist, peaceable, pluralist, spontaneous, 'civic', and inclusive as many theorists and proponents of civil society have suggested, or is this simply a more 'theorized' and updated version of the earlier Whiggish national myth? How far does the grand narrative propounded by present-day civil society theorists bear any relation to real historical structures, institutions, ideas, individuals, and events?

Paradoxically, the characterization of Britain by theorists of 'civil society' as the classic arena of peaceful and inclusive societal change coincided with a moment when detailed research by social and political historians, rooted in archival and other primary sources, was increasingly pointing in a rather different direction.

---

[8] Habermas, *Public Sphere*, 17, 57–67, 78–9, 93–4, 167–8, *et passim*; Dahrendorf, *Society and Democracy*, 53–4, 70, 272–4.

[9] Below, Ch. 5.   [10] Below, Ch. 1.

[11] For classic accounts of this national self-awareness, see Richard Titmuss, *Problems of Social Policy* (1951); Paul Addison, *The Road to 1945* (1975).

Several major historical studies of the 1970s, 1980s, and 1990s drew attention to the many *failures* of inclusion within mainstream British institutions of various minority and even majority groups (for example, the very late arrival of formal democracy, the prolonged life-span of aristocratic and quasi-feudal power, the absence of women from the public sphere, the very limited popular access to courts of law, and the chronically fraught condition and ultimate failure of the union between Britain and Ireland). Such studies highlighted certain historic acts of violence perpetrated both domestically and imperially by agents of the British state; and they gave prominence to the fact that the state itself (albeit a relatively slimline and semi-invisible state) had played a much more powerful role in the shaping of economic, financial, social, and cultural relations than had often been supposed. Studies of the 'fiscal-military state', the 'policeman-state', the 'over-extended state', and many aspects of the mid-twentieth century 'welfare state' all cautioned against underestimating the discretionary, coercive, and interventionist powers of British governing institutions, not simply since the Second World War, but over much longer periods of time.[12] And this questioning of the identity of Britain's past coincided with a degree of disenchantment about the present time as institutions forged in the cross-currents of earlier eras were increasingly perceived as failing to adjust to the post-industrial, multicultural, egalitarian, and 'globalizing' pressures of the later twentieth century. By the mid-1990s some of the very same voices that only a few years earlier had been to the fore in identifying Britain as an archetypal 'civil society' were now equally prominent in commenting adversely on Britain's collapse of 'civility' and widespread civic decline.[13] At the end of the twentieth century many enthusiasts for the revival of 'civil society' appeared to have shifted away from the Anglo-centric narratives of mainstream British history; they were looking instead for its embodiment either in the more concrete and intimate sphere of local communities and 'voluntary association' or in the more abstract, legalistic, and impersonal sphere of institutions campaigning for universal 'human rights'.[14] By a strange reversal of fortunes normative ideas about 'civil society', long seen as inspired by the evolutionary political culture of the Anglo-Saxon countries, now began to emanate from a quite different cultural

---

[12] J. Brewer, *The Sinews of Power: War, Money and the English State 1688–1783* (1989); F. M. L. Thompson (ed.), *The Cambridge Social History of Britain 1750–1950* (Cambridge 1990), iii. chs. 1, 2, 5; L. Stone (ed.), *An Imperial State at War* (1994); V. A. C. Gatrell, *The Hanging Tree: Execution and the English People 1770–1868* (Oxford, 1994); J. Brewer and E. Hellmuth (eds.), *Rethinking Leviathan: The Eighteenth-century State in Britain and Germany* (Oxford, 1999).

[13] R. Weatherill, *Cultural Collapse* (1994): Ralf Dahrendorf, 'Prosperity, Liberty, Civility: Can We Square the Circle', *Proceedings of the British Academy* (Oxford, 1996), 223–35; Ralf Dahrendorf, *After 1989: Morals, Revolution and Civil Society* (Basingstoke, 1997).

[14] Peter Stokes and Barry Knight, *Organising a Civil Society* (Foundation for Civil Society, Working Paper No. 2, 1997); David Green, *Civil Society. The Guiding Philosophy and Research Agenda of the Institute for the Study of Civil Society* (2000); G. B. Maddison, *The Political Economy of Civil Society and Human Rights* (1998); M. Glasius, M. Kaldor, and H. Anheier (eds.), *Global Civil Society* (Oxford, 2002).

inheritance—from the European Union, continental civil law, and the Strasburg-based Court of Human Rights.[15]

All this begs a second question, however, which is: what precisely is 'civil society'? What have its numerous theorists and protagonists understood by the term, both in past epochs and at the present time, and what have they had in common? In current debates many who talk and write about civil society, both as a theoretical concept and as a desirable programme or goal, appear to assume that its content and frame of reference are self-evidently clear and exact. Yet the idea of 'civil society' has had an immense variety of complex and often arcane intellectual roots—in Roman law, in medieval Christian theology, in early-modern positivist jurisprudence, in classical political economy, and in different strands of idealism, liberalism, and Marxism.[16] Resonances of all of these ancestries can be heard in current uses of the term, but often in forms very remote from those intended by their original authors. Some of these lineages overlap or are closely linked together, whereas others entail totally different, even antithetical, outlooks on such basic issues as the role and character of states, communities, markets, religion, families, and self-governing private associations. Many nuances of meaning have been both lost and added in translation, with the Latin terms *Societas* and *Civitas*, the German *bürgerliche Gesellschaft* and *staatliche Gesellschaft*, and the French *société civile*, all being anglicized and homogenized as 'civil society'.

The result has been that commentators in Britain and elsewhere have differed widely on the scope and definition of civil society—on whether it refers primarily to institutions in the *public* sphere, to arrangements in the *private* sphere, or to a special area of interaction or 'interface' between the two. Many classic English and Scottish writers on the subject (Hobbes, Locke, Adam Ferguson, Henry Maine) portrayed the state itself as the fundamental institution of civil society; whereas most nineteenth-century German authors (Hegel, Marx, Riehl, Emminghaus) used the term to refer to various institutions and processes distinct from the state (among them markets, vocational corporations, and the organs of municipal government).[17] Despite the widespread perception of Britain as a classic civil society, recent commentators have more often followed the German usage in applying the term to 'non-governmental' bodies outside the state, including both those which act in partnership with the state (such as

---

[15] Colin Crouch and David Marquand (eds.), *Re-inventing Collective Action. From the Global to the Local* (Oxford, 1995); G. Teubner (ed.), *Global Law Without a State* (Aldershot, 1997).

[16] J. N. Figgis, *Studies of Political Thought from Gerson to Grotius, 1414–1625* (Cambridge, 1907); Anthony Black, *Guilds and Civil Society in European Political Thought from the Twelfth Century to the Present* (1984); John Ehrenberg, *Civil Society: The Critical History of an Idea* (New York, 1999); below, Ch. 1.

[17] W. H. von Riehl, *Die bürgerliche Gesellschaft*, vol. 2 of Riehl's *Naturgeschichte des Volkes* (Stuttgart, 1856); A. Emminghaus, *Das Armenwesen und die Armengesetzgebung in Europäischen Staaten* (Berlin, 1870); Frank Trentmann (ed.), *Paradoxes of Civil Society. New Perspectives on Modern German and British History* (Oxford, 2000), Introduction, and chs. 3 and 4. On British writers about civil society, see below, Ch. 1.

denominational schools or housing associations) and those which are detached from or hostile to it (such as protest movements and pressure groups). Some authorities (such as the American sociologist Amitai Etzioni) have used 'civil society' more or less interchangeably with the idea of 'community'; whereas for others (such as Dahrendorf) the two concepts are deeply antithetical ('civil society' entailing free-standing individuals, contractual relations, and impersonal legal rules; while 'community' implies close-knit kinship, ethnic, neighbourhood, and confessional ties that are often 'given' rather than 'chosen').[18]

Similar ambiguity surrounds the role of markets. To many commentators 'civil society' is closely identified, for better or worse, with capitalism and 'market society'. But within this approach there are many different shades of understanding about whether it is *markets themselves* that form the core of civil society—or whether it refers rather to the framework of laws, regulations, and moral restraints that make markets to some degree publicly accountable.[19] And, at the same time, there are others who treat civil society as though it were the very opposite of market society—as a sector in which social exchanges take place, for a variety of reasons and motives, outside the economic context of prices, payment, and profit. This latter view again embraces a very wide spectrum of theory and opinion, ranging from those ethically and ideologically committed to non-profit-making 'public service', through to those within the Gramscian strand of Marxism, for whom 'civil society' means non-economic cultural and social institutions that nevertheless implicitly support a wider framework of capitalist domination.[20] In the sphere of law, the technical language of 'civil society' has been much more conspicuous in the Roman-based civil law systems of continental Europe and of Scotland than in the common law systems of England and Wales, the British Commonwealth, and the United States: a fact which makes it all the more remarkable that, until very recently, it has often been common-law countries in which observers of civil society have perceived its principles as being most concretely and historically embodied. Over many centuries theorists both high and low have largely concurred in linking civil society to ideas about voluntarism, individual autonomy, and rational choice; but a very long history of conceptual mutation lies behind the evolution of 'voluntarism' in the sense used by medieval moral theology (the Augustinian

[18] Amitai Etzioni, *The Spirit of Community: Rights, Responsibilities and the Communitarian Agenda* (New York, 1993) (though see the same author's much more critical approach to civil society from a communitarian perspective, in Etzioni, *The Monochrome Society* (Princeton, NJ, 2001); Dahrendorf, *Society and Democracy*, 120–32.

[19] Habermas, *Public Sphere*, 29–31; Antonio Estache, *Politics, Transaction Costs, and the Design of Regulatory Institutions* (Washington, 1999); Sandra van Thiel, *Quangos: Trends, Causes, and Consequences* (Aldershot, 2001).

[20] For a wide variety of such views, see Lester M. Salamon, *Global Civil Society: Dimensions of the Non-profit Sector* (Baltimore, 1999); Susannah Morris, *Defining the Non-profit Sector: Some Lessons from History* (2000); Robert Whelan, *Helping the Poor. Friendly Visiting, Dole Charities and Dole Queues* (2001); P. Anderson, 'The Antinomies of Antonio Gramsci', *New Left Review*, 100 (1976–7), 5–78; Antonio Gramsci, *Pre-Prison Writings*, ed. Richard Bellamy (Cambridge, 1994), xii–xvi, xxxvii–xxxviii, 8–18, 51–3, 73–4.

doctrine of 'free will'), into the self-regulating 'voluntary action' and private choice often identified with civil society at the present day.[21] Similar diversity surrounds the relation of civil society to notions of 'good citizenship': some authorities claiming that the two are coterminous, whilst others assert that the very essence of a civil society is quite the opposite—that it rests on just laws, fair procedures, and sound civic institutions, *not* on the qualities of personal character, altruism, and public spirit displayed by the individual citizens of whom it happens to be composed.[22]

Many of these ambiguities have remained unresolved, and often even unnoticed, in recent civil society debate. In the *mélange* of prescriptive ideas, social theories, and historical perspectives that swarmed around in British, European, North American, and post-colonial public cultures at the turn of the twenty-first century, civil society was clearly a powerful and compelling theme that captured the imaginations of many, but its precise meaning and provenance have remained obstinately obscure. In a British context, prominent political figures as various in outlook as William Hague, David Willetts, Chris Patten, David Blunkett, and Gordon Brown have all concurred in prescribing a renewal of Britain's unique historic legacy of 'civil society' as a remedy for the country's current social ills; but whether they mean the same thing by this appeal to earlier ideas and practices seems doubtful.[23] Similar diversity has prevailed in the sphere of public persuasion. While the Institute for the Study of Civil Society (founded as an offshoot of a free-market think-tank, the Institute of Economic Affairs, in 1998) has interpreted its remit as being primarily the historical analysis and practical promotion of voluntary self-help, the Centre for Global Civil Society (founded at the London School of Economics in 2000) focuses on cross-national promulgation of universal human rights (to be imposed 'preferably by consent, but by force if required').[24] Likewise in academic and media debate, many who thirty years ago were stern critics of *bourgeois* society have now become no less powerful advocates of *civil* society (regardless of the fact that, in one strand of linguistic origin and in the usage of many both past and present, the two concepts are one and the same).

The present collection of studies has arisen out of a shared sense of dissatisfaction among its authors with all this ambiguity and muddle. The collection is

[21] See below, Ch. 1.

[22] Dahrendorf, *Society and Democracy*, 299–311; Thomas Janoski, *Citizenship and Civil Society: A Framework of Rights and Obligations in Liberal, Traditional, and Social Democratic Regimes* (Cambridge, 1998); below, pp. 17, 23–4, 27, 36, 275–91.

[23] David Willetts, *Civic Conservatism* (1994); William Hague, *Speaking with Conviction* (1998); Chris Patten, *Respect for the Earth: Sustainable Development* (2000); David Blunkett, *Politics and Progress: Renewing Democracy and Civil Society* (2001); J. Gordon Brown, *Civic Society in Modern Britain*, ed. by John Wilson (Amersham, 2001).

[24] David Green, *The Guiding Philosophy and Research Agenda of the Institute for the Study of Civil Society* (2000); Mary Kaldor, *Global Civil Society* (Cambridge, 2001); BBC Radio Four, interview with Mary Kaldor, October 2001; *Global Civil Society*, ed. by Marlies Glasius, Mary Kaldor, and Helmut Anheier (Oxford, 2001–3).

the product of a series of seminars, workshops, and informal discussions organized in Oxford by a small group of modern historians, and historically oriented
political theorists and social scientists, between 1998 and 2001. The discussion
drew upon the very diverse research interests of the group's members, in such
areas as political thought, social policy, imperialism, urban and military history,
voluntary associations, rational choice theory, class relations, and constructions
of gender. The participants embarked upon these discussions united only by
their sense that 'civil society' appeared to have some bearing upon many historical settings—but that its usefulness and cutting edge as an historical concept
were often fatally undermined, not just by vagueness in uses of the term, but by
the fact that, wherever it *was* sharply defined, it meant quite different and mutually contradictory things in different intellectual, national, temporal, and cultural contexts. There seemed little point, for example, in discussing whether
Britain over several centuries had been the 'unique exemplar' of civil society in
respect to its traditions of grass-roots association and voluntary philanthropy,
if what civil society really meant was (as some authorities maintained) the uni-
versalization of free markets or (as others maintained) an over-arching regulatory 'impartial state'. Was there any connection, other than an arbitrary freak
of language, between the ideas of the grand theorists and the recent claim by a
spokesman of the British Football Association that the game he represents
should have its own public regulator because 'football has become a unique
institution of our civil society' (a statement interesting both in its own right, and
as evidence of the far-reaching popular resonance of the term in the early
twenty-first century)?[25] In the end, the decision was taken to eschew any single
unitary model, but to explore different aspects of social, intellectual, and institutional life in Britain over several centuries, with a view to finding out where—
if anywhere—the various off-the-peg models of civil society seemed to fit (or,
alternatively, where they seemed irrelevant or historically inappropriate).

The results, as suggested below, came up with some perhaps rather surprising conclusions about how a supposedly 'classic' civil society operated in real
life. They indicate that certain assumptions about the definitive attributes of
civil society often ascribed to it by its current theorists and protagonists are—at
least in the case of the history of Britain—often inapplicable or false. From the
eighteenth century there certainly developed in Britain a large layer of dynamic
social interaction that closely resembled Habermas's 'bourgeois public sphere'
in being distinct both from purely private life and from courtly or 'high' politics;
but this intermediate social layer was both much more actively involved in the
various organs of government and public administration than Habermas had
suggested, and also much less uniformly 'bourgeois' (at least in the English
understanding of that malleable term).[26] Civil society as it was understood in
Britain was never a pure form, but coexisted at different times and in different
ways with many other forms of social organization and identity, based on such

[25] BBC interview, Sport on Four, 24 Nov. 2001.   [26] Below, Chs. 3, 5, and 6.

factors as family, ethnicity, gender, locality, inheritance, patriotism, and religious belief. Virtually nobody, for example, after the end of the seventeenth century thought that patriarchalism (arguably the extreme obverse of civil society) was an adequate basis for constitutional rights and governmental power; but this did not preclude the persistence of many residues of patriarchy in the spheres of property relations, gender, professional organizations, and family life. The civic peace of 'civil society' (based on law, contract, and guarantees of personal freedom) was often favourably compared with the supposed disorders of 'natural society' (the latter based on personal protection networks, tribalism, and mafia-like extended families). But again this did not prevent patronage and kinship connections, or the lack of them, from having a powerful impact on an individual's prospects in the arena of 'open competition' promoted by civil society. The operation of markets (seen by some as a *sine qua non* of civil society) could stimulate the activities of voluntarism, self-help, and self-governing associations, but it might also in certain circumstances frustrate and undermine them; as could be seen in the 'crisis of voluntarism' among Edwardian and inter-war friendly societies, or in the 'bowling-alone' phenomenon of the later twentieth century. ('Bowling alone' itself, seen by Putnam and others as a signal of the recent *decline* of civil society, would be seen by some as its defining characteristic—embodied in the person of the free-standing, freely choosing, rational individual, 'unencumbered' by societal ties other than transient and tradable ones).[27]

On the other hand, several of the essays included here seem to demonstrate very clearly certain institutional and cultural traits and practices that corresponded to *some* past and present definitions of civil society; and they may help us to piece together a picture of how far the term may or may not be applicable to the history of Britain. They suggest, for example, that there was no necessary incompatibility between voluntary action and strong central government—that an active and flourishing civil society could on occasion be the precondition of highly effective collaboration between the two.[28] Voluntarism *per se*, however, was never directly equated with civil society by any British commentators before the 1980s, and there seems reason to doubt how far it is appropriate to do so now.[29] Civil society is often assumed, and was assumed in the past, to be categorically 'secular' in outlook (with religious practice either occupying its own separate public sphere, or being deemed inherently personal and private). But several of the theorists and advocates of civil society studied in this collection maintained exactly the opposite view—that only a cultural framework linked to some form of publicly organized religion could make modern mass society genuinely both 'social' and 'civil', and that religious practice in its this-worldly manifestations might in itself be a component of civil society.[30] In this respect

---

[27] Robert Putnam, *Bowling Alone: The Collapse and Revival of American Community* (2000); Ferdinand Tönnies, *Community and Civil Society*, ed. Jose Harris (Cambridge, 2001); Patrick Joyce, *The Social in Question: New Bearings in History and the Social Sciences* (2002); below, Chs. 4 and 7.
[28] Below, Chs. 4 and 9.   [29] Below, Chs. 1 and 4.   [30] Below, Chs. 1, 2, and 12.

much eighteenth–century Anglican thought bore a close resemblance to certain strands of moderate Islamic thought on civil society at the present day.[31] Another point which emerged was that the role of particular groups within civil society ebbed and flowed in different periods and contexts; women, for example, were sometimes acknowledged as active participants and fellow-citizens, at other times were demoted and obscured; they were promoted by some variants of civil society (such as philanthropy, sociability, and voluntary action), while being simultaneously sidelined by others (such as entrepreneurship and political representation).[32] Religious dissenters were seen in some contexts as potential subverters of civil society, in others as its supporters and beneficiaries. Similarly, there was little evidence to support the commonly held view that civil society was a quintessentially 'urban' phenomenon, dependent on the close contacts and information networks of city life. This might have been true in the early eighteenth century, when communications and 'publicity' were relatively localized and limited; but by the second quarter of the twentieth century rural communities in many parts of Britain appeared to have established an associational, participatory, and self-regulatory culture that was no whit less active, multifaceted, and 'public' than its equivalent in cities and towns (while recent debate on the erosion of civil society has identified symptoms of its structural decline in both urban areas and rural ones).[33]

A general conclusion is, not that the term is so protean as to be meaningless, but that it makes much more sense if seen as locally variable and culturally specific; as a phenomenon shaped and modified by different historical contexts, rather than as a universal and predefined analytical model. Many of the classic British theorists of civil society (Hooker and Hobbes, Ferguson and Smith, even the historically minded Sir Henry Maine) conceived of their ideas as having some kind of general or 'universal' application. But universalism often clashed with stubborn historic reality, as manifested in the romantic and corporatist conceptions of 'civil society' (quite different from those of Victorian liberalism) that British observers encountered in nineteenth-century Germany; or in the civic revival of family, village, religion, and nation that secular missionaries for British-style 'modernity' discovered in early twentieth-century India. Similarly, the centuries-old saga of relations between European settlers and indigenous peoples—investigated here through colonial and post-colonial treatment of Australian Aborigines—suggests that what appear to be fundamental tenets of civil society may in certain circumstances be in deep tension and contradiction with each other.[34] And even within very similar frameworks of language, liberalism, and the common law, conceptions of the 'regulatory' aspects of civil society could evolve quite differently in different institutional settings (as suggested

---

[31] M. Khatani, *Islam, Dialogue, and Civil Society* (Canberra: Australian National University, 2000); S. H. Hashmi (ed.), *Islamic Political Ethics: Civil Society, Pluralism and Conflict* (Princeton, NJ, 2002).

[32] Below, Chs. 3 and 11.   [33] Below, Chs. 2 and 10.   [34] Below, Chs. 5, 7, and 15.

by comparison of public/private economic partnerships in Edwardian London and New York).[35] Within Britain itself the late nineteenth-century trade-union movement—if judged by the criterion of active, self-governing, 'voluntary association'—appeared to represent the very essence of a vital civil society; but nevertheless trade unionists resolutely resisted the other face of civil society, in the form of public regulation of their collective activities by statute and common law.[36] Similarly middle-class pressure groups might act as the disinterested moral conscience of the public sphere; but they could also lapse on occasion into something remarkably like the networks of 'sinister interest' and 'old corruption' that civil society was widely supposed to have discredited and displaced.[37] There appeared to be no single path to 'civil society', not one single prototype but many, even within the public culture identified by Habermas and Dahrendorf as its classic historical site.

The chapters of this book are all derived from the ongoing research interests of the contributors, and contain historical materials and intepretative arguments unpublished anywhere else. However, each chapter is written in a way designed to be accessible to readers outside a particular area of technical research, and to engage with issues that are current not just in academic history and the social sciences but in wider public debate in Britain, Europe, Japan, North America, and elsewhere. Although the chapters stretch over several centuries and address a wide range of historical contexts (including comparative material on Germany, Ireland, India, Australia, and the United States), they are fused together by the common theme of exploring and defining the multiple meanings of 'civil society' and their relevance or otherwise to particular events and institutions in the history of Britain. Although each chapter has been written by a separate author, the whole work has benefited from the comments and suggestions of other contributors. As will become apparent, there was some diversity of opinion about how 'civil society' should be conceived and defined, but an overall consensus that—at least in the context of British history—the state itself had been an important element in either *shaping* or actually *constituting* civil society, and could not be left out of the reckoning.

Quite apart from the centrality of the theme of 'civil society' in current historical and social-science debate, the collection highlights the importance of linking broad conceptual interpretations of history to primary archival and textual research, and offers a series of case-studies showing how this may be done in practice. These studies also demonstrate many ways in which key aspects of current (and apparently novel) debate were replicated or anticipated in many earlier historical settings. The book is in no sense exhaustive in its coverage: indeed the contributors became acutely conscious of how much more work

[35] Below, Ch. 7.
[36] Thus, most British civil society theorists who considered the issue of trade unions thought that they should accept the status of legally defined corporations, as giving them ultimately greater independence from the powers of the state (below, Ch. 1).
[37] Below, Chs. 4, 6, and 13.

From Richard Hooker to Harold Laski: Changing Perceptions of Civil Society in British Political Thought, Late Sixteenth to Early Twentieth Centuries

JOSE HARRIS

I

Current discussion of 'civil society' in Britain and elsewhere draws extensively though often unconsciously upon two distinct intellectual lineages that are in certain respects deeply antithetical. One is a tradition that evolved in Germany during the late eighteenth/early nineteenth century, which saw 'civil society' as consisting of a range of semi-private and corporate institutions (including economic production and markets) separate from and outside the state.[1] In much nineteenth-century German thought a central problem for law and government was how to harmonize and incorporate those often dissonant lesser institutions into a larger political whole; but more recent variants of that tradition have re-emphasized the autonomy of 'civil society' and its distinctness from formal governing institutions. The second tradition that continues to inform current debate was set in train by the French Revolution. Deriving from Rousseau and refined by Kant, it saw civil society as embodying the equal and identical political and legal rights of citizens, purged of any qualifying reference to kinship, status, religious confession, and inherited privilege (and to other forms of

---

[1] *Hegel's Philosophy of Right*, trans. with notes by T. M. Knox (1952), paras. 182–256; W. H. von Riehl, *Die bürgerliche Gesellschaft* (Stuttgart, 1851); Karl Marx, *Early Writings*, ed. by L.Colletti (Harmondsworth , 1975), *passim*. It should be noted that, with the exception of the essay 'On the Jewish Question' (1843), Marx's most important comments on civil society, such as *The German Ideology*, were not available even in German till the mid-twentieth century.

'difference' that came to be seen over the course of time as similarly arbitrary).[2] This latter tradition was in the past implicitly, and often explicitly, *hostile* to intermediate, particularist, semi-private bodies except where these were directly licensed and endorsed by the state (or by some more universal sovereign authority in a hypothetical 'internationalist' polity of the future).[3]

Nineteenth-century Britons detected both these ways of thinking in the respective institutions of their continental neighbours—in the 'incorporating' policies of Prussia and Wilhelmine Germany, and in the centralizing, codifying, 'macadamizing' tendencies of post-revolutionary and post-Napoleonic France—and they were conscious of living in Britain under a set of social arrangements that was distinctively different from either.[4] British society as it had evolved over many centuries was full of a vast and burgeoning array of 'spontaneous' self-governing voluntary associations—religious, commercial, educational, charitable, scientific, local, or merely peculiar—whose existence was either wholly unknown to the law and public authorities, or only very lightly regulated by them.[5] Many of these voluntary bodies—like the London Stock Exchange, the ancient universities, and major philanthropic organizations—performed functions that in France and Germany would have been closely monitored by government and public law, but that in Britain for long remained subject only to private laws relating to companies, trusts, or charities (and then to a large extent only if they specifically chose to be so).

Contrary to what is often supposed, however, this plethora of voluntary arrangements, distinct from government or 'the state', was *not* what Victorians and Edwardians or their forebears had in mind when they talked (as they did from time to time) about 'civil society'. There *was* an Anglophone tradition of thinking about civil society, that developed spasmodically over the course of time from the sixteenth through to the early twentieth centuries, but it was only indirectly concerned with the many and various kinds of private voluntary association. Language of course is plastic and dynamic, and the fact that people used a term in the past to mean something quite different from what they mean by it in the present does not thereby invalidate current usage. But because this shift has been largely overlooked or glossed over, there is some danger that in current narratives of civil society those earlier resonances and frame of reference will be misinterpreted or lost. This chapter will attempt to trace the shifting

[2] Jean Jacques Rousseau, *The Social Contract and the Discourses*, ed. by G. D. H. Cole (1955 edn.), xxviii–xxxviii, 208–12, 236–42; *Kant's Political Writings*, ed. by Hans Reiss (Cambridge, 1970), 22–35, 45–9.

[3] F. W. Maitland, 'Moral Personality and Legal Personality' (1903), in *The Collected Papers of Frederick William Maitland*, ed. by H. A. L. Fisher (Cambridge, 1911), i. 312–13. On Rousseau's interest in a possible wider polity, see 'A Discourse of Political Economy', in *Social Contract and Discourses*, 236–7.

[4] Maitland, 'Moral Personality and Legal Personality', 313; below, Chs. 4 and 5.

[5] Martin Nadaud, *Histoire des Classes Oevrières en Angleterre* (Paris, 1873) suggested for every one voluntary association supported by the French, the English supported seven. This was doubtless a misleading figure, but it reflected a widely held nineteenth-century view that England was the Mecca of voluntary association.

contours of that earlier tradition, and to identify ways in which civil society (or its close synonyms) was imagined, theorized, and written about by political commentators in different contexts and periods of British history. No suggestion is intended here that 'ideas' about civil society necessarily shaped the ways in which society behaved, but simply that the expression of such ideas is a major clue to what people at the time thought was true and important. Unsurprisingly, over several centuries nuances of language and perceptions of social reality changed, and a way of conceptualizing social relations that was central to political thought in some generations lapsed into largely redundant cliché in others. It will be suggested, however, that despite wide diversity in their immediate concerns, British theorists of civil society over the course of four centuries held certain distinctive core assumptions in common. Moreover, although it shared many ancient roots with conceptions of civil society on the continent, this British tradition parted company at a certain point from both German and French understandings of the term (or, perhaps more accurately, all three diverged from what had hitherto been a common tradition throughout Western Europe).[6] And, even more markedly, past understanding of civil society in Britain significantly differed from many current Anglo-American uses of 'civil society' at the start of the twenty-first century.

II

'Civil society' first emerged in vernacular languages in the late sixteenth and early seventeenth centuries, in response to controversies about religious diversity, the role of monarchy, relations between church and state, the dismantling of personal fiefdoms and private armies, and the endemic threat of civil war. In both Britain and Europe writers drew heavily on earlier Latin uses of the term— on the Ciceronian idea of the *civitas* as an arena of neutral public space above private family and tribal connections; on Roman law notions of contract (*obligatio*) and partnership (*societas*); and on the attempts of late medieval theorists to define and demarcate the respective spheres of divine, natural, and positive law.[7] Throughout early modern Europe the idea of a 'civil society', meaning a collective public identity shaped by shared political and legal institutions, long preceded any conception of 'society' in the more modern sense, as a totality of self-sustaining social relationships distinct from any such politico-legal

---

[6] Anthony Black, *Guilds and Civil Society in European Political Thought from the Twelfth Century to the Present* (Cambridge, 1984), xi–xii, 32–43, 76–8, 93–4, 96–109, 203–5; Anthony Black, 'Concepts of Civil Society in Pre-modern Europe', in Sudipta Kaviraj and Sunil Khilnani (eds.), *Civil Society: History and Possibilities* (Cambridge, 2001), 33–8; Fania Oz-Salzburger, 'Civil Society in the Scottish Enlightenment', in Kaviraj and Khilnani, 61, 78–83.

[7] Otto Gierke, *Political Theories of the Middle Age*, trans. by F. R. Maitland (Cambridge, 1900), 9–21, 73–87; J. N. Figgis, *Studies of Political Thought from Gerson to Grotius 1414–1625* (Cambridge, 1916), 31–54; John Ehrenberg, *Civil Society. The Critical History of an Idea* (New York, 1999), 45–54.

framework: indeed the very idea of such an extra-political totality was scarcely thought of anywhere prior to the eighteenth century, and even then in only the most tentative and embryonic terms. Much of the meaning of 'civil society' evolved negatively, from attempts to define what it was *not*: it was not the rule of clans, or patriarchs, or private militias, or the universal church, or charismatic personal leaders, though in practice it might contain and coexist with large residues of any or all of those forms of power. It was also typically couched in largely abstract terms, as a set of model principles often illustrated by historical examples, rather than a description of actual social arrangements at a particular moment of time.

The first systematic invocation of civil society in English came from the 'Anglican' theologian Richard Hooker, who at the end of the sixteenth century made use of the term in his attempt to construct an institutional *via media* between the theocratic claims of Calvinists and the Papacy, the 'separatist' claims of religious independents, and the 'absolutist' claims of secular kingship.[8] Drawing upon the ideas of Aquinas and of late medieval 'conciliar' thought, Hooker's *Of the Laws of Ecclesiastical Polity* used the term 'civill society' interchangeably with 'politique society', 'publique society', and 'civil regiment',[9] and made it clear that what he was referring to was a set of governing institutions exercising authority over a given national community. Such institutions were 'voluntary' only in the sense that all persons living under them were deemed to be doing so, not by *force majeure* or even force of habit, but by their own willed and rational 'consent'. In the prior sphere of nature, 'natural law' was morally binding but in practice unenforceable: all were 'defenders of themselves', partial to their own interests, and judges in their own causes, with the result that 'strife and troubles' were 'endless'. Dwellers in 'natural society' therefore agreed (tacitly or explicitly) to transfer defence of their persons and their interests to 'some kind of regiment' in the form of 'civill society'.[10]

Civil society was thus the system of 'public government' that men were deemed to have placed themselves under for personal security, impartial judgement of disputes, material prosperity, and the enhancement of 'sociability' (the latter an attribute that Hooker believed to be latent in all mankind).[11] The task of civil society was enforcement both of universal 'natural laws' and of 'positive laws' belonging to a particular time and polity. Such laws required an executive 'prince or potentate', but the 'lawful power of making laws to command whole politique societies of men belongeth . . . properly to the same entire societies'.[12]

---

[8] Richard Hooker, *Of the Laws of Ecclesiastical Polity, Book I* (1593) in *Folger Library Edition of the Works of Richard Hooker*, ed. by W. Speed Hill (Cambridge, Mass.: Belknap Press, 1977), Vol. I. On Hooker's political thought, see W. D. J. Cargill Thompson, 'The Philosopher of the Politic: Richard Hooker as a Political Thinker', in W. Speed Hill (ed.), *Studies in Richard Hooker* (Cleveland, Oh., 1972); Arthur S. McGrade (ed.), *Richard Hooker and the Construction of Christian Community* (Tempe, Ariz., 1997); Alan Cromartie, 'Theology and Politics in Richard Hooker's Thought', *History of Political Thought*, 21: 1 (2002), 41–66.

[9] 'Regiment' meaning 'rule' or 'government', as in John Knox's 'monstrous regiment of women'.

[10] *Ecclesiastical Polity*, i. 95–103.   [11] Ibid., i. 96, 107, 139.   [12] Ibid., i. 98–100, 102.

Moreover, 'law' itself as enacted by civil society had an abstract status and potency that was absent from the *ad hoc* commands of the prince; and 'disordered' hotheads who would not 'stomach' the one, would often acquiesce in the other.[13] Princes and potentates were themselves bound to obey and execute both universal and immutable natural laws and the currently existing positive laws of their particular era and culture ('law-makers must have an eye to the men where, and to the men amongst whom', wrote Hooker, '. . . one kind of laws cannot serve for all kinds of regiment').[14]

Civil societies in Hooker's view might be purely secular bodies (attainable among pagans and unbelievers no less than among Christians) or they might also relate to the non-transcendental aspects of Christian church organization (which needed structures of legal and administrative authority no less than the mundane practices of civil life and commerce).[15] In either context Hooker drew a careful distinction between good members of civil society and 'good men', between the everyday morality of obedience to positive law and the higher morality of eternal salvation. Among his own opponents he discerned many 'whose betters amongst men would be hardly found', but whose obsession with personal piety rendered them unfit and 'unframable' to perform their civic duties.[16] In an ecclesiastical civil society no less than in a secular one, Hooker distinguished between immutable divine laws, and lesser matters of ceremonial taste and administrative convenience (permitting a degree of variation and 'inclusion' that was intended to reconcile religious pluralists both to the union of 'politic society' with the Church of England, and to the monarch's governorship of the latter).[17] This was a very 'national' view of civil society; but in Hooker's account of both religious and secular civil societies there were nevertheless hints of a broader, more 'internationalist' dimension. As a remedy for contention over 'polity, order, and regiment in the church' he recommended a revival of the 'general councils' of churches throughout Christendom, that had lapsed since the later middle ages. And his account of secular civil society likewise stressed the advantages of sociability, not just between neighbours and fellow-countrymen, but in the form of 'courteous entertainment of foreigners and strangers', 'commerce between grand societies', 'a kind of mutual society and fellowship even with all mankind', and a citizenship 'not of this or that commonwealth, but of the world'.[18]

III

Hooker's discussion of civil society was clearly addressed at least in part to the immediate *Realpolitik* of the Elizabethan church settlement.[19] Nevertheless, his

---

[13] Ibid., i. 102.   [14] Ibid., i. 104.   [15] Ibid., i. 137–9.   [16] Ibid., i. 139–40.
[17] Christopher Morris, introduction to Hooker, *Laws of Ecclesiastical Polity* (1958 edn.), v–xiii.
[18] *Ecclesiastical Polity* (Folger edn.) i. 107–10, 139.
[19] On Hooker's sensitivity to the charge that he was writing in the hope of preferment, see *Ecclesiastical Polity*, i. 56.

account anticipated many themes that were to shape discussion of the subject for several centuries to come. Among them were the contrast between civil and natural society, the link of the former to the rise of 'traffic' and 'commerce', the distinction between good men and good citizens, the search for a form of flexible but structured 'inclusion', and his portrayal of natural human sociability as not just a psychological trait but something catalysed by 'civil society' into a powerful force for historical and socio-political change. Thomas Hobbes, writing half a century later in the context of the English civil wars, echoed several of Hooker's central assumptions,[20] though drawing from them starker, or more starkly expressed, conclusions. Like Hooker, Hobbes's *Leviathan* and *De Cive* portrayed civil society as coterminous with effective governing institutions, embodied in the 'Commonwealth', the '*Civitas*', the 'City', or the 'civil state'.[21] And, like Hooker, Hobbes portrayed 'civil society' as the obverse of a disorderly 'state of nature' in which men lived untrammelled by government. But, whereas in Hooker's account clusters of small family groups might gradually evolve into civil societies, in Hobbes's view 'in all places, where men have lived by small families, to rob and spoil one another has been a trade'.[22] Similarly Hobbes allowed much less room than Hooker for conscientious dissent. There could be no appeal to any '*ghostly authority* against the *civil*'; 'private men' who pretended to be 'supernaturally inspired' caused the 'dissolution of all civil government'; and it was a 'doctrine repugnant to civil society . . . that whatsoever a man does against his conscience, is sin'.[23] Hobbes like Hooker portrayed the route out of natural conflict into civil society as embodied in a compact or contract; but the parties to Hobbes's compact were driven by no admixture of Hooker's 'convenience' and 'sociability', simply by fear, or acquiescence in physical force. There was also a marked difference in the status of Hobbes's sovereign authority: whereas Hooker's prince was himself subject to positive law, and his subjects gave such law their continuing consent, Hobbes's sovereign (whether a prince or a popular assembly) was no party to the compact that brought civil society into being, nor was he (or it) bound by civil society's laws.[24]

Hobbes's 'civil society' may therefore sound like an obtuse parody of what many of its protagonists were to understand by the term at the end of the twentieth century. The whole thrust of his argument was deeply opposed to any suggestion that there could be an independent societal counterweight to sovereign

---

[20]   Though it is unlikely that Hooker was a direct influence on Hobbes, who would have found *societas civilis* in Bodin, Grotius, and other writers on Roman and civil law.

[21]   Both *Leviathan* and *De Cive* made many references to 'civil society'. The Latin version of *De Cive* (The Citizen), published in Paris in 1642, appeared in translation in 1651, then was not republished in English until the 1840s. It reveals even more than *Leviathan* the extent to which Hobbes equated 'civil society' with governing institutions, and his debt to Roman civil law (Thomas Hobbes, *De Cive; or, Philosophicall Rudiments concerning Government and Society*, ed. by Howard Warrender (Oxford, 1983). The term 'City' was frequently used by civil society theorists throughout the 17th and 18th centuries to mean not an urban community but a polity or polis.

[22]   *Leviathan*, ed. by M. Oakeshott (Oxford, 1957), 109, 155.

[23]   Ibid., 211, 212, 214–15.   [24]   Ibid., 212.

power. The role of intermediate, self-governing corporations (such as universities and chartered trading companies) was viewed with deep suspicion, as a form of incipient conspiracy against the public interest;[25] and 'civil society' itself was embedded in, indeed largely synonymous with, the overarching structures of law, government, and public administration. The element of consent had no reference to ongoing popular endorsement of laws, merely to tacit acceptance of the original compact.[26] Hobbes's system not merely favoured an Erastian church establishment but saw any deviation from outward conformity as a menace to civil peace; the main practical purpose of religion was to make men 'the more apt to obedience, laws, peace, charity and civil society'.[27] There were, nevertheless, certain features of Hobbes's polity that suggested a rather different slant, and which did not altogether foreclose upon the kind of diversity and autonomy that many later authorities were to look for in civil society. One of these was 'the silence of the laws', by which men were deemed free to do anything that their sovereign had not explicitly forbidden (which might in practice allow for almost unlimited associational life *below* the political sphere).[28] Another was Hobbes's claim that civil society was concerned only with 'the conservation of men in multitudes': in other words, self-destructive *private* acts might be forbidden by the law of nature, but civil institutions were not concerned with enforcement of personal virtue or enhancement of private good.[29]

IV

The version of civil society set out in John Locke's *Two Treatises of Government* (composed as an oblique contribution to the royal succession debates of the 1670s and 1680s) contained many resonances of the earlier models of both Hooker and Hobbes.[30] It was none the less more complex and multi-layered than either, particularly in the fact that Locke's account addressed not just the threat of conflict among warring individuals but the possible abuse of power by the civil authority set up to mediate between them.[31] A group of men who in a state of nature were free, equal, and had a right to acquire whatever they could in the way of material goods, were deemed to have entered voluntarily into a pact or agreement, to protect their persons and possessions from each other and from external aggression. This agreement transformed a mere 'number' or 'aggregate' of men into 'one People, one Body Politick under one Supreme Government'— the latter consisting of a legislature, an executive, and a system of 'Law and Judicature' for settling disputes by 'standing rules' that applied equally to all

---

[25] Ibid., 151–2, 224–5.   [26] *De Cive*, 135–6.   [27] *Leviathan*, 73.
[28] Ibid., 143.
[29] Ibid., 103; for Hobbes's dislike of public interference in private matters, see *The Correspondence of Thomas Hobbes*, ed. by Noel Malcolm (Cambridge, 1994), ii. 702–3.
[30] John Locke, *Two Treaties of Government*, ed. by Peter Laslett, rev. edn. (New York and Cambridge, 1965).
[31] Ibid., 456–64.

parties.[32] Private powers were transferred to the public sphere and 'the Community comes to be Umpire'—displacing the state of nature, where everyone was his own 'judge' and 'executioner'. Wherever such a transformation took place, wrote Locke, 'there and there only is a *Political, or Civil Society*'.[33]

Thus far, Locke's account largely coincided with the story set out by Hobbes, but it then diverged in a number of fundamental ways. Unlike Hobbes, Locke was very far from allowing that all forms of government which effectively maintained civil peace automatically constituted civil societies. On the contrary, absolute governments not bound by positive law could not be seen as genuine civil societies, even where they *did* successfully keep the peace. This was because of the lurking danger that the sovereign power itself, if unanswerable to any process of legal appeal and popular consent, might threaten the property and persons of its subjects: people could 'never be safe nor at rest, *nor think themselves in Civil Society*, till the Legislature was placed in collective Bodies of Men, call them Senate, Parliament, or what you please'.[34] Locke would have nothing to do with Hobbes's view that an individual's goods and services were legitimately at the disposal of the sovereign at any time; on the contrary 'the chief end' of civil society was precisely the protection of those 'Lives, Liberties and Estates, which I call by the general Name, *Property*'.[35] On both consent and property rights, Locke's account was much closer to that of Hooker than of Hobbes; but there was a third point on which he differed from them both, and that was the relation of civil society to the organs of 'civil government'. That Locke, no less than his predecessors, viewed civil society as coterminous with 'political society' and as embodied in the different branches of government, cannot be doubted;[36] but nevertheless, while the dissolution of civil society automatically brought about the collapse of governing institutions, Locke denied that the opposite was necessarily true. Where breakdown of government led to anarchy, or where 'Conquerours Swords . . . cut up Governments by the Roots, and mangle Societies to pieces', then there was little point in pretending that civil society survived.[37] But Locke seemed to envisage that there might well be cases where a mere temporary hiatus in government occurred, arising either from a ruler's abuse of trust or simply from the fact that a particular legislature was of limited duration. In such a case, there was no instantaneous reversion to nature, and the 'Body of the People' remained a 'Society' able to act as its own 'proper Umpire'.[38] The first act of such a 'Society', Locke believed, would be to

---

[32] Locke, *Two Treaties*, 367–8.

[33] Ibid., 368.

[34] Ibid., 373. Thus Locke believed that France under Louis XIV, perceived by many as the epitome of 'civilized' society, was nevertheless not a 'civil society' because of the large element of arbitrary royal power, and attacks on the rights of Huguenot subjects.

[35] *Leviathan*, 213; *Two Treatises*, 366, 395.

[36] John Dunn, 'The Contemporary Significance of John Locke's Conception of Civil Society', in Kaviraj and Khilnani, *Civil Society: History and Possibilities*, 39–47.

[37] *Two Treatises*, 454, 459.   [38] Ibid., 476.

set up new political institutions, particularly a legislative body, without which social life could not survive. But there was an interesting sleight of language here between 'civil government', 'civil society', and mere 'society'; suggesting perhaps the dawn of an idea that, conceptually if not in practice, there might be a fine distinction to be drawn between 'Society' (as a group of people with a communal identity) and 'Civil Society' (as the institutional framework of legislation, government, and enforcement of rights).[39]

V

Many recent interpreters have identified the eighteenth century as the period in which civil society (in many of its 'modern' connotations) first materialized in many parts of Western Europe, and particularly in England and Scotland. Markets and communications, urban living and 'policing', conversation and good manners, philanthropic and voluntary associations, and ideas about civil equality—all have been seen as hallmarks of a new kind of self-regulating 'public sphere', distinct from family and private life but distinct also from the seats of government and royal courts which had defined and dominated national life in earlier eras.[40] Such changes manifested themselves rather more patchily than is often supposed, but none the less there is overwhelming evidence that alert contemporaries were themselves conscious of living within a new kind of social order. Many of those who commented on such changes at the time also made use of the language of civil society, which ceased to be confined to the realm of high theory and became part of the everyday currency of sermons, salons, poetry, journalism, morality, and the market-place.[41] In the process of popularization, civil society took on certain new meanings, with manuals on polite behaviour (often translated or adapted from the French) offering 'Maxims for Civil Society', 'Reflexions on the ridiculous in civil society', and model anecdotes on 'morality, history, politics and the various events of life' as affording 'inexhaustible sources of Polite Conversation'.[42] A denizen of civil society in this new sense of the term should avoid jesting 'with Country Folks and Fools', practise 'vertuous Celibacy' as against 'the fashionable and barefac'd example of the *Grand Monde*', and facilitate rational intercourse by cultivating 'Discretion', 'Complaisance', 'Good Humour', and 'Sincerity' (though opinion differed on

---

[39] Ibid., 459, 476–7.   [40] See Introduction, above, pp. 2–3, 8–9.

[41] On the celebration of civil society in verse, see Bernard de Mandeville, *The Fable of the Bees; or, Private Vices, Publick Benefits* (1714), ed. by F. B. Kaye (1924), Vol. I; Richard Payne Knight, *The Progress of Civil Society. A Didactic Poem in Six Books* (1796); Anon., *Ode on the Fluctuations of Civil Society* (1797).

[42] Jean Baptiste Morvan be Bellegarde, *Models of Conversation for Persons of Polite Education. Selected and translated from the French* (1765); *Reflexions upon the Politeness of Manners; with Maxims for Civil Society. Being the Second Part of the Reflexions upon Ridicule* (1710 and 1767); see also Ch. 3, below.

this latter point, some maintaining that 'in all Civil Societies men are taught insensibly to be hypocrites from the cradle').[43]

This portrayal of civil society as the medium of affluent and well-informed sociability, distinct from both the rude pleasures of country folk and the dissipations of aristocratic fashion, clearly had implications for the emergence of a new kind of public culture, and there was a close affinity between perceptions of the 'political' and the 'polite'. Nevertheless, although the new politeness certainly impinged upon the language of political thought, it was never its main constituent. On the contrary, political and legal theorists, economists and philosophers in eighteenth-century Britain continued to identify civil society as the 'frame' or 'framework' of legal and governing institutions that made private and voluntaristic social and commercial developments conceivable and possible. Despite a slowly emerging, somewhat hazy awareness of a new thing called 'society', in these more systematic writings 'civil' society meant, as it had done in earlier thought, not private life nor the new extra-governmental public sphere, but the organs and powers of the state as the indispensable progenitor and guardian of those lesser affiliations. Nor was it seen as something peculiar to the new commercial age; it was detected wherever there was a settled polity ruled by impartial laws (thus China, for example, was seen as a civil society because it had been governed for many centuries by a rational bureaucracy and a unified system of law, despite its social and commercial stagnation).[44]

This traditional, constitution-centred, understanding of civil society was evident even in the writings of those most acutely conscious of the onset of powerful self-generating forces of social change. Bernard de Mandeville's influential *The Fable of the Bees* (1714) notoriously conjured up a picture of 'the Social System' as a vast interlocking network of mutual exchange relationships, in which even pathological pressures such as vice, vanity, and greed all contributed to the functioning of the social whole: 'the whole Superstructure is made up of the reciprocal services which men do to each other'. This may sound like the description of a new kind of 'spontaneous social order' independent of government, but Mandeville was very insistent that this was not what was meant. On the contrary, civil society was explicitly a 'Body Politick'. 'Laws and Government are to the Political Bodies of Civil Societies, what the Vital Spirits and Life itself are to the Natural Bodies of Animated Creatures': and 'no species of Animals is, without the Curb of Government, less capable of agreeing long together in Multitudes than that of Man'.[45] David Hume, writing in the lowlands of Scotland a generation later, poured scorn on the stereotype of distinguishing 'civil' from 'natural' institutions—both were equally the invention of men, and 'civil society' was the product not of abstractions like 'consent' and

---

[43] *Reflexions upon . . . Maxims for Civil Society*, 1–2, 91, 158, 213, 239–43, 284–5; Mandeville, *Fable of the Bees*, 349.

[44] David Hume, *Political Essays*, ed. by Knud Haakonssen (Cambridge, 1994), 66.

[45] Mandeville, *Fable of the Bees*, 3, 41, 347.

'contract' but of human experience and practical utility.[46] Like his predecessors, however, Hume identified the heartland of civil society as 'authority', 'good government', and 'good police', rather than commerce, civilization, and good manners (though he hoped that the former processes would facilitate the latter).[47] The conservative theorist Bolingbroke likewise dismissed the tortuous dichotomy of the 'civil' and the 'natural'. He argued that 'civil society' had evolved historically and incrementally from a mixture of sociability, self-interest, and family life; but once again its defining medium was the emergence of formal governing and law-making institutions.[48]

A rather different perspective appeared to be suggested by Adam Smith, who went further than any of his contemporaries in elaborating the idea that a 'society' might have internal relations and dynamics that could be steered only very remotely by government and politics—'in the great chess-board of human society, every single piece has a principle of motion of its own, altogether different from that which the legislature might chuse to impress upon it'.[49] But by 'society' (a term that he employed frequently and loosely) Smith usually meant something quite different from 'civil society' (a term that he employed very sparingly and always in conjunction with government and law-enforcement).[50] 'The public magistrate is under a necessity of employing the power of the commonwealth to enforce the practice of . . . [justice]. Without this precaution, civil society would become a scene of bloodshed and disorder, every man revenging himself at his own hand whenever he fancied he was injured . . . the magistrate, in all governments that have acquired any considerable authority, undertakes to do justice to all.'[51] As a rule, Smith maintained, the growth of civil society (i.e. government) and the growth of society were mutually reinforcing; but there was also a recurrent hint in Smith's writings of civil society acting as a form of moral safety-net *against* the dangerous exuberance of mere 'society'. It was a means by which the genuine 'citizen' ('disposed to respect the laws and to obey the civil magistrate') might stand out against the transiently 'fashionable and popular' and promote thereby 'the welfare of the whole society of his fellow-citizens'.[52]

---

[46] David Hume, *A Treatise of Human Nature* (1739) ed. by Ernest C. Mossmer (Harmondsworth, 1969), 590–8. (The two traditions were closer than was often supposed, Hume seeing utility as akin to a non-transcendental version of natural law.)

[47] Hume, *Political Essays*, 22–3, 66–70.

[48] Isaac Kramnick, *Bolingbroke and his Circle. The Politics of Nostalgia in the Age of Walpole* (Harvard, 1968), 88–98.

[49] Adam Smith, *The Theory of Moral Sentiments* (1759), ed, by D. D. Raphael and A. L. Macfie (Oxford, 1974), 234.

[50] 'Usually', because Smith on occasion also used 'society' to mean simply government and law enforcement (i.e.'civil society'). The interpretation of Smith's position suggested here differs fundamentally from that adopted in Hiroshi Mizuta, 'Moral Philosophy and Civil Society', in Andrew S. Skinner and Thomas Wilson (eds.), *Essays on Adam Smith* (Oxford, 1975).

[51] *Theory of Moral Sentiments*, 340; Adam Smith, *Lectures on Jurisprudence*, ed. by R. L. Meek, D. D. Raphael, and P. G. Stein (Oxford, 1978), 129–39.

[52] *Lectures on Jurisprudence*, 129–30; *Theory of Moral Sentiments*, 231.

Adam Smith's 'civil society' therefore meant something not dissimilar to that of Hooker and Locke, though the element of mere 'society' had become more autonomous, and the role of the upright citizen more actively moralistic than in those older narratives. A much stronger version of this stress on civic morality came from Smith's Scottish contemporary Adam Ferguson, whose *An Essay on the History of Civil Society* (1767) tried to fuse together the new language of sociability and commerce with an older ideal of 'active and strenuous' personal loyalty and service to a small close-knit community.[53] Ferguson rejected the 'atomistic' model of man latent in Smith and the 'social compact' theorists. Instead, human beings were born to live in groups and were far more likely to become isolated and fearful in advanced commercial societies than in more intimate and primitive ones.[54] The genesis of civil society came not from competition and fear between neighbours, but from common defence against an external enemy; it was organization for war that gave rise initially to obedience to a personal leader, and thence to the specialized structures of the legalistic modern state. It was not inclusiveness and universalism but differentiation against an external 'other' that gave the inhabitants of civil society, particularly its menfolk, their sense of purpose and cohesion; and throughout Ferguson's narrative there ran a powerful thread of the 'civic republican' tradition in political thought which many commentators have seen as the obverse of civil society.[55] Property, trade, competition, and specialization of functions—all brought about by civil society and government—were in Ferguson's view essential to the advance of prosperity, knowledge, and the arts: but there was also an ever-present danger that civil society might become the victim of its own success, that security and luxury would sap the sources of civic patriotism and virtue and 'the occasion of farther exertion be removed'.[56] More than any other writer on civil society, Ferguson rejected the distinction made by earlier theorists between the law-abiding citizen and the good man; the strength of a nation, he argued, depended above all on 'the character of its people', and 'the most important lesson of civil society' was the habit of 'implicit obedience' to a leader in times of danger.[57]

Ferguson's *Essay* was to be published in seven editions over the course of the eighteenth century, and was translated into several European languages. It was particularly popular in Germany, where it has been credited with influencing the semantic migration of the concept of civil society away from state and government into the arena of competitive private interests (the *bürgerliche Gesellschaft*

---

[53] Adam Ferguson, *An Essay on the History of Civil Society*, ed. by Fania Oz-Salzburger (Cambridge, 1995).

[54] *History of Civil Society*, 23–4.   [55] Ibid., 24–9, 45–50, 246–7.

[56] Ibid., 168, 212, 241; for a critique of the frequent confusion between 'civil society' and 'civic republican' ideas in recent thought, see Adam B. Seligman, 'Animadversions upon Civil Society and Civic Virtue in the Last Decade of the Twentieth Century', in John Hall (ed.), *Civil Society. Theory, History, Comparison* (Cambridge, 1995), 200–23.

[57] *History of Civil Society*, 62, 143–4, 220, 231.

of Hegel and Marx).[58] This was not, however, the way in which Ferguson's ideas, nor those of other writers of the Scottish school, were interpreted in Britain. In British discourse civil society remained firmly attached to ideas about law, government, and the constitution—with the main theoretical debate coming to rest on whether civil society and its institutions were rooted in contract, utility, or natural rights.[59] Throughout the eighteenth century the concept was frequently invoked on ceremonial public occasions, such as assize sermons, loyal addresses, and patriotic celebrations, to remind audiences of the legitimacy of 'limited' monarchy, the links of government with natural and divine as well as positive law, and the moral duty of both civil and religious obedience.[60] Such resonances were reinforced after 1789 by the onset of revolutionary upheaval in France. More explicitly than ever before 'Albion' was depicted as the *locus classicus* of civil society, France as the unhappy victim of deluded notions of primordial rights, and George III himself was portrayed in some quarters as civil society's ideal 'impartial magistrate', revered for his slogan of 'My Office before my Person'.[61]

It would be a mistake to suggest, however, that such developments were uniformly uncritical and conformist in tone; indeed a striking feature of the civil society theme in late eighteenth- and early nineteenth-century Britain was its invocation in support of a very wide spectrum of political causes and beliefs. Although it was used to defend property and obedience, the idea of a civil society—embodying popular consent, and an entitlement to have certain inalienable rights defended by civil government—was also employed in radical rhetoric to attack slavery and the slave-trade, to defend habeas corpus, and to champion the claims of the destitute to statutory public relief.[62] This latter theme was a

[58] Ibid., introduction, xvii; Fania Oz-Salzberger, 'Civil Society in the Scottish Enlightenment'; Kaviraj and Khilnani, *Civil Society, History and Possibilities*, 78–9. Ferguson's German influence was particularly marked, however, in Tönnies's famous dichotomy of 'Gemeinschaft' and 'Gesellschaft', which adhered to the traditional view that civil society included the institutions of the state (Ferdinand Tönnies, *Community and Civil Society*, ed. by Jose Harris (Cambridge, 2001), xxi, xxxvi, 64).

[59] Thomas Gisborne, *The Principles of Moral Philosophy investigated, and briefly applied to the Constitution of Civil Society* (1795).

[60] Robert Burrow, *Civil Society and Government vindicated from the charge of being founded on, and preserv'd by, dishonest arts* (1723); George Fothergill, 'The Importance of Religion to Civil Societies', in *Nine Sermons on Severall Occasions* (Oxford, 1734–5); Richard Green, *The Benefit of Oaths to Civil Society considered* (1744); George Horne, *The Influence of Christianity on Civil Society* (Oxford, 1773); William Langford, *Obedience to the established Laws and respect to the person of the Administrator are the joint support of Civil Society* (1793).

[61] Gisborne, *Principles of Moral Philosophy*, 307; Langford, *Obedience to the established laws*, 5–7; Payne Knight, *Progress of Civil Society*, 150–1; *Ode on the Fluctuations of Civil Society*; W. D. Conybeare, *The Origin and Obligations of Civil and Legal Society* (Oxford, 1834), 18–19. George III was reputed to have uttered these words when insisting that an assize procession headed by a judge should take precedence over the royal coach.

[62] Thomas Gisborne, *Remarks on the late decision of the House of Commons, respecting ABOLITION of the SLAVE TRADE* (1792), and below, Ch. 3; Frederick Page, *The Principle of the English Poor Laws Illustrated and Defended, by an Historical View of Indigence in Civil Society* (Bath, 1822).

recurrent strand in debate on the English Poor Laws, with Tom Paine in the 1790s and William Cobbett in the 1820s arguing that a public relief system was a necessary corollary to that 'safeguarding of private property' which many viewed as civil society's primary rationale. Such communal protection in time of need was *'essential to the lawfulness* of civil society', wrote Cobbett in *The Poor Man's Friend*, since it was inconceivable that rational beings would have relinquished their natural right to fend for themselves on any other terms. 'Before this state of civil society, the starving, the hungry, the naked man, had a right to go and provide himself with necessaries wherever he could find them . . . When civil society was established, it is impossible to believe that it *had not in view some provision for these destitute persons* . . . The contrary supposition would argue, that fraud was committed upon the mass of the people in forming this civil society . . . It is impossible to believe this. Men never gave their assent to enter into society on terms like these.'[63]

VI

'Civil society' was thus a commonplace in much social and political discourse of eighteenth- and early nineteenth-century Britain, widely used both in writings on high theory and in pulpits, drawing-rooms, and popular oratory. From the 1820s onwards, however, its currency began to dwindle in all these contexts, surviving often as little more than a conventional synonym for civilization, the constitution, or the 'rule of law'. The reasons for this decline are not fully clear, though it may have been linked to the emergence of new and more precise conceptions of 'the state', 'government', 'local government', and their respective public roles.[64] The term was avoided by Jeremy Bentham and John Austin, who preferred to speak of 'political society' ('political' being perhaps less imbued with non-utilitarian notions of social contract and natural rights).[65] Despite certain similarities of language, 'civil society' was not used by the disciples of Dr Thomas Chalmers and other early Victorian proponents of civic philanthropy and voluntary self-help.[66] Nor, despite their debt to the broad-based labour and

[63] William Cobbett, *The Poor Man's Friend* (1829), paras. 10–11; Thomas A. Horne, *Property Rights and Poverty. Political Argument in Britain 1605–1834* (Chapel Hill: University of North Carolina Press, 1990), 201–51.

[64] See Ch. 2, below. Other possibilities are that 'civil society' became associated with post-revolutionary French uses of the term, and with the spread on the continent of Roman law-based civil codes, perceived by English commentators at this time as inimical to personal liberties—a large theme, beyond the scope of this chapter.

[65] Jeremy Bentham, *A Fragment on Government*, 2nd edn. (1823), in *The Collected Works of Jeremy Bentham*, ed. by J. H. Burns (1977), 425–48; John Austin, *The Province of Jurisprudence Determined* (1832), ed. and intro. by H. L. A. Hart (1965), 193–202, 211–12, 217–18.

[66] Chalmers had used 'civic economy' to describe 'voluntarist' assistance to poor families, and 'civil government' to describe what many of his contemporaries referred to as civil society, i.e. government and law-enforcement (Thomas Chalmers, *The Importance of Civil Government to Society, and the Duty of Christians in regard to it* (Glasgow, 1820); *The Christian and Civil Economy of Large Towns* (Liverpool, 1823).

property theories of Locke, was civil society part of the vocabulary of Owenite socialists, the co-operative movement, early trades unionists, or the Chartists. Similarly it played little explicit part in the new language of colonization and empire, where earlier discussions that had assumed the timeless universality of civil societies, or at least their universally latent possibility, gave way to a much more relativist sense that they were fragile and historically unusual.[67]

This did not mean that civil society wholly vanished from British political thought, but that for many Victorian thinkers it was a much less potent theme than it had been in earlier periods. Evidence both of what was understood by the term and its diminishing purchase may be noted in the writings of John Stuart Mill. Mill was closely familiar with civil society debates of the seventeenth and eighteenth centuries (familiar not merely with their political substance but with the various philosophical and theological nuances that lay behind them). His essay on Coleridge, composed in the late 1830s, contained a brief but suggestive digression on the origins of civil societies and the problems involved in maintaining them. In Mill's view, civil society—which he defined as 'the very first element of the social union, obedience to a government of some sort'—was much more difficult to establish and much easier to fall away from than was usually supposed. So great was the repugnance of 'brave and warlike' men to submitting their natural freedom to a 'common umpire' that early civil societies had always been ascribed to a divine origin. In more complex cultures, the survival of civil society depended on maintaining a fine-tuned balance between 'habitual submission to law and government' and the 'vigour and manliness of character' that would initially have resisted any such submission (a clear echo here of the civil society/civic republican paradox of Adam Ferguson). Such a conjunction was in turn dependent on what Mill identified as three 'essential requisites'. These were, first, 'a system of *education* . . . of which . . . one main and incessant ingredient was *restraining discipline*'. The second was a 'feeling of allegiance, or loyalty' to some transcendent idea—be it God, a constitution, or a set of laws or principles, 'which men agreed in holding sacred'. And the third was a sense of common national identity—not 'vulgar' nationalism, but 'a strong and active principle of cohesion among the members of the same community or state', whereby no part of the inhabitants 'consider[ed] themselves as foreigners with regard to another part'. Institutions which embodied these core principles, even in an antiquated form, 'could not without great peril be left vacant'—as could be discerned from the disastrous policies of the French Revolution, which had thrown away 'the shell without preserving the kernel' and attempted to 'new-model society without the binding forces which hold society together'.[68]

Mill was sufficiently pleased with this passage to reproduce it some years later in *A System of Logic*, where he used it to demonstrate the importance of an understanding of history to a 'general science of society'.[69] Yet 'civil society' was

---

[67] J. S. Mill, *Collected Works* (Toronto, 1969), x. 136; xviii. 119–47; Ch. 15, below.

[68] Ibid., x. 132–8.   [69] J. S. Mill, *A System of Logic* (1843), in *Collected Works*, viii. 921–4.

not a term that Mill invoked in his later more overtly political writings, and at no time did he identify it with pluralism, voluntary association, franchise extension, or secularization of public institutions—though all these causes were closely linked with his name, and were to feature prominently in historical portrayals of Victorian civil society a hundred and fifty years later.[70] Mill's analysis seemed to confirm that civil society *per se* was still understood in a British context as referring to the realm of government and the state (and as such was simply taken for granted by most people). But it also implied that it was coming to be seen as part of the much larger and more elusive entity to which it had given birth—i.e. the totality of human relationships, or 'society in general'.

A similar emphasis on civil society as 'ultimate political authority', but with hints of further subsidiary meanings, appeared spasmodically in other writings of the Victorian era. Henry Maine in *Ancient Law* (1861) briefly reverted to the subject in order to expound a cyclical interpretation of economic history. In Maine's account, 'civil society' had surfaced wherever large-scale, multicultural, trading polities had superseded and swallowed up small-scale patriarchal ones—the prime example being the absorption of such petty communities, including the city of Rome itself, into the Roman empire. The motor behind civil society was not mutual fear but the imperative of harmonizing and legally regulating the processes of international trade. Its central principle was to lay down general rules, which treated individuals as subjects and agents rather than as members of tribal or status groups; and its characteristic device was the contract—not the 'social contract' of Hooker, Hobbes, and Locke, but the mutual exchange of pledges and promises between private traders.[71] Such pledges generated book-keeping, rational administration, the law of contract, systematic jurisprudence, and the overarching institutions of law enforcement—all constituting the substance of what came to be known as 'civil society'. If and when such trading empires collapsed then, in Maine's words, 'civil society no longer cohering, men universally flung themselves back on a social organisation older than the beginnings of civil communities'—on 'the lord and his vassals', the patriarchal household, infeudation, and primogeniture. Thus Maine's perception of civil society, though no less political and governmental than that of his predecessors, was of a set of institutions specifically geared to the needs of market society.[72]

Lord Acton's classic essay on nationality, published a year later, differed from Maine in suggesting that the reciprocal powers and property rights established under feudalism had also constituted a civil society, no less than the 'absolute sovereignty' ruling over a 'formless combination of atoms' characteristic of a universal empire. In the same essay Acton also drew attention to what he

[70] e.g., *Urban History*, 25: 3, (1998), Special issue on 'Civil Society in Britain'; John Garrard, *Democratisation in Britain. Elites, Civil Society, and Reform in Britain since 1800* (2002).
[71] Sir Henry Sumner Maine, *Ancient Law. Its connection with the early history of society and its relation to modern ideas* (1861, 1897 edn.), 166–70, 304–47.
[72] *Ancient Law*, 235–6.

perceived as two totally different strands in the civic and political culture of con-temporary Europe. One was the 'Roman' inheritance of unlimited 'sovereign power', 'abstract nationality', personal 'equality' between citizens, and the 'abrogation of all intermediate powers', which he associated with the post-revolutionary heritage of nineteenth-century France (and to a lesser extent with nationalist movements in Spain and Italy). The other was the 'Teutonic' inheritance of limited sovereignty, pluralistic nationalities, the existence of 'independent authorities not derived from the state', and the ideal of personal liberty, of which 'the model would be England'.[73] One may question here Acton's over-simplified rendering of contemporary historical facts; but it is not difficult to discern in this contrast the template of what would emerge in the later twentieth century as two very different conceptions of the identity of civil society. Yet such discussion remained on the margins of mainstream Victorian political thought. When a decade later the idealist philosopher T. H. Green began to deliver in Oxford his seminal *Lectures on the Principles of Political Obligation*, he critically reviewed the civil society theories of Hobbes, Locke, Spinoza, and Rousseau.[74] But he made no use of the term when setting out his own theory of the state, which he portrayed as rooted (even when initially based on force) in the evolution of common consciousness and an 'idea of social good'.[75] Like many of the idealist school, Green laid great emphasis on the expression of active citizenship through voluntary associations and organized philanthropy—an ideal that would be instantly identifiable as a form of 'civil society' to many of its advocates in the early twenty-first century. But neither Green nor his disciples applied the term in this way. Indeed, his criticisms of earlier theorists rested not on their conception of civil society but their reliance on the fiction of a pre-political 'contract' or 'compact'. For Green, no less than for Hobbes and Locke, civil society itself meant not voluntary association but the institutions and processes of the body politic.[76]

VII

There was, however, an exception to this relative Victorian neglect. As indi-cated above, much of the earlier commentary on civil society had assumed a close conjunction between the state and organized religion. And, despite its vir-tual disappearance from other aspects of political thought, civil society remained an important strand in discussion of relations between church and state. For much of the Victorian era there was an undercurrent of liberal

[73] J. E. E. Dalberg-Acton, 'Nationality', *Home and Foreign Review*, 1 (1862), 2–25.
[74] T. H. Green, *Lectures on the Principles of Political Obligation* (1911 edn.), 55–80, 130–1, 135, 143–4, 159, 244–7.
[75] Green, *Lectures*, 135, 144. See also H. J. W. Hetherington and J. H. Muirhead, *Social Purpose. A Contribution to a Philosophy of Civic Society* (1918), where 'civic society' was also identified with the consciously willed political order. For a fuller discussion, see Ch. 14, below.
[76] Green, *Lectures*, 58, 70–8.

Protestant thought that portrayed the advance of civil society, organized Christianity, popular sovereignty, and 'the idea of man as a free personality' as all running in tandem.[77] These views were rivalled, however, by a growing mistrust of close relations between church and state and of the assumption made by many earlier civil society writers that the one necessarily buttressed the other. This questioning arose initially *within* the established church, where adherents of the old 'high church' party reacted to the enfranchisement of dissenters (including Roman Catholics) and to increased parliamentary control over church matters, by reasserting the autonomous 'catholic' status of the Anglican church *against* 'state interference'. Protestant dissenters likewise became much more confident in their questioning both of political regulation of religious matters and of the general principle of a 'state church'. A series of very diverse measures and movements—the secession of the Free Church of Scotland in 1843, the disestablishment of the Church of Ireland in 1868, the sustained campaigns of English nonconformists against tithes, church rates, and denominational education—all operated to prise apart the earlier view that 'civil society' implied close identification between secular and religious establishments.

A principled critique of any subjection of church to state was most powerfully expressed in certain quarters of the renascent Roman Catholic church, which in 1851 reintroduced its own episcopal hierarchy in Britain for the first time since the Reformation. Catholic apologists of an 'ultramontane' bent strongly resisted the view that such a measure implied any absorption of the Catholic church into 'civil society', and criticized the readiness of their co-religionists in France and Germany to enter into concordats and accommodations with state authorities. A series of articles in the 1860s and 1870s by Edward Lucas—an associate of Cardinal Manning and one of the very few Victorian authors explicitly to address 'civil society' as a central theme—repudiated any suggestion that civil society should include, or take precedence over, or even coexist on equal terms with, 'the Society' of the universal church.[78] On the contrary, civil society *per se* was a mere circumstantial convenience that had long preceded the divine society of the Christian church, and prevailed in some form or another wherever human beings lived side by side, often in active rejection or total ignorance of Christianity.[79] In so far as civil societies were genuinely 'civilized' this was because, at a crucial stage in their history, their existence had been protected and fostered by the church; and wherever these roles were reversed, the secular authority 'either gives nothing, or it gives persecution'. Catholics who deluded themselves otherwise, Lucas predicted, were laying themselves open to the kind of attacks inflicted by secular rulers of the sixteenth century.[80] Far from

---

[77] e.g., Samuel Smith Harris, *The Relation of Christianity to Civil Society* (1883).

[78] Edward Lucas, 'Christianity in Relation to Civil Society', Parts I–V, in H. E. Manning (ed.), *Essays on Religion and Literature*, Vols. I–III, (1865–74). Lucas, a Roman Catholic convert from Quakerism, was the brother and biographer of Frederick Lucas, MP, founder of the Catholic journal *The Tablet*.

[79] Lucas, in *Religion and Literature*, i. 290, 334–6, 338.   [80] Ibid., i. 313–14; ii. 365–6:

'Christian Society' being 'subject to the abstract idea of "the State"', Lucas claimed that 'the government of civil society is in great measure dependent on that of the Christian society'. This priority had been legitimized both by divine ordinance and by 'the social benefits bestowed on mankind' over the previous seventeen centuries.[81] The notion that organized religion should retreat into the private sphere or be subordinate to the civil power was mere Zoroastrian 'dualism', falsely inseminated into political thought by the peculiar circumstances of early Christianity's struggle for survival under pagan rule. The aim of a Christianized civil society of the future should be the quest for 'a true City of God' where 'the federation of the world shall be united under one government'.[82]

Edward Lucas's vision of a civil society answerable only to a universal church met with a muted response among his mainly Catholic readers, who complained that his articles were 'tedious' and shed little 'light'.[83] Nevertheless his arguments were echoed by a number of thinkers who approached the subject from a very different angle. As shown above, an important thread in earlier constructions of civil society had been the assertion of popular 'consent' against both arbitrary government and anarchy. Over the course of the nineteenth century, however, the advance of democracy, mass society, and political nationalism began to awaken fears of a quite different kind—that the main threat to individual or group rights might come from democratic majorities, mass public opinion, or state bureaucracies claiming to represent the 'general will' (dangers seen as exemplified by Bismarck's *Kulturkampf* and by the attacks on voluntary and religious bodies launched by the French Third Republic). The 'Gladstonian' administrative reforms of the 1860s and 1870s, which transferred to parliament and secular law courts control over many social and religious matters that had previously been the concern of self-regulating private bodies, likewise appeared to some to be transforming the nature of the British state; and similar anxieties were to be stirred by certain landmark legal decisions, particularly the Taff Vale case and the Scottish church controversy, during the 1890s and 1900s. A response to these developments, which was partly to redefine the perception of civil society, came from a loose grouping of 'pluralist' thinkers, some of them mainly concerned with the autonomy of denominational groups, whilst others saw churches as a test case for the treatment of all kinds of 'voluntarism' and free association whether religious or secular.

The pluralists were few in number, but their fewness was counterbalanced by their close familiarity with intellectual debates on church, state, community, and society over the previous two millennia. A common thread of their writing was the question of how far the wide variety of social groups that existed under the general protection of the secular state possessed a self-sustaining 'reality' independent both of the state itself and of their constituent members. Such

[81] Ibid., i. 316–17, 376–7; ii. 160–1.   [82] Ibid., ii. 204–5, 238–40; iii. 202.
[83] Ibid., iii. 174–5.

groups existed in all modern societies; but as Mill, Acton, and many others had pointed out, they were peculiarly numerous and independent in Britain, and had been so for several centuries. Nevertheless, to pluralist theorists their status both in English law and in public doctrine was paradoxical and precarious, leaving them vulnerable to attacks on their autonomy and corporate life which, if less overtly authoritarian than such attacks on the continent, were none the less similar in kind.[84] The writings of the pluralist legal historian Frederick Maitland criticized the legacy of 'absolute' state sovereignty and mistrust of lesser organizations that had been mediated into English thought by Hobbes and Austin, and suggested that the 'real personality' of such lesser bodies needed to be strengthened and acknowledged in English law. Such acknowledgement would promote the flourishing of modern 'multicellular' group life as a counterweight to the overweening power of the 'absolute' state, and reduce the latter to its proper status of being merely one 'society' among many (albeit a society with the special and all-inclusive role of maintaining civil order and enforcement of law).[85]

Maitland's references to what he called 'mere "Civil Society"' were casual and infrequent;[86] but its relation to the pluralist cause was addressed much more explicitly by Maitland's Anglican disciple J. N. Figgis. Figgis's prime concern was to promote the uncoupling of what he believed had become an intolerable degree of state control over the doctrines, property, and internal management of the various churches of Britain (both 'free' and 'established'). But he argued that 'the problem of the relations of Church and State cannot be considered in isolation'. It involved the free corporate life of associations of all kinds, and 'raises topics which go down to the root of all political philosophy, and forces us to face the whole problem of the true nature of civil society'.[87] A proper understanding of civil society, so Figgis claimed, had been dogged and distorted throughout the history of Christianity by its origins under an empire that had outlawed the very existence of private associations except as a 'concession' from the 'single all-absorbing omnicompetent power' of the Roman imperial state. When Christianity itself became the hegemonic power, then both Papacy and empire had been happy to take over this concessionary idea, so there had been 'no need for men to worry themselves with forming a totally new doctrine of the structure of civil society'.[88] Though challenged from time to time in medieval thought, the 'concession theory', with its 'doctrine of the unity of sovereign power and the complete non-existence of all other real authorities' had survived into the era of the modern secular state, reinforced by the pan-European revival of Roman law.[89]

---

[84] Maitland, *Collected Papers*, 212, 212–19; J. N. Figgis, *Churches in the Modern State*, 2nd edn. (1914), 3–53.

[85] Maitland, *Collected Papers*, 29–32; Otto Gierke, *Political Theories of the Middle Age*, introduction by Frederick William Maitland (Cambridge, 1900), x–xii, xxvi–xxvii, xxxi–xxxii.

[86] *Political Theories of the Middle Age*, xxv.   [87] Figgis, *Churches*, 170.

[88] Ibid., 60–2, 74–5, 202–3.   [89] Ibid., 73, 76–7, 82–4, 195.

Yet such a doctrine in Figgis's view was not merely illiberal and tyrannical: it also flew in the face of sociological reality, and of the 'religious heterogeneity' of contemporary European, and particularly British, social life (the latter further complicated by Britain's connections with a multivarious world empire).[90] Rather than assuming 'an abstract doctrine of unity', it made much more sense to proceed by 'observing the facts of life as it is lived, and trying to set down the actual features of civil society'. The outcome of such observation, Figgis concluded, was 'not, surely, a sand-heap of individuals, all equal and undifferentiated, unrelated except to the State, but an ascending hierarchy of groups, family, school, town, county, union, Church, &c. &c.'[91] Within that ascending hierarchy of different 'societies'—all overlapping in personnel, but each with its own special function and sphere of authority over its own members—the function of 'civil society' was simply the maintenance of order and enforcement of law.[92] Members of other societies—such as churches, families, companies, and trade unions—had no more right to impede or interfere with the proper functioning of civil society, than *it* had to impede or interfere with *theirs*.[93] This meant that there could be no special privileges under civil law for members of churches and other voluntary associations, but at the same time they should have absolute freedom to manage their own generic doctrines and internal affairs. 'What we claim is freedom within the limits of civil society . . . we neither claim to be outside the law nor to exercise control over politics'.[94]

Not all Edwardian pluralists were as pessimistic as Figgis about the monopolistic potential of the twentieth-century British state. Indeed some, like Ernest Barker, thought just the opposite: that constitutional theory, common law, and the concrete practices of everyday life all meant that the state as envisaged in Roman civil law scarcely existed in Britain—the nation's chief defining characteristic being the vast network of sub-political, self-governing associations and partnerships that managed its private and most of its public affairs.[95] What is important here, however, is not Figgis's accuracy or otherwise as a contemporary social analyst, but his use of political language. There can be no doubt of his desire to see a much diminished state, a greatly enhanced role for intermediate 'societies', and a much clearer definition and entrenchment of small-group rights. Yet, nevertheless, it was still the policing and peacekeeping functions of that slimmed-down state that constituted the sphere of 'civil society', *not* the mass of self-governing voluntary associations to which a peaceful, law-abiding public order had given rise. A rather different emphasis may, however, be detected in the early writings of Harold Laski, who agreed with Figgis

---

[90] Ibid., 84–5, 100, 113–14.　　　　　　　　　[91] Ibid., 87.

[92] Ibid., 103–5, 251.

[93] Ibid., 112–13, 125–9, 224–5. Thus Figgis held that churchmen *qua* churchmen had no right to tell the civil authorities what to do on questions of social welfare, though they had every right (and duty) to press for such action as citizens of the state.

[94] Ibid., 103–6, 120–1.

[95] Ernest Barker, 'The Discredited State. Thoughts on Politics before the War', *Political Quarterly*, 2 (1915), 102–21.

that religious freedom was 'in reality . . . but part of the larger problem of the nature of civil society'.[96] Laski applied Figgis's analysis to a series of case-studies of clashes between church and state in recent European history, using them to develop a new theory of the nature and distribution of secular power. Like Figgis, and against the account of Ernest Barker, he portrayed the previous three centuries of British history as a story of continuous displacement, not just of self-governing voluntary associations but of numerous intermediate *public* bodies, by an over-centralized unitary sovereign state.[97] Writing in 1917 from the external vantage-point of Harvard university, Laski argued that—quite contrary to the prevailing national self-image—there was in normal times a far more vigorous and autonomous culture of local and civic self-government in Germany than in Britain, where local authorities were merely an 'anaemic reflex of the central power'.[98] Laski's implied solution (developed much more fully in later works) was the dilution and dispersal of sovereign power downwards and outwards into the hands of self-governing groups, each recognized as sovereign in its own sphere. The 'worship of a supposed logical necessity in unified governance' would give way to a recognition that the 'sovereignty of the State does not in reality differ from the power exercised by a Church or trade union'.[99] This sounds like the language of Maitland and Figgis, but the degree of 'dissipation of sovereignty' envisaged was much greater; and unlike his mentors Laski made no mention of retaining a separate role for civil society, as the 'society' charged with the special function of public order and defence. On the contrary, civil society appeared to be dissolved into 'the essential federalism of society' and its 'constituent parts'.[100] One can identify here a clear prefiguring of an important strand in much late twentieth-century thinking about 'civil society'—as a virtuous alternative to, rather than concrete embodiment of, the powers and functions of national governments and nation-states.

VIII

After 1918 the category of 'civil society' faded from political language in Britain even more completely than it had done in the Victorian era.[101] This eclipse has often been ascribed to the fact that the era of two world wars led to a massive resurgence of the 'omnicompetent' state, both as a tool of popular welfare and as a tool of oppression, thus crowding out the lesser and intermediate sphere of civil society. But this scarcely seems an adequate account, in view of the fact

---

[96] Harold Laski, *Studies in the Problem of Sovereignty* (New Haven, Conn., 1917), 208.
[97] Ibid., chs. II and III.   [98] Ibid., 279–80.   [99] Ibid., 65–6, 270.
[100] Ibid., 65, 268–75. 'Civil society' disappeared from Laski's subsequent works, though the development of his views about the diffusion of sovereignty not merely downwards but upwards to international agencies, and the evolution of multi-cultural societies guaranteed by those agencies, bore a recognizable resemblance to some models of civil society current at the present day (Harold Laski, *A Grammar of Politics* (1925), chs. 2–3, 6–7, 11).
[101] Though see Ch. 11, below.

that—in Britain at least—the history of civil society over more than three centuries had been so closely identified with the activities of government. A fuller explanation both of the decline of the notion of 'civil society', and of its late twentieth-century resurgence in a guise quite different from its traditional one, cannot be attempted here. But its role in the history of political thought in Britain suggests a number of points that deserve further comment and enquiry.

One of these points is that the concept of 'civil society' needs to be disentangled and much more clearly differentiated from that of 'society' in general. The idea of a *societas* originated in Roman law as a voluntary partnership for any purpose between two or more free persons, with a *societas civilis* being a partnership for maintaining peace and public order (and therefore necessarily extending to a much larger group). At the beginning of the modern era, a civil society was still a much broader and grander category than any mere 'society'. In the language of Hooker, Hobbes, Locke, and even of de Mandeville and Adam Smith, civil society was the 'frame' or 'framework' within which lesser, private, social activities and relationships were able to happen. In these same writings, however, one can observe the very gradual crystallization of the idea of 'society' as something potentially larger and more all-encompassing than the state itself. This was the sense of a 'grand' or 'great' society, hinted at casually by Hooker and Adam Smith, theorized about by J. S. Mill, but not fully articulated until social theorists like Robert Park and Graham Wallas brought it to the fore in the early twentieth century.[102] Many of the shifting nuances of 'civil society' occurred as a counterpoint to the almost imperceptible evolution of this wider and quite different idea, of 'society' as a massive spontaneous network of human interaction outside and distinct from politics and civil government. This 'spontaneous social order' (to use Hayek's phrase) might be composed of the sum of the free choices of rational individuals; but its overall shape and purposes—unlike those of civil society—were largely beyond the reach of individual 'choice' and 'consent'.[103]

A further point is that, although British understanding of civil society was so closely linked to the institutions of the state, it was in many respects not the same kind of state as that which was conceived of by theorists on the continent. Although people in Britain talked only rarely about 'the state', they had other words which meant much the same thing, such as 'polity' or 'commonwealth' or 'the King's government'; but no British writer on civil society would have suggested (as Hegel did in *The Philosophy of Right*, for example) that such activities as police, public administration, and enforcement of law were not part of this overarching political authority. In other words, the state in Britain was perceived as something much less 'untrammelled', much more embedded in the

---

[102] Above, pp. 17, 23; Graham Wallas, *The Great Society. A Psychological Analysis* (1914), 3–20, 305–40.

[103] See R. G. Collingwood, *The New Leviathan* (Oxford, 1942), 130–7, for a suggestive discussion of this theme. A further complication that it has been impossible to explore fully here is the term 'political society', often but not invariably used to mean 'civil society' in the sense discussed in this chapter.

structures of everyday life, than the more abstract and 'reified' regimes of continental Europe, particularly where the latter were permeated by Roman and modern civil law. Such 'trammelling' (another image favoured by British writers on this theme) perhaps helps to explain why no gulf emerged between the concepts of state and civil society in English discourse before the later twentieth century. Moreover, despite Britain's role as the historic crucible of economic change, very few British commentators saw civil society in primarily economic terms, and some explicitly criticized the Hegelian school for doing so.[104]

While the overall tradition of civil society thought in Britain was thus distinctively different from that which developed in Europe, there were also many important ways in which British interpreters of civil society differed among each other. Most civil society theorists from Hooker through to Harold Laski were concerned in some way or another with a vision of political 'inclusiveness'; but perceptions of who was eligible for inclusion varied enormously in different periods and contexts—indeed the very 'openness' of civil society continually generated new categories of people with claims to inclusion who had not previously been thought of as civil 'persons' (such as property-less men, nonconformists, women, and migrants). Some commentators proclaimed Britain, or England, or 'Albion', as the triumphal prototype of a civil society; but a more common approach among serious writers was to see civil society as an ideal or model against which different aspects of real institutions and practices could be measured and found wanting. Thus J. S. Mill, for example, cited England as a country which, at an internal level, had attained one of his major criteria for civil society 'in the strongest degree'; but in relation to Ireland was nevertheless 'one of the most signal examples of the consequences of its absence'.[105] Despite fears of a relapse into 'natural' disorder, many British commentators from Hooker onwards assumed a degree of 'natural sociability' in mankind. But there were other accounts—most notably that of Hobbes—which seemed to presage the abstract, free-standing, socially 'unencumbered' personality found in some accounts of civil society at the present day. There were those like Ferguson and Mill, for whom the flourishing of civil society was crucially dependent on the moral character of its citizens; others like Hooker and Hume, for whom a positive merit of civil society (as opposed to more intimate communities) was that well-ordered institutions made it possible to by pass difficult questions of personal virtue. For all its more recent identity as a largely 'secularizing' concept, British discourse on civil society down to the early twentieth century was closely engaged with controversies about church and state (both as a major issue in its own right, and as a surrogate for other kinds of public/private relationships). But, as shown above, these ideas encompassed a very broad spectrum of intellectual positions, ranging from support for a hegemonic church establishment through to extreme religious pluralism. Similarly, within a framework of

[104] Ernest Barker, *Political Thought in England 1848 to 1914* (1915), 67.
[105] Mill, *Collected Works*, x. 136.

constitutionalism, the term civil society was used at various times to legitimate a very wide range of political positions, ranging from ultra-loyalism and civic obedience through to championship of welfare rights (in the case of William Cobbett), and implicit sponsorship of revolution (in the case of John Locke). Such extreme diversity of application suggests that the moral resonances and frame of reference of civil society have been much more complex and multifaceted than is often imagined. British ideas on the subject drew upon a common European heritage of legal and political thought that stretched back for nearly two millennia; but they were also constantly redeployed and reshaped by immediate circumstance. This suggests that both as an idea and as a set of institutions civil society should more properly be seen as part of the ongoing subject-matter of history, rather than as a fixed category of cross-cultural historical analysis.

2

Central Government 'Interference': Changing Conceptions, Practices, and Concerns, *c.*1700–1850*

JOANNA INNES

I

During the mid-nineteenth century, much argumentation went on around the loosely connected themes of 'centralization' and 'government interference' on the one hand, the 'principles' of 'non-interference' in economic matters and of 'local self-government' on the other. 'Interference' and 'centralization' were commonly reprobated (though might be argued to have merit in particular cases). 'Local self-government' was commonly extolled. These attitudes were associated with a widely held belief that society was most likely to flourish and develop—to become more prosperous and more civilized—through the efforts of freely associating individuals. Though especially associated with liberalism, this view was not peculiar to it: conservatives, Chartists, and Owenites can all be found endorsing variants of it—though they might differ sharply about their implications in any given case. Still, much discussion was conducted against a broadly consensual background.[1]

Historians often suggest that these values and attitudes had deeper roots in British culture: in formal theorizing (about the limits of state power in matters of property, for example); in embedded practices (in long habits of parliamentary government, and local 'self-government at the king's command'); and in

---

* Among various people who have discussed these themes with me, I should especially like to thank Simon Devereaux and Andrew Hanham for sharing their findings about terminology.

[1] For (ambivalent) Chartist and Owenite attitudes, Paul Pickering, *Chartism and the Chartists in Manchester and Salford* (Basingstoke, 1995), ch. 4; and G. Claeys, *Citizens and Saints. Politics and Anti-Politics in Early British Socialism* (Cambridge, 1989), 279, 309–18. W. C. Lubenow, *The Politics of Government Growth. Early Victorian Attitudes towards State Intervention 1833–48* (Newton Abbot, 1971) analyses the range of philosophies and ideas expressed in similar terms. I write of 'interference' rather than 'intervention' throughout this chapter because I do not find the latter word much used in this context before 1850. 'Interference' at this time did not have wholly negative connotations, and was sometimes urged rather than resisted.

widely held prejudices (against 'tyranny' and 'arbitrary power'; for 'liberty'.)[2] This chapter sets out to explore some of the antecedents of, and patterns in the development of, mid-nineteenth-century views. To that extent its theme is continuity. But interpretatively, it stresses *discontinuity*. It argues that there was much that was novel both about the forms these ideas took in the mid-nineteenth century and about the contexts in which they were invoked. The very terminology of discussion was novel. In eighteenth-century Britain, people did not talk about 'centralization' or indeed about 'central' or 'local government'. Though they did talk about the 'state' and about 'government', not until the 1780s did they use these terms to refer to ministers and their policies. Eighteenth-century Britons occasionally complained about legislative interference—but the form of interference they complained about most was the interference of peers in elections!

The central argument of the chapter is, thus, that the ideas and attitudes identified at the outset were historically specific: products of a particular time and place. The chapter tries to illuminate this specificity by explaining in what ways and why eighteenth- and even early nineteenth-century concerns were different. At the same time, it acknowledges continuities, and tries to historicize these: to show, as it were, elements of the mid-nineteenth-century picture moving into place, while emphasizing that, at other times, these parts were parts of other wholes.

The subject is too large to be easily mastered, and the chapter does not pretend to undertake more than a preliminary enquiry.[3] It falls into two main parts. The first offers a broad sketch of changes in the way that government was constructed and operated, and in the problems it was seen to pose, between the late seventeenth and mid-nineteenth centuries. The second surveys changing patterns of debate in relation to two issues: policing; and poor relief. In the mid-nineteenth century, much debate about the nature and limits of government focused on such topics. They were less central to eighteenth-century debate—because of which, the terms of earlier discussion are not always easy to reconstruct. I shall suggest that some nineteenth-century concerns were foreshadowed, but that both the nature of these concerns and the ways in which they were expressed initially differed from one policy field to another. Only in the nineteenth century did such debates begin to converge around common themes and preoccupations.

This enquiry is relevant to the concerns of the current volume inasmuch as the substantially self-regulating and self-propelling society in which so many nineteenth-century Britons thought they lived, and which they sought to

[2] Thus Richard Bellamy, 'Introduction', in Richard Bellamy (ed.), *Victorian Liberalism. Nineteenth-Century Political Thought and Practice* (1990), 2; Eugenio Biagini, *Liberty, Retrenchment and Reform. Popular Liberalism in the Age of Gladstone 1860–80* (Cambridge, 1992), 6, 84–5, 93–6, 139, 144.

[3] Because the topic is diffuse, complex, and underexplored, it is not easy to footnote. My footnotes are minimal; secondary works cited supply further references.

enhance, resembles what some recent commentators have meant by a 'civil society' though, as Jose Harris suggests in the previous chapter, few contemporaries would have understood the term in this way. 'Civil society' *was* often invoked in the eighteenth and early nineteenth centuries, but not to aid thought about setting limits to government. Conventionally, 'civil society' was contrasted with the 'state of nature'. People made their world 'civil' by practising various forms of interaction, both formal (setting up governments, making other legally-enforceable agreements) and informal (trucking and bartering, trying to impress each other). One could, in this tradition, ask how government might best operate, civil society being the kind of organism that it was. But such an enquiry was not normally conceptualized as an enquiry into how government might best interact with another entity, 'civil society'. Rather 'civil society' denoted the structured whole, of which government was a part

Although nineteenth-century German theorists began to distinguish 'state' from 'civil society', in the British tradition it was commonly government and 'society' *tout court* which came to be counterposed. Interestingly, those early nineteenth-century writers who continued to write of 'civil society' often seem to have done so in the course of justifying what others might have termed 'government interference'.[4] 'Civil society', as they portrayed it, offered benefits to its inhabitants by instating a series of correlative rights and duties. Thus, in civil society, in contrast to the state of nature, people had a right not to be left to starve, so long as there were sufficient resources to support everyone. The correlative duty to maintain had to be borne by someone. In advanced societies, this was most effectively and fairly discharged by government. Even in the 1820s, when such arguments were sometimes made, it was nevertheless relatively unusual to argue about public policy by reference to a concept of 'civil society'. Subsequently the term dropped almost entirely from use.

Taking recent conceptions of 'civil society' as my reference point (and recognizing their variety), I have, none the less, thought that an enquiry into how people in the eighteenth- and nineteenth-century Britain talked about the proper nature and limits of government operations in society would be relevant to this volume. My emphasis on the historical specificity of conceptions of that relationship should have wider resonance.

II

In seventeenth-century Britain, arguments about government exceeding its authority focused on such matters as these: monarchs proceeding without reference to parliament, especially in relation to taxation; parliaments proceeding without adequate reference to the people; use of military force to enforce

---

[4] e.g. Frederick Page, *The Principle of the English Poor Laws Illustrated and Defended, by an Historical View of Indigence in Civil Society* (Bath, 1822); T. A. Horne, *Property Rights and Poverty: Political Argument in Britain, 1605–1834* (Exeter, 1986); above, pp. 25–6.

unpopular policies; arbitrary and oppressive treatment of critics of government; high-handed dealing with chartered bodies, and intrusion upon freedom of conscience in matters of religion. Attempts to dictate to county elites how they should govern their localities, or to bully them into supporting unpopular royal policies undoubtedly caused resentment, as did puritanical attempts to control moral conduct, but there was relatively little principled argument about those matters.[5]

Many of these concerns persisted into later centuries. Parliament's representativeness, the role of the army, the extent of respect for freedoms of speech and assembly, the conduct of political trials, and the role of the state in relation to religion all remained live issues through the 1840s and 1850s—but at the same time, new concerns arose (and older ones changed in character) as structures and practices of government and forms of public life changed and new ways of thinking developed.

In surveying the eighteenth-century scene, I shall both note what was new and emphasize certain things that did not apply as yet. The 'Glorious Revolution' of 1688 gave parliament an unwontedly central role. In this context, new modes of governing were developed which changed ideas as to how kings and their ministers were most likely to abuse power. In terms of substantive policies, ministers focused their efforts quite narrowly. They showed little interest in restructuring what we might term 'local government', or in shaping policy in the sorts of matters with which local authorities were most concerned. Local authorities had their own problematic features, and were by no means routinely idealized, though local groups showed some ingenuity in developing alternatives. Voluntary associations proliferated, undertaking some quasi-governmental functions. The language of 'liberty' had wide currency, and was used to criticize various 'arbitrary' and 'oppressive' practices. Developments in social and economic theory made it increasingly common to posit a 'system of natural liberty', such that individuals pursuing freely chosen courses would contribute to general benefit—but arguments based on that premiss only occasionally surfaced in public debate.

Let us enlarge on this sketch. First, some aspects of usage might be clarified. 'Government' in eighteenth-century use—at least, until the century's final years—commonly denoted the dynastic regime, or the principle and activity of governing, or the framework of institutions through which government was carried out. Discrete parts of the system were referred to by discrete names, thus the king's ministers, magistrates, and so forth. A distinction was sometimes drawn

---

[5] Michael J. Braddick, *State Formation in Early Modern England* (Cambridge, 2000) surveys seventeenth-century government practice, and some of the controversies to which it gave rise. John Locke was much concerned to identify proper limits to government power—but chiefly in relation to property and religion. Though he took an interest in both poor relief and education, in these cases he was more concerned with substantive good practice than with implementing agencies. See Locke, *Some Thoughts Concerning Education* (1695); R. G. Bouyer, *An Account of the Origin, Proceedings, and Intentions of the Society for the Promotion of Industry . . . by Mr. John Locke* (3rd edn., 1789).

between 'superior' and 'inferior' parts of government—'inferior' roughly corresponding to what we might term 'local government'.[6] I shall not disdain anachronistic usages when they are convenient, but shall try to show some respect for contemporary habits of expression.

The establishment of parliament as a central element in government after 1688 made it necessary for the king's ministers to develop new ways of mobilizing support for their policies. To this end, they refined the art of employing money and patronage to win friends and influence people (particularly people who served in parliament and their key supporters); at the same time, they cultivated ideologically based loyalties. In this new context, critics argued that although parliament seemed well placed to check such arbitrary tendencies as kings or their ministers might display, in practice, 'influence' and 'faction' usually disabled it. Tax policies, policies in the development and use of military force, religious policies, and the treatment of political opponents consequently remained problematic.[7]

Ministerial initiatives relating to the ordinary work of domestic government received little critical attention—mainly because there were few such initiatives. Whereas in continental Europe at this time, a number of states, starting with France, developed new systems to oversee local agencies so as to further the state's military and fiscal performance, British ministers developed fiscal and military support systems substantially independent of traditional local government. They could therefore afford to let that continue substantially unreformed. Ministers also made little effort to promote domestic legislation, other than on fiscal, military, constitutional, and some religious matters: they commonly left it to backbenchers to propose improvements to criminal justice, welfare, highway maintenance, and so forth. This was not a recipe for ambitious domestic legislation—though nor was it a recipe for stagnation. There were many such piecemeal initiatives, though these reached the statute book only if they won spontaneous support from enough MPs.[8]

The apparatus of local government was heterogeneous, and had its own problematic features. In the counties, the key authorities were justices of the peace (also called magistrates) who were appointed by the Lord Chancellor. Magisterial appointments were politicized in the 1680s and continued on a party-political basis down to the accession of George III, in 1760. Urban corporations, by contrast, enjoyed substantial autonomy, but might none the less

[6] For my preliminary thoughts on terminology: J. Innes, 'Changing Perceptions of the State in the Late Eighteenth and Nineteenth Centuries', *Journal of Historical Sociology*, 15 (2002), 107–13. See also J. A. W. Gunn, 'Eighteenth-Century Britain: In Search of the State and Finding the Quarter Sessions' in John Brewer and Eckhart Hellmuth (eds.), *Rethinking Leviathan. The Eighteenth-Century State in Britain and Germany* (Oxford, 1999).

[7] For this 'country' critique: H. T. Dickinson, *Liberty and Property. Political Ideology in Eighteenth-Century Britain* (1977).

[8] J. Innes, 'The Domestic Face of the Military-Fiscal State: State and Society in Eighteenth-Century Britain', in L. Stone (ed.), *An Imperial State at War: Britain 1688–1815* (1993), 96–127, and 'Parliament and the Shaping of Eighteenth-Century English Social Policy', *Transactions of the Royal Historical Society*, 5th ser., 40 (1990), 63–92.

be captured by local partisans. Many corporations were self-recruiting, so that a party that gained ascendancy might perpetuate its hold. Both magistrates and corporations could therefore be seen as caught up in webs of 'influence' and 'faction'. In town and country alike, the parish was a key lesser administrative unit. Parish affairs were often controlled by a group of large ratepayers; many parishes had 'select vestries' which might again be self-recruiting. In London, hostility to select vestries bubbled up at several points during the century. None of this implies that these bodies were not also valued as defenders of local interests. However, they also encountered criticism; some town corporations attracted sustained opposition.[9]

Reservations about existing local arrangements provide part of the context in which some eighteenth-century innovations should be set. In a small way from the 1690s, increasingly as the eighteenth century unfolded, there emerged a practice of local property holders applying to parliament to obtain legislative sanction for the establishment of a special statutory 'corporation', 'trust', or 'commission' to provide specified services, and to finance these by means specified in the act. Detailed arrangements varied, but efforts were often made to ensure accountability to those whose payments funded services (for example, by providing for some form of election). Efforts were made too to prevent these new bodies from becoming tools of faction by dispensing with such membership qualifications as traditional corporations imposed (such as having been apprentice to, or the son of, a member) and by making membership free of any form of religious test. As Paul Langford has argued, these bodies embodied new values, more consonant with the world-view of eighteenth-century propertied society than many older forms of agency. But these values did not as yet provide the basis for any concerted assault on the older institutional order.[10]

Also burgeoning in the eighteenth century and embodying, at least latently, alternative value systems were voluntary associations. Some of these existed primarily to sustain sociability or mutual aid; some were in effect pressure groups; some political organizations. But some discharged quasi-governmental functions: thus maintaining hospitals or providing other charitable aid; putting special constables on the streets to combat 'vice and immorality'; or prosecuting frauds or crimes against subscribers. Voluntary organizations of this kind again commonly emphasized accountability and transparency in their operations—especially in relation to their own members, but also in relation to a wider public, from whom they hoped to elicit support.[11] As we shall note shortly, they

---

[9] David Eastwood, *Government and Community in the English Provinces 1700–1870* (Basingstoke, 1997) for a recent overview.

[10] J. Innes, 'The Local Acts of a National Parliament: Parliament's Role in Sanctioning Local Action in Eighteenth-Century Britain', in D. Dean and C. Jones (eds.), *Parliament and Locality* (Edinburgh, 1998), 23–47 for an overview; Paul Langford, *Public Life and the Propertied Englishman* (Oxford, 1991), chs. 3–4 for much illuminating detail and interpretation.

[11] Peter Clark, *British Clubs and Societies 1580–1800: The Origins of an Associational World* (Oxford, 2000).

provided the basis for at least one form of developed challenge to official patterns of provision.

Whoever initiated and implemented them, domestic policies were, of course, always open to criticism in substance. Some eighteenth-century proposals and practices were attacked as inimical to liberty. At mid-century, a series of proposals under discussion—to conduct a national census, to establish lazarettos to quarantine incomers carrying infectious diseases, and to improve the 'police' of London—attracted intemperate criticism from one MP on the grounds that these were all French notions.[12] In debates on matters of this kind, however, arguments of this sort were exceptional. Although the limitations of the written record make it hard to be confident about trends in debate, my impression is that criticisms invoking concepts of liberty became more common in the second half of the century. If so, this would fit with J. A. W. Gunn's suggestion that the language of liberty was more variously applied in the late than in the early eighteenth century.[13]

The courts had long held that the law should favour liberty, and therefore interpreted statutes restrictive of economic activity, for example, as narrowly as possible. Enthusiasm for the benefits of relatively unregulated economic activity was expressed in various contexts during the century; at mid-century, thus, ministers contemplated repealing laws regulating apprenticeship on those grounds. In 1772, laws against forestallers and engrossers—people who breached traditional rules of market conduct for gain—were repealed.[14] The development of more systematic forms of economic theory, expounding the benefits of a 'system of natural liberty'—notably, in Adam Smith's *Wealth of Nations* (1776)—may have encouraged resort to the argument that 'interference' was *per se* objectionable. One can certainly find, in the 1790s, instances of 'interference'—usually, if expanded, 'legislative interference'—being denounced in parliamentary debate, most commonly in an economic context. In 1802, cotton manufacturers campaigning against the first factory act thus argued that it created 'an unquestionable power of inspection over and interference with the manufacture of the country which hitherto has flourished free'.[15]

Against this background, the following developments in the years down to 1830 need to be noted. First, ministers came to play a more active role in shaping domestic policy-making. Second, the parish gained in importance as a politico-governmental forum. Third, early moves to improve checks on abuse

---

[12] William Cobbett (ed.), *Parliamentary History*, 36 vols. (1806–20), xiv. 1318–26.

[13] J. A. W. Gunn, *Beyond Liberty and Property. The Process of Self-Recognition in Eighteenth-Century Political Thought* (Kingston, Ontario, 1983), ch. 6.

[14] There exists no convenient general overview. Deregulation of marketing has received special attention because of Edward Thompson's influential work on 'the moral economy'. See E. P. Thompson, *Customs in Common* (Harmondsworth, Middlesex, 1991), chs. 4–5 and similarly, but more generally, Douglas Hay and Nicholas Rogers, *Eighteenth-Century English Society. Shuttles and Swords* (Oxford, 1997), ch. 7.

[15] J. Innes, 'Origins of the Factory Acts: The Health and Morals of Apprentices Act 1802', in N. Landau (ed.), *Law, Crime and English Society 1660–1830* (Cambridge, 2002), 252.

by creating new supra-local bodies provoked some principled defences of local government. Fourth, the popularization, and vulgarization, of political economy helped to diffuse opposition to government interference as a form of ideology—a development reinforced by other shifts in thought.

Increasing reference to 'interference'—as problem or, sometimes, as desirable remedy—apart, the early nineteenth century saw two other noteworthy changes in usage. First, in a series of developments from the 1780s, people seem to have started to talk more about 'the state', and to speak more commonly of both 'the state' and 'the government' not just as socio-institutional complexes, but as entities that might *do* things. The phrase 'His Majesty's Government' came into widespread use meaning (commonly) ministers.[16] Secondly, the adjective 'central' came into use in connection with government and other forms of organization or institution. The earliest references of this kind have mainly European referents. 'Centralization' was an early nineteenth-century French neologism, descriptive of processes underway in post-revolutionary government. In post-Napoleonic France, a lively debate developed about the pros and cons of centralization.[17] I have not yet found references to 'centralization' or indeed to 'central government' in Britain before 1830, but the adjective 'central' did come into fashion; by the 1820s, increasingly ramified voluntary associations might boast 'central committees'.[18]

What more common reference to ministers as 'the government' and conception of 'government' as an active force had to do with the conduct of ministers is not easy to say. However, ministers did become somewhat more active in shaping domestic policy from the 1780s, with the establishment of a distinct 'Home Office', and the challenges associated with the Revolutionary and Napoleonic Wars.[19] In parliament, ministers continued on the whole to leave it to knowledgeable backbenchers to take new initiatives—but increasingly if such an initiative aroused wide interest, yet failed to produce agreed legislation,

[16] Innes, 'Changing Perceptions'. With help from Simon Devereaux, I have now identified some examples from the 1780s and 90s of the terms 'executive government' or 'government' denoting ministers or the central executive departments: thus, from the 1780s, it would be impracticable for justices of the peace to revive transportation 'without the Assistance of Government'; 1784, 'it would be likely to create trouble were the intentions of Government known'; 1792, 'if this Plan is lost, it is lost for want of the common exertions of Government in the House of Commons'; 1799, 'the expences attending [convicts'] custody must be borne by Government instead of being defrayed by the respective counties.' My impression is that such uses were new to these decades.

[17] The *Oxford English Dictionary*'s earliest citation is 1801: William Dupré, *Lexicographia-Neologica Gallica. The Neological French Dictionary* (1801), 44; Rudolf von Thadden, *Restauration und napoleonisches Erbe: der Verwaltungszentralismus als politisches Problem in Frankreich, 1814–30* (Wiesbaden, 1972).

[18] I am grateful to Joshua Civin for advice on the use of the term 'central' by voluntary associations. Note, however, that implicitly 'government' in some of the passages cited in n. 16 above *meant* what would later be termed 'central government'.

[19] On the Home Office, Simon Devereaux, 'Convicts and the State: The Administration of Criminal Justice in the Eighteenth Century during the Reign of George III', unpublished Ph.D. thesis, University of Toronto, 1997; for the impact of the wars, Clive Emsley, *British Society and the French Wars 1793–1815* (1979).

ministers would step in to try to achieve some result (not least, a result palatable to them).[20]

These years saw much vigorous charitable, evangelical, improving, and political activity, some of it channelled through associations, some through local institutions of government. For our purposes, the most notable development in the local context was probably the rise of the parish as a dynamic politico-governmental forum. Since the sixteenth century, parishes had borne certain governmental responsibilities, notably, for the administration of poor relief. In the eighteenth and early nineteenth centuries, local improvement acts enhanced some parishes' powers: thus, urban parishes often equipped themselves with proto-police forces in the form of an enhanced night-watch. In the 1790s and early nineteenth century, parishes also emerged as political fora: holding meetings and drafting petitions on national affairs; battling with other bodies and interests over the proper conduct of local affairs. In London and some other cities, 'parish radicals' emerged as a radical subtype. In this context, an act of 1819, initially proposed by William Sturges Bourne (chairman of a Commons select committee), offering to parishes the option of vesting poor-law responsibilities in the hands of an executive committee, elected by a system which gave more votes to those who owned more property, was potentially controversial. In fact, it helped to set in train a move to obtain legislative sanction for more democratic forms of parish government, which achieved its formal goal with Hobhouse's Act of 1830.[21]

The reforming climate of the early nineteenth century was associated with much highlighting of abuse, both administrative and social. In this context, creative effort from various quarters was directed towards developing systems to monitor and constrain abuse. Visiting and inspection were favoured devices. Charitable societies maintaining infirmaries, Sunday and day schools developed routines of visiting. Justices of the peace were authorized to inspect madhouses, prisons, workhouses, and factories.[22] Continuing complaints raised doubts about the efficacy especially of official systems, however. In 1816, following the report of a Commons select committee, it was proposed that a special commission be established with powers both to license and to inspect madhouses. This encroachment on the powers of justices was not universally welcomed. Somerset justice Thomas Poole wrote: 'I am afraid those permanent commissioners will be another permanent job. Justices in the neighbourhood I should think the best judges of the propriety of licensing.' As he saw it, the proposal departed 'from the genius of our Government, from our greatest glory (as M. Neckar called, in my hearing, the unpaid magistracy of this country), to

[20] Eastwood, 'Men, Morals and the Machinery of Social Legislation 1790–1840', *Parliamentary History*, 13 (1994), 190–205.
[21] The only general study of the parish as an administrative unit at this time remains Sidney and Beatrice Webb, *The Parish and the County* (1906), Book 1; Elaine Reynolds, *Before the Bobbies: The Night Watch and Police Reform in Metropolitan London, 1720–1830* (1998).
[22] Early statutes enjoining visiting were 14 George III c.49; 24 George III s.2 c.54; 30 George III c.49, and 42 George III c.73.

introduce more *paid* executors of our laws than are absolutely necessary.' To the student of terminology, it is of interest that although Poole here clearly articulated a preference for local government over centralization—in the context of a comparison with Europe—he did not employ those terms. This vision of the distinctive 'genius of [English] government' was still under development.[23]

The changes outlined helped to shape discussion about how different levels of government might interact. Many contemporary statements about the pros and cons of 'interference' were cast in more general terms, however: they focused on questions about whether government in *any* form should 'interfere' in matters arguably outside its sphere. In the early nineteenth century, perhaps especially in its second decade, it seems to have become more common for people to profess relatively abstract and schematic convictions in this regard. MPs thus began to invoke (or contest) a 'principle of non-interference'.[24]

One influence here was undoubtedly 'political economy', which gained in popularity in the years after 1815, as a new generation of educated young men strove to master this challenging science, and its theories were propagated and debated on the burgeoning public lecture circuit. The spread of prejudice against interference was assisted when theologians appropriated such analyses to illuminate God's providence. God, they characteristically insisted, intended the earthly state to be a state of probation, a test of character; naturally therefore he had arranged things so that there were limits to what government could do. More diffusely, suspicion of 'interference' was promoted by post French revolutionary anti-utopianism. Radical and emergent 'liberal' suspicions of big-spending governments prone to deploy power to maintain themselves and reward their supporters could also be synthesized with other forms of liberty preference.[25]

---

[23] M. E. Sandford, *Thomas Poole and his Friends*, 2 vols. (1888), ii. 284. He presumably met Necker while visiting Switzerland in 1802. I would tentatively date to the years following British triumphs in the Seven Years War (1757–63) a flowering of European admiration for governmental arrangements which effectively engaged the energies of ordinary people.

[24] Thus Hansard, *Parliamentary Debates* 92 vols. (1812–20), 39 (1819), 343, 1432. Equally, more self-consciously pro-interference philosophies began to take shape: see David Roberts, *Paternalism in Early Victorian England* (1979); Kim Lawes, *Paternalism and Politics. The Revival of Paternalism in Early Nineteenth-Century Britain* (Basingstoke, 2000).

[25] For the diffusion of interest in political economy, see Barry Gordon, *Political Economy in Parliament 1819–23* (1976); and Gregory Claeys, 'Political Economy and Popular Education: Thomas Hodgskin and the London Mechanics Institute 1823–8', in Michael T. Davis (ed.), *Radicalism and Revolution in Britain, 1775–1848* (Basingstoke, 2000). For religiously inflected anti-intervention theories, Boyd Hilton, *The Age of Atonement: The Influence of Evangelicalism on Social and Economic Thought 1795–1865* (Oxford, 1988); and A. M. C. Waterman, *Revolution, Economics and Religion: Christian Political Economy 1798–1833* (Cambridge, 1991). Radical thinkers of libertarian/liberal views included William Godwin (his *Principles of Political Justice* is best consulted in *Political and Philosophical Writings of William Godwin*, ed. by Mark Philp, 7 vols. [(1993), Vols. 3–4]); and Thomas Paine, on whom see esp. Gregory Claeys, *Thomas Paine: Social and Political Thought* (1993). Proponents of anti-interventionist radicalism included Francis Place, Richard Carlile, and Joseph Hume. Bentham's attitude was ambiguous: in effect, he provided a framework within which the pros and cons of intervention could be discussed: James Steintrager, *Bentham* (1977), ch. 3.

To note that these themes increasingly surfaced in debate is not to imply that they drove policy. In fact, the period is notable for many kinds of innovative, legislatively sanctioned government action.[26] Yet some efforts were made to develop forms of action that worked with these concerns. One interesting example was the practice of offering grants from national funds to match funds raised by local taxation or voluntary subscription: the basis on which parliament sought to encourage the building of new churches in large towns from 1818. The intention was clearly to foster, not supersede, local effort. Forms of policy intended to foster individual striving were also well regarded: thus, substantial sums of public money were spent on the building of a reformatory prison, Millbank, and numerous acts were passed to encourage the formation of mutual aid societies.[27]

Developments post-1830—especially in the reform decade, the 1830s—added further elements to the picture. This decade saw, first, ministers assuming unprecedentedly wide-ranging responsibilities for domestic policy-making; second, on their initiative, the passage of legislation which restructured local agencies of government—poor-relief systems and municipal corporations—in unprecedentedly ambitious ways; and third, the creation, in the form of the Poor Law Commission, of a body exercising exceptionally wide and continuing powers over local authorities: it was this development which launched in Britain a variant of the debate about centralization already in train in continental Europe.

To elaborate: although, as I have noted, a trend favouring ministerial initiative was evident before 1830, the Reform Ministry stood out for its willingness to initiate legislation—often bold, far-reaching legislation at that—across a broad front. This seems to have been partly because its members wished to distinguish themselves from their immediate predecessors who, as they saw it, had left many pressing issues unresolved.[28] Two measures sponsored by this ministry effected unprecedentedly sweeping changes in local institutions: the Poor Law Amendment Act of 1834, which promoted new-style Poor Law Unions over parishes as the chief decision-making and administrative bodies in relief matters; and the Municipal Corporations Act of 1835, which replaced English municipal corporations with new bodies whose constitutions were determined by statute. Governing bodies in both cases were to be elected by ratepayers (in the first case, on a weighted franchise). Though not democratic enough to please

---

[26] There is a large historiography on 'government growth', mainly dating from the 1960s and 1970s. Gillian Sutherland, *Studies in the Growth of Nineteenth-Century Government* (1972) for an influential collection. Lawrence Goldman, *Science, Reform and Politics in Victorian Britain. The Social Science Association 1857–86* (Cambridge, 2002), 272–3 for further references.

[27] A. B. Webster, *Joshua Watson. The Story of a Layman 1771–1855* (1954), ch. 5; Robin Evans, *The Fabrication of Virtue. English Prison Architecture, 1750–1840* (Cambridge, 1982), ch. 6; P. H. J. H. Gosden, *The Friendly Societies in England 1815–1875* (1971). See also Eric Stokes, 'Bureaucracy and Ideology: Britain and India in the Nineteenth Century', *Transactions of the Royal Historical Society*, 5th ser., 30 (1980), 131–56.

[28] The Reform Ministry's activism is stressed by Jonathan Parry, *The Rise and Fall of Liberal Government in Victorian Britain* (New Haven, 1993), chs. 3–5.

radicals, these acts did generalize features of good practice as evolved, especially in local acts, in preceding generations. The radical MP Joseph Hume campaigned, unavailingly, for elective government to be extended to the counties.[29]

A further significant feature of the Poor Law Amendment Act was that it brought into being what was intended to be a permanent body of 'Poor Law Commissioners' with wide-ranging powers to determine policy and to impose good practice upon local boards. Regionally based Assistant Commissioners linked them to the localities. No real precedent existed for such a body—and indeed it had, and for a long time thenceforth would have, no parallel in continental states. Most criticism of the bill in parliament focused on this experiment in 'centralization': it appears to have been above all in the context of this debate that the concepts of 'centralization' and 'local self-government' were popularized.[30] Parishes provided a key base for practical resistance to the new measure (where it was resisted).[31] In the case of municipal corporations, it can be argued that 1830s reforms helped to relegitimate and revitalize local government structures. In the case of the Poor Laws, however, though novel local authorities were similarly conceived, it was the administrative unit intended to be largely superseded, the parish, which came to be championed. The merits of the parish as a unit of government formed a central theme in crusades carried out in the name of an ideal of local self-government in the mid-nineteenth century.[32]

III

Both the challenges and the opportunities provided by new developments in the 1830s were thus crucial to the crystallization of the themes outlined at the start of this chapter as central themes in public debate. I turn now to survey developments in relation to two specific issues: policing and poor relief. In both cases, the story that emerges will be compatible with the chronology sketched. But it will not merely illustrate it. Policy debates on these different topics took different forms—though both were marked by larger changes in thought and practice, and by the middle decades of the nineteenth century were being framed in terms of some common themes and preoccupations.

[29] Josef Redlich and Francis W. Hirst, *The History of Local Government in England*, 2nd edn., ed. by Bryan Keith-Lucas (1970). David Philips and Robert D. Storch, *Policing Provincial England 1829–1856. The Politics of Reform* (1999), discuss both Hume's efforts to this end, and his success in 1833 in obtaining legislation to facilitate the establishment of ratepayer-controlled lighting and watching boards: 76–8, 94.

[30] The report itself—*PP* (1834) 27, esp. 162–9—employed a vocabulary of 'local authorities' and 'central boards' which must have helped to set the terms of debate. The commissioners also adumbrated a critique of the 'local', as partial, capricious, and irrationally heterogeneous, which had been prefigured in the debate over metropolitan policing. Eastwood, *Government and Community*, 166, for a London vestry resolution invoking the right of local self-government against the commissioners.

[31] N. C. Edsall, *The Anti-Poor-Law Movement 1834–44* (Manchester, 1971).

[32] J. T. Smith, *Local Self-Government and Centralization* (1851); *The Parish: Its Obligations and Powers; Its Offices and their Duties* (1854). Smith acknowledged but sought to rebut the anti-local argument: *Local Self-Government*, 32.

Policing

The term 'police' came into use in English debate—to denote the regulation of social life generally, and the maintenance of law and order on the streets more particularly—in the middle of the eighteenth century. It was already in standard use in France, where it was also applied to bodies of men charged with responsibility for 'la police'. Though the term was promoted by some English advocates of an improved police, it was always possible for critics to denounce it as un-English.

In fact, however, during the first three-quarters of the eighteenth century there is little if any evidence of anxieties about most of the *activities* we might term 'policing', so long as these were carried on by ordinary public authorities and not presented in provocative ways.[33] England was not a badly policed society by contemporary European standards: the network of manorial and parish constables across the country, supplemented by night-watchmen in towns, provided reasonable coverage.[34] Across the course of the century, considerable effort was invested in trying to improve these forces. Local improvement acts often provided for an improved night-watch; by the end of the century many urban districts had uniformed watch forces that undertook regular patrols.[35] Constables were not proactive, but did provide a resource for victims of crime. Importance was attached to such provision, not just for practical reasons but also because of a prevailing ideology which stressed the importance of punishing petty misdeeds to prevent greater offences. This was a standard theme of chairmen's charges to quarter sessions. The Whig magistrates who dominated the bench in the early eighteenth century sometimes linked such injunctions with their favourite theme, liberty, stressing that liberty could be safeguarded only by the rigorous enforcement of law.[36] Had ministers tried to create new forms of police force more directly under their control, and had there been moves radically to extend licensing and monitoring, probably there would have been objections. But no such moves were made.

[33] See John Styles: 'The Emergence of the Police: Explaining Police Reform in Eighteenth and Nineteenth-Century England', in *The British Journal of Criminology*, 27 (1987), 15–22; and 'Sir John Fielding and the Problem of Criminal Investigation in Eighteenth-Century England', *Transactions of the Royal Historical Society*, 5th ser., 33 (1983), 127–49.

[34] See e.g. J. M. Beattie, *Policing and Punishment in London 1660–1750: Urban Crime and the Limits of Terror* (Oxford, 2001), chs. 3–5, 8. Note Adam Smith's judgement that French-style policing was associated with more, rather than less murders and robberies, in Smith, *Lectures on Jurisprudence*, ed. by R. L. Meek, D. D. Raphael, and P. G. Stein (Oxford, 1978), 331–3: in his view this reflected the role culture, as opposed to institutions, played in promoting civil peace.

[35] Reynolds, *Before the Bobbies*, chs. 1–6.

[36] Douglas Hay's influential essay 'Property, Authority and the Criminal Law', in Hay *et al.* (eds.), *Albion's Fatal Tree. Crime and Society in Eighteenth-Century England* (Harmondsworth, 1975) suggests otherwise—but he seems to me to have been over-influenced by Paley's late eighteenth-century analysis, discussed below. For an early eighteenth-century Whig magistrate's view, Bodleian MS Eng Hist. b. 209–10 f. 27 ff.; other charges are collected in G. Lamoine (ed.), *Charges to the Grand Jury 1689–1803*, Camden, 4th ser., vol. 43 (1992).

What did cause concern were forms of private-venture policing: the moral policing sponsored by reformation of manners societies in the late seventeenth and early eighteenth centuries, for instance. Reforming constables were seen as harassing and intrusive—and were moreover accused of running protection rackets under pretence of upholding moral standards. Freelance 'thieftakers' gained a bad reputation as corrupt bounty-hunters. Henry Fielding's efforts to improve the forces at his disposal as a Westminster magistrate earned him criticism in part because he was seen as endorsing these dubious characters.[37]

In the last two decades of the eighteenth century, liberty and police were more commonly counterposed. A much-cited case in point is that of William Paley. In his influential *Principles of Moral and Political Philosophy*, first published in 1785, this Cambridge don suggested that one reason why capital punishment was prevalent in England was because concern for liberty inhibited the development of continental-style policing. In fact, this analysis does not convincingly account for *how* English practice developed: policing had not been intentionally under-developed (even if it had been developed in particular ways), nor had capital punishments been intentionally proliferated, still less had the one consciously been traded off against the other. Paley's sense that there were choices to be made more directly relates to the circumstances of his time. Recently, the merits of capital punishment had been debated throughout Europe. According to the Tuscan writer Cesare Beccaria, the problem with the death penalty was that most criminals did not expect to incur it, and in practice did not. More would be gained by enforcing laws rigorously and having to hand an appropriately graded range of punishments, such as prison sentences of varying lengths. English interest in these themes was just developing when the outbreak of war with America precipitated a penal crisis. For half a century, most of those convicted of serious crimes had been transported to the American colonies; when the ending of the war confirmed the loss of America and brought the usual post-war crime wave, English authorities found themselves at a loss. Should they respond by executing more criminals? Or by developing schemes of hard labour and imprisonment as alternatives? Could they reduce the scale of the problem by new approaches to policing? Debate was framed in part in terms of concern that whatever solution was found it must be suitable to a land of liberty. Paley's analysis reflected the terms of this debate.

Metropolitan policing provided a special focus for concern at this time. Even before the post-war crime wave broke, there had been a flurry of discussion about metropolitan arrangements. The devastating anti-Catholic 'Gordon Riots' of 1780 illustrated the deficiencies of the 'civil power' in the capital: order had been restored by troops, who themselves caused many deaths. Distressed by this, and seeking a way to make political capital out of an incident that threat-

[37] Robert B. Shoemaker, *Prosecution and Punishment. Petty Crime and the Law in London and Rural Middlesex, c. 1660–1725* (Cambridge, 1991), ch. 9; Ruth Paley, 'Thieftakers in London in the Age of the McDaniel Gang c.1745–1754', in Douglas Hay and Francis Snyder (eds.), *Policing and Prosecution in Britain 1750–1850* (Oxford, 1989).

ened to provoke a backlash against popular reforming politics, Whigs and reformers sought to focus attention on the need for police reform. In their analysis, a large part of the problem was that ministers sought to keep power in the hands of their political allies. The quality of the magistracy was consequently lower than it should be. Ministers had also failed to do all that might have been done to mobilize civic spirit in the cause of public security. Concrete proposals for change emerged only five years later, against the background of the post-war crime wave: in 1785 the Solicitor-General brought to parliament a bill to improve metropolitan policing arrangements. This proposal was objected to on three main grounds. First, it overrode the privileges of the City of London. Second, inasmuch as it involved the creation of a special salaried magistracy, it could be seen as an attempt to extend government influence. Third, proposals to allow the arrest of suspicious persons were thought to give law-enforcement officials too much leeway. When the first objection was dealt with by exempting the City from the scheme, there was enough support for the remainder for a version to emerge as legislation in 1792.[38]

Over the next few decades, there were repeated efforts to improve co-ordination and efficiency in metropolitan policing, and some progress was made at a local level. Such parliamentary initiatives as there were were complicated by the tendency of parish vestries—the bodies through which night-watches were characteristically organized—to want to preserve their autonomy. The radicalization of some vestries further complicated the task. A wary Commons select committee, having listened to many hostile representations, concluded in 1822 that if improved policing could be achieved only at the price of reducing liberty, then that price might be too dear. Complaints about the inadequacies of existing arrangements none the less persisted. Against this background, the recently appointed Home Secretary, Robert Peel, took it upon himself to negotiate an acceptable solution. Elaine Reynolds—to whose careful analysis I am indebted—suggests that he was able to achieve this in the late 1820s partly because of a momentary weakening of 'parish radicalism': as some parishes came under fire for corruption, and Sturges Bourne legislation made it possible to wrest control of others from radical hands. When in 1830 Hobhouse's Act opened the door to the establishment of more democratic forms of parish government, parish radicals lambasted the new police.[39]

In the 1830s, the police debate became national. The 1835 Municipal Corporations Act required all municipal corporations to establish watch committees to superintend watch forces. This left the counties as the main districts under-supplied with civil forces subject to overall direction and control. Agricultural, industrial, anti-Poor Law, and finally Chartist disturbances

[38] For oppositional police reform plans, Cobbett, *Parliamentary History*, xxi. 1305–25; D. Williams, *A Plan of Association on Constitutional Principles* . . . (1780); Granville Sharp, *Tracts, concerning the Ancient and Only True Legal Means of National Defence* . . . (1781). For bills of 1785 and 1792, Reynolds, *Before the Bobbies*, ch. 5.

[39] Reynolds, *Before the Bobbies*, ch. 8.

suggested that this was a real problem. Widespread consultation revealed that many county benches feared what they termed the 'centralizing' effects of national legislation (that term had, by contrast, apparently not featured in debates on metropolitan police). In fact, once it became clear that what the government intended was to place new county police under the superintending power of local magistrates, many objections fell away. In the counties, as in the metropolis, some still objected to the imposition of uniformity on previously diverse practice; and to new opportunities for jobbery expected to spring from the creation of new forms of salaried post. The most recent historians of this episode, David Phillips and Bob Storch, suggest that, though 'government interference' and 'centralization' were attacked as such, more important in shaping decisions by individual counties to opt in or out of what was (in its initial form) an optional system were financial considerations. Had a central government subsidy been forthcoming, they suggest, there might have been more immediate take-up. Then, as in the closing decades of the nineteenth century, country gentlemen worried about rate burdens were for that reason in practice not ill disposed towards well-financed 'centralizing' measures.[40]

Although attempts by parliament and government to determine the form of local policing arrangements were attacked as 'interference', and although certain kinds of policing proposal were challenged as threatening to 'liberty', it is notable that the provision of policing as such was not generally characterized as 'interference' by doctrinaire proponents of 'non-interference'. On the contrary, it was commonly posited that the minimal 'night-watchman state' *should*—as that name suggests—provide a night-watch. At the level of theory, this may have represented a hangover from the common premiss of natural law/social compact theories that the primary reason why people accepted restrictions arising from law and government was to enhance the security of their persons and property. In 1848, in his *Principles of Political Economy*, J. S. Mill mischievously questioned this assumption. He asked why government interference in such matters should not also be seen as detrimental to independence? Mill's object does not appear to have been to encourage vigilantism. Rather, he hoped to promote a more open-minded attitude to the rights and wrongs of all forms of 'interference'.[41]

Poor relief

Whereas in the case of policing, the principle that some form of provision should be publicly organized was rarely directly challenged, in the case of poor relief that challenge was repeatedly issued over several centuries. One reason for this difference was undoubtedly that whereas, in the case of England at least, the origins of public policing were lost in the mists of time, tax-funded poor relief was

[40] Philips and Storch, *Policing Rural England*.
[41] J. S. Mill, *Principles of Political Economy* (1848), Book V, ch. 1, §3. I am not sure when or with whom the phrase 'nightwatchman state' originated.

of recent invention, dating no further back than the sixteenth century. Moreover, from the middle of the eighteenth century it was commonly (if not entirely accurately) observed that most other countries had 'no poor laws'. Even in Scotland, poor rates were much more rarely levied than in England, where, by the end of the seventeenth century in almost every parish they were a routine annual charge.[42]

Scepticism about the practice of tax-funded relief is evident from the start of printed debate on the poor laws in the late seventeenth century. The counter-arguments were essentially threefold. First, it was argued that tax-funded relief undermined private charity: potential charitable donors held back because they thought the law would provide. This, in turn, was regrettable for several reasons: because charity was a Christian virtue; because it promoted good feelings between people of differing social standing; also because, in a spirit of charity, the rich might dig deeper into their pockets than they would readily dig under compulsion. A second argument was that tax-funded relief was not easily targeted on the most deserving, and often ended up instead in the hands of the idle but clamorous, whose idleness was thereby encouraged (this too could be turned into an argument for private charity, inasmuch as private donors were suggested to be more discriminating). A third argument was that it was not a good idea to employ such funds even to set the poor to work—because, although that might discourage 'idleness', it would tend to depress wages.[43]

In the late seventeenth century, private charity was commonly envisaged as deriving from charitable individuals, or from hybrid institutions, such as statutory local 'corporations of the poor', which were expected to appeal for charitable donations as well as administering the proceeds of poor rates. In the course of the eighteenth century, however, a new species of collective charity came into being and multiplied. These new-style charities depended wholly on charitable gifts and subscriptions. They might, like most charitable infirmaries, depend in important part on charitable endowments, or like many non-institutionally based societies, largely or wholly upon annual gifts and subscriptions. By the second half of the eighteenth century, it was common to group individual charity and such collective charity together under the rubric 'voluntary charity'. By the early nineteenth century, the compulsion-based alternative was commonly termed, by contrast, 'legal charity'.

---

[42] For these differences, J. Innes, 'The State and the Poor: Eighteenth-century England in Comparative Perspective', in J. Brewer and E. Hellmuth (eds.), *Rethinking Leviathan: The Eighteenth-Century State in Britain and Germany* (Oxford, 1999), 225–80; and 'The Distinctiveness of the English Poor Laws 1750–1850', in P. O'Brien and D. Winch (eds.), *The Political Economy of British Economic Experience 1688–1914* (Oxford University Press for the British Academy, 2002). These and J. Innes, 'The "Mixed Economy of Welfare" in Early Modern England: Assessments of the Options from Hale to Malthus (1683–1803)', in Martin Daunton (ed.), *Charity, Self-interest and Welfare in the English Past* (1996), 139–180 amplify and provide references for the next few pages.

[43] See [Daniel Defoe], *Giving Alms no Charity* (1704) for this last argument—the concrete and pragmatic way in which Defoe argued presents an interesting contrast with later, more abstractly formulated, analyses.

Though attempts to model social interaction as the result of self-interested calculation were widespread in the seventeenth and eighteenth centuries, the implications of such modelling were not initially commonly worked through to illuminate the pros and cons of alternative ways of addressing poverty. The Dutch emigré physician Bernard Mandeville, in his provocative *Fable of the Bees*, came closest among early eighteenth-century writers to addressing that task. Mandeville focused, however, on forms of charity directed to ends the state did not address, notably, charitable provision of schooling. Mandeville was sceptical about charity. He argued first, that while charitable donors pretended to be moved by public spirit, in fact they were self-interested: they wanted to be admired. Secondly, he questioned whether they did in fact benefit society by educating the poor above their station or more generally by trying to reform character: society worked as well as it did because people were self-interested: vicious, not virtuous in conventional moral terms. We might expect that Mandeville would have been sceptical about many if not all forms of effort to relieve distress, on the grounds that the poor needed the goad of necessity to impel them to labour—but he did not directly enter that debate.[44]

In the late eighteenth century, by contrast, some attempts were made to theorize the impact of compulsory poor relief upon society. Henry Home, Lord Kames, addressed himself to this task in his *Sketches of the History of Man* of 1774. In characteristically Scottish fashion, Kames was chiefly concerned to develop a speculative history of poor relief in the context of certain general ideas about human conduct and social development. Kames's efforts probably helped to inspire Wiltshire clergyman Joseph Townsend's *Dissertation on the Poor Laws* of 1786. T. R. Malthus, by far the most influential of those who theorized in this vein, later claimed not to have read Townsend's work when he first published his *Essay on the Principle of Population* in 1799, though he did read it, and acknowledged common ground, before he put out a second edition, in 1803. All these writers suggested that systems of legal relief had serious, unintended ill effects—mostly along the lines that previous writers had indicated. Townsend and Malthus both added to the list of ill effects a tendency to encourage the poor to beget children they could not support—and thus to increase population overall without reference to the capacity of available resources to sustain increased numbers. Both Townsend and Malthus focused their criticisms especially upon systems of legal relief, and wrote more warmly of voluntary charity—though in neither case is it entirely clear why they thought this a safer way to proceed. The theory was perhaps that charity did not create the same confident expectation of relief, and moreover was likely to be more discriminatingly given.[45]

In the early nineteenth century, it fell to Scottish evangelical minister Thomas Chalmers influentially to push the argument for charitable restraint one step

---

[44] Bernard Mandeville, *The Fable of the Bees; or, Private Vices, Public Benefits* (1714; subsequently revised and extended to 1733).

[45] Innes, 'Mixed Economy of Welfare', 165–6.

further. Chalmers argued that voluntary relief was also demoralizing; charitable effort should ideally take the form not of material relief but of spiritual uplift.[46]

Over the same period—from the late eighteenth through the early nineteenth centuries—increasing emphasis was placed on the oppressiveness of the poor laws. On the one hand, they were said to be oppressive to ratepayers, especially marginal ratepayers, some of whom had little to spare and might have to be forced to contribute by distraint. The laws—or particular features of the laws—were also argued to be oppressive to the poor. Workhouses, where these existed, were said to be little better than prisons. A wave of enthusiasm for workhouse building in East Anglia in the 1760s and 1770s, and proposals that this be treated as a model for the nation, evoked critical responses cast in part in those terms. Settlement laws were criticized for exposing the poor to harassment and constraining their mobility. More generally, it was suggested that the relief system forced the poor into an attitude of slavish deference.[47]

The fact that the poor laws could be criticized both as too generous and as too oppressive helps to explain the breadth of criticism they attracted, not least from numerous champions of liberty and popular rights. Opponents of the laws might at the same time lament the distresses of the poor, and concede that it was beyond the poor themselves to do much to alleviate these—but, they argued, better means of relieving distress, ideally, of diffusing prosperity, should be found (perhaps, for example, by reducing the weight of taxation).[48]

As early as the 1690s, ministers had seen a case for reforming the poor laws, and had commissioned the Board of Trade to look into this. During the eighteenth century, reform proposals normally emanated from backbenchers. Radical reform proposals were floated, and discussed in parliament, in almost every decade. It proved hard to mobilize parliamentary majorities behind alternatives, however—not least because both problems and opportunities differed from one region to another. In this context, statutory change chiefly took the form of piecemeal, local legislation.

Rising prices for grain and other consumables from the 1760s against a background of lagging wages led some contemporaries to argue that the problem of poverty was in fact becoming more severe. A proposal to allow magistrates to set rural wage levels, in an attempt to shift wage norms, was canvassed. Any such interference with the relationship between master and servant was, however, argued to be impracticable, as well as unwise. Having discountenanced this scheme, the prime minister, William Pitt the Younger, exceptionally

---

[46] Stewart C. Brown, *Thomas Chalmers and the Godly Commonwealth in Scotland* (Oxford, 1992).

[47] e.g. Thomas Mendham, *A Dialogue in Two Conversations between a Gentleman, a Pauper and his Friend* . . . (Norwich, 1775); Thomas Butterworth Bayley, letter to *London Chronicle*, 20–2 March 1787; Paley referred to the poor laws in the context of the general undesirability of restraint, *Principles*, 442. See also Andrew, *Philanthropy and Police*, chs. 5–6 for new values animating late eighteenth-century charity.

[48] The approach suggested by Thomas Paine in his *Rights of Man*, Part 2.

brought in a poor law reform bill of his own, which reflected changing ideas inasmuch as it offered a miscellaneous package of benefits—including education—intended to promote and facilitate self-help. This too, however, was shot down as over-complicated and over-ambitious.[49]

Following the conclusion of the Napoleonic Wars in 1815, against a background of economic depression, several currents of thought converged to bring criticism of the poor laws to a peak. The laws had by this time, however, also attracted robust defenders, who argued that they could be constructively administered, especially if run in harness with efforts to promote self-help. Many who would ideally have liked to do away with them, moreover, recognized a pragmatic case for continuing them in the face of widespread distress. Ministers resisted calls for 'government' to take the lead, arguing that any policy adopted should be seen to reflect a consensus in parliament, and not the view of a party—though they did seek to influence the outcome.[50] The legislation which eventuated, known by the name of the chairman of the Commons select committee, Sturges Bourne, addressed itself primarily to the task of improving local systems of control by offering to any parish whose inhabitants chose to take this course the option of strengthening the hand of greater ratepayers, and employing paid overseers to manage the distribution of relief.

The New Poor Law of 1834 in effect continued the same strategy, but did so by more innovative means. It retained tax-funded relief as a safety net; reconstructed local administrative arrangements across the board; and superimposed upon the whole a Board of Commissioners with wide-ranging powers to determine policies. In practice, local boards were chivvied into adopting policies intended to minimize any temptation to become relief-dependent: all but the sick were to be given relief only at the price of entering a workhouse. Success was gauged by the extent to which the poor were inspired to seek other means of improving their situation—by joining friendly societies, or moving in search of work—and by the effective capping of expenditure: absolute spending totals in fact did not rise significantly for the rest of the century. New Poor Law practices were, exceptionally, vigorously opposed in the industrial North, where they were never fully implemented. But, in general, they were sufficiently consonant with current values, and sufficiently effective, to take the steam out of abolitionism, and to remove relief policy from governmental and parliamentary agendas for several decades.[51] 'Centralized' administrative structures, though ultimately accepted as an accustomed part of the institutional landscape, provoked opposition that proved harder to satisfy. Litigation established the right of localities which already had statutory endorsement for their own chosen

---

[49] J. R. Poynter, *Society and Pauperism. English Ideas on Poor Relief 1795–1834* (1969), ch. 3 remains the best discussion.

[50] See Hansard, *Parliamentary Debates*, 39 (1819), 409.

[51] Alan Kidd, *State, Society and the Poor in Nineteenth-Century England* (Basingstoke, 1999) for a recent survey. Note the low profile of the relief issue among the concerns of the mid-century Social Science Association: Goldman, *Science, Reform*.

form of reformed administrative structure to continue, if they chose, to operate through that. Not only in the industrial North, where many aspects of the new regime were resisted, but also in metropolitan London, 'centralization' was denounced and the parish exalted, both in practice and increasingly stridently in theory, as a bastion of local self-government.[52]

IV

By way of conclusion, I should like to underline first (to avoid misunderstanding) some things this chapter *has not* claimed; secondly, certain things it has claimed.

I have not sought to resurrect the thesis, whose origins lie in some later nineteenth-century accounts, that public policy came in the course of the early nineteenth century to be driven by individualistic and *laissez-faire* principles—principles later modified or discarded. No single theory drove early nineteenth-century public policy. The preoccupations and attitudes I have been tracing coexisted with other concerns and ideas.

Moreover, these attitudes did not constitute a coherent 'theory'. When the early nineteenth century is compared with the eighteenth century, the relative frequency of appeal to underlying principles in debates on social policy—principles more or less loosely linked into a range of economic, social, and religious analyses of human society and its functioning—is striking. But to the extent that theories framed debates they were diverse, and left much scope for argument.

What I *have* sought to argue is that from the 1830s, particularly in the field of what we might broadly term 'social policy', much reference was made to such phenomena as 'centralization', 'government interference', 'local self-government', and 'liberty'. Although people employed these terms variously, they did highlight certain themes of common concern. By the middle of the century, numerous widely differing public policy issues were discussed in these terms.

Elements of those themes and concerns can be discerned in the thought and practice of the previous century. Yet they were, none the less, to an important extent, historically specific. They arose out of growth in the ambitions and capacities of central government, and in perceptions of those capacities; out of changes in the nature and functioning of 'inferior' agencies of government; out of the burgeoning of the voluntary sector, and out of a host of developing ideas—political, economic, and religious—about the power and value of spontaneous human striving.

Concern about the proper nature and limits of state power emerged in the course of the eighteenth century in relation to a number of what we might term

[52] For the legal battle to defend local incorporations, see Andrea Tanner, 'The Casual Poor and the City of London Poor Law Union, 1837–1869', *Historical Journal*, 42 (1999), 184. For the ultimate triumph of the London vestries, John Davis, *Reforming London. The London Government Problem 1855–1900* (Oxford, 1988), ch. 2.

'social policy' issues. Older forms of concern were thus interestingly supplemented. But both issues and attitudes varied from one policy field to another.
They would, of course, continue to differ through the nineteenth century. Yet
that century saw more cross-referencing between debates, and more conscious
attempts to conduct debate and frame policy with reference to a common stock
of principles.

In the later eighteenth century, both Adam Smith and William Godwin
attempted to produce general analyses of the proper role of government in a
society conceived (if in rather different ways in the two accounts) as primarily
impelled by individual striving. In both analyses, the kinds of issues I have
focused upon here figured. Of these two, Smith had much more impact on
public debate. But neither really founded a tradition of *theorizing* about such
matters.[53] In the early nineteenth century, economic treatises increasingly
focused on the analysis of economic relationships; questions of public policy
were marginalized.[54] When John Stuart Mill decided to devote a chapter of his
1848 *Principles of Political Economy* to an attempt to theorize questions about
when governments should and should not 'interfere', he accordingly represented himself as a pioneer.[55] Questions about the proper nature and limits of
state power, especially in relation to public policy in the domestic sphere, subsequently stood at the centre of much later nineteenth-century political, social,
and moral theorizing.[56] We should not allow the abstract ways in which these
discussions were framed to blind us to the particular circumstances out of which
they emerged and by which they were sustained.

[53] Smith, *Wealth of Nations*; Godwin, *Principles of Political Justice*.
[54] Ellen Frankel Paul, *Moral Revolution and Economic Science. The Demise of Laissez-Faire in
Nineteenth-Century British Political Economy* (Westport, Conn., 1977) is useful, but tends to exag-
gerate the anti-interventionism of the writers dealt with—when not chastising them for failing to
follow their principles through to the bitter end!
[55] Mill, *Principles*, Book V, ch. 11.
[56] See e.g. M. W. Taylor, *Man versus the State. Herbert Spencer and late Victorian Individualism*
(Oxford, 1992). In so far as such notions helped to structure A. V. Dicey's *Lectures on the Relation
between Law and Public Opinion in England during the Nineteenth Century* (1905), they provided
an important source for later historians' ideas about the shape and logic of nineteenth-century developments—contested in the 'government growth' controversy, for which see n. 26.

3

'Opinions deliver'd in conversation': Conversation, Politics, and Gender in the Late Eighteenth Century

KATHRYN GLEADLE

This chapter, by analysing the diaries of a late eighteenth-century gentlewoman, Katherine Plymley, and her wider network, investigates some of the complex and often conflicting ways in which women were able to construct themselves as members of a wider civic polity. Whereas recent scholars have noted how women played a central role in public debate through their lively contribution to print culture;[1] or were able to forge identities of cultural authority in such fora as coffee-houses, salons, and intellectual institutions,[2] here we shall be concerned primarily with the domestic site. This endeavour has been greatly informed by recent studies that have problematized the dichotomy of 'public' and 'private'. Lawrence Klein, noting the multivalence of these terms during the period, suggests that there were in fact a number of interrelated yet distinct 'publics'. In particular, Klein points to the domestic-based culture of eighteenth-century politeness, with home-based rituals, such as tea-drinking, functioning as a critical forum for the expression and cultivation of genteel civility. This, he suggests, forged a third zone operating 'between the intimately private and the officially public'.[3] The existence of this intermediate sphere of sociability was often alluded to by contemporary Enlightenment theorists. As Mary Catherine Moran has observed, leading figures in the Scottish Enlightenment, such as John Millar and William Robertson, conceptualized the domestic as a 'social

---

[1] Ann K. Mellor, *Mothers of the Nation. Women's Political Writing in England, 1780–1830* (Bloomington, 2000).

[2] Elizabeth Eger, Charlotte Grant, Cliona Ó Gallchoir, and Penny Warburton (eds.), *Women, Writing and the Public Sphere, 1700–1830* (Cambridge, 2001).

[3] Lawrence Klein, 'Gender and the Public Private Distinction in the Eighteenth Century: Some Questions about Evidence and Analytic Procedure', *Eighteenth-Century Studies*, 29 (1995), 92–109.

sphere'.[4] Hence, the domestic was not simply elided with intimacy, or 'private life' but was problematized as an additional, intermediary locus of civic import.

A consideration of the ways in which the home could be invested with wider political and civic significance will form the basis of this chapter. In order to analyse the gendered processes involved, and the implications of this relationship between the home and the 'public sphere' for women, I shall focus upon the cultural politics of conversation. Conversation held a vital place in contemporary analyses of social manners, whilst also being invested with potent political significance. In a widely diffused metaphor, conversation was taken to be the currency of civil society, an act of social exchange that helped to define the relationship between the individual and society.[5] The political and social value of free conversation emerged strongly during the course of the eighteenth century. The institutions spawned by the urban renaissance, in particular debating societies, book clubs, coffee-houses, and philosophical institutions became associated with political debate and could serve as centres of parliamentary opposition.[6] Indeed the public sphere, so famously conceptualized by Jürgen Habermas, was constructed upon just such opportunities for free converse. As historians are now becoming aware, these public fora were but part of a wider culture of social exchange that drew upon domestic-based activities such as reading circles, salons, dinners, and tea-parties.[7] However, by the 1790s, the decade with which this chapter is particularly concerned, the role of conversation was becoming deeply contested. Many progressives were beginning to cast conversation as a critical tool in the reformation of both the domestic and civic worlds. Meanwhile, repressive legislation and loyalist action were seeking to fetter the processes of political exchange—with the 'Gagging Acts' of November 1795 perceived as an attempt to stop the very mouths of radicals. As women sought to negotiate their own political identity in these troubled days, the nature of women's social intercourse, became, as we shall see, particularly problematic.

It is useful to begin with a brief consideration of recent discussions concerning the cultural and political significance of female conversation. As Gary Kelly has observed, in many eighteenth-century discursive contexts, female conversa-

[4] Mary Catherine Moran,' "The Commerce of the Sexes". Gender and the Social Sphere in Scottish Enlightenment Accounts of Civil Society', in Frank Trentmann (ed.), Paradoxes of Civil Society. New Perspectives on Modern German and British History (New York and Oxford, 2000), 61–84.

[5] Leland E. Warren, 'Turning Reality Round Together: Guides to Conversation in Eighteenth-Century England', Eighteenth Century Life , 8, n.s. 3 (1983), 65–87; see also Jack Prostko, ' "Natural Conversation Set in View": Shaftesbury and Moral Speech', Eighteenth Century Studies, 23: 1 (1989), 42–61. 'Conversation' could also function as a metonym for all kinds of social interaction. See Betty A. Schellenberg, The Conversational Circle. Rereading the English Novel, 1740–1775 (Kentucky, 1996), ch. 1.

[6] Kathleen Wilson, The Sense of the People. Politics, Culture and Imperialism in England, 1715–1785 (Cambridge, 1995), especially ch. 1.

[7] Lawrence E. Klein, 'Gender, Conversation and the Public Sphere in Early Eighteenth Century England', in Judith Still and Michael Worton (eds.), Textuality and Sexuality. Reading Theories and Practices (Manchester, 1993), 100–15; Amanda Vickery, The Gentleman's Daughter. Women's Lives in Georgian England (New Haven and London, 1998), ch. 6.

tion was conceptualized as central to the imagining of civil society. This was particularly so for David Hume, whose thesis concerning the progress of civil society emphasized the ways in which individuals might restrain their own inclinations so as to prompt and promote those of one's companions. Here, women were assigned an essential task of civilizing and refining their companions.[8] 'What better school for manners', wrote Hume, 'than the company of virtuous women, where the mutual endeavour to please must insensibly polish the mind, where the example of female softness, and modesty must communicate itself to their admirers, and where the delicacy of that sex puts every one on his guard'.[9] In some contexts female sociability, constructed as it was upon the values of domestic affection and friendship, could also have a particular political resonance. Hence Kelly has illustrated the role of bluestocking salons in the delineation of a concept of civil society that was sharply differentiated from the corrupt world of courtly culture.[10]

None the less, despite (or perhaps because of) such celebrations of the civil potential of female conversation, attitudes towards women's converse were frequently ambiguous. Thus Michèle Cohen has pointed to persistent anxieties concerning the possible 'excess' of female conversational influences. William Alexander feared that too great a participation in female converse might soften men; whilst others warned that it threatened to emasculate male company and weaken its capacity for 'sound reason'.[11] Furthermore, alongside the ideal images of female polite conversation persisted the recurrent gibes at women's inability to curb their tongues, with numerous commentators configuring the tea-table as a subversive site for female intrigue.[12] Towards the end of the eighteenth century, such warnings became woven into particular ideological agendas. Evangelicals such as Hannah More and Thomas Gisborne cautioned against women's propensity for unguarded, undisciplined conversation, and Gisborne in particular counselled on the virtues of female silence.[13] Moreover, particular aspects of polite conversation were now constructed as peculiarly fitting for female discourse. Whereas such behaviour as the value of adapting oneself to the assembled company, of affecting a wide but not deep knowledge of conversational topics, and avoiding the pitfalls of over-assertiveness had previously been promoted as virtues of polite gentlemanly discourse[14]—they were

[8] Klein, 'Gender, Conversation and the Public Sphere'.

[9] Quoted in Gary Kelly, 'Bluestocking Feminism', in Eger et al., Women, Writing and the Public Sphere, 166.

[10] Kelly, 'Bluestocking Feminism', 163–80.

[11] Michèle Cohen, Fashioning Masculinity: National Identity and Language in the Eighteenth Century (1996), 109–10.

[12] Beth Kowaleski-Wallace, 'Tea, Gender, and Domesticity in Eighteenth-Century England', Studies in Eighteenth-Century Culture, 23 (1993), 131–45.

[13] Cohen, Fashioning Masculinity, 70; Thomas Gisborne, An Enquiry into the Duties of the Female Sex (1777), ch. 6.

[14] Lawrence E. Klein, Shaftesbury and the Culture of Politeness in Early Eighteenth Century England (Cambridge, 1994), 5. Stephen Copley, 'Commerce, Conversation and Politeness in the Early Eighteenth-century Periodical', British Journal for Eighteenth-Century Studies, 18: 1 (1995), 67–8.

increasingly promoted as female ideals. Hester Chapone, for example, advised her female readership of the dangers of pedantry, and counselled them to 'exert your own endeavours to please, and to amuse, but not to outshine' their companions.[15] Similarly, Hannah More's novel, *Coelebs*, argued that the ideal female conversationalist was one who had perfected the ability to draw others out in conversation. Moreover, in *Coelebs* women are not required to refine male discourse. In the ideal Evangelical family, male conversation is, in itself, pure and rational.[16]

Discourses on the nature of conversation, and women's role within it, were then diffuse and often contradictory. By the late eighteenth century the 'third sphere' of domestic converse had established a tradition of mixed-sex socializing, in which female participation was viewed not only as critical, and of civic significance, but also as potentially dangerous. Moreover, the growing spread of Evangelical ideas was beginning to introduce a further strand to the debates on social interaction. The emphasis the Evangelicals placed upon the integrity of intimate family relationships and the sanctity of the home as a site of virtue, was predicated upon a more restrictive code of female manners.

In many ways, the cultural and political world of Katherine Plymley, the subject of this chapter, operated on the cusp of these overlapping models of social intercourse. Katherine Plymley (1758–1829) was a well-educated spinster, and an accomplished watercolourist and botanist, who lived just outside Shropshire with her brother, the Archdeacon of Salop, Joseph Plymley (later Corbett). Together with her sister, Ann, Katherine Plymley helped to supervise the upbringing of Joseph Plymley's twelve children.[17] Their proximity to Shrewsbury opened up a wide range of opportunities to participate in the cultural and political life of this thriving leisure town.[18] On the whole, however, Katherine Plymley's social and intellectual life remained rooted within the domestic environment established by her brother. Joseph Plymley, who was adored and revered by his sister, presided at the heart of an eclectic social network. This embraced Shropshire ironmasters, such as the Reynolds family; the cultural élite of the local Anglican clergy including the much beloved Archdeacon Clive and the radical Rector of Abberley, Mr Severne; many of Shrewsbury's radical dissenting ministers; as well as experimental scientists and doctors living in the environs of the town.[19] But the Plymleys also moved on the

---

[15] Mrs Chapone, *Letters on the Improvement of the Mind. Addressed to a Lady* (1801), 144–6, 156–7.

[16] Hannah More, *Coelebs in Search of a Wife* (Bristol 1995, first published 1808), 60–1, 80.

[17] I discuss in greater detail Katherine Plymley and the wider opportunities for female civic engagement in late eighteenth-century Shrewsbury in a forthcoming essay, 'Women, Civic Identity and Domestic Virtue in Late Eighteenth-century Provincial Culture'. See also Ellen Wilson, 'A Shropshire Lady in Bath, 1794–1807', *Bath History*, 4 (1992), 95–123.

[18] A. McInnes, 'The Emergence of a Leisure Town: Shrewsbury 1660–1760', *Past and Present*, 120 (1988), 53–87.

[19] For useful contextualization, see Barrie Trinder, *The Industrial Revolution in Shropshire* (London and Chichester, 1981).

peripheries of bluestocking circles, enjoying slight acquaintances with female literati such as Hester Piozzi and Elizabeth Carter; one of their closest friends, Dorothy Alison (the daughter of John Gregory, author of *A Father's Legacy to his Daughters* (1774)), was the ward of Elizabeth Montagu (with whom Joseph Plymley was also acquainted).[20] In addition, Joseph Plymley was a pivotal figure in the provincial anti-slavery movement. His activities in this field brought him and his family into close collaboration with the likes of William Wilberforce and Josiah Wedgwood, as well as more progressive activists including Granville Sharpe. In particular, the family formed close ties of friendship with the leading abolitionist Thomas Clarkson—a man venerated by Katherine Plymley. Thomas Clarkson was, at this period, engaged in a series of gruelling tours of the provinces to mobilize opinion in support of the anti-slavery cause. He frequently used the Plymley home as a base for his activities in the region. Clarkson's dogmatic and indefatigable dedication to the cause combined with his progressive politics (he attempted to collect subscriptions for France's National Assembly) brought Katherine Plymley into contact with the world of the professional political activist. This was a politicizing experience for Plymley, although it may also have reinforced her own sense of inferiority in public matters in the face of such ardent, and widely recognized talent.[21]

The ideas and activities of the Plymley family present an unexpected picture of the cultural and political milieu of the Anglican hierarchy in this provincial setting. Many in this network, in addition to Clarkson, sponsored highly radical political views. Whilst Joseph Plymley was often constrained to affect an ignorance of their sentiments in his public capacity, in private he was to be found lending both financial and moral support to radical causes. For example, he suggested that an abolitionist tract written by a former sailor in Liverpool should be suppressed, fearing that its extreme political radicalism would damage the anti-slavery cause. However, he none the less contributed to a subscription for the author's benefit.[22] A number of those whom the Plymleys entertained during these years were also at the vanguard of revolutionary politics. Theophilus Houlbrooke, their close friend, was to become a member of the Scottish Convention; Archibald Alison, one of their most intimate associates, was in favour of a republican government; and Lord Daer, another respected guest, only narrowly escaped prosecution for treason. In 1800 Katherine Plymley professed herself 'delighted' with the company of W. Todd Jones, the

---

[20] Plymley Notebooks, Shropshire Record Office 1066/24 (1794); 1066/41 (1796) hereafter Plymley (cited by kind permssion of owners of Plymley archive); Sylvia Harcstark Myers, *The Bluestocking Circle. Women, Friendship, and the Life of the Mind in Eighteenth-century England* (Oxford, 1990), 267.

[21] For Thomas Clarkson, see Ellen Gibson Wilson, *Thomas Clarkson. A Biography* (Basingstoke, 1989); and J. R. Oldfield, *Popular Politics and British Anti-Slavery. The Mobilization of Public Opinion Against the Slave Trade, 1787–1807* (Manchester, 1998), chs. 3–4. In later years Katherine Plymley was to admit that she had been something of 'an enthusiast' concerning Clarkson and she subsequently began to note fondly the idiosyncrasies of his manner and conversation. Plymley 1066/48 et ff.

[22] Plymley 1066/46 (1797).

author of a prohibited work on insurrection in Ireland.[23] Perhaps equally surprising is that a significant number in the Plymley network, including Charles Bage (son of the progressive novelist, Robert Bage) and Robert Townson (a local doctor), also professed a profound religious scepticism. This made for a lively and earnest coterie who relished and valued the opportunity for debating current affairs within the privacy of the home environment.

This commitment to the importance of free discussion provided, as we shall see, one of the ways in which this network conceptualized the relationship between the individual and the polity. None the less, alternative configurations of civil society simultaneously complicated the Plymleys' intellectual terrain. As Evangelical Anglicans, the Plymleys may also be contextualized within another discourse of civil society that was being actively promoted at this time by Anglican (and particularly Evangelical) clergymen such as Thomas Gisborne, John Lowe, John Robert Scott, and George Horne. This dwelt upon the need to discipline the self as a precursor to engagement as a member of civil society. Such a process, it was repeatedly argued, would enable the recognition of social and religious duties, and facilitate an active engagement in society. Critical to these accounts was the role of establishment religion in civil society, and its importance in maintaining hierarchical social and political structures. Civil society, in this discourse, emerged as a restraining influence, keeping unruly passions and irresponsible aspirations in check.[24] George Horne, for example, wrote of 'this command of the passions, this self government, that qualifies a man to discharge properly all the relative duties of life; that endears him to a community, and renders him a truly useful and valuable member of society.'[25] The Plymleys, who exhibited a deep commitment to the role of the gentry in guiding local social and political life, closely accorded with such a view. They themselves attempted a self-disciplined lifestyle that would promote the good of the wider community. Indeed, the command of the passions was central to their concept of civic virtue. During times of food shortages among the poor, for example, they abstained from eating bread,[26] and Katherine Plymley particularly praised Thomas Clarkson for giving up 'everything the world calls pleasure' to devote himself to the cause of abolition.[27]

Whilst the ideals of radical democratic converse and the Anglican concept of civil society were fundamental to the Plymleys' cultural landscape, others within their acquaintance were experimenting with more unorthodox discourses. In 1796 the local MP for Ludlow, Richard Payne Knight, published his lengthy

---

[23] Plymley 1066/12 (1792); 1066/26 (1794); 1066/53 (1799).

[24] For example, Thomas Gisborne, *The Principles of Moral Philosophy investigated, and briefly applied to the constitution of civil society* (1789); John Lowe, *The Duties of Man as a Member of Civil Society. A sermon [on Matt. vii. 12] preached before the . . . Society of Gregorians at their Anniversary Meeting, at Pontefract, the 11th of July, 1792* (1792); John Robert Scott, *A Dissertation on the Influence of Religion on Civil Society* (Dublin, 1777).

[25] George Horne, *On the Influence of Christianity on Civil Society. A sermon [on Tit. ii. 11, 12] preached at . . . Oxford at the assizes* (Oxford, 1773), 12–13.

[26] Plymley 1066/59 (1801).   [27] Plymley 1066/1 (1791).

poem, *The Progress of Civil Society*. This work considered the emergence of modern society, tracing the evolution of civilization through the various stages of hunting, agricultural developments, and political changes, as well as noting the importance of the arts and commerce. Most memorably, it dwelt upon the role of sexual love and desire in promoting social change and artistic endeavour, and made a tentative suggestion for the relaxation of the divorce laws.[28] *The Progress of Civil Society* thus drew upon a culture of Enlightenment libertinism that was frequently practised among the cultural élite of the day. This included, of course, such figures as Erasmus Darwin, a figure with extensive local connections to the Plymley network.[29] The Plymleys themselves were certainly fairly relaxed towards the sexual peccadilloes of some of their friends.[30]

Varying models of citizenship were, therefore, entwined in the Plymley network. The notion of civil society for these individuals was not a static concept, but a contested and fluid phenomenon. In order to probe the implications of this for women's political identity I shall now turn to the diaries of Katherine Plymley. Her record (comprising some two hundred notebooks) permits a close scrutiny of the myriad, gendered, and often conflicting processes by which individuals, through the social conduit of conversation, were able to imagine and confirm themselves as subjects within a wider polity.

Conversation was pivotal to Plymley's record. In her detailed accounts of the many visitors received in her brother's house, it was their conversational gifts upon which her assessments frequently focused. In this her judgements were steeped in the mores of polite society. She particularly esteemed, for example, the demonstration of a wide general knowledge. Mr Howell, she was pleased to report, was a great conversationalist, registering his ability to talk on diverse subjects such as natural history, chemistry, mineralogy, botany, and household economy, as well as his stimulating discussions of politics and religion.[31] Dr Babbington was similarly praised for his ease in discussing botany, chemistry, the classics, and philosophy.[32] The ability to converse well on such subjects was important to Plymley. It confirmed the existence of a distinct cultured and genteel élite—one that was fitted to serve and lead the community.[33] Plymley's own membership of such a class was critical to her civic identity. She wrote often of the social, political, and cultural duties of the gentry class, and her paternalistic relationship with local tenantry, electors, and servants is a recurring theme of

---

[28] Richard Payne Knight, *The Progress of Civil Society. A Didactic Poem, in Six Books* (1796), see especially pp. 54–60. Knight, a member of the Society of Dilettanti, had earlier found himself in trouble for publishing an essay on the worship of Priapus. See Nicholas Penny, 'Richard Payne Knight: A Brief Life', in Michael Clarke and Nicholas Penny (eds.), *The Arrogant Connoisseur: Richard Payne Knight 1751–1824* (Manchester, 1982), 1–18.

[29] Roy Porter, *English Society in the Eighteenth Century* (Harmondsworth, 1982), 259–60.

[30] Katherine Plymley herself makes casual mention of the mistress and illegitimate children of her close friend, Mr Howell. Plymley 1066/107 (1815).

[31] Plymley 1066/19 (1793); 1066/52 (1798).   [32] Plymley 1066/35 (1795).

[33] Joseph Plymley insisted, e.g., that magistrates should play a leading role in their communities. Trinder, *The Industrial Revolution in Shropshire*, 209.

the diaries.[34] An accomplished botanist herself, and with a keen interest in contemporary science and religious debate,[35] such social interchanges affirmed and deepened her sense of cultural authority.

It was slightly different acquirements, however, that she praised in the conversation of a Mr Heber and Mr Otter, reporting it to be 'particularly interesting & instructive, they have both travelled & seen much of the world, & are cheerful & communicative'.[36] As this extract hints, the ease of male access to wider cultural opportunities could render them attractive conversational companions to women such as Plymley, who led more sheltered lives.[37] It was, as we have seen, almost a commonplace in many eighteenth-century texts to speak of the edifying influence of female conversation. In contrast, for Plymley it was male conversation that was salutary for women. Thus, Plymley recounts with pride her presence at a discussion between Thomas Clarkson and her brother: 'Mr C and my Br now proceeded to converse in a strain of calm wisdom & true goodness that was highly gratifying & edifying to be present at. I am most thankful to have sat in such company.'[38] As in More's *Coelebs*, Plymley did not privilege women with possessing any unique, improving influence.

Significantly, for Plymley, it is male political privileges that can render men particularly instructive speakers. She was gratified that her brother should choose to take his teenaged daughter, Josepha, to the trial of Lord Melville, noting that this was 'one of the few opportunities a woman can have of hearing any of the speakers in the House of Commons'.[39] The capacity to speak well on politics (and particularly on radical politics) is a quality Plymley often records with favour. She recalls approvingly of a colleague of her brother's, a Mr Trowd, that 'In politics & all other subjects he is very liberal; an advocate for the just liberty of the subject.'[40]

Plymley's comments indicate a perception that the home could function as a site of civic import not merely because of the complementary values women supposedly brought to male political practice, but because of the instruction some women might receive in current affairs. Plymley frequently copied into her diary lengthy political conversations she had witnessed between her brother and his guests, and then elaborated upon and explained their meanings.[41] This does not mean that Plymley considered political discussions to be a predominantly male prerogative. It is evident that Plymley could be loquacious on such topics with her female acquaintances. This is clear from her relationship with Mrs Vaughan of Otley Park, (a wealthy local widow), whose stimulating conversation Plymley clearly relished. Their discourse frequently turned on politics, with the

---

[34] Plymley 1066/15 (1793); 1066/32 (1795); 1066/38 (1795); 1066/67 (1806).

[35] Katherine Plymley attended, for example, chemistry lectures in Shrewsbury. Plymley 1066/62 (1804).

[36] Plymley 1066/109 (1815).

[37] Although Plymley accompanied her brother's family on various leisure trips around the country on several occasions, she often alludes to her comparative isolation. Plymley 1066/50 (1797).

[38] Plymley 1088/12 (1792).   [39] Plymley 1066/67 (1805–6).   [40] Plymley 1066/46 (1797).

[41] See , e.g., Plymley 1066/16 (1793).

two women sharing a firm belief in the 'liberty of the subject'—a position, which as Plymley tellingly noted, meant they agreed on a whole raft of issues extending beyond the scope of the strictly 'public'.[42]

Plymley's relationship with Vaughan indicates the political potential of female sociability. Whilst Plymley gives the impression that her conversations on political matters were at their freest in such situations, neither this nor her awe at male privilege and knowledge meant that she was content merely passively to absorb the wisdom of her male companions. Conversation was still expected to be a process of mutual interaction. In common with the traditions of genteel etiquette, Plymley was critical of those whose speech was too self-referential, or ill-sufficiently sensitive to the feelings of their companions. She complained of Mr Severne, whose conversation was marred by his self-preoccupation,[43] and observed wryly of a local judge, 'there is nothing but listening required to keep up a conversation, if I may so call it, with him.'[44] By contrast, she approves of those such as the young Mr Iremonger, who, according to the classic tenets of eighteenth-century conversation, 'not only listened well, but if he knew the subject better than the speaker, he never betrayed the least impatience'.[45]

However, whilst Plymley expected a courteous attention to her words, too great an emphasis upon her speech could be disarming. Although Mr Howell (of whom Plymley was particularly fond) is praised as a good listener, she confesses that he is so attentive to the comments of herself and Ann that they find it embarrassing, not feeling that their comments were worthy of such attention.[46] Clearly, despite her considerable intellectual attainments,[47] Plymley lacked the confidence to engage in this conversable milieu on equal terms with men. Indeed, Plymley readily acquiesced in a set of finely constructed gendered behaviours—distinctions that ensured that the female experience of domestic sociability was subtly different from that of their male companions. After describing in considerable detail the radical political views of an Irish MP, that had emerged during the course of his visit, she then noted approvingly that 'with women he will converse on the lighter subjects of literature seemingly with great pleasure'.[48] Whilst the Plymley network was clearly impressed with examples of egalitarian conduct, this did not incorporate any substantial revision of gendered behaviours. Plymley praised the behaviour of an African prince at a dinner held in his honour. She was gratified at his refusal to acknowledge the attempts of the local grandee, Sir Richard Hill, to mark him out with 'distinctions to his rank', yet lauded the prince's great 'courtesy to the ladies'.[49]

---

[42] Plymley 1066/48 (1797); although the relationship later soured when Mrs Vaughan's illness rendered her a demanding companion 1066/66 (1805).

[43] Plymley 1066/108 (1815).   [44] Plymley 1066/114 (1817).

[45] Plymley 1066/123 (1820).   [46] Plymley 1066/107 (1815).

[47] Plymley's notebooks contain extensive references to her wide reading, including such authors as William Godwin, Paley, Mme de Staël, Voltaire, Butler, Blair, Goethe, Hester Chapone, and Dugald Stewart. Plymley 1066/149–80.

[48] Plymley 1066/17 (1793).   [49] Plymley 1066/14 (1793).

In part, then, the functioning of the conversable world within this milieu depended upon the reinstatement of gendered hierarchies. Women were to be treated with a marked courtesy and charm, thus underlining their separate and distinct status. However, the home should not be conceptualized as a mono- lithic forum. Gendered behaviours and discourses impacted differently and were variously enacted within the discrete spaces and processes of domestic activity: women's utterance and social interaction assumed new meanings and involved delicately differentiated behaviours in, say, the nursery, the dining room, or the drawing room. Of course, the custom of ladies retiring after dinner immediately excluded them from certain conversational practices. (Katherine Plymley was grateful to her brother for reporting back to her the con- versations she missed.[50]) Gendered practices could also be delineated less overtly, however. Plymley records happily her relaxed conversations with local intellectuals such as Dr Babbington and Dr Dugard on wide-ranging issues including radical millenarianism, metaphysics, and French revolutionary politics.[51] Such encounters typically occurred in intimate and informal settings (usually with only herself and sometimes her sister present). Similarly, whilst Plymley reported of Thomas Clarkson that there was no one with whom she was 'more unrestrained in conversation',[52] this did not mean to say that Plymley would feel able to converse with equal ease with Clarkson in all domestic situa- tions. Most of the conversations she reports between herself and Clarkson occur in the interstices of formal entertaining—early in the morning, whilst waiting for breakfast; or whilst playing with her nephews and nieces. Her garrulity in these circumstances is in marked contrast to the political conversations between Clarkson and her brother, in which, as we have seen, she portrays herself as a privileged spectator.

Plymley's self-presentation as an onlooker to the political discussions that occurred within her home is a recurring phenomenon. After recording, for example, a conversation between the Revd Archibald Alison and Theophilus Houlbrooke on constitutional reform she writes, 'I *observe* an idea gaining ground very fast among men of an enlightened & upright mind that some reforms are become very necessary, and if not obtained it will be likely to pro- duce a greater change' [my emphasis].[53] Similarly, dinners given to local polit- ical allies and candidates during a general election are assiduously documented by Plymley, but she is sensitive to her ambivalent presence during such meetings. She often validates her report of what was said by explaining, rather proudly, 'I was there'. She portrays her presence to be a privilege, and often expresses gratitude to her brother for allowing her to attend such functions.[54] It is clear that the conversation of male associates gathered together within the home to

---

[50] Plymley 1066/1 (1791). The restricted nature of mixed-sex conversation among the British élite was often commentated upon by foreign visitors: Peter Burke, *The Art of Conversation* (Cambridge, 1993), 117.

[51] Plymley 1066/65 (1805).   [52] Plymley 1066/12 (1792).   [53] Plymley 1066/10 (1792).

[54] Plymley 1066/70 (1807).

discuss political or professional matters had a formal significance, and that women's participation on such occasions would (in this circle at least) be muted.

Plymley's cognizance of the wider import of these occasions was in keeping with the high political significance afforded to conversation in such networks. This was made explicit by the Revd Archibald Alison (1757–1839).[55] Alison, best known today for his work on aesthetics, was, during these years a Shropshire vicar, and one of the Plymleys' closest friends. For Alison free discussion embodied an ideal strategy for political change. He was envious of (what he perceived to be) the role of the conversable public sphere in revolutionary France, maintaining that the National Assembly made decisions by gauging the opinion of the people. This was done, he argued, by judging the state of discussions in such fora as the coffee-house.[56] Alison's ideas are very close here to those of French philosophes such as the Abbé Morellet, for whom the public sphere, as embodied in democratic sites of conversation, provided a consultative role.[57]

Within the Plymley milieu it is evident that the home was viewed as a further appropriate site for such democratic discussion. For example, another of the Plymleys' friends, a religious sceptic by the name of Dr Townson, articulated the importance of what he termed 'free discussion' during the course of his visits.[58] Yet, the use of the domestic site as a third sphere of political sociability did not provide women with an unproblematic conduit into political discussion. Although women may have been included in these politico-social rituals, their engagement in such an environment could be fraught with ambiguity.[59] That is to say, women's participation at a dinner could have very different meanings and implications from that of a male diner. This dissonance was unwittingly conveyed by a young associate of Joseph Plymley, Mr Dean. For Dean, a barrister, the ability to talk and debate with fellow professionals around a dinner table was resonant with political implications. It exemplified, he explained to Katherine Plymley, at one such dinner, the 'excellence of our constitution, & the upright administration, of our laws'.[60] Dean, a liberal Whig, further observed to Plymley that the opportunity to talk without 'rank and distinction' 'on an equality no

[55] For Archibald Alison, see Mark Salber Phillips, 'William Godwin and the Idea of Historical Commemoration: History as Public Memory and Private Sentiment', in Dario Castiglione and Lesley Sharpe (eds.), *Shifting the Boundaries. Transformation of the Languages of Public and Private in the Eighteenth Century* (Exeter, 1995), 202–5; John Brewer, ' "The Most Polite Age and the Most Vicious". Attitudes Towards Culture as a Commodity, 1660–1800', in Ann Bermingham and John Brewer (eds.), *The Consumption of Culture, 1600–1800. Image, Object, Text* (1995), 351–2.
[56] Plymley 1066/10 (1792).
[57] Daniel Gordon, ' "Public opinion" and the Civilizing Process in France: The Example of Morellet', *Eighteenth Century Studies*, 22: 3 (1989), 302–28.
[58] Plymley 1066/68 (1806).
[59] This was not necessarily the case of all social networks, however. See pp. 74–7 below. See also Sarah Richardson ' "Well-neighboured Houses": The Political Networks of Elite Women, 1780–1860', in Kathryn Gleadle and Sarah Richardson (eds.), *Women in British Politics, 1760–1860. The Power of the Petticoat* (Basingstoke, 2000), especially pp. 60–8.
[60] Plymley 1066/67 (1806).

matter where they are in the profession, upon any subject' was the hallmark of a free society. Such a beguiling picture, which, in many senses captures the essence of 'civil society' as Alison would present it, is based, however, upon male professional identities. Whilst Plymley is present at such dinners, it is the men's egalitarian prerogative to question each other, no matter what their professional rank, that is the critical defining point. Plymley is thus situated in a curiously liminal position. Her conversation with the barrister functions as a peripheral commentary to the seemingly more significant discourse taking place around her.

Thus far it would seem that in many ways, the Plymley network bears out the observations of recent scholars—that the domestic site functioned not as an antithesis to the public but rather as a further forum for sociability and political interchange. Whilst this may have enhanced female exposure to democratic discussion, it did not necessarily imply the full integration of women as independent political subjects. This duality in female engagement—that women could inhabit the same space as men and yet remain excluded from the civic meanings perpetuated therein—lies at the heart of the problematic relationship between women, the domestic site, and civil society. Yet this was not a static phenomenon. Shifts in political events could subtly alter the meanings attached to domestic conversability, and dissolve some of the boundaries of female political alterity. As Plymley herself was keenly aware, during the mid-1790s, the civic significance of free discussion changed swiftly. During these years, as fears of revolution and invasion swept Britain, contemporary cognizance of the potentially subversive role of conversation emerged starkly. Many features of urban associational life were directly affected, as institutions such as literary and philosophical societies were frequently forced either to close or to ban political conversation.[61]

Significantly, it was not merely public conversation that was viewed as potentially subversive: private discussions also became the subject of scrutiny. In 1793 Katherine Plymley reported with alarm on the establishment of loyalist clubs that called for the prosecution of 'seditious' writings, as well as the policing even of 'opinions deliver'd in conversation'.[62] The advisability of curbing the tongue was early pressed home to those in the Plymley circle. This is because conservative political opinion frequently allied the cause of anti-slavery with that of democratic reform.[63] In the rapidly changing climate of political fear, abolitionists felt it imperative, therefore, to dissociate themselves from radical activity.[64] Thomas Clarkson's inability—or refusal—to restrain his speech on such questions as the desirability of an English revolution rapidly became a bone of contention among more moderate campaigners. William Wilberforce admitted to Joseph Plymley that he no longer felt able to entertain Clarkson in his own home as, 'his conversation was so very unguarded in politics'.[65]

---

[61] John Brewer, *Pleasures of the Imagination: English Culture in the Eighteenth Century* (1997), 508, 511.

[62] Plymley 1066/15 (1793).

[63] Plymley 1066/27 (1794).

[64] Oldfield, *Popular Politics and British Anti-Slavery*, ch. 3.

[65] Plymley 1066/41 (1796).

Katherine Plymley usually deferred to the judgement of her brother, Joseph. However, she was unable to concur with his disapproval of Clarkson's dogged persistence in giving voice to revolutionary views.[66] Katherine Plymley's evident determination to support the right of Clarkson and others to express insurrectionary beliefs is particularly significant. Her persistence in reporting and recording the conversation of male radicals amounted in this atmosphere (when repressive legislation had all but extinguished the circulation of printed radical material) to an act of sedition. In a move indicative of her growing political awareness and confidence, she used her knowledge of the current political climate, her careful reading of local newspapers, and a familiarity with works written by prohibited radicals, including Thomas Paine, to consider her acquaintances' radical political analyses.[67] Plymley was herself a radical Whig, rather than a republican or a democrat. She none the less agreed with key facets of the political analyses of many of the radicals in her network, being bitterly critical of government policy, desirous of constitutional reform, and assessing that revolution was just around the corner.[68] (She even muses, at one point, upon the part that Clarkson might play in a revolutionary situation.[69]) Plymley herself acknowledged that anyone expressing a desire for even a moderate reform of the constitution was likely, in the climate of the revolutionary years, to find themselves positioned as seditious.[70] This was particularly so after the passage of the 'Gagging Acts' in 1795. A piece of legislation that horrified Plymley, she was angered at its attempt to 'repress liberty of speech' 'even in private conversation'.[71] Whilst continuing to position herself as a spectator in the conversations and expression of radical politics that took place around her, she therefore acted as a subversive citizen in circulating, recording, and often validating many of the ideas of the extreme radicals. Indeed, Plymley's record serves as a private history of radicalism among the cultural élite.[72]

We have seen, above, the reluctance of figures such as Wilberforce to permit their domestic space to be used for the airing of radical political sentiments. Katherine Plymley, in contrast, clearly provided a sympathetic and receptive audience for figures such as Theophilus Houlbrooke, Archibald Alison, Granville Jones, Thomas Clarkson, Lord Daer, and W. Todd Jones, who wished to continue to air and debate insurrectionary ideas. The encouraging eye and responsive mien adjured by Hannah More, Thomas Gisborne, and the like here emerge as a conscious political act in themselves, especially given the high

---

[66] Plymley 1066/41–2 (1796).

[67] Plymley's detailed observations and comments on revolutionary politics form a dominant theme of the notebooks. See 1066/15 (1793); 1066/16 (1793); 1066/21 (1793); 1066/23 (1794); 1066/26 (1794); 1066/27 (1794); 1066/29 (1793); 1066/34 (1795); 1066/42 (1796).

[68] Plymley 1066/16 (1793); 1066/29 (1794); 1066/34 (1795); 1066/38 (1795).

[69] Plymley 1066/42 (1796).   [70] Plymley 1066/15 (1793).

[71] Plymley 1066/38 (1795). The acts made any criticism of the king or the government a treasonable offence.

[72] Without Plymley's testimony it is unlikely that scholars would have been made aware of the extent of Thomas Clarkson's radicalism, for example.

stakes now associated with the act of listening.[73] Whilst she may have frequently conceptualized her role to be that of an auditor, rather than an interlocutor, Plymley demonstrated that even within such perimeters, women could construct themselves as political actors.[74] Plymley and her sister, Ann, were clearly shaken one day when confronted by some angry locals, who challenged them to defend their political opinions and those of their family.[75] Women's presence at political debate, however muted, immediately positioned them as radical citizens—an act for which they could be called to account.

For Plymley, then, the home did indeed function as a sphere of conversability and political significance. Even within the contours of a tightly defined gender role, Plymley was able to assist in creating a sympathetic forum for the diffusion of a visionary politics. At a time when public political activity was so tightly subscribed, and surveillance threatened also free expression within more intimate contexts, such opportunities were of considerable importance to the likes of Todd Jones and Thomas Clarkson. Yet Plymley, whilst welcoming the exchange of revolutionary ideas, none the less simultaneously championed, as we have seen, a male-dominated model of polite conversation founded on genteel accomplishments and the cultivation of a studied civility.

For others, however, the project of democratic politics was doomed unless personal interaction was restructured upon new, egalitarian modes of conduct. Within this model, the family itself was to be privileged as the basis for wider civic reform. In order to examine some of the implications of such a strategy I wish to turn to a circle of radicals with which Plymley was herself acquainted: that of Thomas Clarkson's wife, Catherine (née) Buck, and her close friend, Sarah Jane Maling. Buck was from a nonconformist family in Bury St Edmunds, Suffolk. Their family home formed a lively focus for political and intellectual debate, in which women appear to have been accorded an equal role. Katherine Plymley reported with interest the comments of a mutual friend, Mr Jones, who noted, after visiting the family, that 'the ladies in general, on the eastern side the kingdom are well versed in politics, & conversed with freedom on the subject'.[76] Plymley, who, as we have seen was ambivalent as to the role of women in political debate, was intrigued to learn that Catherine Buck was 'a great politician' and gifted in political argument.[77] Other sources also testify to Buck's vigour as a conversationalist. Julia Smith, the daughter of MP William Smith, whose

[73] For a broader consideration of the diverse meanings of silence, see Burke, *The Art of Conversation*, ch. 5.
[74] For a textured and highly sophisticated account of other processes whereby women might construct themselves as political subjects within the context of domesticity, see Harriet Guest, *Small Change. Women, Learning, Patriotism, 1750–1810* (Chicago, 2000).
[75] Plymley 1066/15 (1793).   [76] Plymley 1066/35 (1795).
[77] Katherine Plymley did not meet Catherine Buck until 1805. For further information on Buck, see Kathryn Gleadle, 'British Women and Radical Politics in the Nonconformist Enlightenment, 1780–1830', in Amanda Vickery (ed.), *Women, Privilege and Power. British Politics 1750 to the Present* (Stanford, 2001), 134.

sister Patty was a close friend of Catherine's, recalled that Catherine Clarkson was 'in conversation quite brilliant sometimes'.[78]

Many in dissenting circles were prepared to transgress conventional etiquette concerning the gendered basis of social entertaining. Maling and another female acquaintance, for example, successfully insisted that they should be invited to a gentleman's party.[79] Recent research on other centres of political and religious dissent is beginning to reveal similar patterns of mixed-sex sociability else-where. Helen Plant, for example, notes the extent to which nonconformist women in York were actively involved in a wide range of discussant activities—including book societies and debating clubs.[80] Within such environments female conversation could easily slide over the boundaries of established norms. Jane Rendall observes that in Edinburgh the lively discourse of progressives Eliza Fletcher and Mrs Millar led to Lord Jeffrey teasing them as 'women that would plague him with rational conversation'.[81]

Sarah Jane Maling, however, soon made the bitter discovery that dissenting families might exhibit very different levels of tolerance to unconventional female conversation. Her wish to engage in democratic intercourse, stimulated by lengthy visits to the Buck family, was frequently frustrated by the more con-ventional sensibilities of her family and their acquaintances. They were clearly exasperated by her speech, and her willingness to divulge feminist and atheistic views. Whereas Plymley evidently felt content to fulfil a tangential function in political debate, for Maling, the opportunity to converse on equal terms was a critical right. In contrast to Plymley's tacit participation, silence was experi-enced by Maling to be a fundamental denial of her political integrity. Maling admitted to Buck that she was 'so much in the habit of conversing in a certain strain, that I find it impossible to keep my hands before me, hold up my head & behave in all respects like a pretty *modest*, well-educated miss'. She spoke of the 'monstrous exertion' required in stifling her conversation, talking potently of the need to 'strangle' her thoughts.[82] This she attempted to do when, over din-ner, a family acquaintance began to abuse William Godwin for his supposedly free love doctrines. Maling described her outrage at his 'incessant babbling' on the topic, but noted that 'After saying a severe thing or two, I held my peace in contempt.' Maling bitterly resented the pressures upon her to '*think* but *say*

---

[78] Cambridge ADD 7621/15 TS recollections of Julia Smith, p. 3. This was thought to be in marked contrast to the serious intensity of her husband. BL Add. MSS 72839A Typescript of Family life 1803–6 (William Smith family), 11–12.

[79] Sarah Jane Maling to Catherine Buck, 30 Nov. 1803, BL Clarkson Papers, Add. MS 41, 267 B, f. 19.

[80] Helen Plant, 'Gentlewomen Dissenters: Women of the Rational Dissenting Élite in Yorkshire, 1770–1830', unpublished paper delivered at the Feminism and Enlightenment Colloquium, 27 May 2000, Senate House, London.

[81] Jane Rendall, ' "Women that would plague me with rational conversation": Aspiring Women and Scottish Whigs, c.1790–1830', unpublished paper delivered at the Feminism and Enlightenment Colloquium, 27 May 2000, Senate House, London.

[82] Sarah Jane Maling to Catherine Buck, 10 Sept. 1794, St Johns College, Cambridge, Slavery Box 1, by permission of the Master and Fellows of St Johns College, Cambridge.

nothing'. For Maling such proscriptions were deeply hypocritical given the widespread dismissal of female intellectual and political significance. 'I might have been permitted to talk harmlessly enough', she complained, 'Would any one have ever been disposed to adopt a notion because maintained by an obscure illiterate young *woman*?'[83] Such comments were a little disingenuous, however, as she was rarely so circumspect. On one occasion, when the dinner conversation turned to the subject of 'love and women', Maling bluntly articulated her own views as to the debased nature of contemporary marriages. Despite the protests of the rest of the company she was proud to report that she would not 'flinch an inch'. When one of the gentlemen present attempted to assert the dignity of his own marriage, Maling proceeded to, in her own words 'interrogate him'.[84]

Maling's repeated attempts to assert her right to converse with freedom were part of a wider political project to reform the conventions of social exchange. When her father gave a toast to the newly married Clarksons, Maling tried to insist that it should be given not to 'Thomas and Catherine Clarkson', as her father proposed, but to 'Catherine and Thomas Clarkson'.[85] A similar desire to recast the forms of personal dialogue is evident in Catherine Clarkson's and Maling's use of revolutionary modes of address, replacing the customary 'miss' with the politically provocative 'Citoyenne'.[86]

For radicals such as Maling, these challenges to conventional etiquette were part of a more fundamental attempt to reconfigure personal relationships. She attacked the mores of polite society directly in her refusal to make herself agreeable to others. 'I know I am not formed to please people in general', she confessed to Catherine, '& I am generally not liked at all'.[87] On occasion, she criticized her friend for failing to live up to her own standards of egalitarian conduct. Claiming that she sometimes detected a certain 'caprice' in Catherine's behaviour she grumbled, 'I despise the *indiscriminate smile*, & *appearances*, which contradict *reality*.' Complaining that Catherine appeared to prefer the company of the genteel, Maling affirmed that she would remain, 'true to my *democratic* principles, I stoop to no-one, I *court* the favour of no-one'.[88]

Maling's ambition to transform the nature of personal relationships was perfectly in keeping with the programme propounded by her intellectual mentor, Mary Wollstonecraft. As Sylvana Tomaselli has recently suggested, the

---

[83] Sarah Jane Maling to Catherine Buck, 1 Dec. 1795, BL Clarkson Papers, Add. MS 41, 267 B, f. 13.

[84] Sarah Jane Maling to Catherine Buck, 10 Sept. 1794, St Johns College, Cambridge, Slavery Box 1.

[85] Sarah Jane Maling to Catherine Buck, 29 April 1796, BL Clarkson Papers, Add. MS 41, 267 B, f. 16.

[86] Sarah Jane Maling to Catherine Buck, 10 Sept. 1794, St Johns College, Cambridge, Slavery Box 1.

[87] Sarah Jane Maling to Catherine Buck, 28 May 1793, BL Clarkson Papers, Add. MSS 41, 267B, f. 5.

[88] Sarah Jane Maling to Catherine Buck, 30 Nov. 1793, BL Clarkson Papers, Add. MSS 41, 267B, f. 7.

endeavours of radicals such as Wollstonecraft to re-examine the nature of private life formed an integral facet to their wider political programme. 'The family', Tomaselli argues, 'was the most public sphere of all because it made or broke public-spiritedness.'[89] Tomaselli's discussion focuses upon Wollstonecraft's insistence on the need to promote a concept of virtue that might be practised equally by men and women and, ultimately, to unite the values of the public with the private. However, some radicals sought to look beyond the construction of civic values. They also attempted, at the most intimate and practical level, to reorientate the very ways in which family members interacted with one another. Families such as the Galtons (who were related to the Darwins), for example, sought to educate their children in 'democratic manners', and encouraged them to question parental authority and assert their rights.[90] The reformed domestic site was to form the starting-point for the diffusion of new egalitarian practices into the wider spheres of civil society.[91] The attempts of radicals to create alternative customs of egalitarian converse were not lost on contemporaries. Laetitia Matilda Hawkins, for example, ridiculed the attempts of British radicals to practise democratic behaviour with their wives, children, and servants.[92] Significantly, the reassertion of tight conversational rules for women was a feature of conservative reaction in the coming decades. This is evident from works as disparate as Hannah More's *Coelebs* to Stodart's *Every Day Duties* (1840).[93] Well might the feminist author Geraldine Jewsbury complain in her novel, *The Half-Sisters*, of the way in which women were 'crushed down under so many generations of arbitrary rules for the regulation of their manners and conversation'.[94]

In recent assessments of female civic engagement, there has been an inevitable tendency to focus upon the more forthright and exceptional models of female political activity. To excavate the sensibilities of less publicly active (and in Plymley's case, self-effacing) women can help to reveal an extremely diffuse and complex narrative of the relationships between domesticity, politics, and gender. Those women who felt bound by convention and social duty to tread a circumspect path could nevertheless forge intricate ideological connections with a broader 'civil society'. Indeed, Plymley's analysis of the nature and import of

[89] Sylvana Tomaselli, 'The Most Public Sphere of All: The Family', in Eger *et al.*, *Women, Writing and the Public Sphere*, 254.

[90] Mary Schimmelpennick, *Life of Mary Anne Schimmelpennick* (1858), 222–3; Gleadle, 'British Women and Radical Politics', 135.

[91] These concerns are central to my own work in progress on the relationship between family culture and political expression. K. Gleadle, 'Radical Parents and the Politicization of the Domestic Site, 1780–1860', paper delivered to the conference 'Parenthood in Early Modern Europe', Institute of Historical Research, January 1999; Kathryn Gleadle, ' "The Age of Physiological Reformers". Rethinking Gender and Domesticity in the Age of Reform', in Arthur Burns and Joanna Innes (eds.), *Rethinking the Age of Reform* (Cambridge, forthcoming, 2003).

[92] Laetitia Matilda Hawkins, *Letters on the Female Mind, its powers and pursuits. Addressed to Miss H. M. Williams* (1793), 2 vols., ii. 71.

[93] M. A. Stodart, *Every Day Duties: In Letters to a Young Lady* (1840) has chapters on female conversation and politeness.

[94] Geraldine Jewsbury, *The Half-Sisters* (Oxford, 1998, first published, 1848), 159–60.

conversation reveals the ways in which the home could function as a critical site for the construction of political identities through the interchange and reception of ideas. If, in Plymley's network, there was a tendency to recreate a gendered 'third sphere' within the domestic environment, this was but one possible way to configure the home as a site of democratic exchange. For those such as Maling, conversation and modes of social interaction were important not merely to facilitate the spread of democratic ideas, they were an essential means by which personal relationships might themselves be reformed.

A consideration of these very different approaches to the cultural role of conversation does reveal certain commonalities. For both Maling and Plymley the creation of a political identity was a fluid and often unstable process. (Witness Maling's violent fluctuations between attempts at conformity and her bitter outbursts; or Plymley's uneasy incorporation of a radical political agenda within her broader, paternalist outlook.) It is particularly evident in the case of Plymley that contrasting forms of civil society were constantly overlapping and evolving. Her social relations involved elements of a number of contrasting models: the female sociability of the bluestocking world, the Evangelical ideal of self-control and regulation, and the democratic (if largely androcentric) concept of free political exchange. This in itself reveals the rich if uneven possibilities open to women to forge their own civic identities within a largely domestic milieu. If Maling's vision of an egalitarian social practice that might dissolve the boundaries between public and private interchange had a greater unity and cohesion, it was strongly contingent on political events, and ultimately fleeting. By the early 1800s, when the radical project was largely in abeyance, Maling's (and Catherine Clarkson's) letters have assumed an air of weary conformity, and there is no further evidence of their revolutionary views. Discrete formulations of the relationship between the self and the wider polity might enjoy very different trajectories. The idea of civil society was in the constant throws of creation and revision; and even those women who played but a minor role in public activity might contribute and interact with this process.

4

Civil Society by Accident? Paradoxes of Voluntarism and Pluralism in the Nineteenth and Twentieth Centuries

BRIAN HARRISON

The importance to democracy of 'civil society' became a modish preoccupation among intellectuals in developed societies during the 1990s. This reflected their sense not of its vitality but of its actual or potential demise. They were concerned not only that the social underpinning necessary for democracy was lacking within the USSR and its former satellites after Communist control had been removed, but also that even in Western societies participatory and voluntarist social institutions could not be taken for granted. In Britain such preoccupations were reinforced by a more parochial concern: Labour leaders sought a non-statist philosophy that would distance their party from its painful legacy of the 1970s, but which would also make it electable by accepting many of the free-market and libertarian ideals that Thatcher had revived after 1979. Fiercely repudiating Thatcher's remark of 1987 that 'there is no such thing as society' (in fact lifted totally out of context),[1] 'New' Labour found its answers in what it initially called 'community', then reclassified as 'civil society' (though how far these terms are interchangeable remains controversial). A revived 'civil society' involving reciprocal rights and duties would rebuild the Edwardian 'new Liberal' consortium. Given this theoretical component, the Blairite 'project' would then be on course for reuniting the Liberal and Labour traditions: under Blair as under Asquith, the left would be able to force the Conservatives on to the defensive. Outlining his philosophy of the 'third way' in September 1998, Blair pronounced it 'the grievous 20th century error of the fundamentalist left' to suppose that the state could replace civil society and thereby advance freedom; 'a key challenge' for progressive politics was to use the state 'as an enabling force, protecting effective communities and voluntary organisations'.[2]

---

[1] Interview in *Woman's Own*, 31 Oct. 1987, p. 10.
[2] *Independent*, 21 Sept. 1998, review section, p. 4.

Thatcher would not have disagreed. In her comment about society, as she later explained, she had meant 'that society was not an abstraction, separate from the men and women who composed it, but a living structure of individuals, families, neighbours and voluntary associations . . . The error to which I was objecting was the confusion of society with the state as the helper of first resort'.[3] She told the Women's Royal Voluntary Service's annual conference in 1981 that voluntary bodies are welcome 'because either they can do things which the government cannot do, or they can do them better'. William Hague maintained in 1998 that Conservatives 'have a long and rich tradition of championing civil society', believing as they do 'in strengthening those institutions which stand between the individual and the State'.[4] So an all-party consensus built up in the 1990s to the effect that voluntary associations lie near the heart of 'civil society'. Robert Putnam's *Bowling Alone* (2000) conveyed a similar message within the United States, and was influential there.

The phrase 'civil society' was rarely used in twentieth-century Britain before the 1990s, not because its reality was absent but because its presence was so completely taken for granted that it needed no discussion.[5] If defined to include families, neighbourhoods, community structures, and non-governmental economic institutions—voluntary associations are central to 'civil society'. Their role is integral to Cohen and Arato's six components of the phrase: individual rights, privacy, formal legality, free association, plurality, and free enterprise.[6] The aim here will be to shed historical light upon deliberately articulated rather than spontaneously emerging voluntarist structures: that is, upon the diverse types of organized pressure on government from without, whether overt and altruistic or covert and self-interested, that emerged between the industrial revolution and the present. Their diverse components include cause or opinion groups and interest groups—all conventionally covered by the umbrella term 'pressure group'. Even these organizations rarely use the phrase 'civil society', though the concept was implicit behind phrases they frequently *have* employed: self-help, self-improvement, charity, think-tank, philanthropy, crusade, lobby, and civic culture. After a brief chronology of pressure groups and voluntary movements in Britain since the industrial revolution, first the affinities and then the tensions between them and 'civil society' will be explored.

[3] M. Thatcher, *The Downing Street Years* (1993), 626.
[4] Thatcher in *The Times*, 20 June 1981, p. 5; Hague speech on 27 July 1998, *Independent*, 29 July 1998, p. 4.
[5] For a survey of the volunteer's importance in twentieth-century Britain, see B. Harrison and J. Webb, 'Volunteers and Voluntarism', in A. H. Halsey with J. Webb (eds.), *Twentieth-Century British Social Trends* (2000), 587–619.
[6] J. Cohen and A. Arato, *Civil Society and Political Theory* (Cambridge, Mass., 1992), quoted in B. Knight and P. Stokes (eds.), *The Deficit in Civil Society in the United Kingdom*, Foundation for Civil Society Working Paper, No. 1 (1996), 4.

I

The voluntarist component in nineteenth-century civil society was powered by a combination of industrialization, Enlightenment values, and pluralism in religion. Government in an industrializing society needs to ensure that it is fully informed both about the unprecedented day-to-day practical issues that arise, and about long-term shifts in public opinion. On issues of government policy—taxation, the armed forces, health and safety, for example—interest groups, trade-union, and professional structures were forced to mobilize in self-defence and self-advancement, and spontaneously made their expertise available to those in authority. Yet to the newly emergent power groups of industrial society government seemed regionally and socially remote, and so crusades and cause groups—championing causes from anti-slavery and religious liberty to free trade, feminism, franchise extension, and pacifism—emerged as vehicles of public opinion. They drew heavily upon the libertarian, humanitarian, and participatory traditions of nonconformity, and readily responded to puritan resonances. The pace was set within the new industrial towns, as Richard Cobden, the radical spokesman for free trade, pointed out in 1850. Urging tenant farmers into self-defence, he referred to Lancashire's industrial leaders: 'if it had been a question affecting one of our mechanical trades in Lancashire and Yorkshire, the persons connected with that trade would have met together, and would have discussed among themselves exclusively what should be the course to be pursued under the circumstances'.[7]

An inspiring story—even a myth—was assembled from pressure-group history. The professions, trade unions, employers' organizations, and chambers of commerce saw themselves as ousting corruption and servility and as challenging metropolitan, aristocratic, and Anglican ignorance through self-organized group-voluntarism. So great was their vitality and range that they could afford sometimes to quarrel among themselves, thereby nourishing further their shared libertarian and participatory values. They were continuously accumulating settled procedures, expertise, and standards of conduct, preferably operating behind the scenes in relation to practical issues. They saw no necessary conflict between their own interests and those of the wider community, and were well able, on occasion, to mount the platform for more generalized causes. The National Association of Factory Occupiers, the National Free Labour Association, and the Liberty and Property Defence League were all formed to resist interventionist governments and over-mighty trade unionism.

More flamboyant in their altruism, however, were the 'cause groups' that were concurrently emerging, often run by the same people in their spare time. Overcoming the many obstacles to spontaneous agitation in what was only

[7] R. Cobden, speech at Aylesbury on 9 Jan. 1850 in R. Cobden, *Speeches on Questions of Public Policy*, ed. by J. Bright and J. E. T. Rogers (1870), i. 447.

slowly becoming a pluralist society, they continuously refined agitational technique in response to earlier crusading successes. The protectionist MP George
Finch presciently pointed out in February 1846 that 'if Ministers . . . yield to the
clamour of the Anti-Corn-Law League, they would have plenty of other
leagues—leagues for cheap religion, cheap Government, and cheap everything'.[8] The protectionists' champion Benjamin Disraeli claimed that the
Conservative prime minister Robert Peel's concessionary response to outside
agitation 'literally forced the people out of doors to become statesmen', and that
O'Connell's movement for Roman Catholic emancipation, the Birmingham
Union for franchise reform and the Anti-Corn Law League were all his 'legitimate offspring'.[9]

With the mounting self-confidence of dissenting and provincial culture, the
enthusiasts for reform gravitated from one single-issue cause to the next,[10] so
that the prominent Chartist William Lovett in 1847 saw the need for a 'general
association of progress' which could draw the reformers together. He stressed
the need for franchise reform, disestablishment, free trade, lower taxes, cheaper
justice, better education, temperance, peace, and housing reform, adding that 'I
still entertain the hope that the day is not distant when some such general organization of the friends of progress will take place'.[11] The *National Temperance
Chronicle* in 1851 highlighted the existence not only of a 'circle of the sciences'
but also of 'a *circle of moral and philanthropic movements*; so that he who
begins in seeking the welfare of his fellow-men in one thing is led step by step to
seek it also in other things'.[12] Moving on to the next cause was in some cases
only half-conscious: 'the vitality of our Crusade appeared . . . to cause it to break
through the boundaries of its own particular channel', wrote Josephine Butler,
the crusader against state-regulated prostitution, 'and to create and fructify
many movements and reforms of a collateral character'.[13] The Unitarian
reformer F. W. Newman, however, was entirely self-conscious: he told the pro-
hibitionist United Kingdom Alliance in 1865 that it would succeed like its four
great predecessors: the attack on religious disabilities, the destruction of the rotten boroughs, the abolition of slavery, and the Anti-Corn Law League. It 'would
make the fifth great struggle in this century, and it would be as successful and as
triumphant as the others'.[14]

Mid-Victorian politicians had to respond, if only to moderate the pace or
guide the direction of these movements, and Joseph Chamberlain's National

---

[8] *House of Commons Debates* (H.C.Deb.) 26 Feb. 1846, c.173.
[9] B. Disraeli, *Lord George Bentinck*, 5th edn. (1852), 309.
[10] I have discussed these interconnections further in 'A Genealogy of Reform in Modern Britain',
in C. Bolt and S. Drescher (eds.), *Anti-Slavery, Religion and Reform. Essays in Memory of Roger
Anstey* (Folkestone, 1980), 119–48.
[11] W. Lovett, *Life and Struggles* (1876), 324–5; cf. p. 329.
[12] Quoted in A. Tyrrell, 'Personality in Politics: The National Complete Suffrage Union and
Pressure Group Politics in Early Victorian Britain', *Journal of Religious History*, December (1983),
382.
[13] J. Butler *Personal Reminiscences of a Great Crusade* (1896), 83.
[14] *Alliance News*, 28 Oct. 1865, p. 344.

Liberal Federation after 1877 aimed to systematize this process so that the Conservative enemy could no longer divide and rule. And with Conservatives increasingly learning from the Liberals, a cumulative voluntarist-assisted two-party late-Victorian shift towards pluralism built up. Although pluralism conflicted with some aspects of the Conservative tradition, the sheer need for electoral survival forced Conservatives to refine their approach to public opinion, and even on occasion—in the Association movement, the Anti-League, the Church Defence Institution, and the Tariff Reform League—to mount crusades of their own. The careers of Wellington, Peel, and Disraeli show that merely to shelter behind established structures and privileged groups had become for Conservatives a waning option: conservative opinion had to be mobilized for Conservative Party purposes, and was the more effective when not bearing the Conservative label. In 1926 over 300,000 and perhaps half a million people volunteered to work during the General Strike,[15] yet their self-image was entirely non-party.

Far from emerging to challenge this voluntarist structure and mood, the Labour Party grew out of it—though Tony Blair in 1999 told the National Council for Voluntary Organizations that in later years Labour 'at times forgot its own roots in self-help, friendly societies, co-operatives and voluntary organisations'.[16] The party was not at first at all statist in outlook. Its 'prefigurative strategy' led it to set up miniature welfare communities within party and trade-union branches, and later within Labour-controlled local authorities, long before notions of a centralized, bureaucratic, and impersonal 'welfare state' gained any currency. So in many parts of the country socialism was incorporated into daily life long before it had been incorporated into national legislation.[17] There was much grass-roots utopianism in the early labour movement, together with the same wary suspicion of government structures as alien, the same belief that power corrupts—as middle-class Liberal and dissenting organizations had earlier displayed. As with the Liberals, free trade was Labour's aim in foreign relations, and trade unions combined their dispute pay, their old-age pensions, and their sickness, accident, and funeral benefits with commitment to what they came to call 'free collective bargaining'; even in their mid-twentieth-century prime they felt restive when tied in to central-planning structures and priorities.

Yet attitudes were changing. The First World War nourished both voluntarist and statist structures, but in generating the Federation of British Industries in 1916, and two years later the National Confederation of Employers' Organizations, it drew employers' organizations and trade unions into a more centralized policy-making process. In setting precedents for centralized control of the economy, the two world wars helped to advance corporatist ideas, and

[15] G. A. Phillips, *The General Strike. The Politics of Industrial Conflict* (1976), 153.
[16] *Guardian*, 22 Jan. 1999, p. 10.
[17] S. Yeo, 'A New Life: The Religion of Socialism in Britain, 1883–1896', *History Workshop Journal*, 4 (Autumn 1977), 36.

thereby to advance statism within the Labour Party. Labour's presence in national government and the advance of nationalization and 'planning' moderated trade-union hostility to state structures, which now seemed diminishingly remote. Producers, regionally and organizationally more concentrated than consumers, were relatively alert to their interests and readier to turn the state to their own purposes. The move towards twentieth-century 'corporatism' was not continuous or one-way: it advanced fast during the two world wars, but markedly slackened between them. By 1951, however, a statist Labour Party, allied with trade unions that were at least nominally socialist, seemed so powerful that Conservative governments from then until 1964 did not mount any serious challenge. Two-party competition from then until 1979 became in effect a debate about which party could manage corporatism most effectively. Pluralism persisted, but it increasingly took the form of a group-pluralism in which trade unions, welfare pressure-groups, and statist employers' organizations—all with their eyes on government funds—moved towards continuous consultation with central government, especially over the attempt to operate 'incomes policies'.[18]

Meanwhile voluntarism of the individualist type gravitated towards the right wing of the Conservative Party. In the 1970s the drawbacks of group-voluntarist corporatism were advertised through the privatized policy-formation conducted by think-tanks like the Centre for Policy Studies and the Adam Smith Institute. 'What we can do', said Dr Madsen Pirie, President of the Adam Smith Institute in December 1987, 'is to introduce ideas into the public arena and make it acceptable to talk about them'.[19] Of these ideas, Thatcherism was the beneficiary and pressure groups for collectivism were the victims—if only because the abandonment of incomes policies and the retreat from 'planning' freed governments from dependence on trade unions, welfare pressure groups, and employers' organizations. During the 1980s the 'volunteer' and the entrepreneur resumed their appeal for the Conservative Party, whereas the volunteer's pejorative left-wing analogue, the 'activist' became a term of abuse within the Labour Party. 'New Labour' increasingly emphasized duties rather than rights: to quote Gordon Brown in his budget speech of March 2000, 'a strong civic society is built not by rights alone but by rights and responsibilities and by the shared pursuit of the common good'.[20]

This shift in voluntarist fashion—from crusading activist towards entrepreneur and volunteer—had its social underpinning in a social as well as politico-economic privatization. Earlier pointers to a growing concern that John Stuart Mill's ideal of the active citizen was not being realized included the disappointment expressed in the later nineteenth century by old working-class radicals and

---

[18] For this key trend from the 1940s to the 1970s, see my 'Incomes Policies in Britain Since 1940: A Study in Political Economy', in C. Bruland and P. O'Brien (eds.), *From Family Firms to Corporate Capitalism: Essays in Business and Industrial History in Honour of Peter Mathias* (Oxford, 1998), 269–96.

[19] *Guardian*, 22 Dec. 1987, p. 13.   [20] H.C.Deb. 21 March 2000, c.866.

Chartists about the working people whom they had earlier helped to enfranchise, as well as C. F. G. Masterman's exposure of Edwardian middle-class suburban quietism in his *Condition of England* (1909). Domesticity, whose alliance with humanitarianism and respectability made it seem at first the ally of voluntarism, ultimately turned against its progenitors and provided excuses and incentives for opting out of the political process altogether. Within the comfortable urban home, both sexes—with their planned families, their hobbies, their television, their do-it-yourself, and their individualized transport in the family car—could feel entirely self-sufficient. From the early 1950s the mass membership of political parties went into decline, and the concomitant rise of the opinion poll ensured more attention for the politically passive at the expense of the politically active. Influential inter-war intellectuals had made a cult of the private as distinct from the public virtues, and from the 1940s on from both left and right there even came theoretical justifications of political quietism—most notably in Crosland's *Future of Socialism* (1956) and Oakeshott's essay 'The Claims of Politics'. Secularized personal priorities can be seen in retrospect to have undermined both new-model Thatcherite and old-style communitarian socialist strategies, both of which were premissed upon the ideal of citizen activism in one form or another. So by the 1990s Putnam's worries about American civic culture had resonance in Britain too.

II

How close is the affinity between these voluntarist structures and the ideals of 'civil society'? Voluntarists seldom spell out their long-term assumptions and hopes: their concerns are so specific and often so pressing that there is small inclination for fundamental principles. Their mood is unhistorical, unreflective, and severely practical; besides, abstract discussion might risk unnecessary dispute. Nor did Britain's cultural environment encourage anything different: parliament, epitomizing the national mood, showed 'an aversion . . . for anything approaching to abstract reasoning, an indifference to any considerations which do not promise a distinct practical advantage';[21] and in drawing together such broad spans of opinion from centre to left and from centre to right, the two-party system so central to the House of Commons blurred disagreement within and between political parties.

Yet reading between the lines, pressure groups do seem to feed into 'civil society' in important respects. For the cause-group voluntarist operating within a libertarian environment progress comes through the free exchange of ideas, and for the interest-group voluntarist from the free exchange of goods. A major advantage of free trade was that it minimized potentially corrupt commercial

---

[21] Lord Robert Cecil [later the prime minister, Lord Salisbury], *Saturday Review*, 17 Sept. 1864, p. 358.

pressures on government: when Philip Snowden attacked the McKenna duties in his budget of 1924, he was shocked by the self-interested pressures protectionism nourished. It was, he recalled, 'one of the greatest dangers of a tariff system' that it corrupted the political process. 'The lobbies at the House of Commons were crowded out with representatives of vested interests bringing pressure to bear upon members of Parliament to oppose the repeal of these duties.'[22] But whether free trade or protection prevail, the *cause* group's voluntarism subjects the *interest* group's voluntarism to continuous public scrutiny by preventing locality, tradition, and personal or group interest from elbowing aside discussion of national policy questions. In this way a highly educative clash of opinions is promoted. Press, procession, and petition illuminate dark corners, ensuring that influence is open and direct, and that freedom of trade and opportunity give quality products and talented people their due. Furthermore, the conflict between rival cause groups—Anti-League and Anti-Corn Law League, friends and opponents of women's suffrage—encourages public debate and civic involvement. When one cause group is wound up, its promoters gravitate into new enthusiasms in what becomes in practice, though not explicitly, a continuous reforming sequence. And at a time when political participation took place directly through face-to-face encounters rather than 'virtually' through electronic devices, much mutual learning, much generation of mutual tolerance, was the result. Activists within a face-to-face society found it both necessary and feasible to reach an accommodation.

All these movements worked with the grain—that is, compatibly with the aroused consciousness and self-confidence of groups hitherto socially and politically subordinate. The voluntarist saga is one dimension of Britain's middle-class success story since the industrial revolution, whereby upper and lower social extremes were drawn towards the centre. Middle-class allies included dissenters, respectable working men, moral and ethnic minorities, and women—but also newly assertive regional groupings: town as against country, north as against south, subordinate nationalities as against England. Working-class, dissenting, and progressive missionaries radiated out from the towns in search of rural allies and converts. Both interest and cause groups either directly or indirectly challenged an English male-dominated, traditionalist, Anglican, and aristocratic society. Conservatives who mimicked their progressive opponents by stirring into action their traditionalist allies—tenant farmers in the Anti-League, women in the National League for Opposing Woman Suffrage—were playing with fire, for this risked rendering restive people who were required to display only their contentment.

Cause groups continually sought to identify and encourage new categories of citizen. For opponents of state-regulated prostitution in 1871 the prostitute might be 'the meanest of citizens, yet she does not cease to be a citizen, much less

---

[22] P. Snowden, *An Autobiography* (1934), ii. 650.

to be a woman'.[23] Emmeline Pankhurst, championing women's suffrage in February 1912, wanted 'to make women feel as men have always felt, that great human causes and great human needs transcend all our private duties'.[24] The aim of the National Union of Townswomen's Guilds, which grew out of the women's suffrage movement, was in 1933 'to encourage the education of women to enable them as citizens to make their best contribution towards the common good'.[25] Then, after three decades of campaigning, a future Labour minister Chris Smith, a self-confessed homosexual, could tell parliament in February 1994 that 'yes, we are different. We have a different sexuality. But that does not make us in any way less valid or less worthy citizens of this country.'[26] Nor is it only political voluntarism that enhances civil society, for non-political voluntary structures help to initiate the isolated and potentially subversive individualist into political processes and democratic relationships. They also cut different cross-sections through society and encourage strangers to collaborate. Hensley Henson, as Bishop of Durham, acknowledged in 1911 the 'ludicrous solemnities' involved in being admitted as a freemason, yet his memoirs welcomed the resultant contacts: freemasonry, he wrote, 'must be counted among the soundest factors in the national life', and as 'a force which makes for cohesion and social stability'.[27]

Cause groups were driven on by the ideal of the 'active citizen': by the energetic and often prickly reformer who readily breaks off from parent organizations to create a splinter group. Well-managed cause groups (the RSPCA under John Colam, the Charity Organization Society, the National Union of Societies for Equal Citizenship, and the National Council for Social Service) actually encourage such people to hive off into a useful, more specialist, and nominally independent offshoot. Spontaneity and diversity of ideas and opportunity were the ideal, with leaders responding to initiatives that bubbled up from below. Behind all this was a humanitarian and libertarian ideal of personality, continuously refined through the exercise of unconstrained choice. Self-improvement did not (unlike some superficially similar late twentieth-century self-help groups) nourish mere solipsism: it led directly into public life, thereby undermining prescriptive roles and deference. Citizens responsible for their own fate—mature, independent, creative, entrepreneurial, and spontaneous, if sometimes eccentric and even perverse—continuously advanced the open and prosperous society.

The voluntarist sum was always greater than its parts: voluntarist organizations not only broadened participation in the political system they invigorated the political parties. Formally often hostile to them and wary of central government,

[23] Memorial from conference delegates opposed to the C.D. Acts printed as appendix D to Royal Commission on the Contagious Diseases (CD) Acts, *Parl. Papers* 1871 (C.408), XIX.

[24] E. Pankhurst, speech at the Connaught Rooms, *Votes for Women*, 23 Feb. 1912, p. 319.

[25] NUTG, *Annual Report* 1932, 28.   [26] *H.C.Deb.* 21 Feb. 1994, c.112.

[27] H. Hensley Henson 'MS Diaries', Vol. 17, f. 416 (quoted by permission of the Bishop of Durham); *Retrospect of an Unimportant Life* (1943), ii. 288.

cause groups preferred the liberty of opposition, at least until a governmental political party had been converted. Yet in practice they brought the political parties ideas, recruits, and impetus. Sometimes they even themselves set up new political parties, or pseudo-parties. One of these, originating as an interest group within the Liberal Party, became the Labour Party, and eventually ousted its parent. Cause groups were not confined to the left: effective conservative crusades could be mounted when necessary—against the French Revolution in the 1790s, against Home Rule after 1885, against redistributive taxation through promoting tariff reform after 1902, against socialism after 1931, and for Thatcherism in the 1970s—though the career of Sir Robert Peel illustrates the early Victorian Conservative Party's difficulty about accommodating spontaneous 'pressure from without' without appearing to capitulate. None the less, Conservative leaders from Disraeli onwards did eventually learn the art of prudent and timely (though often only tactical and/or insincere) concession. The Labour Party, too, had its difficulties, given the tension between *laissez-faire* trade unionists and interventionist socialists, anti-state libertarians, and collectivist paternalists. Still, a two-party system worked well enough from the mid-nineteenth to the early twenty-first century, partly because so accessible to outside pressure. Through the Liberal Party, and to a lesser extent through Labour, even cranks and eccentrics were drawn into the system, and were thereby tamed, neutralized, or trained to become constructive.

The volunteer's expertise was legislatively useful, especially at a time when there were few civil servants. Alertness to a new source of suffering, a new hazard, a new injustice, or a new remedy could as likely come from a volunteer as from a civil servant. Anthony Sampson noted in 1962 the growth of 'new institutes' which provided politicians with 'a kind of shadow civil service':[28] the Royal Institute of International Affairs (complementing the Foreign Office), the National Institute of Economic and Social Research (complementing the Treasury), and the Institute for Strategic Studies (complementing the Ministry of Defence). Businessmen helped the Attlee governments to plan the economy, just as think-tanks helped the Thatcher governments to revert to the free market forty years later. Voluntarists in, say, the Centre for Policy Studies or the Adam Smith Institute could broaden the bounds of public debate by floating policy ideas which sympathetic politicians could then take up. Pressure groups could also help with enforcement. The RSPCA relished the fact that 'in other countries the intervention of the State would be invoked, and an organization of public prosecutors and overseers would be established, but in England it was their pride to do these things themselves, and to trust to the State nothing they could accomplish by local efforts'.[29] This was no mere Victorian response: Sidney Webb pointed out that in social work 'the Public Authority and the

---

[28] A. Sampson, *Anatomy of Britain* (1962), 242–3.
[29] S. Laing at a public meeting in 1870 inaugurating the society's Sussex branch, *Animal World*, 1 Feb. 1870, p. 96.

salaried official can only do the work in gross; they are apt to be blunt and obtuse; to have no fingers, but only thumbs', and that 'we need the voluntary worker to be the eyes and fingers of the Public Authority'.[30] And without voluntary bodies the Heath government could not have organized so effectively the reception and absorption of Ugandan evacuees in the early 1970s—a success which no doubt encouraged its appointment in 1973 of a government minister to manage its aid to voluntary organizations.[31]

Politicians need expertise not only on specialist matters but on public opinion, and pressure groups know a lot about that. In a complex and democratic society, they could help politicians to mobilize the consent their measures required. Politicians could even, especially during the two world wars, create the pressures to which they ultimately intended to respond, for a voluntary movement could give them the broadened community contacts that planning requires. In 1967 the Minister of Overseas Development, Reg Prentice, told an OXFAM National Hunger Lunch that public pressure made it easier for government to help, 'and this government and governments of the future ought to be nagged and bullied by those who care strongly about these things'.[32] The education was mutual: parliament educated—even discreetly moderated—the tribunes of the people at the same time as they in turn 'handled' opinion in the country at large. There was, of course, a tension between crusader and politician, but the responsiveness of politicians like Lord John Russell, Peel, Gladstone, Asquith, Lloyd George, Baldwin, Bevin, and Wilson ensured that significant lines of contact remained open at the most dangerous moments: 1831–2, 1845–6, 1866–7, 1885–93, 1912–20, 1926, 1931, 1940, and 1974–6.

The successful interaction of insider with outsider, nourished by the polarity between government and opposition, raised the tone of a political life that was all too prone to murky compromise. Gladstone became the most brilliant among the system's nineteenth-century political brokers, and when he told Granville in May 1877 that 'the Government will only be kept even decently straight by continuous effort and pressure from without',[33] the gamekeeper was indeed turning poacher. Intermediaries like this helped to reconcile human nature as it is with human nature as it should be. Nor did the British political system's moral preoccupations die with Gladstone: in the twentieth century they merely assumed new forms. Edwardian 'New Liberalism' put much faith in individual moral progress, and its increasingly collectivist routes towards it were carried forward by an increasingly collectivist Labour Party. Labour's moralism was less individualist in mood, in that it reared up the virtues of a

[30] Quoted by Eleanor Rathbone in *H.C.Deb.* 30 Apr. 1936, c.1195.

[31] See E. Heath's speech to Buckinghamshire Conservative Associations, *The Times*, 14 July 1973, p. 3.

[32] Quoted in M. Black, *A Cause for Our Times. OXFAM. The First 50 Years* (Oxford, 1992), 117.

[33] Gladstone to Granville, 17 May 1877 in A. Ramm (ed.), *The Political Correspondence of Mr. Gladstone and Lord Granville 1876–1886* (1962), i. 29.

newly politicized working class against the vices of an allegedly declining political élite. Moralistic middle-class causes thereafter distributed themselves between the parties, with Labour laying greater claim to feminism, environmentalism, and opposition to nuclear defence, while the Conservatives appropriated support for family life and the moralistic element in entrepreneurial values. The Labour Party responded with a 'New Labour' that was highly moralistic at more than one level, and was as heavily preoccupied as early Thatcherism had been with refurbishing the purity of civic institutions (though doing so in such a way as to arouse suspicion in many quarters that they were subverting rather than rejuvenating established constitutional procedures).

Pressure groups liaising with the politicians could help them to channel protest towards parliament and away from the street violence of participatory-revolutionary and authoritarian-reactionary movements. They could secure a continuous interaction between government and governed, not only at general elections but between elections. British trade-union leaders in the 1970s often stressed the need for this. The trade-union leader David Basnett pointed out in February 1973 that democracy means more than periodic elections: 'it means the elected government respecting the views of minorities, and protecting their welfare; it means the obtaining consent through persuasion, and not coercion; it means according a greater weight to the views of those with a special interest in the resolution of a particular issue than to those whose interest is peripheral'.[34] In their stabilizing role, pressure-group leaders were quite self-conscious: 'as for the public', Cobden declared in 1846, 'its voice is never heard in France unless it be in the street for "three days" behind barricades, and this is after all a very clumsy way of settling questions of political economy'.[35] For the former Chartist Henry Vincent, in May 1850, public meetings were 'the safety valves of society: they let off the steam'.[36]

Pressure groups saw themselves as educating the élite on economic and moral realities, but also their own members in self-confidence and articulateness. Thereby they enlisted into the political process the nation, or (with Irish nationalists and militant suffragettes) a subsection of the nation. As Cobden put it in 1845, 'we have been teaching the people of this country something more, I hope, than the repeal of the Corn-laws'; that is, through the Anti-Corn Law League the middle classes were learning their moral power, and positioned themselves to guide the working classes towards non-violent agitation. Whig aristocrats reinforced this popular view from above with their appeal to history and shrewd concessionary tactics—most memorably in delivering what Trevelyan called that 'bull's-eye of legislative marksmanship',[37] the Reform Act of 1832, though

[34] General Secretary of the General and Municipal Workers' Union, *The Times*, 1 Feb. 1973, p. 16.
[35] Cobden on 9 Sept. 1846 in J. A. Hobson, *Richard Cobden. The International Man* (1918), 44.
[36] Speech at Abingdon in *Oxford Chronicle*, 25 May 1850, p. 3 (a reference I owe to the late Raphael Samuel).
[37] R. Cobden, speech of 18 June 1845 in his *Speeches*, i. 305; Trevelyan quoted by D. C. Moore in his 'Political Morality in Mid-Nineteenth Century England: Concepts, Norms, Violations', *Victorian Studies*, September 1969, 32.

less effectively in Gladstone's attempt at home rule after 1885. Nor was the Whigs' subtle approach to political participation laid up in a napkin: through twentieth-century Liberal defections to Labour and the Conservatives it permeated the entire twentieth-century two-party system, promoting political participation and stability in its wake.

So voluntarists since the mid-eighteenth century have performed a sixfold service for civil society: they enhanced the free exchange of ideas, recruited new groups into citizenship, cultivated the democratic personality, fuelled the two-party system, facilitated informed and therefore effective legislation, and, by raising the tone of politics, helped to ensure that the system retained contact with the disgruntled idealist, whose direct action might otherwise have subverted democratic government. Yet the discussion cannot stop there, for on closer inspection each of these affinities between voluntarist movements and 'civil society' has its undemocratic obverse, and each needs to be discussed in turn.

III

J. S. Mill thought democracy should not only mould the political system, but should pervade its subordinate institutions—self-government in 'the business of life' being his route to adult education.[38] Yet many nineteenth-century Liberals took a more narrowly political view of democracy: within the family, the chapel, and the business firm the values of the earthly or divine and precariously benevolent paterfamilias were by no means necessarily liberal, and women rarely enjoyed formal authority within trade-union and nonconformist structures. Furthermore, the need for confidentiality hinders democracy in commercial interest groups and in law-breaking cause groups, and many pressure groups are (in Kornhauser's terminology) 'radical' rather than 'liberal' organizations[39]—that is, authoritarian in origins, beliefs, and instincts. To take an extreme case, a male-enforced secrecy and exclusiveness were integral to the world of freemasonry, yet the freemason's fraternal and philanthropic role seemed to exemplify civil society's constructive pluralism. The philanthropist could be as authoritarian as the entrepreneur in outlook, the two roles often being run in harness. 'I am essentially what may be called a strong man, *i.e.*, I rule', said Dr Barnardo;[40] the voluntarist careers of Octavia Hill and Lady Reading provide female analogues.

It is questionable, too, how far a voluntarist regime really benefited the subordinate social groupings mobilized (or in some cases patronized) by voluntarist structures: provincial dissenters, working men, women, the very poor, and

---

[38] J. S. Mill, *Principles of Political Economy*, ed. by W. J. Ashley (1909), 948; see also p. 949.

[39] W. Kornhauser, 'Social Bases of Political Commitment: A Study of Liberals and Radicals', in A. M. Rose (ed.), *Human Behavior and Social Processes. An Interactionist Approach* (1962), 333–4.

[40] Quoted in S. L. Barnardo and J. Marchant, *Memoirs of the Late Dr Barnardo* (1907), 300.

subordinate nationalities. Because their leaders inevitably come from groups
with the leisure necessary for voluntary work (or in more recent times the
necessary education to take on paid, professional roles in non-governmental
organizations) voluntarist structures do not necessarily empower those who
most need a voice, nor does the general interest necessarily emerge from the
clash between groups of the organizable. Hence nineteenth-century working-
class interests were at risk of distortion from middle-class mediators of political
power, while those in extreme poverty had little to hope for from the self-help
organizations of more prosperous workers. Dissenting and Catholic interests
were in tension with those of the Anglican establishment; women's interests
with male supremacy; and the rationalistic priorities of experts with those of
emotional populists. Likewise in gaining a public hearing the twentieth-century
producer had the edge over the consumer, the motorist over the pedestrian,
and the organized worker over the unorganized. The Labour politician
C. A. R. Crosland was sceptical about environmentalist lobbyists in the early
1970s: rural working-class jobs needed defending, he thought, against 'a set of
middle- and upper-class value judgements' whose exponents (often suburban
and self-interested) sought 'to kick the ladder down behind them'. In such a situation, a neutral government—concerned for the welfare of all, fuelled by direct
access to ordinary voters and responsive to altruistic pressure groups—may
need to hold the ring. 'We are the trade union for the pensioners and children',
said the Conservative prime minister Edward Heath, seeking an impartial image
when embattled against strikers in February 1974, 'the trade union for the disabled and sick . . . We are the trade union for the nation as a whole'.[41]

Nor is it clear that voluntarist structures necessarily nourish the democratic
temperament. Sociologists have asked some awkward questions. Bernard
Barber and Robert Michels highlight potential conflicts of interest between leaders and led, and they find some support in the history of twentieth-century
British corporatism. Its participating structures were wracked by the tension
between sharing the government's generalized benevolence and promoting their
members' special interests. Corporatist conspiracies against the public all too
easily resulted, with both trade unions and employers' organizations hovering
between three roles: cause group (their initial role); interest group (their subsequent role), and arm of government (a projected role, ultimately aborted).
There is not only the latent or actual conflict of interest between the full-time
employee and the subscribing member, which may tempt the employee into
rigging the structure against the member; there is also the conflict, even within
a democratic movement like Chartism, between dominant and defeated faction.
Dissidents from Feargus O'Connor's Chartist dominance after 1840 were, said
William Lovett, 'crucified' in the columns of its leading newspaper, the
Northern Star, 'and the fawning pack of intolerants . . . were hounded on to

[41] Crosland in Fabian pamphlet, quoted in *New Statesman*, 8 Jan. 1971, p. 40; Heath's speech at
the Free Trade Hall, Manchester, *Guardian*, 21 Feb. 1974, p. 6.

hunt and clamour down those presumptuous sticklers for individual right and freedom of action'.[42] The voluntarist temperament has not been invariably tolerant, pluralist, democratic, or 'civil', in the way that some late twentieth-century proponents of civil society have claimed.

What, then, of the continuous mutual fertilization between pressure groups and political parties? This was always hindered by the non-party image that such groups cultivate. In many pressure groups, such as the League of Nations Union or the Royal Society for the Protection of Birds, the non-party stance is genuine. In others it is imagined or, where exploited to frighten the party hierarchy, simulated. The temperance reformers, Chartists, feminists, dissenters, pacifists, humanitarians, libertarians, and Marxists who brought such pressure on the nineteenth- and twentieth-century Liberal and Labour parties rarely praised and often actively conspired against the more moderate elements in the party of the left which they wished to convert. Nor did Corn Law protectionists, beleaguered aristocrats, empire loyalists, diehard Unionists, and 'hard-faced' champions of twentieth-century corporate capitalism feel much affection for moderate centrists in the party of the right. Pressure groups have prompted recurrent and often fierce splits in mainstream parties, with supposedly 'independent' candidates splitting the vote of their own side and letting the other side in—both at general elections and at by-elections. Such zealots were restrained from splitting off altogether only because the simple-majority electoral system denied them any alternative refuge.

The dislike between the wings of any one mainstream party was often mutual, and the judicious statesman often gained by distancing himself from sectarian, self-interested, or narrowly partisan groups. Prime ministers advocating incomes policies in the 1960s and 1970s regularly portrayed themselves as championing the national interest over lesser ones. Likewise Margaret Thatcher, when *repudiating* incomes policies, claimed to be doing just the same: when asked at a centenary lunch of parliamentary lobby journalists in 1984 how she would like her governments to be remembered, it would be, she replied, for tackling 'vested interests' such as trade unions, nationalized industries, professional monopolies, and local government.[43] The history of political parties witnesses many angry and sometimes dramatic confrontations between pressure-group leaders and the leaders of the party of which they were notionally supporters—whether it is Gladstone confronting the sectarian Edward Miall during debates on the Education Bill in 1870, Baldwin spurning the press barons Beaverbrook and Rothermere in 1930, or Gaitskell speaking up for Labour MPs as 'men of conscience and honour' against unilateralists in 1960. As for the even wider-ranging pluralism that necessarily stemmed from a system that fostered only two parties, cause groups had little taste for it, and even yearned for single-party dominance—though only by the party they had themselves come to dominate. Hence voluntarists, far from strengthening political parties in a

---

[42] W. Lovett, *Life and Struggles*, 296.   [43] *Financial Times*, 19 Jan. 1984, p. 10.

democracy, may actually weaken them with their insistent, sectarian, and often divisive claims.

When it comes to legislating, the cause group's opposition-mindedness also leads it to diverge from the constructive and empirically based policy-formation that comes as second nature to the interest group and is integral to the governmental process. At the climacteric of substantive decision-making, cause groups can be surprisingly bankrupt of precise proposals—whether they are prohibitionists, suffragettes, or Irish nationalists. Of many pressure groups could it be said, as its general secretary Len Murray said of the TUC in 1976, 'we are very good at stopping what we don't like, but not at starting anything'.[44] The cause group's repudiation of practicalities, and of the empirical basis necessary for decision-making, was sometimes quite unashamed. In the 1860s the authorities applied the Contagious Diseases Acts to seaports and garrison towns with the aim of curbing venereal disease there through state-regulated prostitution. In leading the attack on the acts, Josephine Butler showed not the slightest interest in their local impact: 'of the operation of the Acts I neither can nor will speak . . . It is nothing to me whether they operate well or ill, but I will tell you what you wish to know as to my view of the principle of the Acts.'[45] Antivivisectionists took a rather similar line in the same decade.

Both interest- and cause-group leaders can be legislatively unhelpful in a second respect, for both are necessarily specialists, whereas the democratic politician must balance conflicting pressures and priorities. The interest group's expertise can be valuable to the politician, but its preoccupations are relatively narrow, and if only for commercial reasons cannot always be publicly discussed. Cause-group leaders can usually afford to speak out, but they too are specialists, whereas government ministers are inevitably generalists, and cannot refer, as did the distinguished philanthropist Lord Ashley in 1846 to 'my especial questions'.[46] Whereas the House of Commons recruits generalists who relish compromise and diversity, the cause group mobilizes specialists who relish principle and uniformity. Voluntarist spokesmen will not always feel comfortable within such a legislature, and certainly experience strain when forced to address two types of audience: a sceptical and even irreverent parliamentary audience accustomed to compromise; and a passionate and single-minded extra-parliamentary audience with exclusive access to the truth. An MP 'is obliged to weigh his words', wrote C. W. R. Cooke, '. . . and to express not the opinions he really holds, but such as will give least offence to his constituents, or compromise him least when some question now only looming in the dim and

---

[44] *Observer*, 5 Sept. 1976, p. 8.

[45] Royal Commission on the CD Acts, Q.12863. For a fuller discussion of such attitudes, see my 'State Intervention and Moral Reform' in P. Hollis (ed.), *Pressure From Without in Early Victorian England* (1974), 289–322.

[46] E. Hodder, *The Life and Work of the Seventh Earl of Shaftesbury, K.G.* (1886), ii. 168.

distant future comes within the range of practical politics'.[47] The single-issue reformer, by contrast, is free to speak out.

As for elevating the tone of politics, a pressure-group leader can rise so high as to reject the art of politics altogether. Preoccupation with a single issue encourages black-and-white views of the world which readily dismiss difference of opinion as devious, malicious, or corrupt. In this situation, the voluntarist promotes not democratic political education but an over-fastidious half-retreat from the real world. Hopes rest not with patient bargaining, but with trans-forming mechanisms which will solve problems 'in the twinkling of an eye'—no route to adult education in pluralistic values. The mood becomes rather that of Oswald Mosley in *Tomorrow We Live* (1938), where he describes a club-like parliament with its bar, its smoking room, its lobby, and its dinner tables as likely 'very quickly' to 'rob a people's champion of his vitality and fighting power'.[48] The more elevated the cause, the more justified seems coercion in pro-moting it—a coercion incompatible with open structures because these are so vulnerable to penetration by governmental authorities that have wider interests to protect. Militants must be conspiratorial in order to ward off the authorities. This was a major drawback of the Women's Social and Political Union, vehicle of the militant suffragettes: as Teresa Billington pointed out in 1907, when defending secession by the Women's Freedom League, 'if we are fighting against the subjection of woman to man, we cannot honestly submit to the subjection of woman to woman'.[49] To this the Pankhursts' reply was that in a democratic society nobody was compelled to join the union. This was to ignore the power-ful moral pressures that could be brought to bear within such structures upon the individual member—pressures more subversive of individual freedom than anything governments might do.

Intense commitment may even insulate the voluntarist from the public, espe-cially if violent methods or 'direct action' are adopted: suffragettes resisting what they saw as a male-dominated environment; or Irish nationalists fending off a nationality they saw as having been forced upon them. From failing to cul-tivate public support, the cause-group leader may even go up the blind alley that is involved in despising it. 'Oh, how I *hate* the respectable world!', the suf-fragette Lady Constance Lytton exclaimed to her sister Betty in June 1910, impatient with a public so unresponsive to what she saw as patently powerful arguments—arguments powerful enough to send her to prison and to risk her health through the hunger strike.[50] Alternatively, the enthusiastic organized minority nursing its high ideals within an apathetic unorganized majority may even be tempted into substitutionalist politics: the vanguard foists its ideals and

[47] C. W. R. Cooke, *Four Years in Parliament with Hard Labour* (1890), 88.

[48] Quoted in R. Skidelsky, *Oswald Mosley* (1975), 311.

[49] Women's Freedom League, *Votes for Women. Report of the Second Annual Conference of the Women's Social and Political Union, now the Women's Freedom League . . . October 12th, 1907* (n.d.), 5.

[50] Lady C. Lytton, *Letters*, (ed. by B. Balfour, 1925), 207.

ideas upon the majority whom it has failed to convert. Convinced of your own moral superiority, confident in your progressiveness, you may become arrogant enough to assume that coercive short-cuts to utopia are justified. Voluntarists of this type are in no position to stabilize the political system through accurately assessing relevant opinion and presenting it to government's attention. Cause-group leaders may not only misrepresent their own members but may acquire an interest in exaggerating the strength of their movement. They may deliberately create an opinion about opinion manipulatively, as did nineteenth-century utilitarians and evangelicals, or twentieth-century imperialists and Fabians. Some shrewd politicians realized that such assertive groups could be scaled down to size through enlarging the electorate and then deploying the enlarged number of voters against the relatively small number of activists.

So while there is indeed an affinity between voluntarism and 'civil society', and while voluntary bodies do indeed promote Cohen and Arato's six components of civil society, one could say of voluntarism what Marx and Schumpeter said of capitalism: it carries within itself the seeds of its own destruction. The demise of pluralism is not inevitable, but the affinity between voluntarism and pluralism is precarious enough for democracy never to be secure. For the pluralism that emerges from voluntarist activity has in modern Britain been less an embodiment of the voluntarist ideal than a pragmatic compromise between the political system and two types of voluntarist whose instincts are not necessarily democratic at all: the interest group, whose short-term and practical concerns have no necessarily democratic or libertarian implications; and the single-issue idealist, whose instincts can readily be or become authoritarian. So if voluntary organizations *are* ultimately compatible with the pluralism of 'civil society', voluntarist intent may be less responsible for the outcome than appears at first sight. Civil society may owe at least as much to an accidental and even precarious compromise between covert authoritarians. We are drawn back by this analysis, therefore, to the much older tradition of British thought on civil society, where voluntarism and pluralism were civil society's consequence rather than its essence, and where only the non-arbitrary state could render diversity tolerable and constructive.[51]

[51] See above, Ch. 1.

5

Civil Society in Nineteenth-century Britain and Germany: J. M. Ludlow, Lujo Brentano, and the Labour Question

LAWRENCE GOLDMAN

I

The term 'civil society' is used in a variety of ways, of which two are most germane to this chapter. The first, largely confined to academic discourse, denotes a distinct sphere of social relations in all societies. Civil society is understood as the web of relationships, institutions, and organizations generated in some way or another by all communities, whether national or of another type, sometimes within but frequently outside the state.[1] And in recent years a second usage has become common in which 'civil society' is specifically identified with voluntary, community, and private organizations and with a consequent project to re-establish certain sanctioned types of social interaction and association. In Western societies this has taken the form of advocating greater participation, fellowship, and mutuality in communities where these attributes have seemingly declined (often from some past golden age where close-knit social interaction is believed to have been more common). Meanwhile in Eastern European, post-communist societies, the focus on civil society since the 1980s has arisen out of a desire to promote sources of social authority, solidarity, and self-help beyond the reach of, and untainted by, the legacy of the repressive, bureaucratic state. Civil society in this second sense, whether used in East or West, is seen as synonymous with tolerance and social harmony, 'civil' in its manner and tone and in the treatment of subjects and citizens.[2]

---

[1] Above, pp. 5–7, 13–15; Krishnan Kumar, 'Civil Society', in Adam and Jessica Kuper (eds.), *The Social Science Encyclopedia* (1985), 2nd edn. (London and New York, 1996), 88–90.

[2] Frank Trentmann (ed.), *Paradoxes of Civil Society. New Perspectives in Modern German and British History* (New York and Oxford, 2000), ix, 5–8; S. Kaviraj and S. Khilnani (eds.), *Civil Society: History and Possibilities* (Cambridge, 2001), 1–6.

Most Victorians made little use of the term 'civil society'. But nineteenth-century Britain was notable for the development of forms of association—from politics and religion to sport and leisure—which, it is generally held, contributed to the relative stability and cohesion of British society and provided a means by which new or hitherto excluded groups could be integrated easily into the national community. Both the transition from aristocracy to democracy and the integration of groups such as religious nonconformists, workers, and women were assisted by the adaptability and elasticity of a civil society capable of accommodating new sections and providing them with a place and stake. When recent commentators have referred to Britain as a classic example of a historic civil society, it is very often this Victorian culture of voluntary association, and progressive integration of previously excluded classes, that they have had in mind. This chapter will focus on a test-case of such integration: the relatively smooth passage of the institutions of the working class into civil society in Britain during the third quarter of the nineteenth century.

It follows from the two definitions of civil society above—and especially from the second in which civil society is explicitly associated with certain sanctioned social values—that any analysis of the relative strength of 'civil society' in British history must rest on comparative foundations. How can we assess the distinctive features of civil society in Victorian Britain except by reference either to a fixed definition of the term, or to the history of other societies? Any discussion of the stability, pluralism, and 'inclusiveness' of the age implies comparison with other communities or periods in which those features were less evident. From Cromwellian providentialism to Whig parliamentarianism there have been many versions of British (or English) exceptionalism that have sought to explain the special character of national development with reference to religious, institutional, or social arrangements that supposedly set Britain apart. Beyond mythologies and teleologies of this type, there have also been more recent attempts to define 'the peculiarities of the English', whether in relation to the predictions of Marxist social theory or as a contribution to the study of stability itself.[3] In turn, British history has been used as a model against which the distinctive features (and deviations) of other states and societies can be explained—though the paradoxical effect of this has been to turn an apparently 'exceptional' national history into a 'paradigmatic' one. We get a glimpse of Britain through European eyes in the debate on the German 'Sonderweg'—the malign special path supposedly taken by the newly created Second Reich after 1871—which has become central to both the modern history of Europe and the trajectory of liberalism.

In the 1960s and 1970s, in a highly creative phase of post-war German historiography, the peculiarities of nineteenth-century German history were explained in relation to the development of liberal Britain, which served as the

---

[3] See articles by Tom Nairn and Perry Anderson, *New Left Review*, Nos. 23, 24, and 35 (1964–6); E. P. Thompson, 'The Peculiarities of the English', *The Socialist Register*, 2 (1965); Brian Harrison, *Peaceable Kingdom. Stability and Change in Modern Britain* (Oxford, 1982).

model for the direction Germany 'should have' taken but did not. In the work of Ralf Dahrendorf, Hans-Ulrich Wehler, James J. Sheehan, and Gordon Craig the nature of the newly unified nation (and the roots of the German tragedy in the twentieth century) were explained with reference to the German failure to establish a civil society of the British type.[4] In narrowly political terms, this was explained through the failure of German liberals to gain control of the new Reich: dependent on Bismarck and Prussian power for its creation, they were unable and often unwilling to challenge the resulting authoritarian structures that controlled the state. In broader terms it was explained through the failure to establish free institutions, social and religious tolerance, and the inclusivity of a civil society of the British type, relatively free from control by the state. A picture emerged of a society without a politically distinct and influential liberal middle class, which had either been co-opted into the structures and organizations of the state (and shorn of its liberalism, therefore), or had retreated into private disillusion and depoliticization. The German economy had been transformed but the political and social correlates—an open society and representative-democratic government—had not developed in tandem. Instead, Germany remained in thrall to 'pre-industrial élites' who manipulated the politics and economic policy of the new state in their own interests and to the detriment of long-term social stability. The German empire was 'a Bonapartist dictatorship based on plebiscitary support and operating within the framework of a semi-absolutist, pseudo-constitutional military monarchy'.[5]

More recently, this settled interpretation has been challenged in the joint work of Geoff Eley and David Blackbourn, who have probed both parts of the pre-existing interpretation—the supposed existence of a clear and unambiguous British model; and the failure of liberalism and civil society in imperial Germany.[6] They have questioned whether the type of 'bourgeois revolution' which allegedly failed in Germany in the mid-nineteenth century ever occurred anywhere at all. They have also questioned the assumption that a bourgeoisie at the forefront of economic development should have necessarily espoused classical liberalism. What appeared to some historians to be a 'feudalization' of the captains of German industry, who accepted the leadership and political economy of the old Prussian agrarian aristocracy, could be better explained as the product of rational calculation of their best interests.[7] Their fear of a mass

[4] Ralf Dahrendorf, *Society and Democracy in Germany* (1968); Hans-Ulrich Wehler, *Das Deutsche Kaiserreich 1871–1918* (Göttingen, 1973) published in English as *The German Empire 1871–1918* (Leamington Spa, 1985); Gordon Craig, *Germany 1866–1945* (Oxford, 1978); James J. Sheehan, *German Liberalism in the Nineteenth Century* (Chicago, 1978).

[5] Wehler, *The German Empire*, 60. Compare Marx's description in the *Critique of the Gotha Programme* in 1875: 'a state which is nothing but a police-guarded military despotism, embellished with parliamentary forms, alloyed with a feudal admixture, already influenced by the bourgeoisie and bureaucratically carpentered . . .', in Karl Marx, *Selected Writings*, ed. by David McLellan, 2nd edn. (Oxford, 2000), 610–11.

[6] David Blackbourn and Geoff Eley, *The Peculiarities of German History. Bourgeois Society and Politics in Nineteenth-Century Germany* (Oxford, 1984).

[7] Ibid., 124–5.

socialist working class and the advantages accruing from the high tariffs of the so-called 'rye-iron alliance' mandated a different course of action. Blackbourn in particular tried to draw an alternative picture of German civil society (using the term explicitly)[8] to demonstrate the *growth* of voluntary associations and social institutions—'Vereine'—throughout the nineteenth century, and hence to question the assumption that the new Reich endured an impoverished social life dominated by the state. Rather, there was 'an embourgeoisement of German society'.[9] Blackbourn accepted, however, that the development of bourgeois associations and culture took place in isolation from the culture of the working class and largely without the participation of workers,[10] a point that Wehler had emphasized somewhat earlier and which contrasts with the much greater inter-action of the classes in Victorian Britain.[11] As for the British model itself, Eley and Blackbourn argued that the Victorian middle classes had also accepted aristocratic domination, and that the Gladstonian coalition from the 1860s—the model of liberal pluralism against which German development has been tested—was much less secure and united than had been imagined. Germany was less exceptional and more 'civil' than we had been led to believe, they argued; while Britain was the reverse—less 'civil' and more 'exceptional'.

II

This chapter is to be situated against this historiographical backdrop. In a small way it will test the validity of using Britain as a comparator, consider afresh the way in which contemporaries understood German development, and, on this basis, explore the historical relevance of the idea of 'civil society'. Explanations of National Socialism almost invariably include consideration of the special characteristics of German institutions and society which either encouraged, or failed to prevent, its emergence. Historians interested in civil society as a cate-gory of historical analysis have thus looked to modern Germany as a test-case, and have exploited the analytical potential in the already-existing comparative discourse linking German and British history. But their research has not led to a consensus; in a recent collection of essays, John Hall has reaffirmed the intrin-sic civility of modern British society in contradistinction to 'an illiberal German pattern of development', whilst other contributors, particularly those interested in the history of the British empire, have drawn attention to a much closer Anglo-German moral-historical equivalence.[12]

---

[8] Blackbourn and Eley, *The Peculiarities of German History*, 194, 288.

[9] Ibid., 13. See also Geoff Eley, *From Unification to Nazism. Reinterpreting the German Past* (1992), 13.

[10] Blackbourn and Eley, *The Peculiarities of German History*, 226, 233.

[11] Wehler, *The German Empire*, 83–4.

[12] Trentmann, 'Introduction', and John A. Hall, 'Reflections on the Making of Civility in Society', in Trentmann (ed.), *Paradoxes of Civil Society*, 37–9, 54–6.

The present study is based on archival sources that support Hall's position and the earlier model developed by Wehler, Dahrendorf, and Sheehan. Its focus is the 'labour question' in both countries—how to deal with the organizations and aspirations of a mature, mass working class—and it will examine the friendship and opinions of two men who were closely involved with the development of organized labour: John Malcolm Forbes Ludlow, the British Christian Socialist; and Lujo Brentano, the German political economist. The association of both men with types of 'socialism'—Brentano was colleague to many of the 'Kathedersozialisten' (literally, 'socialists of the chair' or professorial socialists) who supported Bismarckian state interventionism—should not obscure their essential liberalism.[13] They were united in their support for free trade, voluntarism, free association, and cultural pluralism, and they shared the desire to integrate the working classes into the established political and social institutions of their respective nations. Ludlow was to play a significant and creative role in establishing this kind of liberalism in Britain; Brentano, conversely, 'as a John Stuart Mill liberal in an environment that was a far cry from Gladstonian England' was to endure a very different experience.[14] They met first in 1868–9, when Brentano made an extended visit as a young researcher to examine forms of working-class association in Britain. Before coming to Britain he had read the German edition of Ludlow's famous study, on *The Progress of the Working Class*, written jointly with the old Owenite co-operator Lloyd Jones, which examined the history of the labour movement between the first and second Reform Acts.[15] He naturally sought out the authors.[16] Thus began a friendship with Ludlow that lasted until the latter's death in 1911 and which is preserved in their letters—the few from Brentano, from before 1870, among the Ludlow papers in Cambridge, and the three hundred from Ludlow, covering forty years, which Brentano preserved among his papers, held in the Bundesarchiv in Koblenz. The regular correspondence between these two men on the social and political life of the workers and the politics of the Reich provides for a unique comparison of their perceptions of German and British 'civil society' in the mid-to-late nineteenth century.

Ludlow had been born in India in 1821 to British parents but, following his father's death, from an early age he was brought up in Paris.[17] He settled in England in the late 1830s, though retaining a pronounced Francophilia. He read for the bar under the tutelage of the leading Whig lawyer Bellenden Ker, whose expertise in the law of partnerships, and particularly the incorporation of joint

[13] Abraham Ascher, 'Professors as Propagandists: The Politics of the Kathedersozialisten', *Journal of Central European Affairs*, 23, Oct. (1963), 282–300.

[14] Herbert Kisch, 'Brentano, Lujo', in D. L. Sills (ed.), *International Encyclopedia of the Social Sciences* (New York, 1968), ii. 148–9.

[15] J. M. Ludlow and Lloyd Jones, *Progress of the Working Class 1832–67* (1867).

[16] Lujo Brentano, *Mein Leben im Kampf um die soziale Entwicklung Deutschlands* (Jena, 1931), 45–53.

[17] N. C. Masterman, *John Malcolm Ludlow. The Builder of Christian Socialism* (Cambridge, 1963).

stock companies, provided Ludlow with an invaluable training for a career that was to be spent assisting working-class associations of different sorts.[18] Through the 1840s Ludlow had some limited contact with extra-parliamentary political groups like the British India Society and Anti-Slavery Association; and he also began voluntary work in the London slums. His life changed in 1848 when he made contact with F. D. Maurice and Charles Kingsley, and placed himself at the heart of the first Christian Socialist movement, co-editing *Politics for the People*, their journal of 1848.[19] Indeed, 'more than anyone else he was responsible both for founding and giving concrete substance to the Christian Socialism of England' and he was 'arguably the most important of the Christian Socialist leaders of the whole century'.[20] His enthusiasm for the associational ventures of French socialists, and his strong desire to turn the movement towards practical achievements, brought him into painful conflict with Maurice, who wished to avoid defining social commitments. It was Ludlow who brought the Christian Socialists into direct contact with Chartists and Owenites in meetings beginning in 1849, and who strove to engage his fellows with the institutions of the organized working class.[21]

Ludlow recognized very quickly the significance of the 'new model unions' established from the early 1850s, and he wrote an important account of the Amalgamated Society of Engineers (ASE) in *The Master Engineers and Their Workmen* (1852). He became 'virtual standing counsel for the ASE, had their cases referred to [him], settled a complete amendment of their rules'.[22] Over the course of the 1850s he emerged as one of the most influential 'friends of labour', advising the trade unions on their legal position, which was then a vexed issue, and using his knowledge to argue their cause on various platforms and in the journals of the day. Described in 1868 'as representing the new and generous, and sympathetic school of political economy—the school which says workmen ought to be considered and treated not as labour machines, but as men',[23] the course of Ludlow's life changed again in 1870 when he became secretary of the Northcote (Royal) Commission on Friendly Societies, and then, from 1875 to 1891, the first Chief Registrar of Friendly Societies under the 1875 Friendly Society Act, which he had himself drafted. In this latter position he regulated the

[18] 'I am no doubt answerable in great measure for the practical part of the Christian Socialist movement. It so happened that I was the only one who was familiar with the legal conditions of associations, & probably at that time there were not half a dozen men in England who were more so', Ludlow to Brentano, 2–3 Aug. 1882, f. 158, Brentano papers, Bundesarchiv, Koblenz.

[19] Torben Christensen, *Origins and History of Christian Socialism, 1848–54*, Acta Theologica Danica, 3 (Aarhus, 1962).

[20] Neville Masterman, 'Ludlow, John Malcolm Forbes', *Dictionary of Labour Biography*, ed. by Joyce Bellamy and John Savile (1974), ii. 249; Edward Norman, *The Victorian Christian Socialists* (Cambridge, 1987), 62. Ludlow underestimated the importance of his practicality and consistency to Christian socialism: 'I have never been anything but a second-rate man, only with sufficient comprehension of what is first-rate to make me not unfit to consort with it. Maurice & Kingsley, & [Thomas] Hughes & Charles Mansfield have all been in their way men of genius; I have only had talent.' Ludlow to Brentano, 7–8 March 1882, f. 153.

[21] Masterman, *John Malcolm Ludlow*, 83, 101.   [22] Ibid., 184.

[23] *The Beehive*, 11 July 1868, p. 4.

major institutions of working-class thrift in Britain, dispensing legal and practical advice to associations with millions of members. His assessments of his achievements were characteristically modest: as he wrote to Brentano in 1869, 'a good deal of my life has been spent in helping, or at least trying to help, lame dogs over stiles'.[24] It was not an ignoble or ineffective vocation.

Ludlow's social philosophy can be summed in a phrase he used in a discussion of the franchise published in *Politics for the People* in May 1848: 'inclusion should be the rule, not exclusion'.[25] He was here advocating the enfranchisement of the respectable majority of workmen but, arguably, *social* inclusivity was more important to him than *political* expansion of the suffrage. His vocation, strongly influenced by his Christian faith, was to bring the working classes and their institutions within the law and within civil society. This would do more than offer legal protection for the different organizations of the working class; it was also a solution to the 'labour question' itself. To offer the working classes a defined, protected, and accepted place in wider society—to integrate them, in fact, though without asking them to sacrifice their independence, for Ludlow was staunch in defence of working-class interests—would be a luminous example of the social harmony that Christian Socialism preached. The lesson he drew from the June Days in Paris in 1848 was that 'capital and labour cannot thus be suffered to remain at issue with one another. They must be harmonised, they must be associated.'[26] One of his letters in 1873 attests to his commitment to social integration by illustrating his deep aversion to its opposite: complaining to Brentano about recent events in Britain, he described the conflict on the Yorkshire coalfields between Lord Fitzwilliam and his colliers, and the infamous judgment of the magistrates of Chipping Norton, Oxfordshire, that the wives of striking agricultural labourers in Ascott-under-Wychwood be sentenced to hard labour for the verbal intimidation of blacklegs, as 'the two greatest blows at social order, the two greatest steps towards social disintegration that I have yet known in my time in the country'.[27] Allowing for exaggeration, the misuse of an employer's power over his workforce (as Ludlow saw it) in the former case and the misuse of the criminal law in the latter case affronted his commitment to the inclusivity of a truly civil society.

In the same way Ludlow was affronted, not to say bemused, by *disintegrative* features in German politics. After a visit from a German aristocrat, Ludlow related to Brentano that 'We were talking about German matters, & I expressed

---

[24] Ludlow to Brentano, 14–16 Dec. 1869, f. 15.

[25] 'The Suffrage—No. 3', *Politics for the People*, 3 (20 May 1848), 43.

[26] 'Warnings of the Late Paris Insurrection', *Politics for the People* (8 July 1848), 197.

[27] Ludlow to Brentano, 16 June 1873, Brentano collection, f. 73. Fitzwilliam threatened to close down his colliery at Low Stubbin when he learned of the intimidation of a miner who would not join the union. Though his principled opposition to the closed shop was applauded, the almost feudal manner in which he addressed and treated his workforce was criticized. *The Times*, 6 June 1873, p. 5; 11 June 1873, p. 11. On the 'Ascott-under-Wychwood Martyrs', see Frederic Harrison, 'The Chipping Norton Case', *The Beehive*, 7 June 1873; Henry Pelling, *A History of British Trade Unionism* (1963), 3rd edn. (Harmondsworth, 1976), 74.

my regret that there should be such a thing as an anti-semitic party, a recognized factor in politics, but he defended it!'[28] That politics might be deliberately conducted on the basis of religious or social discrimination and exclusion—as it undoubtedly was under the Second Reich—rather than striving for tolerance and inclusivity was anathema to Ludlow. He was similarly opposed to interventions by the state that limited the capacity of citizens to take voluntary action in their own best interests. His life was spent assisting the British working classes to assist themselves through self-organization, and he came to believe that a better society would result from voluntary endeavour than from state socialism on the Bismarckian model: 'I cannot tell you how important I feel must have been the part played by our friendly societies in the moral & intellectual development of our working class.'[29] Ludlow's experience was in working to expand the opportunities of the skilled artisans of the mid-Victorian period—roughly between the 1850s and 1880s—and, like the mid-Victorian 'labour aristocracy' whom he represented, he favoured a voluntaristic society where men and women asked for enabling legislation that would allow them to provide for themselves. That he was freely allowed to represent their interests, and then, on the basis of the knowledge and expertise he had so gained, to take a position inside the bureaucracy assisting working-class institutions, is evidence in itself of the existence of a civil society disposed to social integration in later Victorian Britain. He was an object of curiosity to German academics interested in similar questions precisely because of the influence he wielded *inside* the state, in sharp contrast to their own fortunes.

Lujo Brentano was 23 when he met Ludlow. Born in Frankfurt in 1844, he was a member of a distinguished literary family with connections to earlier German romanticism.[30] He studied law and then political economy, writing a thesis on von Thünen's theory of distribution. He then took up an appointment at the Prussian Statistical Bureau under its director, Ernst Engel, and it was as Engel's assistant that he first went to Britain. Engel wanted to investigate the development of profit-sharing in Britain in the 1860s as a possible model for reducing the tensions between labour and capital in Prussia. Together they took a particular interest in the ill-fated co-partnership scheme of Messrs Briggs, coal-owners in West Yorkshire, which bid fair for a few years in the late 1860s to offer a solution to problems between labour and capital.[31] Though it achieved European celebrity, Ludlow, who well knew the real attitude of the Briggs brothers to their workers and to the local miners' union, never supported the

---

[28] Ludlow to Brentano, 5 Aug. 1893, f. 261.

[29] Ludlow to Brentano, 4 June 1881, ff. 142–3. The letter was prompted by the publication of Bismarck's scheme for workers' insurance. See also Masterman, *John Malcolm Ludlow*, 229–31.

[30] James J. Sheehan, *The Career of Lujo Brentano. A Study of Liberalism and Social Reform in Imperial Germany* (Chicago and London, 1966). Masterman, *John Malcolm Ludlow*, 205.

[31] Sheehan, *The Career of Lujo Brentano*, 16–17. J. M. Ludlow, *The Autobiography of a Christian Socialist*, ed. by A. D. Murray (1981), 303–4.

venture, and its collapse in the mid-1870s proved his judgement correct.[32] Ludlow evidently did not think the Briggs brothers the right place to begin a study of the 'labour question', and at his prompting Brentano came to understand the significance of trade unionism for the future of class relations.[33] He had come to Britain at a singular moment when the Royal Commission on Trade Unions (1867–9) was in session, and his contact with leading trade unionists like William Allan of the Engineers, and with their intellectual advocates like Frederic Harrison, the Positivist who played an analogous role to that of Ludlow in guiding the emergent working class of the 1850s and 1860s, convinced Brentano of the merits of strong and disciplined unions as partners with capital. Harrison indeed showed Brentano a draft of his famous minority report to the Royal Commission which influenced the basis of the 1871 trade union legislation.[34] Thereafter, Brentano championed the social and economic advantages of free collective bargaining between unions and masters with a tenacity which evidently troubled his former tutor. It was all Ludlow could do in his letters to try to get his pupil to look again at the full range of working-class institutions and the moral and practical benefits conferred by co-operatives and friendly societies as well.[35] Ludlow also struggled to make him realize in later years that his depiction of the new model unions he had studied at the end of the 1860s was no longer accurate.[36]

While in Britain Brentano travelled widely, attended public meetings including sessions of the Social Science Association,[37] conferred with trade union leaders and their intellectual advocates, and, in his own words, 'made the acquaintance of the finest specimens of the working class in the English working men'.[38] 'Working-men's Associations of every kind, and the History of Labour in England, became the chief objects of my study.'[39] Ludlow described Brentano to W. E. Forster, then a minister in Gladstone's first administration, as 'a very able, very learned & very good fellow, with a great penchant for

[32] Lawrence Goldman, *Science, Reform, and Politics in Victorian Britain. The Social Science Association 1857–1886* (Cambridge, 2002), 213–18. Ludlow to Brentano, 11 June 1886, ff. 221–2. Ludlow had become acquainted with industrial relations on the West Yorkshire coalfield in 1858–9 while researching a contribution to the investigation of trade unions undertaken by the Social Science Association. See J. M. Ludlow, 'Account of the West Yorkshire coal strike and lock-out of 1858', *Trades' Societies and Strikes* (1860), 11–51.

[33] 'You and Max Hirsch both came here originally full of co-operation of some kind or other, and distrusting the trade unions, and I urged you both to look well into the latter as the more important of the two for the moment.' Ludlow to Brentano, 10 May 1873, f. 69.

[34] Brentano to Harrison, 2 March 1873, Harrison papers, File 1/22, British Library of Political and Economic Science, London School of Economics.

[35] Ludlow to Brentano 21 June 1869, f. 3; 10 May 1873, f. 69; 'Easter Sunday 1876', f. 107; 11 Dec. 1876, f. 111.

[36] Ludlow to Brentano, 19 Nov. 1878, f. 126; 2–3 Aug. 1882, f. 156.

[37] Goldman, *Science, Reform, and Politics*, 334. Brentano attended the 1868 congress in Birmingham and meetings in London in 1868 and 1872.

[38] Brentano to Ludlow, 18 June 1869, Ludlow Papers, Cambridge University Library, Add. 7348/14/5 (i).

[39] Lujo Brentano, *On the History and Development of Guilds, and the Origin of Trade-Unions* (1870), v.

England'.[40] He made a special study of the Amalgamated Society of Engineers, which he presented as the embodiment of the future institutional development of the working class in an article published in English in 1870.[41] In the same year he published a study of the historical origins of trade unions as emerging from medieval craft guilds (later to be comprehensively undermined by the Webbs),[42] which he dedicated to Ludlow, 'one of the truest friends to working-men in England'.[43] In 1871 and 1872 he then published in two parts the work that would make him famous and prove to be his most enduring contribution to social and economic literature, *Die Arbeitergilden Der Gegenwart*, based on his researches into British trade unions. It was both an exposition of trade union-ism as conducted in Britain and an argument in favour of the unionization of workers in general as beneficial to society as a whole and not contrary to eco-nomic principles. It was read across the continent and attracted some trenchant, politically-inspired criticism.[44] Brentano was one of the founders of the Verein für Sozialpolitik in 1872–3 which he, at least, envisaged as a forum 'to help the rising unions . . . and to get laws passed which are necessary for the welfare of the working class'.[45] This was never the aim of other founders of the Verein like Gustav Schmoller and Adolf Wagner, however, and the organization was unable to influence the policy of the state on social and economic questions, not least because it was itself divided over these same issues.[46] Indeed Brentano's energy and optimism in the years immediately before and after German unifica-tion in 1871 soon gave way to disillusion with the institutions and policies of the Second Reich. Though he held distinguished positions in several universities including Breslau (1872–82), Strasburg (1882–8), Leipzig (1889–91), and Munich (from 1891 until his death), the rest of his career was to be spent in a vain struggle to promote liberal thinking, liberal policies, and open discussion of social questions in a political system and culture that were closed to ideas and practices of this sort. Coming from a strict Catholic background he was critical of the Reich's policies towards his co-religionists. He opposed the introduction of state insurance for workers as likely to undermine the development of their own independent, collective institutions.[47] He protested at the abject surrender of many German academics to Bismarck's social and economic policies. The growing orthodoxy of the age that politics and scholarship could not and should

---

[40] Ludlow to Brentano, 18–22 March 1870, f. 27.

[41] 'The Growth of a Trades-Union', *The North British Review*, 53 (Oct. 1870–Jan. 1871), 59–114.

[42] Sidney and Beatrice Webb, *The History of Trade Unionism* (1894; 1911 edn.), 11–20.

[43] Lujo Brentano, *On the History and Development of Guilds*, iii.

[44] See Brentano's discussion of the attack launched on him by the National Liberal politician Ludwig Bamberger in his letter to Frederic Harrison, 2 March 1873.

[45] Brentano to Harrison, 2 March 1873.

[46] Dieter Lindenlaub, 'Richtingskämpfe im Verein für Sozialpolitik: Wissenschaft und Sozialpolitik im Kaiserreich, vornehmlich vom Beginn des "Neuen Kurses" bis zum Ausbruch des Ersten Weltkrieges, 1890–1914', *Vierteljahrschrift für Sozial- und Wirtsschaftsgeschichte*, Beihefte 52–3 (1967), Teil I, 1–271; Teil II, 272–482.

[47] Sheehan, *The Career of Lujo Brentano*, 76.

not mix made the type of advocacy developed in Britain by 'the friends of labour', including Ludlow and Harrison, impossible in Germany. Yet it was this style of scholarly engagement in support of social reform and the working classes that had so attracted Brentano when in Britain and which had given such purpose and direction to his early academic career. Like many liberal academics of his generation—and in conformity with interpretations of late nineteenth-century German history which emphasize the failure of liberalism there— Brentano's impotence led to thoughts of a retreat from the public realm and politics. Ludlow complained in 1877 that he did not 'like hearing you talk of giving yourself up to philosophy for 10 years'.[48] Two years later Brentano wrote to Schmoller that

I would prepare a critique of Bismarck if I thought that it would do any good, but after careful consideration I am convinced that I should keep my resolution not to concern myself with contemporary affairs any longer. If I could read Assyrian, I'd start a book on the ancient Assyrian economy, if only to forget the economic policies of modern Germany.[49]

He was not alone. As Ludlow related in a letter at the end of 1878, Adolph Held, professor of political economy in Bonn and then Berlin and another of the several German academics who looked to him for information on the labour question,[50] had written 'saying that he had quite withdrawn from politics, & timidly intimating that he did not agree with Bismarck's statesmanship, but still declaring that no true German could wish him out of office'.[51]

The central theme in the Ludlow–Brentano correspondence until the mid-1880s—after which, all passion spent, they came to recognize that there never would be a liberal Germany as they had hoped—was exasperated criticism of the new state and of Bismarck in particular. One of Brentano's surviving letters from 1869 complained about the absence of an independent Prussian professoriate—'one consequence of which you see in our labour question, where no person (Huber being dead) of respectability dares take the side of our workmen'—and of an independent press 'like your *Spectator* or your reviews'.[52] The defects of civil society in the old Germany were initially expected to be rectified in the new state: Brentano welcomed unification with enthusiasm, but it is clear from Ludlow's letters to him from as early as 1872 that the two friends took a common, hostile view to political developments. 'As far as I can judge', wrote Ludlow in 1874, 'I should think you were quite right as to the extinction of the ideas of right and true liberty in a Teutonic national chauvinisme'.[53]

[48] Ludlow to Brentano, 28 Sept. 1877, f. 119.

[49] Brentano to Schmoller, 1 June 1879, quoted in Sheehan, *The Career of Lujo Brentano*, 94.

[50] Masterman, *John Malcolm Ludlow*, 213.   [51] Ludlow to Brentano, 19 Nov. 1878, f. 129.

[52] Brentano to Ludlow, 18 Aug. 1869, 18 Aug. 1869, Ludlow papers, Cambridge University Library, 7348/14/7. Victor Aimé Huber (1800–69) was a professor of history and languages who advanced the idea of co-operatives and Christian workers' associations in Germany. He met Ludlow in England in the 1850s.

[53] Ludlow to Brentano, 15 Sept. 1874, f. 89.

You hug and glory in your chains. Your press is gagged & muzzled, your representatives are punished for proceedings in Parliament, your judges are so conscious of their own bad name that they write to the papers to defend themselves, your Falck laws reduce all churches to the basest thraldom, your government is as mean as it is oppressive . . . & yet you (I don't mean yourself personally of course, but the nation generally so far as one can judge) are perfectly delighted, & you fancy yourselves the finest fellows in the world.[54]

Ludlow, though at pains to explain that he was 'no pro-Romanist', described the Kulturkampf in 1872 as 'sheer tyranny' and as likely, in reinvigorating German Catholicism, to have the very opposite effects from those intended.[55] In 1878 in sympathy with Brentano, he denounced 'the senseless, abominable [anti-socialist] law against the Social-Democrats'. With considerable prescience he saw the danger in this type of political scapegoating in which majorities were created by chastizing and isolating minorities: 'Possibly Bismarck whilst alive & sitting on the safety-valve may be heavy enough to keep the steam from blowing up, but woe to them who are by when he slips off!'[56] Together they lamented the state of Germany in the 1870s and looked forward to a truly civil society at some future date: 'I feel with you as to German politics. There must be a bitter awakening for Germany some day after her Bismarckianism, as there was to France from her Napoleonism. I trust that when that day comes, it may have as rapid and marvellous a revival of public spirit as France has now.'[57] Bismarck was held accountable for these outcomes: 'anything like a sense of justice seems to me entirely foreign to the man's character so that there is nothing to be wondered at'.[58] To Ludlow he was 'the devil's chief lieutenant on earth at the present day'.[59] But the absence of any revival in German public life was explained by another theme in this correspondence: Ludlow's critical assessment of the capacity and resolve of German liberals whom he blamed for their feeble response to this catalogue of illiberal acts, not to say complicity in many cases. Two letters in 1879 at the time of the 'Second Reichsgründung' when Bismarck definitively switched alliances from left to right and introduced the infamous tariff law of 1879, encapsulate the argument:

I am afraid that there is not much good to be said about politics. In England I often feel inclined to swear at the Tories, but in Germany it is the Liberals that stimulate me to do so. Just because Bismarck turns round—as he was certain to do sooner or later—they are like a set of whipped dogs, sneaking off with their tails between their legs. Instinctively I feel convinced that the events of the last two years will give enormous strength to the Social Democrats, as soon as they are able to show themselves. The people will feel that there is no back-bone elsewhere.[60]

[54] Ludlow to Brentano, 10 Dec. 1874, f. 96. The Falk Laws (1873–5), named after the Prussian minister of public worship Dr Adalbert Falk, subjected church discipline, clerical education, and appointments in the Catholic church to state control.

[55] Ludlow to Brentano, 10 Oct. 1872, f. 60. See Róisín Healy, 'Religion and Civil Society: Catholics, Jesuits, and Protestants in Imperial Germany', in Trentmann (ed.), Paradoxes of Civil Society, 244–62.

[56] Ludlow to Brentano, 19 Nov. 1878, f. 129.   [57] Ludlow to Brentano, 3 March 1876, f. 103.

[58] Ludlow to Brentano, 10 Oct. 1872, f. 60.   [59] Ludlow to Brentano, 19–23 Dec. 1873, f. 80.

[60] Ludlow to Brentano, 29 Aug. 1879, f. 131.

I am afraid that for the time being I have lost interest in German politics. Bismarckolatory, you know, was always odious to me, & until the so-called Liberal party shows itself capable of shaking it off, one can only shrug one's shoulders and look elsewhere. Mill called our Conservatives 'the stupid party'. But I am inclined to think the epithet should be applied to the opposite party in Germany.[61]

The combination of a conservative, authoritarian state and the absence of effective opposition led to disillusion among German intellectuals, and Ludlow tried from time to time to lift the gloom over his younger friend:

You must not give way to pessimism. The world has not always been led by knaves & fools—witness Abraham Lincoln in our century, or George Washington in the last. And even when it is so led, see how they are baffled at the last—whether a 1st or a 3rd Napoleon! I quite understand that there is much in the present moral condition of Germany that is heart-breaking—so there is in France—so there is in England.[62]

Political impotence encouraged a virulence in German academic life that Ludlow deplored and which strained their relationship on occasion. The very frustration of the intellectuals' aim to influence government and wider opinion encouraged violent arguments within the marginalized community of scholars. Ludlow criticized the 'personal tone of controversy' which was 'a terrible blot . . . on German literature' and complained when Brentano used his comments from a private letter in a public dispute: 'it seems to me that when you once get into a controversy you are so anxious to smash your opponent that you cease to care for the moment about the feelings of your friends'.[63] Impotent rage and political disillusion were displaced into internalized struggles over theory, doctrine, and academic precedence. It is a besetting sin of many academic cultures but was especially evident in late nineteenth-century Germany.[64]

III

For two decades the Ludlow–Brentano correspondence was a commentary on the ills of German policy and the incivility of the new society that had been created in 1871. What can it tell us about the historiography of nineteenth-century Germany, the character of civil society in the new Reich, and of 'civil society' in general?

The relationship between the two men and their shared reaction to developments in Germany evidently supports an interpretation of the new state as

---

[61] Ludlow to Brentano, 19 Dec. 1879, f. 141. [62] Ludlow to Brentano, 21 Oct. 1889, f. 238.

[63] Ludlow to Brentano, 16 June 1873; 3 March 1885, ff. 71, 214. The controversy in 1885 was with Wilhelm Hasbach (1849–1920) the economic historian and author of *Das englische Arbeiterversicherungswesen* (Leipzig, 1883) on social insurance, and *Die englischen Landarbeiter* (Leipzig, 1894) on eighteenth-century economic change in Britain. Hasbach, a pupil of Schmoller and Wagner, held pronounced anti-democratic views.

[64] Fritz K. Ringer, *The Decline of the German Mandarins. The German Academic Community, 1890–1933* (Cambridge, Mass., 1969).

illiberal, not merely because the dominant policies and political alliances were anti-liberal in conception but also because liberals themselves failed to oppose the prevailing authoritarianism and intolerance. In the view of Ludlow and Brentano, German liberalism *did* fail. And their laments were consciously set against developments in Britain, which served for them both as a model of how things 'should have' been done and turned out. Ludlow, whose French upbringing and education gave him the character of an admiring and observant 'outsider' in Britain, carried an essential respect for British institutions through his whole career.[65] The very openness of these institutions had allowed an 'outsider' with pronounced and controversial opinions to become an 'insider' working for the state in the interests of the working classes. Brentano's Anglophilia—and his reflexive use of Britain as the standard by which to judge Germany—is manifest in his whole career and caught in his remark to Schmoller at the time of the crisis over the tariff law:

I feel that your views would be different in many respects if you had lived for a longer time in a country [England] where you could have seen the great things freedom can accomplish, where you could have experienced the influence freedom can have on the character of a nation.[66]

Allowance must be made, of course, for the very identities of Ludlow and Brentano: if we take evidence from such quintessential liberal figures we should not be surprised that it fits the dominant interpretation.[67] But in so far as liberal Britons and Germans interpreted events in Germany within a comparative Anglo-German framework, the evidence from this correspondence validates a longstanding view that has focused on 'the failure of German liberalism' and the related rejection of the 'British model' as key themes in German history between 1848 and 1914. Wehler and the other historians who have advanced this view have not imposed an illegitimate template and set of expectations onto German history: some of the historical actors thought in this way themselves and explained contemporary events using the very terms and comparisons that historians have advanced subsequently. This does not disprove the contentions of Eley and Blackbourn: the evidence contained in the history of a single relationship and correspondence is, by its very nature, limited. And their critique was not a new interpretation so much as a set of questions aimed at certain assumptions in the historiography which were worth asking and remain relevant. But the opinions of Ludlow and Brentano undoubtedly reinforce rather than undermine the interpretation at which they took aim.

[65] 'The Colonial System', *Politics for the People*, 14 (22 July 1848), 239–40. 'What a glorious empire would this be when an Englishman could travel from London to Labrador, to Hong Kong, to New Zealand, and find everywhere parishes and boroughs, juries and English judges, churches and schools.'

[66] Brentano to Schmoller, 4 Nov. 1878, quoted in Sheehan, *The Career of Lujo Brentano*, 54.

[67] Sheehan's later analysis of German liberal failure, published in 1978, developed naturally from his initial research on Brentano. Starting from the study of such a life the subsequent argument could be expected, though that does not in any way diminish its force or accuracy.

More specifically, the comparison between British and German treatments of the labour question helps us to understand the nature of civil society in Victorian Britain. In the year of the 1871 Trade Union Act Ludlow noted the remarkable alteration in attitudes towards trade unions inside a generation:

The change in public opinion on the subject is so wonderful that in reading the Times or the Pall Mall [Gazette] I have sometimes almost to rub my eyes to make sure that I am not dreaming. Positions which 20 years ago my friends & myself were scouted for taking up as revolutionary socialists form now part of the common fund of thought.[68]

The growing acknowledgement from the 1850s in Britain that the institutions of organized labour merited inclusion in civil society, and the developments that flowed from this—from their legal recognition to the extension of the suffrage to working men—should be compared with the prevailing hostility towards organized labour in the new Reich, the banning of the Social Democratic Party between 1878 and 1890 under the Anti-Socialist Law, and the attempt to undercut working-class self-organization by the state's welfare laws. Civil society in Victorian Britain proved flexible, plural, and elastic as new groups claiming social recognition and political equality were gradually brought 'within the pale of the constitution' (as the Victorians described the process themselves). Arguably, this was as much a technique of social incorporation to secure against general disruption as it is evidence of the essential 'civility' of the society as a whole. We might say that the extension of pluralism was a means by which British society could be stabilized and hence a tool of government first, and perhaps represented the settled, liberal convictions of the propertied and privileged classes only second. But however we view it—whether as the defining liberal principle of Victorian society or as a mechanism for dealing with challenges to that society—we may note its success as reflected in the social solidarity and cohesiveness that German authors believed they saw in British society of this period.[69]

Beyond this, the case-study presented here has implications for a more general understanding of civil society itself. Many contemporary usages treat civil society as the web of voluntary relations and institutions outside and beyond the realm of politics, and also as separate from the state. It has become fashionable to imagine that a regenerated civil society of this type in which active citizens in community organizations take on greater civic responsibility will solve a range of social ills that cannot be, or have been unsuccessfully, addressed by the state. But such definitions are not relevant to the history of social institutions as examined through the relationship of Ludlow and Brentano and may be generally suspect. It is axiomatic in their letters and commentaries that the faults and deficiencies of German society are the product of state policies and political institutions whether in the context of national disaggregation before 1871 or

---

[68] Ludlow to Brentano, 17–20 Nov. 1871, f. 50.
[69] See, for example, G. von Schulze-Gaevernitz, *Social Peace: A Study of the Trade Union Movement in England* (1893), xx.

unification after it. They lament the state of German society and place the blame squarely with 'Bismarckism' rather than any inherent failure among Germans to develop pluralism and tolerance. Indeed, the burden of their shared analysis was that Bismarck and the political interests that he represented had deliberately used the state to prevent the natural development of a civil society. From this historical example it would seem that the character of civil society is strongly influenced—if it is not in fact determined—by the nature and policies of the state, and hence, that definitions of civil society as an autonomous sphere of purely social interactions are insufficient and misleading.[70]

Finally, we should note that the relationship between the two men was severely strained at the moment of national unification in 1870–1, as the young Brentano rapturously welcomed the new German state and seemed to glory in the defeat and occupation of France and the annexation of Alsace and Lorraine. It was more than Ludlow's natural Francophilia that produced his harsh and damning response to 'Prussian rapacity' and Brentano's attack of 'Blut—u[nd]—Schwert Pan-Germanism':[71]

I could not have believed, if I had not read it under your own hand, that you could become a prey to such a fit of German chauvinisme as your letter received today indicates. You are exactly copying Napoleonism. The question between you and me on your letter is really whether there be a *Christian* civilization, capable of recognizing the rights of nations & of individuals, or whether we are still to be shut up to the old Pagan civilization in which the greatest man & the greatest nation alike are those who succeed in grabbing to themselves the largest slice of the earth's surface, imposing their will on the largest number of its inhabitants . . . If these frightful historical *vendette* are allowed to hold their ground between nation and nation, what peace can there be in the world? . . . Get rid of your war-fever, my dearest man, & be once more the sensible, right-feeling one you were.[72]

Ludlow was at pains to contrast German nationalism and militarism with British neutrality and the humane response of Britons to the suffering caused by the war: 'Our working classes are, thank God!, French now in their sympathies almost to a man—not from the slightest ill-will to Germany, but simply from the honest human abhorrence of a war of conquest pursued with a cruelty daily more relentless.'[73] To employ a social characteristic Brentano had so admired—the superior virtues of British working men—as an argument against German actions was a highly effective way for Ludlow to make his case.

Ludlow's letters in 1870–1 not only opposed Prussian methods and arrogance but also point towards the vulgarity and atavism of nationalism itself as essentially incompatible with the liberal attitudes and civility required of a truly civil society. Violence, force, and conquest are intrinsically hostile to the conduct

---

[70] Cf. Trentmann, 'Introduction' and Daniel A. McMillan, 'Energy, Willpower, and Harmony: On the Problematic Relationship between State and Civil Society in Nineteenth-Century Germany', in Trentmann (ed.), *Paradoxes of Civil Society*, 31–2, 188.

[71] Ludlow to Brentano, 21–3 Aug; 3–9 Dec. 1870, ff. 34, 41.

[72] Ludlow to Brentano, 5 Sept. 1870, f. 37.   [73] Ludlow to Brentano, 3–9 Dec. 1870, f. 42.

required of civilized communities; the hysteria of nationalism is incompatible with the tolerance and reason of a civil society. It is a remarkable feature of British history since the seventeenth century that it has been relatively untouched by the explosive forces of nationalism on the British mainland—though they have disfigured Irish history for at least the past two centuries. If we return to the theme of British exceptionalism, it may be that in the peculiar case of Britain the absence of nationalism allowed for the growth of a distinctively 'civil' civil society able to devote itself in the nineteenth century to the careful inclusion of excluded social groups precisely because the nation-state had already been built and was not in question. And it may also be the case that, in general, nationalism has been, and is still, a dissolvant of civility in other societies—though this would hardly be an original speculation. Responding to criticism from his older and wiser friend, Brentano was able to collect his senses, apologize to Ludlow—though their friendship was never as close thereafter[74]—and then observe how quickly a state created in war turned inwards to conduct different types of aggression on sections of its own population. But for the new nation as a whole it was less easy to attain such objectivity and detachment. The means of its creation—and the consequent popular support for 'Bismarckism', the authoritarian state and militarism—prevented the development of a civil society on the British model and foreshadowed the turbulent history of Germany that followed. As Ludlow presciently warned his young friend in 1870, 'a peace so shameful will only beget a war yet more terrible than the present one'.[75]

[74] Masterman, *John Malcolm Ludlow*, 207–9.
[75] Ludlow to Brentano, 21–3 Aug. 1870, f. 34.

6

Altercation Over Civil Society: The Bitter Cry of the Edwardian Middle Classes

PHILIP WALLER

Civil society is conventionally identified with the hegemony of a disinterested middle-class public, guaranteed to withstand the brigand rapacity of selfish parties, whether aristocrat or artisan, plutocrat or pauper, who are intent on feathering their nests at the expense of the common good. This presumption is tested here through a case-study of the conceptions of civil rights and duties held by middling sorts of people when a perceived crisis compelled them to contemplate such things. They were Edwardian England's Charlie Chaplins, petty folk who felt bullied by myriad forces: labour, capitalism, landlordism, and statism. The context is the debate about public services and apportionment of liability between ratepayer and taxpayer. Specifically, it revolves around six articles, 'The Bitter Cry of the Middle Classes', by George R. Sims, published in the new Liberal daily *The Tribune*[1] in July 1906. These generated 'a large number of letters from all quarters' (21 July), over seven weeks. That the debate was so sustained is one measure of its importance. Commonly, newspapers drop a topic in short order as sensation succeeds sensation. The Bitter Cry persisted, even through the Bank Holiday when normally controversial kit was discarded for bathing costume. This was not a Silly Season story. The correspondents constituted a wider circle than those habitual writers to newspapers: that is, the official and officious, the cranks and crackpots—not mutually exclusive categories. True, there were repeat offenders, who contributed several letters and pursued private quarrels; and the usual suspects who inflated the postbag of any Edwardian newspaper could not be silenced now. Thus Bernard Shaw paused from composing *The Doctor's Dilemma*, to fire two broadsides (14, 15 August); so did the Chestertons, G. K. (24 July) and Cecil (15 August), the

---

[1] *The Tribune* was founded by a syndicate headed by Franklin Thomasson. A member of the family of Bolton cotton-spinners, Thomasson was among the new intake of Liberal MPs (for Leicester) in 1906. For an explanation of *The Tribune*'s failure after eighteen months: Viscount Camrose, *British Newspapers and Their Controllers*, 1947, 5–6. All references cited below are to correspondence and other matter arising from Sims's articles, printed in *The Tribune*, unless otherwise stated.

latter, in a magnificent sacrifice, interrupting his sojourn in the Hotel de la Paix at St Valerie-en-Caux to set the world to rights. Other prominences peddled predictable wares. The eugenicist Arnold White finger-wagged about the state practising a 'vicarious philanthropy', which contradicted 'the laws of Mother Nature' (3 August); by contrast, the Fabian S. G. Hobson (11 August) prescribed Socialism for the middle classes, as did F. W. Pethick Lawrence (8 August). Still, such celebrated chatterers authored only a fraction of the nearly 200 letters that *The Tribune* published; rather, this subject, which concerned their financial and social security, roused numbers of ordinarily quiescent individuals. Historians will ponder the degree to which the clamour was manufactured.[2] Striking similarities obtain between this Edwardian ding-dong and the uproar about the Loony Left in the Thatcher years; but in both cases the argument lasted the distance because it tapped real fears and grievances.

The timing of Sims's articles was plainly no coincidence. They fell during that interval between the formation of a New Liberal ministry, chivvied by the first Labour party in Parliament, and the Progressives' loss of control of the London County Council (LCC) for the first time since its creation in 1889. Sims's articles also chimed with the proceedings of a Commons' Select Committee on Income Tax, which was weighing graduation and differentiation. More broadly, the division between local and central government, and contingent costs between ratepayer and taxpayer, remained vexatious, following the Royal Commission on Local and Imperial Taxation (1896–1901) and Inter-Departmental Committee on Physical Deterioration (1904). This pot was being stirred continually by pressure groups such as the Liberty and Property Defence League, by Ratepayers' Associations, and by speeches and polemical literature *On Municipal and National Trading*—as Lord Avebury's book of 1906 was entitled.

Historians further need to understand the peculiarity of the protagonist, George R. Sims, because his name triggered in part the scale of the response. It is difficult now to convey how exceptionally famous he was. In 1983, the *DNB*'s *Missing Persons* accorded him belated recognition; but this was insubstantial, only one column, and managed to mislay one of his three wives. In many dictionaries of quotations, Sims is memorialized by a solitary line, 'It is Christmas Day in the workhouse', plucked from *Dagonet Ballads* (1879). Dagonet was his pen-name on the sports and entertainments Sunday, *Referee*; the ballads sold 100,000 copies in twelve months. If historians also take a spin through the *Oxford English Dictionary* and stumble across 'up-to-date', they will encounter Sims again, cited as co-librettist of a Gaiety variety *Faust-up-to-date*, which played for several seasons from 1888 and inaugurated a new meaning in the language. 'Up-to-date' in the sense of 'right up to the present time' had currency from the 1860s, but 'up-to-date' in the sense of being modish or stylish was

---

[2] Previous historians to notice this debate include H. V. Emy, *Liberals, Radicals and Social Politics 1892–1914* (Cambridge, 1973), 172–3; and Avner Offer, *Property and Politics 1870–1914* (Cambridge, 1981), 306–7.

introduced by Sims's play. As an up-to-date celebrity, Sims has been ignored by most literary historians because he did not write Literature. Instead, he penned melodrama and burlesques. His first hit was *The Lights o' London* in 1881. When he wrote his memoirs, it had been playing somewhere in the world for thirty-five years. His royalties on that play alone were reputedly £72,000 by 1894;[3] four years later, he was wrestling with the Revenue over his tax assessment.[4] An addictive gambler, Sims squandered money as fast as he made it. His gimmicks included his own brand of hair restorer Tatcho (motto: 'Always Young You Can Be'). *The Tribune* apparently saw no conflict of interest in positioning a blazoning advertisement alongside Sims's second Bitter Cry article. Tatcho, readers were told, can 'be procured from Druggists or Stores in almost every quarter of the globe, so widespread is the knowledge and appreciation of this preparation' (19 July); but, before today's follicly-challenged seek after this miracle, they should note that Sims's club, the Devonshire, required him to remove his hat indoors, so that the relentless retreat of his own locks could be monitored.[5]

In his prime, living at Clarence Terrace, Regents Park, Sims cut a figure about Town. He had an affair with the stage beauty Mrs Patrick Campbell;[6] he was also an active reformer. It is in this connection that, while overlooked by literary historians, he is recognized by social historians. In 1882–3, Sims's articles 'How The Poor Live' and 'Horrible London', together with a pamphlet (written anonymously by a Congregationalist minister, Andrew Mearns) entitled *The Bitter Cry of Outcast London*, inspired an emerging crusade against slum housing—by highlighting landlords' neglect, desperate shortages, pestilent overcrowding, and the threat to society. Sims discountenanced the idea that sermonizing the poor about vice could correct the structural problems. State intervention was required: to demolish slums and build model tenements; to enforce sanitary standards and provide public parks; and to extend cheap tramways and encourage healthier suburban living. Here was an emergency programme, to avert sansculottism. Sims further justified state action as 'ordinary paternal care'; yet in another breath he warned against crookedness—'much of the worst property in London is held either by vestrymen or by persons who have friends in the vestry'. Anthony Wohl has concluded:

Sims was a brilliant agitator, for his articles contained all the right ingredients in just the right proportions—wit, broad humour, sympathy, pathos, moral indignation, dire warnings, optimism, practical suggestions; his appeals were never annoying or wearisome. His writings on the London slums were more detailed and sympathetic than Mayhew's, and warmer and more effective than all the previous reform articles. His photographic

---

[3] Sandra Kemp, Charlotte Mitchell, and David Trotter, *Edwardian Fiction: An Oxford Companion* (Oxford, 1997), 363.

[4] Newman Flower (ed.), *The Journals of Arnold Bennett, 1896–1910* (1932), 81–2.

[5] Douglas Sladen, *My Long Life: Anecdotes and Adventures* (1939), 159.

[6] Margot Peters, *Mrs Pat: The Life of Mrs Patrick Campbell* (1984), 64–7, 87–9, 92–3.

and sensational descriptions, couched in the style of reasoned emotion, marked a new type of popular reform journalism.[7]

Here was a publicist of ability and reputation. Historians must reckon this in assessing the impact of Sims's crusade in 1906 when he addressed the plight of the middle classes. That Sims now disclosed himself as a social imperialist and protectionist only heightened Progressives' sense of betrayal; but Sims felt no inconsistency. He proudly recorded that a grandfather had been a Chartist and his mother a friend of the suffragists Francis Power Cobbe and Lydia Becker.[8] Moreover, he had not ceased to act as a missioner for the downtrodden. Since the 1880s, he had campaigned in defence of the unemployed and aged poor, against harsh Poor Law administration and the white slave trade, and for various children's causes.[9] He promoted the continental Sunday, to enlarge popular amusements and end kill-joy sabbatarianism; and he was a doughty fighter in defence of victims of misjustice. His championship of a Norwegian national, Adolf Beck, twice imprisoned from mistaken identity, secured Sims a place in every legal textbook: it led to the creation of the Court of Criminal Appeal[10]— and earned Sims an honorary knighthood from the King of Sweden and Norway.[11] The editor of the *British Weekly*, Robertson Nicoll, who was a barometer for Liberal Nonconformity, wrote on Sims's death that he 'had a really kind heart and was a good man. He was one of those Christians who will be astonished by being told at last that they were Christians and that what they had done to the poor they had done to Christ.'[12]

With Sims, therefore, the historian is dealing not only with a propagandist of proven appeal but also with one who tendered unimpeachable humanitarian credentials; hence, the stir when Sims pronounced—in his opening article—'my contention is that the limits have been passed and that we are today faced not with the peril of neglect, but with the peril of pampering; that we have in many directions overstepped the bounds of justice to one class in our desire to be generous to another . . . Still struggling to remain independent, thousands of honest and industrious citizens are to-day forced to deny themselves necessities in order that the class which has abandoned the struggle may have luxuries.' Sims warned of 'the danger to the State threatened by the ever-increasing efforts of Socialism to exploit the middle classes for the sole benefit of the labouring

[7] Anthony S. Wohl, *The Eternal Slum: Housing and Social Policy in Victorian London* (1977), 205. Quotations from Sims's *How the Poor Live and Horrible London* in Wohl, *The Eternal Slum*, 125, 204.

[8] George R. Sims, *My Life: Sixty Years Recollections of Bohemian London* (1917), 9, 53.

[9] J. S. Hurt, *Elementary Schooling and the Working Classes 1860–1918* (1979), 106, for the *Referee* Children's Free Breakfast and Dinner Fund, co-founded by Sims.

[10] A. H. Manchester, *A Modern Legal History of England and Wales 1750–1950* (1980), 187–8; Leon Radzinowicz and Roger Hood, *The Emergence of Penal Policy in Victorian and Edwardian England* (Oxford, 1990), 765–6.

[11] Sims, *My Life*, 119, 323.

[12] Letter to Professor John Adams, September 1922, in T. H. Darlow, *William Robertson Nicoll: Life and Letters* (1925), 437–8.

class, the unemployable class, and the pauper class. Squeezed between the Capitalist Party on the one side and the Labour Party on the other, the brain-worker, the shopkeeper, and the man with the limited income, are rapidly having their vitality crushed out of them' (17 July).

What were these grievances which so moved Sims's sympathies? A preliminary to note is that the Bitter Cry came not from the middle classes but from the lower middle classes. This was signalled in the first letter which *The Tribune* published in reaction to Sims's inaugural; and its qualification was iterated over the following weeks. That first correspondent took the *nom de plume* Two Hundred A Year, on which income he was struggling and inclined to endorse Sims's every word except for this matter of identifying the faces contorted by their Bitter Cry. Two Hundred A Year perceived the middle classes in reality broken into three sections. The first he termed 'the well-to-do'; the second those who pretended to be well-to-do. Neither sort had uttered a whimper, which issued instead from a third section, the despairing lower-middle class. Indeed, this fragmentation was part of the problem:

It is because of the selfishness and snobbishness of the first two sections . . . that the third section suffers so much. The 'poorly paid professional man', as Mr Sims calls him, is the man who can speak out and write; yet he does not use his voice or pen in the cause of justice to those a little below him in worldly wealth. He toadies to the rich, demands credit from his tradespeople, pays his children's governess less than a living wage, and keeps more servants than he can afford in order to 'keep up an appearance'. True his rates are scandalously high, true he grumbles over his wine at municipal extravagance, but neither on platform nor in the Press does he give honest expression to his opinions. Meanwhile, the small shopkeeper goes struggling on against deadly competition, oppressed on the one hand by the selfishness of those above him and by the loudly-voiced necessities of the very poor who bleed him because of their own vice and inefficiency. (18 July)

This assertion, that it was the lower middle classes, earning, say, between £2 and £4 per week, classically the clerk, small shopkeeper, or tradesman, who suffered most from the economic climate and tax system, was pretty unanimously accepted by other correspondents, even by Socialist spokesmen and unsympathetic critics. It was echoed too by the many newspapers and periodicals which monitored the Bitter Cry debate. Thus the *Leeds and Yorkshire Mercury*:

This class of people of small income is very heavily taxed—taxed, indeed, out of all proportion to its taxable capacity. Its members are very largely persons who are punished by the State and municipal taxing authorities by their praiseworthy ambition to live in decent homes, to dress themselves and their children well, and to lead thrifty, virtuous, estimable lives. And it is true that this class is largely exploited between capital and labour. Economically, it belongs to neither. Capital is far beyond its reach; it cannot dig, to beg it is ashamed. In the modern phrase, it is not organized, and is incapable of organization. Politically, despite the franchise, it is declared to be voiceless. (2 August)

It was further charged that the middle middle and upper middle classes were not just denying support to the groaning lower middle classes, but actively conspiring to increase their misery. Lord Welby, interviewed by *The Tribune* some

three weeks into the controversy, argued this forcefully. A former chairman of
the LCC (in 1900), Welby was then chairman of its Finance Committee; equally
relevant, he was an old Treasury hand, its permanent secretary 1885–94, and
ardent 'exponent of rigid economy in all branches of the public service'. So
wrote the editor of *The Economist*, F. W. Hirst, who was chipped from the same
fiscal block. Hirst shared Welby's horror at Lord Salisbury's flippant question,
responding to one of Welby's regular orations in the cause of retrenchment:
'Who are we that we should try to swim against the tide?'[13] Perhaps no better
could be expected from a professional pessimist like Salisbury, who in any case
represented the patriciate. What really dismayed Welby was the dereliction of
the once dependable middle classes. He acknowledged that state and local
taxation fell disproportionately on persons with marginal incomes, typically the
£200-a-year man, who faced fixed costs of around £160 for the upkeep of
his family and was crippled by rates and taxes eating away the rest.
Correspondingly, the middle classes with annual incomes of £500–£2,000, feeling these rising demands much less, appeared almost insouciant:

Where people used to talk shyly about thousands they now light-heartedly dispose of
millions. For example, there was a proposal before the Traffic Commission to build a
road to the Crystal Palace, at a cost, if I recollect, of over 20 millions; and only the other
day, in his address to the British Association, Professor Ray Lankester advocated that the
spending of some millions a year on medical research would be an economical enterprise
. . . These are indications—happily in most cases indications only—of the laxity of public opinion on public expenditure.   (7 August)

Welby argued that most people were now prone to public extravagance when it
served their short-term interest. Thus workmen clamoured for another six bat-
tleships because they knew that money would be spent on wages, even though
half these ships might be scrapped a few years ahead and they like everyone
would bear the cost of this waste. The middle classes too encouraged recklessness. Welby instanced the electrification of the LCC's tram system:

There was much to be said in favour of completing the southern scheme before under-
taking the work in the north.[14] But the pressure from North London overcame all such
financial considerations. That is the spirit animating the entire system of local government at present. All classes are urging the expenditure of money on their own pet
schemes. But you cannot have your cake and eat it.   (7 August)

Welby's incomprehension and exasperation were firm indications that new
forces were at work. That such a once influential civil servant, superintending
national fiscal policy, should feel utterly impotent to curb the expansive expenditure of local government was a measure of the powerful interests involved.[15]

---

[13] Quoted in Hirst's notice of Welby, *DNB 1912–1921*, 563.
[14] Sir Gwilym Gibbons and Reginald W. Bell, *History of the London County Council 1889–1939*
(1939), 616–18 for the north–south Thames tramways controversy.
[15] Ibid., 164–5, for Welby's failure 'to stay expenditure, especially capital expenditure, which in
his opinion was imprudent, even though he was supported by some Progressive leaders, notably

Welby's frustration was matched by his former colleague, Sir Thomas Farrer. Farrer once steered commercial policy as permanent secretary at the Board of Trade (1865–86) and, when released into retirement, maintained objections to every deviation from economic orthodoxy. He discharged salvoes against sugar bounties, bimetallism, mismanagement of the sinking fund, rising expenditure on the armed services, and subsidy of local government through grants-in-aid. To practise what he preached, he stood for the LCC, was elected at its inception in 1889 and served until 1898, the year before his death. His prestige was amplified in 1893 when he was made a peer, and he became the LCC's vice-chairman; yet it was to no avail. His 1892 memorandum 'The London County Council's Labour Bill, Market Rate or Fancy Rate' failed to arrest that movement which saw the LCC and many municipalities acquire reputations as model employers, by establishing direct labour departments and awarding exemplary wages and conditions of work.[16]

Socialists of whatever stripe seemed obvious culprits. This charge was the more easily sustained by reference to the Poplar Board of Guardians. Reports of the Local Government Board's inquiry into its affairs ran parallel with the Bitter Cry. In Poplar, according to Sims, class war was crudely pursued. Socialists lumped together as capitalists anyone who was not a manual worker; and they determined to bleed them of incomes and independence. By their perverse reckoning, 'the working man earning from £2 to £4 a week represents Labour; the clerk earning 30s a week, the little shopkeeper whose profits are not a hundred a year, the brain-worker and the professional man who may only make two or three hundred a year, all are Capitalists in the sense in which the word is used for the purposes of political warfare.' Municipalities' 'mad recklessness' was driving these people out of business, into the workhouse itself, or, more commonly because such folk were proud, into struggling penury. They were 'ruined in order that municipal enterprises may be carried on with wanton waste and heavy loss, that Socialist guardians may boast that their paupers may have the best that money can buy, and that they buy it regardless of cost.' This 'Everything Free' programme mollycoddled 'the least industrious and the least deserving class of the community' and devitalized the hard-working and provident (17 and 19 July).

Yet Socialists did not rule every municipality and still public expenditure escalated. The spotlight turned on those well-placed middle classes who benefited from greater government: by professional job creation, fund-holding, and, it may be, insider dealings over contracts. One correspondent put it bluntly: 'Middle-class men hold the best-paid offices under local governing bodies, and if . . . these officials are responsible for extravagant expenditure, again the blame

Mr (Sir) Andrew Torrance, who, unfortunately for the fortunes of his party, somewhat harshly stigmatized the course which was being followed as "the rake's progress".' See also A. M. McBriar, *Fabian Socialism and English Politics 1884–1918* (Cambridge, 1962), 222–9.

[16] William Carr's notice of Farrer, *DNB Supplement II* (1901), 201–2.

attaches to the middle class.' Furthermore, 'municipal securities are "gilt-edged" and are largely held by middle-class investors' (A. Cooke, 25 July). The West Ham Guardians' malpractices, now exposed by the local government board's auditor, resembled old-fashioned graft more than newfangled Socialism. He surcharged the chairman and other members as penalty for their treating to celebrate the opening of their new infirmary. The Forest Gate Ratepayers' Association, led by Marcus Cohen, complained that this infirmary, costing £250,000, was the most expensive in the land. He jibbed at everything, from £10,000 blown on architect's fees, down to the furnishings of the master's house—'A bed-room suite cost £48 10s, a bedstead £25, and a mahogany cabinet £25'. Moreover, 'a magnificent carpet' had been bought for the board-room where, Cohen maintained, 'you will find a regular ring—contractors' daughters who have married guardians' sons and that kind of thing. Jobs were frequently found for relatives of members.' And when board members visited institutions they travelled third class but claimed first class expenses (1 August).

A similar indictment was submitted by Croydon's elective auditor, H. B. Matthews, who averred that Sims was wrong to blame Socialists for the escalation of municipal borrowing and spending. During 1902–5, Labour representatives comprised only four or five in a council of 48; yet Croydon's borrowing increased from £1.17 million to £1.65 million (41 per cent) and rates from 6s 4d to 7s 8d (21 per cent), of which 5d (31 per cent of the increase) went on servicing the debt. Matthews did not think Croydon an isolated case. Accordingly, he felt it vital to disclose his experiences:

I have during the past eighteen months conducted a campaign against municipal extravagance. Who have been my principal opponents? The reply is—the middle-class aldermen and councillors, who have not hesitated to sneer and jeer at me, denounced me at council meetings, but have not had the courage to meet me at public meetings. A few days ago I appeared at a Local Government Board inquiry, the council having made application to borrow money for street improvements. On this occasion the street improvement was, I submitted, the improvement of certain land to enable owners to sell at a better price. The application was strongly supported by a middle-class councillor, who is a retired tradesman. I asked the inspector to refuse the loan, and so teach the councils throughout the country that it is not, as the councils at present are of opinion—that they have only to ask and they will receive.

Matthews demanded a reformed system of borough audit:

The audit here is a farce. Elective auditors have no powers. Information has been denied me, and the Local Government Board inform me that the Department has no jurisdiction over the accounts of county [borough] councils such as Croydon. The middle-class council here is, therefore, supreme . . . I submit that the real cause of municipal extravagance is the rapid growth of the power of officialism and the 'close friendship' of the corporation officials with the councillors. The duty of the officials, so they think, is to spend money. By so doing they justify their position and so increase their responsibility which means, as we ratepayers know by experience, applications for increase in salaries, 90 per cent of which are granted. (3 August)

The position was complicated again by the quantity of *Tribune* correspondents who defended public spending not, as Croydon's elective auditor suspected, because they had some pecuniary motive or vested interest, but from principle, to correct past omissions and to enlarge the common good. There was, therefore, another way of estimating what one correspondent decried as a profligate policy that enticed 'the lower classes to marry improvidently and to breed incontinently, trusting to the ratepayer to support their families . . . to bring them up in luxury, even, in these modern Ritz establishments still called workhouses, or to give them the comforts and advantages of home life in pretty villas, to educate them in schools of ornate architecture, and to scholarship them up to university' ('M.R.C.S.', 11 August). 'Who . . . would seriously advocate a return to conditions prevailing twenty-five years ago?', rejoindered Charles Shaw of South Woodford (30 July), a state of affairs sardonically spelled out by A. E. Shippobotham of Cardiff: 'no increase of rates [meant] no street improvement, no Public Health Acts, no Factory Acts, no Housing Acts, no Public Libraries Acts, no Free Education Acts, no Truck Acts, nor any of the numerous irritating attempts to raise the status of the workers' (24 July). And J. O. Jubb from Retford asked, 'Can you wonder at the British working-men wanting more?' when one in three subsisted below the poverty line and another third so precariously that a month out of work would pitch them into starvation (4 August)—evidence, incidentally, of how Booth's and Rowntree's surveys were being dramatized in the progressive cause. 'A Liberal of Sixty Years' Standing' was sure that 'the labouring class . . . are now getting the justice which had previously been denied them' and that the New Liberal government was imbued with a 'high, patriot, unselfish and noble' mission to deliver 'the greatest good to the greatest number' (6 August). There were rights more sacred than property, argued John Evans of Harlesden: the child's right to food, shelter, and education, and the labourer's right to a fair wage for a fair day's work. He pleaded for 'a deeper sense of public duty' in support of the helpless, and condemned Sims's Bitter Cry as 'a gospel of selfishness' (8 August). A.G.W. from Hackney agreed that

the advantage is on the side of the working-class. They have a good cry: 'Give us education, clean environment, a living wage, constant employment, facilities for cultivation', and so forth. Have their rate-burdened opponents any effective counter-cry? No: for nobody's soul is stirred by an exhortation to help a class to maintain its pretentiousness and false standard of living. (24 July)

Augustus West, of Battersea council, even had the cheek to attribute to Sims himself some credit for this new concept of government, by the heart-rending articles he had once written, which enlisted sympathy for the unfortunates of the workhouse (26 July). Not a few correspondents pointed out that the benefits of public activity were available to all, and the middle classes were fools if they failed to take advantage of free education, free libraries, subsidized trams, and the like, or pharisees if they did so and then bemoaned their cost. One, who inhabited a 'commodious villa', set in several acres, described what went on in his rural parish, whose council he served as treasurer. The short answer was that nothing went on. The rates there were minimal and the annual parish expenditure totalled £15, of which £5 was a retaining fee for the fire engine. 'I am a strong Individualist', announced this correspondent, 'and Keir Hardie[17] is an offence to me; but I never go home from town without wishing more power to progressive county councils, and envying my compeers of the middle classes the great advantages they possess over us by being able to reap, at the price of ratepaying, the crop of splendid services gratuitously rendered by public men in various departments of municipal activity' (27 July). Public amenities served all, so this argument ran; even if it was the working classes who consumed most, the middle classes gained indirectly through having a sturdier workforce to overcome American and German competitors. And, if public expenditure must be reduced, there were better targets than municipal services. Cut out imperial adventures and cut down the army and navy, so as to provide for old age pensions and other social reform, was the standard response of the Progressive party to the correspondence.[18]

None of this answered the fundamental sense of unfairness felt by the lower middle classes. Embodied in their Bitter Cry was an assumption that society's contractual relationships should function like a romantic novel in which vice and virtue received just deserts. Thus a failure to act responsibly, as was supposed about the generality of the working classes, or a failure to contribute at all, as was supposed about the inveterate pauper class, must reduce or forfeit altogether their claims on society's goodwill. Correspondingly, those who conducted themselves considerately and competently should be rewarded or, at worst, not mulcted by government. Were this tacit contract disregarded, protest was warranted. Whether protest might be pursued to the point of civil disobedience was a moot issue; in theory, because this could subvert the orderliness they wanted to bolster; in practice, because this could incite the real enemies of civil society to seize the moment. In the Edwardian period, two such protest campaigns were evident. One was the female suffrage movement; and mainstream lower middle-class attitudes towards this may be gauged from the *Daily Express*. Its columns recommended various cures for suffragette violence: a fire hose, 'hard labour and salts and senna', the birch, strait-jackets, incarceration 'say for about an hour, with half a dozen mice', transportation to St Helena, and marriage.[19] It was the militant Amazonian phase of the movement that unhinged the *Express* and its circle. Suffragism was considered more temperately at the outset, initially in October 1900, shortly after the paper's foundation

---

[17] Hardie celebrated his fiftieth birthday during the Bitter Cry. *The Tribune*, 15 August 1906, carried a eulogy from R. C. K. Ensor.

[18] Prominence was given in *The Tribune*, 28 July 1906, to the new Liberal government's navy estimates for the coming year, involving savings of £2.5 million; and to the proceedings of the Disarmament Conference at the Hague. See also the interview with Ramsay MacDonald, 8 August.

[19] James McMillan, *The Way We Were 1900–1914* (1978), 94, 101.

by Arthur Pearson. Starting out on *Tit-Bits*, he built up his own press empire with *Pearson's Weekly* (1890), *Home Notes* (1894), *Pearson's Magazine* (1896), *M.A.P.* (1897), and *Royal Magazine* (1898); and the wooing of a female readership was part of Pearson's strategy.[20] It was a popular author, Mrs George Corbett, who was first given the freedom of the *Express* to promote suffragism. Notwithstanding her conventional title, she was the joint, possibly principal, breadwinner in her marriage. Her husband, a merchant navy engineer, was irregularly employed, while Mrs Corbett manufactured a large output of fiction.[21] 'I can honestly claim', she told the *Express*, 'to have provided a wholesome entertainment for millions of readers and employment for thousands of workers. I am compelled to pay the same rates and taxes as if I were a man, and I am also compelled to do my share towards paying for the free education of children, who are thus enabled to compete with those of the professional and highly-taxed classes.' Indeed, so many women were now supporting themselves, giving employment to men, and contributing to the revenue, that only the benighted could maintain that they were less deserving of the franchise than the dim-witted agricultural labourer or 'drunken loafer who is a burden upon the community from childhood to old age'. Warming to her theme, Mrs Corbett contemptuously assessed the many male voters such as those milling 'about our docks':

Their ignorance is only equalled by their degraded mode of life. Their earnings are chiefly spent in public houses. And their political knowledge is entirely derived from tap-room oratory or the Anarchistic utterances of men who covet the proceeds of other people's industry and brains.[22]

There was a correlation, therefore, between aspects of the suffrage movement and the lower middle-classes' Bitter Cry. But most jobs categorized as 'women's work' were low status, low paid, and ill-organized. Even the 'New Woman' was not generally an economically confident and socially assertive creature, rather a bag of nerves who was unsure of her role in the world and apprehensive about her relationships with men, outside and inside marriage. Such distempers were accentuated among women whose fathers, brothers, and husbands were in business, by the pressure to extend rights for workingmen whose social class and cultural outlook were judged inferior to their own. A paradox about the Edwardian middle classes is that, when reckoned collectively, their economic and social power appeared enormous, yet when counted individually few enjoyed security of position and income; and the lower down their ranks the greater these feelings of uncertainty and distress. No more than the working classes were they immune from business recessions or from the misfortunes attendant on sickness and death in the family and advancing age.

---

[20] Sidney Dark, *The Life of Sir Arthur Pearson Bt., GBE*, n.d., 67.
[21] On Mrs Corbett (1846–1930), see Kemp *et al.*, *Edwardian Fiction*, 76–7.
[22] Mrs Corbett's article in the *Daily Express*, reproduced in McMillan, *Way We Were*, 87–8.

The second protest campaign that developed into civil disobedience was the nonconformists' refusal to comply with the 1902 Education Act by mass non-payment of rates. Their grievances in 'single-school' parishes were not new. Without opportunity of establishing a Board School, these parents had been compelled to send their children to the parish church school, yet all the while harboured the hope that this Anglican monopoly would eventually perish from want of voluntary donations. The 1902 Act dashed that pipedream by endowing the church schools with public funds or, as nonconformists saw it, perpetuated their injury and added insult by requisitioning their rates. Moreover, public control over church schools was largely nominal in their opinion; and these schools were exempted from the Cowper-Temple clause of the original 1870 Act, specifying an 'undenominational' religious teaching beloved by nonconformists. Hence the sense of being cheated; and the nonconformists' protest took the form of passive resistance before the Liberals' electoral landslide in 1906 promised redress.

The passions that educational questions aroused are understandable because of the central place these occupied in family and religious life. Correspondents to *The Tribune* during the Bitter Cry dwelt on this subject, yet made little mention of its sectarian aspect. Indeed, there was a strong feeling that sectarians had hijacked the education debate and that government was ignoring the real injustice. This was confirmed by a ten-pages open letter, 'The Burden of the Middle Classes', in the *Fortnightly Review*. It emanated from seven individuals, each in self-styled 'middling circumstances': a solicitor, insurance agent, broker, tradesman, 'employer', journalist, and civil servant. The last, Shan F. Bullock, was also a novelist; and his subscription was significant, presaging his *Robert Thorne: The Story of a London Clerk* (1907) which C. F. G. Masterman acknowledged as an authentic account of 'the attempt of a "twopenny clerk" to provide for the needs of a family on an exiguous and precarious income'.[23] All seven co-signatories had voted Liberal in 1906 but were unenthused by their government's activity so far and especially disappointed by its Education Bill which 'can effect nothing for our own children' or, they thought, anyone else's. Six of the seven attended places of worship and all affirmed Christianity; yet they castigated Dr Clifford—architect of the passive resistance—for politicizing nonconformity, and 'we give it as our opinion that the clergy, all of them, should be kept from our schools altogether'. Their chief concern was the poor standard of education available. The seven had thirteen children and each spent about £30 per annum on schooling (£195 in fees, plus £20 in education rates), achieved only by self-denial and household economies. The top private schools were unaffordable, and the second-class sort to which they sent their children turned them out 'half-instructed'. Why not then, because they all had 'good democratic' intentions, consign their children to State schools? One once did, and

---

[23] C. F. G. Masterman, *The Condition of England*, 1909, 6th edn. (1911), 71. On Bullock (1865–1935) and *Robert Thorne*, see Kemp *et al.*, *Edwardian Fiction*, 49, 344.

within a year his boy contracted 'measles, ringworm, whooping cough, vermin, ill-manners, bad language, and a cockney dialect'. This was not the way to prepare for the professions.

Let us be frank. We emphatically do not want our lads to consort with lads from the Board schools, not even with lads of their own class who may have received elementary instruction there. Call us snobs, or vulgarians; say that we are narrow, and prejudiced and foolish. It matters nothing. First and foremost, . . . we are parents, men who love their children and would do our utmost for them—and it is in our capacity as parents rather than as men, or politicians, or citizens, that . . . we desire to have our children kept as much to themselves as are the children of the classes above us.[24]

Perhaps if they lived outside London things would be better, but their impression was that State schools in Britain, unlike in France, Germany, and America, were generally (to use our pejorative) bog-standard and 'never intended to provide education for the children of people like ourselves'. They deplored having to pay both education rates and private fees, without receiving value from either. State education was not just inadequate; its schools seethed with resentments, in classrooms and playgrounds, where working-class children did not get on with clerks' and tradesmen's children. The seven signatories' ideal was not separate schools for separate classes; rather it was a nationally integrated system, with a mix of all classes and delivery of efficient education; but they despaired of such a system being constructed in time to affect their own children's schooling.

The vileness of council schools and impossibility of sending their children there was a refrain of middle-class correspondents to *The Tribune*, such as Laura Hain Friswell from Wimbledon who begrudged the fact that 'many, such as curates, journalists, and clerks, who earn little more than £100 a year, and yet have to pay to educate the children of men who earn twice their income'; that is, 'the so-called working classes [who] have been so pampered and pauperized that they are degenerates of the most virulent type; scarcely any of their duties do they perform properly, and especially their parental duties do they try to shirk, therefore their children are most insolent and insubordinate' (25 July). Remarkably, the country's best-known educationist T. J. Macnamara, who would shortly become a Liberal minister, expressed qualified agreement when interviewed by *The Tribune* (2 August). A leader of the National Union of Teachers, editor of its journal *Schoolmaster*, and member of the London School Board until its abolition in 1903, Macnamara had been board-school educated.[25] He also sent his own children to state schools but only, he conceded, because they lived in a relatively salubrious area. He would have decided otherwise if the schools had contained a large intake of slum children whose habits were 'such as would strike dismay into the mind of the anxious middle-class parent'. For the rest, Macnamara loyally defended the quality of council

[24] *Fortnightly Review*, 80 (Sept. 1906), 411–20.
[25] Robin Betts, *Dr Macnamara 1861–1931* (Liverpool, 1999).

schools, to which a (in his view, generous) system of scholarships to higher education had now been added. There was no need for the middle classes to avoid council schools 'in districts populated by artisans in regular employment', thus to incur ill-afforded fees of '£20 or even £50 or £60 a year' for an inferior private education. This verdict was shared by 'A City Clerk' from Brockley (3 August) and 'A Clerk' from West Central London (4 August), who distanced themselves from the supposed snobbery of their class; yet Macnamara's admission—that 'we shall have to work steadily for the extinction of certain personal habits, and so on, from amongst the children of the poor parts of our great cities, which are now a legitimate stumbling block to the general use of the elementary schools'— was a significant endorsement of the Bitter Cry. Moreover, while urging the middle classes to 'broaden their outlook, and be less snobbish and "uppish"', Macnamara pronounced them to be 'the most estimable class in the community', applauding their hard-working, god-fearing, sober habits, and how they saved through building societies to buy their own homes and embraced their duty to look after aged parents.

Such appreciation appeared so much flannel to the seven signatories of the open letter:

To belong to the middle class nowadays—at all events, to the lower sections of it—seems to us anything but a privilege. We are beset on all sides. Living is dearer than it used to be, much dearer. Competition is fiercer and more unscrupulous. A higher standard of respectability is required of us. Our families need and claim more in the way of amusements, holidays, clothing.

To stay in the race, they all worked harder and longer; but this 'feverish labour adds little, if anything, to our incomes. We have absolutely nothing. We are always anxious, always trying to make ends meet, always afraid—afraid.' They envied the prosperous future of working men whose votes and organization compelled politicians' 'servile respect':

Social rules and observances do not affect him. He may swear in public, smoke shag cigarettes on the tramcars, ride in corduroys to work and the races on his high-grade bicycle. His children are educated free, will soon be fed, clothed, and physically developed at the expense of the State. If you wish to know how cheaply he can live, contrast the prices of food in Lambeth Walk or the Borough with the prices of precisely the same food in a suburb like our own . . . He has cheap trains, cheap concerts, cheap clubs, amusements, pleasures. He scorns us. We know it. We feel that we deserve his scorn. For we are incompetent, ridiculous, inept; capable of doing nothing for ourselves but complain of inequalities and injustices, which, were we only capable as he is capable, would speedily be rectified.[26]

They closed by calling for the establishment of a Middle-class Party.

It was professed Socialists who most clearly articulated another view, that the lower middle classes who denounced increased taxes were not just reactionaries

---

[26] *Fortnightly Review*, 80 (Sept. 1906), 419–20.

but represented a superannuated element of society; as 'V.H.M.'[27] of Trinity College, Cambridge, put it with some superciliousness, 'The small section that shrieks against Socialism is mostly composed of those unsuccessful ones who, unable to find just cause for their failure in their own selves, rail at a largeness of mind they cannot understand, and these are joined by all such as do not think because they cannot' (31 July). Both Bernard Shaw and Cecil Chesterton identified clerks as a black-coated proletariat, the weaklings of the middle classes who were destined to be crushed between capital and labour. And a good thing too, they thought, because clerks and other lower middle-class types would thereby recognize that they were pseudo-middle class and shared more interests with the working classes. They ought, therefore, to organize, not in Middle-class Defence Leagues inveighing against public expenditure, but in trade unions to improve their lot by collective bargaining.[28] 'Between the growth of trusts and combines on the one hand and the growth of Socialism on the other, their present position will soon become untenable', Chesterton prophesied (15 August); and Shaw urged them to press for 'not a restriction but an energetic extension of municipal enterprise' (14 and 15 August).[29]

Shavian paradoxes performed better in the theatre. Opponents of municipal trading countered with statistics from seventy-eight principal towns, contending that municipal indebtedness and rates were rising out of control. Where a profit was shown, this was illusory and 'generally due to badly-kept accounts and lack of proper auditing'; for example, making 'no provision for depreciation of plant and machinery' (Geo. S. Potter, secretary of the Wimbledon branch of the Middle-class Defence Organization, 4 August).[30] Henry Wilson, a 'private trader' from Farnborough, advised people to ignore the expense, horrendous though that was, and to focus on the politics: 'The real evil is not the

[27] This was Vernon Henry Mottram (1882–1976), later an eminent physiologist and nutritionist: see *DNB 1971–1980*, 604–5. I am grateful to Dr Mark Curthoys for helping to identify him. Mottram was first president of the Cambridge University Fabian Society. For Ben Keeling's account of Mottram disguising himself as Keir Hardie, to draw off the bloods who planned to prevent the real Hardie from speaking in Cambridge: E. Townshead (ed.), *Keeling Letters and Recollections* (1918), 10–12.

[28] For other letters urging clerks and shop-workers to join trade unions and to stop voting Conservative, see those from Charles N. L. Shaw of South Woodford (30 July) and George F. Millin of Brixton (4 August). Membership of the National Union of Clerks was tiny, about 150 in 1906, though it rose rapidly to 43,000 in 1919–20, principally during the war years and mostly from clerks in the engineering trades who were denied membership of the AEU. Damaging to wider recruitment was the decision to call itself a trade union rather than professional association, to join the TUC, and to affiliate to the Labour party in 1907. See Barbara Nield's notice of H. H. Elvin (1874–1949), the NUC's first full-time general secretary, 1909–41, in Joyce M. Bellamy and John Saville (eds.), *Dictionary of Labour Biography* (1982), vi. 105–9.

[29] Significantly, the subject of the Fabian Society's forthcoming winter lecture season was 'Socialism for the Middle Classes'. Shaw, Chesterton, H. G. Wells, S. G. Hobson, and R. C. K. Ensor were among the speakers advertised in *The Tribune*, 7 August 1906. Wells's contribution was published as 'Socialism and the Middle Classes', *Fortnightly Review* (November 1906), 785–98.

[30] *The Tribune*, 25 July 1906, for the LCC session at which the Moderates/Municipal Reform party denounced the Progressives' financial management, accusing them of cooking the accounts to show a pretend profit. Criticism was especially directed at the LCC's Thames Steamboat services and tramways investment, on which see Gibbons and Bell, *London County Council*, 612–19.

amount of the extortion, but the fact that it is caused by Government under-taking many things which it cannot do and has no business to attempt.' State enterprise was, by implication, unenterprising. It disregarded ordinary com-mercial considerations of market risk, product efficiency, and service quality; worse, it used its privileged position to smother independent competition, stifle innovation, and squander public money. It was grotesque that 'men without special knowledge attempt in the fag end of their time to manage concerns which take the whole time of an expert to conduct successfully, to say nothing of the opportunities for peculation' (14 August).[31] This effectively ruled out the course recommended by H. C. Hissett from Liverpool, who demanded better value for ratepayers' money. For him, the root problem was that every muni-cipality wanted to run its own show, like the thirty or forty separate tramways operating in south Lancashire. They should imitate the railway companies' amalgamations to obtain economies of scale and rate reductions (10 August). This was a prospect resolutely opposed by those who anathematized combina-tion of any kind, whether public or private. The level of rates was almost imma-terial to the small trader who was going out of business, unable to survive against a department store or retail chain. 'I can assure Mr Sims', wrote 'H.W.', a wholesale grocer,

if he will get these monopolizers abolished, my [local grocer] friends and myself could well afford to pay the rates, and get some of our money back in pride of our town improvements. The shop monopolizers are really working for Socialism far more effec-tively than the 'Socialists', municipal or otherwise. They, and all big 'combines' in every business, are upsetting the equilibrium of society by destroying the middle class and bringing capital and labour face to face. It will not take much to induce labour to 'take charge' of capital when the time comes. Germany and Austria already see the danger and are doing what they can to avert it by taxing the big monopolizers to the breaking point, and so compelling them to keep up prices.   (25 July)

A few years later, the opening ceremony at Whiteley's new store in Queen's Road, Bayswater, provided an almost perfect parody of this Bitter Cry. The store, whose 16 acres of floors were connected by a marble staircase, was com-pleted in just over a year; and the ceremony, preceded by a luncheon 'attended by the heads of most of the large stores in the West of London', was performed by the lord mayor, Sir Thomas Crosby.[32] Proposing a toast to 'The Firm',

[31] *The Tribune*, 17 July 1906, reported a speech in the House of Lords by the veteran opponent of state interference and founder (in 1882) of the Liberty and Property Defence League, the Earl of Wemyss, who sought to block the ability of the LCC to acquire powers to supply electric light equip-ment. Approaching his ninetieth year, Wemyss recalled the days of oil lamps and said that, had the government of London in his youth possessed its own whaling fleet, it would doubtless have con-spired to prevent the transition to gas lighting. Now, he prophesied, if the LCC were allowed to invest in electricity, it would later resist the adoption of a more efficient system. He impugned the representatives' competence: 'I would have every county councilor after his election obliged to pass an examination before a Government official in all the subjects in which the Council might propose to deal.'

[32] On Crosby (1830–1916), *Who Was Who, 1916–1928*, 248. A Conservative, he was a former surgeon at St Thomas's and medical officer to life insurance companies.

Crosby was uneasy. Critics had questioned whether the lord mayor should officiate at this event, because 'the store was likely to extinguish smaller and rival businesses. He did not look upon it in that light. He considered the enterprise as an element in the commercial rivalry between ourselves and foreign nations.' Equally defensive, Whiteley's general manager emphasized that '80 per cent of the goods sold in their store were British-made'; whereupon he presented the lord mayor with 500 sovereigns to swell Mansion House charities for 'the poor and needy', which Whiteley's directors 'considered the best way to mark this occasion'. Afterwards, 'the Lady Mayoress, Miss Crosby, made the first purchase, in the shape of a gold bag from the jewellery department'.[33]

A more constructive strategy than shaking a fist at the march of monopoly, whether big business or big government, was to exhort the lower middle classes to campaign to alter the incidence of taxation. It was best expressed, as may be expected, by Mr Waller, W. Waller from Clapham, who believed that Socialism was validated by economic, ethical, and historical argument; that municipal services could not be slashed without injury to the community; and that the middle classes ought to 'direct their anger towards the privileged classes, who are the real cause of their oppression, and not seemingly begrudge the lower classes their progress towards emancipation' (14 August). This idea of relieving their tax burden by redistributing it or by discovering new sources appealed to a volume of correspondents. A few warned that this was a delusion. R. Raywood from Bournemouth was sceptical about the site-value rating movement, because it was supported by so many 'spendthrift councils, having exhausted the present ratepayer'. He suspected that councils were simply looking to tap new pools of revenue and had no intention of checking extravagance or sparing the existing ratepayer (14 August). A. M. Scarff, of the Income-tax Adjustment Agency, also forecast that the working classes could not continue to enjoy immunity:

It is inevitable that the better class of working men will soon have to bear their share of the tax. Thousands of them earning their £3 10s and £4 a week have never paid a penny of Income-tax in their lives. It is absurd that the clerk struggling on £4 a week, and sending his children to a private school, should be made to pay, while the mechanic on £4 a week, who sends his children to the Board School, should go scot-free. I expect that before long employers will be asked to make returns of all their workmen, as well as all their clerks, who are liable to pay Income-tax.   (1 August)[34]

Generally, this idea of broadening the basis of taxation was the favoured rescue plan for the lower-middle classes—not, be it whispered, via indirect taxation such as Tariff Reform, which was off-limits in a Liberal paper like *The Tribune*, but via rating and income tax reform. Attacking landlordism was preferred

---

[33] *The Times*, 22 Nov. 1911.
[34] The exemption threshold was lowered from £160 to £130 in 1915: B. E. V. Sabine, *A History of Income Tax* (1966), 152.

above all;[35] as Sydney Peet from Kew put it, instead of berating Socialists and social reformers, the Bitter Cry party would show more sense if 'municipally— as well as nationally'—it aimed to tax

the big landowners who 'toil not, neither do they spin' . . . If social reformers have incidentally hit the man who lives snobbishly in a little suburban villa, and keeps an overworked and underpaid general domestic to suit a lazy, extravagant wife, then it is simply because this little snob has refused to help the social reformer in his efforts to make the avoidably idle rich pay their equitable share of taxes. The 'middle classes' will infinitely better their position if they will but support and co-operate with the social reformers in the fight against monopoly and privilege and for the public well-being, instead of aping in private and social life those who will take no notice of them.   (25 July)

'The right and really effective remedies', according to Peet, 'are to be found in the nationalization of the education, poor and highway rates, and accompanying the nationalization of these rates should be a graduated Income-tax' (23 July). Henry Georgeites too came out of the woodwork, such as W. G. C. Reed of North London who represented himself as a humble member of the middle classes. He proposed the single land tax solution:[36] urban growth meant that all surplus wealth, 'which is created by the presence and industry of the community', was absorbed in rising land values, and 'wrongly appropriated by an idle class. Do this, and the "bitter cry" will be for ever hushed' (21 July and 10 August).

The Bitter Cry was not hushed; rather, it became cacophonous. In his sixth submission (28 July), Sims endeavoured to restore harmony by publishing a four-point programme of action for the middle classes. Point one advised attending closely to all reports of Socialist speeches, so as to understand their vicious ambitions. Point two demanded an independent audit of every borough, so as to 'reveal irregularities and extravagance' and to stir the local government board. Point three required that every voter pay rates *directly*. This would deprive Socialists of one of their most insidious weapons, which was to hoodwink the poor into believing that municipal prodigality brought only benefits. People thereby ignored the penalties involved in rising rents or in bankrupting

---

[35] *The Tribune* enthusiastically advocated Land Reform. Note the leading article, 7 August 1906, apropos the Scottish Land Bill, arguing for a 'diffusion of peasant ownership', thus to end 'the burden of a landless agricultural proletariat'.

[36] Adjacent to its final leader in the Bitter Cry controversy, *The Tribune*, 6 September 1906, published a long article entitled 'BEST GOVERNED CITY IN THE U.S.', being a paean to Tom L. Johnson, friend and follower of Henry George and Mayor of Cleveland. It emphasized that state law presently constrained them from implementing the single tax in full but, if they had this authority, 'they would exempt property and begin to concentrate on land values'. Regarding the corruption rife in American government, 'Mayor Johnson remarked that its source was the power possessed by the municipalities to grant franchises or privileges, or monopolies to corporations or companies, such as gas companies, transportation companies, and the like. Hence graft. The best corrective was an enlightened public spirit and the management of public affairs by municipal authorities sufficiently large and composed of the best men. As to general politics, there had been up to now no really fundamental dividing principle between the two great parties, and they were therefore divided by interest. Office seeking, he was afraid, was the motive power. But questions of principle were rapidly arising—such as municipal ownership, the single tax, i.e., the tax on land values.'

small businesses, with consequent loss of employment. And Point four was a crusade against municipal trading, to scotch the idea that this was remunerative:

Municipalities are now colossal trading concerns, competing in every direction with the private trader who has thus to contribute to trade rivals. So far from the rates having been decreased by these enterprises they have been forced up to a point at which they have become unendurable. The only possible survivors of such a system are the great 'combines' and 'trusts', to whose tender mercies the Municipalities are already handing us over by making it daily more difficult for small traders to remain in business.

A fifth point implicit in Sims's manifesto was that there should be an organizational focus for the movement. One existed already, the Middle Classes Defence Organization (MCDO), founded a few months earlier, whose secretary was L. P. Sidney, based at Hastings House, Norfolk Street, off The Strand, London. The Bitter Cry boosted box-office business for the MCDO which, by the end of July, was claiming 8,000 members, some thirty London branches, and allied organizations in Birmingham, Brighton, Liverpool, Manchester, Newcastle, and Sheffield. Another forty local committees existed and, in towns from Carlisle to Dover, individuals prepared to form the nucleus of activity. A great meeting was planned for the Albert Hall in September, whereupon it was intended to contest council and guardians' elections and eventually parliament. Where they did not run candidates, they should vet those who were standing. 'We want our money's worth for our rates', declared Sidney. 'We want to abolish the absurd pampering of paupers, at the expense of struggling shopkeepers . . . Above all, we want revision of the Income-tax system.' The model for this organization was, ironically, that adopted by one of its enemies:

The Labour Party have put aside their jealousies, have combined into a formidable section of Parliament and are approaching the time when they can hold the balance between the parties. The time has arrived when the middle classes should also combine for the protection of their own interests. Our principle is to eschew the familiar party considerations, and to work for the interests of own class.   (30 July)

Such was the master plan; and *The Tribune* drew recruiting letters from MCDO branch officers. The wisdom in embarking on such an escapade was, however, doubtful. 'A Clerk' wrote: 'I can imagine no better means of embittering everybody against us, and if Mr Sims desires to have the working classes flying at our throats he is likely to attain conspicuous success by his method' (26 July). The fundamental flaw was that the middle classes constituted an incoherent entity; therefore, the idea of consolidating their philosophies and interests was chimerical. The MCDO's secretary, Mr Sidney gave the game away:

It is difficult to say what is the middle class: the character and interests of its various sections differ so much. To meet that difficulty, sectional committees have been appointed, one representing the professional class, another the merchants, traders, and shopkeepers, and a third the clerks. Each committee will regard various questions in their relationship to its own section, and if the interests involved are not inimical to those of the general body of the organization, the recommendations will be acted upon by the general executive.   (30 July)

Did their Bitter Cry go unheard, then? Not at all; as Bruce K. Murray has demonstrated, by extending the range of abatements on modest incomes, as well as by introducing graduated and differentiated income tax and land duties to target the super-rich, and new alcohol and tobacco duties to penalize working-class profligacy, the Liberal government responded. Indeed, 'it was not the working classes but the middle-class income tax payers with earned incomes up to £2,000 who proved the primary beneficiaries of Liberal attempts to reduce the burden of taxation for certain groups in the community. The white-collar, small-business, and professional middle classes gained, in this respect, the most from Liberal finance between 1906 and 1914.'[37] Given this outcome, it is sensible not to overplay the influence of New Liberal ideology on the government's budget-making.

How does this episode bear upon the conceptualization and functioning of Civil Society? The evidence is ambiguous. It may be read, on the one hand, as proof of the relative weakness of a disinterested middle-class public sphere; on the other hand, as proof of the effectiveness of a middle-class interest group in delivering its message to government. Two further reflections are apposite. One is that, if society is to attain and maintain a position of civility, its formal and informal contracts require continuous renegotiation to convince people that responsibilities and rights are arranged in reasonable equilibrium and that it is the national or public interest which is being principally served. This is easier said than done because of the propensity of all classes to equate their sectional interest with the national interest. From this follows a final observation that, increasingly in modern times, it is the tax system which stands as proxy for this, because its structure represents the different classes in relation to each other, and examination of it discloses the winners and losers. As a result, governments generally pursue a policy of conflict containment while, in deference to the democratic shibboleth, pretending that it is the majority—the working classes and the poor: the People—whose interests are being preferred.

[37] Bruce K. Murray, *The People's Budget 1909–10: Lloyd George and Liberal Politics* (Oxford, 1980), 295.

7

Public or Private Ownership? The Dilemma of Urban Utilities in London and New York, 1870–1914

RAPHAEL SCHAPIRO

'Municipal trading', wrote George Bernard Shaw, 'seems a very simple matter of business. Yet it is conceivable that the political struggle over it may come nearer to a civil war than any issue raised in England since the Reform Bill of 1832.'[1] It has been almost a century since issues surrounding the construction of the underground, waterworks, transport infrastructure, and power supply first dominated British local government politics. Yet the issues that voters, intellectuals, and politicians faced in 1900 are the same issues that challenge us today. The terms of present-day debate over how to finance the London underground, how to manage the railways, and how to operate an efficient system for public transport are similar to the questions that prevailed during the late nineteenth and early twentieth centuries. Over the intervening century, the issues were complicated in that many people treated them on a predominantly ethical level and that one of the major national political parties was committed to public ownership as a matter of ideological principle. Current economic policy favours privatization of these services and this has been the trend in Britain and globally since the 1980s. This chapter focuses on a different period of history when different economic and political forces were operating, a time when municipalization and private ownership were both considered to be viable options, and seeks to provide a theoretically informed discussion on the origins and development of public ownership in Britain. Since a comparative glance helps to illuminate the British case more clearly, concurrent issues and developments in the United States of America will also be discussed.

---

[1] G. B. Shaw, *The Commonsense of Municipal Trading* (1908), 1.

I

The broad argument is that, despite much contemporary and historical perception to the contrary, the inexorable absorption of infrastructure services by the public sector was more a product of agency problems than a function of the political complexion of government. Neoclassical economic theory assumes that economic agents are endowed with full information, that they transact costlessly with others, and that these transactions take place in a competitive market. The 'new institutional' economics explicitly identifies the problem of transaction costs and seeks to explain economic behaviour using the transaction as the basic unit of economic analysis.[2] The transaction costs of public utilities are exceptionally high. Large amounts of capital are required to finance asset-specific investments. At the initial stages, entrepreneurs provide the capital and manage the fixed networks that they create in pursuit of rents. Over time, the technology becomes more diffused and more important to urban life.[3] As this process occurs, politicians may need to regulate private firms in order to achieve price and quality benchmarks. Regulation, the process by which government attempts to control the actions of a private firm, can be conceptualized as a long-term contract.[4] Long-term contracts where service is delegated are difficult to write and difficult to enforce. We can identify two parties to such a contract, the principal and the agent. The agency relationship is pervasive in economic life.[5] The difficulty is to ensure that the agent acts in the best interests of the principal. The principal contracts with the agent to accomplish a task, but is often unable to monitor the agent's performance and behaviour due to information asymmetries. If the contract is for a single transaction, the agency problems are minimal. But complexities arise when the relationship extends into the future, especially when the contract involves asset-specific capital investments.[6] Williamson follows Simon in stating that economic actors are 'intendedly rational, but only limitedly so'.[7] This relaxation of the neoclassical assumption of full information implies that contracts are unavoidably incomplete. Hart and Moore argue that it is often impossible for parties to specify all of the relevant contingencies when contracting, either because they cannot foresee them or

[2] For the pioneering article, see R. Coase, 'The Nature of the Firm', *Economica*, 4 (1937), 386–405.

[3] W. Robson, 'The Public Utility Services', in Harold Laski *et al.* (eds.), *A Century of Municipal Progress, 1835–1935* (1935). See also, D. F. Wilcox, *Municipal Franchises*, 2 vols. (New York, 1910), i. 3. For a more recent analysis, see A. Offer, 'Why Has the Public Sector Grown So Large?' *University of Oxford Discussion Papers in Economic and Social History*, 44 (2002).

[4] D. Newbery, *Privatization, Restructuring, and Regulation of Network Utilities* (Cambridge, Mass., 2000); G. Priest, 'The Origins of Utility Regulation and the "Theories of Regulation" Debate', *Journal of Law and Economics*, 36: 1 (1993), 289–323.

[5] K. Arrow, 'The Economics of Agency', in John W. Pratt and Richard J. Zeckhauser (eds.), *Principals and Agents: The Structure of Business* (Boston, 1985), 37.

[6] T. Eggertsson, *Economic Behavior and Institutions* (Cambridge, 1990), 148.

[7] O. E. Williamson *et al.*, *The Nature of the Firm: Origins, Evolution and Development* (Oxford, 1991), 91.

because it is too expensive to enumerate them in extensive detail. A 'complete contract' would never need to be renegotiated or revised, and lack of full information makes this condition unattainable. Most contractual disputes that come before the courts concern a matter of incompleteness.[8] For all but the simplest of goods and services, there is generally a continuing role for government in contract administration. That role involves monitoring, enforcing, and bargaining over unexpected contingencies. As Vickers and Yarrow write, these activities may be one step away from regulation or having the public agency oversee the work directly.[9]

An additional problem of long-term contracting is that agents are prone to opportunistic behaviour. Opportunism occurs when the agent prefers his immediate interests to those of his principal. Parties to a contract may exploit asymmetries of information to realize individual gains. Promises that are unsupported with credible commitments expose the parties to hazard, which in varying degrees constitutes an element of risk. Williamson argues that economic activity should therefore be organized 'to economize on bounded rationality while simultaneously safeguarding the transactions in question against the hazards of opportunism'.[10] 'But for the simultaneous existence of both bounded rationality and opportunism', he writes, 'all economic problems are trivial and the study of economic institutions is unimportant. Thus, but for bounded rationality, all economic exchange could efficiently be organized by contract.'[11] For firms, a solution to the problems of contracting is vertical integration. For governments, a solution is to internalize the provision of services under public control. This ensures that government could always exercise control, engage in long-term planning, and make capital investments to the degree that it chooses. Although this outcome is not perfect, and can result in sub-optimality, it does follow an economic logic. This logic was a driving force behind the municipalization of most of Britain's urban infrastructure, at least as much if not more than the political and ideological forces identified by earlier historians of municipalization. American cities, operating under a different set of institutional endowments, solved the problem of contracting through municipal franchises.

II

To illustrate our argument we shall use the test-case of urban public transport in London. The tramway, or street railway as it was called in America, was the

---

[8] O. Hart and J. Moore, 'Incomplete Contracts and Renegotiation', *Economica*, 56: 4 (1988), 756.

[9] J. Vickers and G. Yarrow, 'Economic Perspectives on Privatization', *Journal of Economic Perspectives*, 5: 2 (1991), 116.

[10] O. Williamson, 'Markets and Hierarchies: Some Elementary Considerations', *American Economic Review*, 63: 2 (1981), 316–25. 'Bounded Rationality', means that the decision making ability of an economic agent is bounded by informational and cognitive constraints.

[11] O. Williamson, 'The Modern Corporation: Origins, Evolution, Attributes', *Journal of Economic Literature*, 19: 14 (1981), 1543.

most frequently used mode of transport in London between 1890 and 1914.[12] Tramways are a good case-study because they involve a public right of way (the street), changing technological specifications (the advent of electricity), and were subject to heated contemporary debates. Today, we are dealing with the same intractable questions relating to public or private ownership that first emerged during the late nineteenth and early twentieth centuries. What is the effect of ownership structure on capital investment, and what form of ownership best responds to the needs of the public?

Regulation of British tramways had first been introduced under the Tramways Act of 1870. The act enabled private entrepreneurs to gain approval for their proposals through the Board of Trade. The terms of the act allowed for private operation of the tramway for a period of twenty-one years. At the conclusion of that period, the local authority had the right to purchase the tramway from the private firm for the depreciated cost of materials, plus the cost of street widening, exclusive of goodwill or any allowance for future profits. The act attempted to create a situation where local authorities owned the track, while private firms managed the operations.[13] There was a standing order in parliament that no clause should be introduced into private bills allowing municipalities to work their own tramways. This standing order was lifted in 1896 only after the town of Huddersfield could not find a private firm to manage its tramways.[14]

The ownership structure of tramways proceeded along three stages. The first stage was private sector operation as stipulated by the Tramways Act. The second stage was the private sector lease, when municipalities contracted with private firms. The third stage was public operation. The reason why tramways moved from the second to the third stage was that the contractual relationship proved difficult to maintain. There were two sets of issues in the contracts: financial and non-financial. The financial issues were resolvable, and the financial terms of the leases were frequently lucrative. For example, in 1897 the London County Council (LCC) concluded a lease with the North Metropolitan Company that provided for a basic rent of £45,000 per year, plus a 5 per cent rent on the purchase price of freehold land and 6 per cent of the value of leasehold depots, plus a 12.5 per cent share of any amount by which the gross profits of the whole company system exceeded gross receipts of 1895. The LCC inserted clauses relating to hours of labour and pay, the running of workmen's cars, repair and maintenance obligations, and the renewal fund. The LCC therefore benefited from a stable source of income without risking any of its own

[12] *London Statistics*, 24 (1914), 477.

[13] Tramways Act, 1870 (33 & 34 Vict.) c78. Section 19 of the Act read: 'But nothing in this Act contained shall authorise any local authority to place or run carriages upon such tramways and to demand and take tolls and charges in respect to the use of such tramways.' See also A. Ochojna, 'The Influence of Local and National Politics on the Development of Urban Passenger Transport in Britain, 1850–1900', *Journal of Transport History*, 4: 3 (1978).

[14] QQ. 99, 108, Minutes of Evidence, Select Committee on Municipal Trading BPP, 1900, vii (305).

funds.[15] The terms of the lease were so good that the Moderates, who were opposed to municipal enterprise, frequently reminded voters that the LCC made more money for rate relief through the lease than they would have done through public operation.[16] Emile Garcke, the managing director of the British Electric Traction Company (BET), the largest private tramways company in Britain, supported this position. BET reported that the accounts for the scheme run by Birmingham corporation had shown a surplus that made possible a reduction of rates by £12,000, but the corporation could have achieved a profit of three to four times that amount if it had leased the lines to a private company.[17]

However, there were non-monetary aspects of leasing that proved to be problematic. Douglas Knoop, who wrote one of the most thorough contemporary accounts of municipal trading, described the problem of contractual incompleteness when he wrote that 'it is practically impossible to draft a lease or franchise embodying the various conditions, in which, sooner or later, one or more serious defects may not prove to exist'.[18] In the case of tramways, the most serious defect of the lease stemmed from electrification. Electrification of tramways had already shown its value in the United States. John Williams Benn, a Progressive London Councillor and chairman of the Highways Committee, reported that according to industry standards, the 1900 profit of a horse tramway was 2.12d per mile run while the electrical tramway profit was 5.5d per mile, largely because of the extra capacity gained through larger carriages powered by stronger engines.[19] Electric traction showed enormous promise to reshape London, and the LCC was keen to electrify.

The problem was what form of electrification to use. There were two types: the conduit system, which had the electric current running from a main within the rails of the tracks to a rod protruding from the train; and the overhead system, which had the power transferred to the carriage through overhead lines. The main disadvantage of the conduit system was that it cost 33 per cent more per mile to install than the overhead line. Its advantages were that it required no overhead wires, did not do any damage to the existing gas and water mains since the conduit was completely insulated, and required less maintenance than the overhead system. The overhead system was cheaper, but eight of the ten affected borough councils opposed it because they objected to both the aesthetics and the safety of the electrified overhead wires.[20] Accidents caused by the overhead

[15] The lease was formalized by the North Metropolitan Tramways Act (1897); Q. 5339, Royal Commission on London Traffic BPP, 1906, xl (2751).

[16] From London Municipal Society Archives, London Guildhall Library: 'Leaflet no. 96', 41 (1903), LMS Box 132; 'London County Council Election 1898, Facts and Arguments', 48–51, LMS Box 106; 'London County Council Election 1904, Facts and Arguments', 104–8, LMS Box 107.

[17] British Electric Traction Company, Report of Proceedings at the Ordinary General Meeting, 1907, 5, BET Archives, uncatalogued (with kind permission of the National Tramway Museum, Crich, Derbyshire).

[18] D. Knoop, Principles and Methods of Municipal Trading (1912), 381.

[19] Q. 4107, Select Committee on Municipal Trading.

[20] Q. 5496–5499, Royal Commission on London Traffic; LCC Minutes, 2 February 1904, London Metropolitan Archives, Open Shelf Access.

wires were common and many European municipalities had also objected to the aesthetics of overhead wires.[21]

The dispute over the type of electrification to be used lasted for years. The LCC had gained the power to run tramways by electric traction in 1900 and had successfully introduced the conduit system on the tramways in south London. The LCC gave notice to the North Metropolitan Company that it wished to introduce electrification into the northern districts in November 1901, but here met with much greater resistance.[22] 'The North of London', Benn recorded four years later in 1905, 'is crying out very properly for the advantages of electric traction to meet the circumstances of the case. We, speaking personally, reluctantly submitted to a compromise which shows half system overhead and half conduit . . . the company will not put up anything else.'[23] Nevertheless, the compromise to which Benn referred was never implemented.[24] James Devonshire, the managing director of the North Metropolitan Company gave evidence to the Royal Commission on the 'seemingly hopeless project of coming to any working agreement' due to the 'implacable attitude of the County Council when the question of electrification arises'.[25] Ongoing problems between the council and the lessor were often referred to parliament, or the law courts, which created a lot of bitterness between the two parties.[26] It was quite natural, Benn conceded, for the North Metropolitan Company not to want to invest in electrification since their lease was expiring in 1910.[27] His Progressive colleague on the LCC, W. H. Dickinson, estimated that the LCC would have to grant a lease term of 40–50 years, as was the practice in New York, in order to make electrification attractive to companies.[28]

The dispute over the type of electrification spilled over onto other areas of the lease, such as repairs and improvements. The LCC Highways Committee Minutes record a continuous exchange of letters between the LCC, the company, and their solicitors. The LCC contended that the company had failed to carry out proper works of repair and renewal according to the lease and had undertaken unauthorized repairs.[29] The company replied that since the lines were to be electrified eventually, it made sense to postpone major repairs until electrification occurred. The LCC filed a lawsuit against the company in order to make it comply with the terms of the lease. It had told the LCC that it would honour its obligations when electrification took place, yet it obstinately refused to agree to electrify using the conduit method. When it was clear that no agree-

[21] J. P. McKay, *Tramways and Trolleys: The Rise of Urban Mass Transport in Europe* (Princeton, NJ, 1976), 87.
[22] LCC Highways Committee Minutes, 21 April 1904, London Metropolitan Archives.
[23] Q. 5523, Royal Commission on London Traffic.
[24] Q. 5438, Royal Commission on London Traffic.
[25] Memorandum of Evidence of James Devonshire, Royal Commission on London Traffic, 664.
[26] Q. 22271, Royal Commission on London Traffic.
[27] Q. 4113, Select Committee on Municipal Trading.
[28] Q. 2508, Royal Commission on London Traffic.
[29] LCC Highways Committee Minutes, 28 January 1904, London Metropolitan Archives.

ment was possible, both parties terminated the agreement in 1906, four years before it was due to expire. The LCC and the North Metropolitan Company negotiated the surrender of the lease in May 1905 and the LCC gained possession of the northern tramway lines in April 1906. The council's annual report for that year stated that 'the tenour [sic] of the negotiations, and the practical difficulties which came to light as the question reached a more advanced state, showed clearly that this work could only be carried out satisfactorily and expeditiously provided the lines were in Council's own hands'.[30]

The approach of Emile Garcke provides evidence of contemporary awareness of the forces affecting the LCC decision, and of the pros and cons of leasing versus direct public ownership. His holding company, British Electric Traction, controlled 40 undertakings and 124 miles of electrified track by 1901, prompting his detractors to call him the 'oligarcke'. Garcke was born in Germany in 1856 and became a naturalized British citizen in 1880. He was the City's leading expert on electrical promotions. In addition to being the chairman of the Electrical Committee of the London Chamber of Commerce, he was also a Fellow of the Royal Statistical Society and a member of the Institute of Actuaries.[31] He stated that 'the problem of a lease is that improvements are discouraged at the end of the tenure—this applies to any specific period.'[32] The only way to ensure that lessees would invest in capital improvements would be to grant them perpetual concessions while maintaining the municipal power to buy out the lease at any time at full market value.[33] Garcke observed that municipalities had an obvious advantage over entrepreneurs arising from their perpetual ownership of public rights of way. 'In the case of gas undertakings, water undertakings, and tramway undertakings too, local authorities have these rights in perpetuity; these rights are granted to private capitalists for specific terms, and unless the private capitalist is very much encouraged, and has facilities offered him, instead of obstacles put in his way, he is very much hampered to supply the commodities and render these public services on anything like the favourable terms that a [municipal] corporation could do.'[34]

However, granting a long lease meant ceding control, and that was problematic in an era of urban growth and swiftly changing spatial organization. E. O. Smith, town clerk of Birmingham, described the problem of being locked-in to a contract. 'If you have leased your tramways, you cannot get hold of them for 21 years, and you cannot make alternatives that may be very necessary in the interests of public safety that you can if they belong to the corporation.'[35] The LCC had learned through experience that it could only exercise control over

[30] Report of the London County Council for the year 1904–1905 (1906), 133, London Metropolitan Archives.

[31] Richard Roberts, 'Emile Oscar Garcke', *Dictionary of Business Biography* (1984), 474.

[32] Q. 1112–13, Select Committee on Municipal Trading.

[33] Q. 1220–3, Select Committee on Municipal Trading.

[34] Q. 1129, Select Committee on Municipal Trading.

[35] Q. 1998, Select Committee on Municipal Trading.

the private sector through extreme pressure and effort. The example of work-men's fares is an illustrative example. The LCC had two possible means of action on workmen's fares. First, it could exert pressure directly on the railway companies to honour their statutory obligations under the Cheap Trains Act. Second, it could pressure for the insertion of clauses into railway bills at the committee stage in parliamentary approval. The Board of Trade, which was the agency responsible for interpreting and enforcing these provisions, did not act except on the submission of a formal complaint. A successful complaint was required to prove in the first instance that an inadequate workmen's service was being offered, and in the second instance that demand existed for that service. The process took considerable time and effort and the LCC considered it to be altogether unsatisfactory.[36] The Progressive councillor W. H. Dickinson sup-ported the creation of a London Traffic Board since questions of workmen's fares, general fares, and workmen's trains had to be fought over every time anew. He hoped that an independent arbitrator would reduce the transaction cost of negotiation and resolution of disputes outside of litigation.[37]

The borough councils (the second-tier units of London local government which replaced the archaic vestry system in 1899) had also had unsatisfactory dealings with the railway companies, and they lacked the political power and influence of the LCC. Alexander Bryceson, the town clerk of Woolwich, com-plained that the railways could only be disciplined on the basis of their statutory commitments. The non-statutory aspects of the relationship, whether omitted from the statute because of lack of foresight or because they were too costly to specify, were in either case outside his sphere of influence. Requests for station improvements, for example, went unheeded.[38] The municipal experience with the railways taught the LCC that a long-term lease created problems of enforce-ment of contract.

The ways in which such agency problems were resolved provides some insight into global electrification of tramways. British electrification lagged behind both America and Germany. The reason for this has been cited as British entrepre-neurial failure compared to German dynamism. The answer is perhaps more related to different levels of civic infrastructure, which in turn created problems of asset-specific investments. There was an effective absence of public control in America until at least the early 1900s.[39] Tramway companies operated under franchises granted by the state and confirmed by the individual cities. New York's formidable tramway development can be attributed to the fact that the early franchises were often perpetual. In Germany, by contrast, exceptionally good relations between local governments and private firms led to long exten-sions of tenure being worked out through negotiation and even some joint

---

[36] Q. 5135, Edgar Harper to Royal Commission on London Traffic.
[37] Q. 2233, Royal Commission on London Traffic.
[38] Q. 9440, Royal Commission on London Traffic.
[39] For discussion of this theme, and the growth of public utility commissioners, see D. Wilcox, *Municipal Franchises*, (New York: 1910) ii, 803.

ventures.[40] Britain only began to catch up between 1900 and 1905, when municipal authorities invested heavily after they gained ownership of the tramways in perpetuity.[41]

The LCC resolved the agency problems of a lease by internalizing the principal–agent problem. The North Metropolitan Company only had a lease until 1910. Electrification in 1901, when the LCC first requested it, would have provided the company with a limited time in which to recoup its capital investment. Its discount rate was therefore high. The LCC faced a time horizon which was equal to the life of the asset, thus reducing its discount rate and enabling it to make the capital investment. There was no alignment between the interests of the principal (the LCC) and its agent (the company). In order for interests to be properly aligned, the term of the lease would have had to be long rather than short or medium term to allow a capital investment to pay for itself. Knoop, despite his objections to public ownership, acknowledged that 'the difficulty of exercising satisfactory control over many monopolistic tramway, water, gas and electricity undertakings affords the principal justification for their municipalisation'.[42] Delos Wilcox, chief of the Bureau of Franchises for the first district of New York, agreed that similar principles applied in America. Wilcox wrote a two-volume analysis on the difficulties of contracting with private firms. He concluded that, based on his description, his readers would 'be eager to accept municipal ownership and operation as the simplest and most logical solution of the public utility problem'.[43] The longer the term of the lease the more difficult it was to write a complete contract, especially in an environment requiring investment in asset-specific technology. These opposing forces created an intractable problem best resolved by public ownership.

III

The American solution to the problems of contracting involved public ownership to a much lesser extent. American cities had more freedom under their state legislatures than British cities had under parliament to contract with private firms. Unless British local governments received parliamentary approval for their proposals, their actions were judged to be *ultra vires*. Any modification of the terms of a contract between a local authority and private provider, even when desired by both parties, required further legislation. In America, the franchise agreement rather than the act of parliament defined the contractual responsibilities of entrepreneurs to local governments. Adjudication of disputes often took place within the legal system, an option unavailable in Britain since the substantive content of acts of parliament could not be contested in courts of

[40] McKay, *Tramways and Trolleys*, 92.
[41] J. Foreman-Peck and R. Millward, *Public and Private Ownership of British Industry, 1820–1990* (Oxford, 1994), 166.
[42] Knoop, *Principles and Methods*, 381.   [43] Wilcox, *Municipal Franchises*, ii. 803.

law. The political and legal context in America was different. From about the 1880s, the courts claimed the authority to set aside legislation that they deemed contrary to constitutionally protected liberties.[44] One of the most important regulatory instruments that emerged was rate-of-return regulation, through which the utilities were awarded what the courts deemed to be a reasonable rate of return on their capital investments. Following from *Munn* v. *Illinois* in 1877, a case which involved the legality of the state regulation of grain elevators, and *Smyth* v. *Ames* in 1898, a large body of case law developed in complexity.[45] A written constitution and a judiciary that was protective of private property rights enabled America to reach an institutional solution without resorting to public ownership.

This system, however, had its disadvantages. One of the consequences of the franchise system was that the awarding and renewal of franchises became embroiled in allegations of serious corruption. Lord Bryce, whose book *The American Commonwealth* helped to propel him to the post of British ambassador to the United States, wrote that 'there is no denying that the government of cities is the one conspicuous failure of the United States'.[46] Walter Fisher, an ex-president of the Municipal Voters League of Chicago, wrote that 'the chief source of corruption in American cities are necessarily public contracts and the granting of special privileges and exemptions'.[47] Companies made large campaign contributions to both Democratic and Republican parties during elections in order to win influence and sought to control nominations before the elections even took place. The companies sought to 'control these governments to avoid being controlled by them in the assumed or real interest of the public'.[48] Politicians were willing and able to oblige. John Commons, a Progressive-minded professor at the University of Wisconsin, wrote that in many cases it was the politicians who blackmailed the capitalists.[49] In 1907, the National Civic Federation, an American research group composed of academics, businessmen and labour leaders sponsored a committee to visit Britain and compare American and British methods of providing urban utilities. The majority report of the committee concluded that 'the success of municipal operation of public utilities depends upon the existence in the city of a high capacity for municipal government'. Public provision in America, however ideologically desirable in theory for the Progressive members of the committee, could only take place when American cities reduced their levels of corruption and improved the level of governance.[50]

---

[44] B. Fried, *The Progressive Assault on Laissez-faire* (Cambridge, Mass., 1998), 43.

[45] *Munn* v. *State of Illinois*, 94 U.S. 113 (1876); *Smyth* v. *Ames*, 169 U.S. 466 (1898). For a discussion, see H. Hovenkamp, 'Technology, Politics, and Regulated Monopoly—an American Historical-Perspective', *Texas Law Review*, 62: 7 (1984), 1263–312. See also Wilcox, *Municipal Franchises*, 43.

[46] J. Bryce, *The American Commonwealth* (New York, 1910), i. 642.

[47] National Civic Federation, *Municipal and Private Operation of Public Utilities*, 3 vols. (New York, 1907), i. 38.

[48] Ibid., i. 94.   [49] Ibid., i. 65.   [50] Ibid., i. 25.

Corruption in American cities often took the form of underpricing inputs. In the case of public transport, for example, the private firms paid for the right to use the public roads. In many cases, bribing the city officials facilitated the acquisition of this right for a below market price. In many cases renewals were granted without being adequately contested or reviewed. The National Civic Federation report describes a range of corrupt practices. A particularly striking example occurred in New Haven, where the mayor was actually an employee of the private water company.[51] In other cases city officials granted perpetual franchises, as was the case in New York. Many American reformers were in favour of public ownership of urban utilities, primarily because they saw it as a means to the end of eradicating corruption and improving the standard of local government.[52]

Despite occasional press campaigns to the contrary, contemporaries in Britain of all political complexions generally thought that British local government was relatively free of the large-scale and deeply entrenched capturing of the public sphere by private interests that was seen as endemic in American political life. Sir Albert Rollit, the president of the Association of Municipal Corporations, boasted that 'neither the Times nor our opponents can or do attribute to our corporations corruption or malfeasance'.[53] However, although public ownership in Britain may have exhibited less of the spoils system, it was not without its faults. Politicians had the electoral incentive to increase workers' wages. When the LCC decided to run the South London Tramways for themselves, one of the first changes they made was to increase wages and improve working conditions. Benn reported that hours decreased from 11–13 hours, seven days a week to 10 hours, six days a week, at 25s per week instead of 22s. The change cost council £14,000 per year, which decreased profits by 16 per cent compared to the previous year under private management.[54] Under cross-examination from the parliamentary Select Committee on Municipal Trading, Benn acknowledged these wages to be a 'gratuitous present' unreflective of the state of the labour market.[55] This was partly motivated by the ideological desire for the council to act as a model employer, but this decision did not harm them during elections. Lord Avebury accused the Progressive bloc of the LCC of wooing residents of the borough of Southwark with higher wages during an election.[56]

[51] Ibid., i. 94.

[52] J. Tarr and C. Jacobson, 'Patterns and Policy Choices in Infrastructure History: The United States, France, and Great Britain', *Public Works Management & Policy*, 1 (1996), 60–75; E. L. Glaeser, 'Public Ownership in the American City', *Harvard Institute of Economic Research Discussion Paper*, 1930 (2001).

[53] Association of Municipal Corporations General Meeting, 1900, 40, PRO 30/72/29.

[54] Q. 4107, Select Committee on Municipal Trading.

[55] Q. 4128, Select Committee on Municipal Trading.

[56] Q. 1548 Select Committee on Municipal Trading. Lord Avebury's publications include, *On Municipal and National Trading* (1906); *On the Real Issues of the London County Council Elections* (1898), and *Municipal Trading: A Speech* (1903).

Lord Farrer, who as mentioned in the previous chapter after retiring from the Board of Trade sat as a councillor on the London County Council, likewise disapproved of paying above market wages. 'The Council will no doubt be a gigantic employer of labour', he wrote in a memo to councillors in 1892, 'and, for purposes connected to labour it will lose its independence, it will be run by the Trade Unions, and it will be bound hand and foot to obey their orders'.[57] Records in the Webb trade union Collection show that the Municipal Employees' Union was active in negotiating better rates of pay for its workers. In a pamphlet sent to workers in 1908, the union listed its achievements as negotiating higher wages for employees working in LCC asylums, agitating against belligerent foreman on the LCC tramways, and achieving better meal arrangements for LCC tramway conductors, drivers, and conduit cleaners.[58] Another pamphlet estimated that there were 70,000 municipal workers around London, among whom about 12,000 were trade unionists. 'What an army of men if all together!'[59] Knoop estimated that up to 5 per cent of registered voters were municipal employees in a sample of English towns.[60] Some contemporaries, including Sir John Ure Primrose, the lord provost of Glasgow, and E. O. Smith, the town clerk of Birmingham, expressed a preference for seeing municipal employees disenfranchised.[61] Public ownership solved the problems of contracting but created the problems of politicians overpaying their workers; private ownership reduced the problems of political employment but created the problems of bribery.[62] This was the dilemma of urban utilities.

IV

By 1914 America and Britain had both arrived at solutions to the dilemma of urban utilities. In Britain, urban utilities were regulated by acts of parliament, which once passed could only be amended by parliament. This created an inflexible regulatory regime without any in-built mechanisms for change over time, or adjustment to contingencies. The exception to this was gas, where the sliding scale system became more common from the 1870s. The problems of contracting were best resolved by internalizing the principal–agent problem under public ownership. This created a different set of problems as the salaries of public employees were susceptible to political pressure. In America, by contrast, urban

[57] T. H. Farrer, *The London County Council's Labour Bill, Memorandum for the Use of Members, Revised with Additions* (1892).

[58] From British Library of Political Science Archives, Webb Trade Union Collection, transport workers and general labourers, collection E, section B, volume 105, item 5.

[59] Webb Trade Union Collection, volume 105, item 7.

[60] Knoop, *Principles and Methods*, 278. The sample included Birmingham, Bradford, Bristol, Leeds, Leicester, Liverpool, Manchester, Nottingham, Salford, and Sheffield.

[61] H. R. Meyer, *Municipal Ownership in Great Britain* (1906), 310–11.

[62] For further discussion, see A. Shleifer and R. Vishny, 'Politicians and Firms', *Quarterly Journal of Economics*, 109: 4 (1994), 995–1025; Glaeser, 'Public Ownership'.

utilities were regulated by contractual agreements adjudicated by the courts. This system proved to be more flexible over time, but also produced ill effects on urban governance. The argument presented in this chapter suggests that these solutions reflected the institutional endowments of both countries.

This is not to say that this was the only cause of public ownership in Britain. Historians have pointed to the ways in which trading profits were used to relieve rates (challenging the view often held by contemporaries that public ownership inexorably led to rate-inflation).[63] This clearly was an issue, but perhaps was not as much of a driving force as has been suggested. As we have seen, there is evidence which suggests that both the LCC and the city of Birmingham could have received a greater revenue stream from leasing their tramways rather than operating them. Another factor was that the linkage of urban transport with the provision of affordable housing meant that municipalities believed that control of tramways was essential to alleviating urban overcrowding.[64] There was also a clear ideological dimension to the question of public ownership. The Fabian Society, for instance, favoured public ownership on principle, although its publications also stressed the pragmatic nature of the question.[65] Although there was a normative undertone to the debates over public ownership, the debate was fought along policy-oriented lines of argument. Proponents of municipal trading argued that local government alone could be trusted to manage a natural monopoly and that private firms were motivated by profits rather than social welfare. Some, like John Burns, even argued that municipal trading strengthened civic institutions and 'democratic' participation in civic life.[66]

Opponents of municipal trading appealed to the cost and benefit of public ownership. Lord Avebury identified the problems of cost as being increased municipal debt, and the hampering of technological innovation.[67] The wealthy opposed public ownership of utilities because they paid taxes for services they did not use. The tramways, for example, catered mostly for the working classes.[68] Private ownership involved financing the service through user fees. Under public ownership, politicians had the electoral incentive to subsidize services below what private firms were charging. This practice was widespread throughout Britain, under conservative as well as radical regimes, and reduced the rate of return for private tramway companies.[69] Again, the London tramways are a good example of this trend. The Moderates beat the Progressives

[63] Foreman-Peck and Millward, *Public and Private Ownership*; E. P. Hennock, *Fit and Proper Persons: Ideal and Reality in Nineteenth-century Urban Government* (1973).
[64] See Edgar Harper's testimony to the Royal Commission on London Traffic (1905), for example.
[65] Fabian Society, *Municipalization of the Tramways*, Fabian Tract No. 77 (1897); S. Webb, *The London Programme* (1892).
[66] National Civic Federation, i. 117.
[67] J. Lubbock, *On Municipal and National Trading* (1906).
[68] Testimony of C. G. Mott, Q. 16521, Royal Commission on London Traffic.
[69] British Electric Traction Company, Report of Proceedings at the Ordinary General Meeting 1910, p. 6, BET Archives. Of the 59 British private tramway companies in which BET did not have an interest, only 23 paid dividends. BET stopped paying dividends on ordinary shares in 1907.

in the 1907 election, partly on a programme of promising to reduce the rates. But, despite their history as the party of fiscal retrenchment, they continued to subsidize the tramways, a fact that Moderate candidates subsequently used to their advantage in the county council elections of 1910 and 1913. They argued that they had electrified more miles and carried more passengers at reduced workmen's fares than the Progressives did before them.[70] By 1914, tramways were largely funded out of the rates. The political complexion of government was less important than the realities of competitive electioneering to a predominantly working-class electorate.[71]

The dilemmas of the nineteenth century remain with us today. Although our analysis has focused on urban tramways, the framework presented here can also be applied to electricity, gas, and water.[72] We see in developing countries the same issues that challenged early twentieth-century Britain and America. The World Bank is in favour of privatization, even though it recognizes that many developing countries lack the institutional endowments necessary for sustaining regulation.[73] Proponents of privatization argue that public ownership is worse, due to waste, inefficiency, and corruption. In the developed world, the issues arising from contractual incompleteness persist. Specifying quality issues has proved to be the most difficult part of public–private partnership schemes. The agreement for the partial privatization of the London tube, drafted in 2001, was 2,800 pages long, with 3,000 separate performance measurements for issues such as graffiti and train cleanliness.[74] History does not provide an answer to these questions, but it does provide perspective.

[70] London Municipal Society, Facts and Arguments for the London County Council Elections 1910, p. 82, Guildhall Library LMS Boxes 108–9.

[71] For a study showing how the working-class vote was larger than historians had previously estimated, see J. Davis and D. Tanner, 'The Borough Franchise after 1867', Historical Research, 69 (1996), 306–27; J. Davis, 'The Slums and the Vote', Historical Research, 64: 155 (1991), 375–88.

[72] For a new institutional study of gas in Chicago, see W. Troesken, Why Regulate Utilities? The New Institutional Economics and the Chicago Gas Industry, 1849–1924 (Ann Arbor, 1996).

[73] B. Levy and P. T. Spiller, 'The Institutional Foundations of Regulatory Commitment: A Comparative Analysis of Telecommunications Regulation', Journal of Law Economics and Organization, 10: 2 (1994), 201–46.

[74] Financial Times, 16 November 2001, front page.

8

British Progressives and Civil Society in India, 1905–1914

NICHOLAS OWEN

I

Debates over the degree to which civil society helps to create and deepen democracy, which were sparked into life by the collapse of communism in Eastern Europe and democratic transitions elsewhere, are not new. They were prefigured in political discussion much earlier in the late nineteenth and early twentieth centuries. In Britain, there was an important colonial dimension to these debates. For the British, and for the inhabitants of their colonies, issues concerning the nature of civil society arose with peculiar force in the empire. The vast array of differences—geographical, cultural, historical, sociological—between the domestic and colonial settings was sufficient to raise doubts as to whether British political practices could simply be transplanted to colonial dependencies. It was widely held, even by those sympathetic to political emancipation in the colonies, that, deprived of the rich soil of civil society, which nourished democracy and progress at home, such transplants would simply wither and die. Institutions might perhaps be exported, but civil society, it seemed, had to be produced locally.

India was the most important setting for this debate and much has been written on nineteenth-century liberal attitudes to Indian reform.[1] This chapter, however, will concentrate on the views of British Progressives at the start of the twentieth century. The later period is chosen because it saw the arrival of a new, complicating development which revitalized the old debate about whether India could develop along Western lines. This was the emergence of a more challenging and less deferential strain of Indian nationalism in the wake of Curzon's partition

---

[1] Eric Stokes, *The English Utilitarians and India* (Oxford, 1959); R. J. Moore, *Liberalism and Indian Politics, 1872–1922* (1966); Javed Majeed, *Ungoverned Imaginings: James Mill's The History of British India and Orientalism* (Oxford, 1992); Thomas R. Metcalf, *Ideologies of the Raj* (Cambridge, 1994); Lynn Zastoupil, *John Stuart Mill and India* (Stanford, Calif., 1994); Lynn Zastoupil, Martin Moir, and Douglas Peers (eds.), *John Stuart Mill's Encounter with India* (Toronto, 1999); Uday Singh Mehta, *Liberalism and Empire: A Study of Nineteenth Century British Liberal Thought* (Chicago, Ill., 1999).

of Bengal in 1905. The focus is on Progressive opinion because it was only among those who believed that India *could* achieve home rule, rather than among those who believed that it could not, that serious debate about the necessary preconditions of political freedom occurred. More precisely, the chapter will examine the impressions of British Progressives who visited India in the years after the renewal of nationalist agitation. These were J. Keir Hardie in 1907, H. W. Nevinson in 1907–8, J. Ramsay MacDonald in 1909, and Sidney and Beatrice Webb in 1911.

II

To nearly all British observers, the main impediment to India's political development on Western lines lay in its traditional social structure, and in particular the strength of loyalties to religion, caste, and extended kinship.[2] Hindu precolonial society consisted, in this view, of an enormous variety of sub-castes (or *jatis*), ordered according to several different hierarchies, based on ritual status, religious authority, and economic influence. These hierarchies, while severally precise in themselves, were mutually incommensurable; that is, an ordering according to one hierarchy could not be weighed against an ordering according to another. This produced what Sudipta Kaviraj has termed an overall 'fuzziness' of identity, in which it was not easy to place the *jatis* into a single ranking, nor therefore for an individual to identify a single, precise 'place' in a society wider than the *jati* itself.[3] Moreover, membership of the *jati*, and the complex social position that followed from it, was ascriptive; that is, assigned to the individual, rather than chosen. Its terms could be neither negotiated nor renounced. The *jatis* comprised a 'circle of circles', each with its own social rules and orderings, but with only very limited communication between each other, each existing in a 'kind of back to back adjacency with the rest'.[4] The members within each circle were bound together by strong bonds of mutual obligation, reinforced by highly prescriptive rules governing social behaviour. These were based on *dharma* (traditional notions of right conduct) rather than evolved consensually in each generation. Furthermore, the sense of mutual obligation they created was highly localized. Thus, collective action on a larger scale, involving co-operation of members of more than one 'circle', was very hard to organize.

[2] M. N. Srinivas, *Social Change in Modern India* (Berkeley, Calif., 1966); Louis Dumont, *Homo Hierarchicus: The Caste System and Its Implications* (1970); Clive Dewey, 'Images of the Village Community: A Study in Anglo-Indian Ideology', *Modern Asian Studies*, 6: 3 (1972), 291–328; Susan A. Bayly, ' "Caste" and "Race" in the Colonial Ethnography of India', in Peter Robb (ed.), *The Concept of Race in South Asia* (Delhi, 1995); Nicholas Dirks, *Castes of Mind: Colonialism and the Making of Modern India* (Princeton, NJ, 2001);

[3] Sudipta Kaviraj, 'On State, Society and Discourse in India', in James Manor (ed.), *Rethinking Third World Politics* (1991). See also his 'On the Construction of Colonial Power: Structure, Discourse, Hegemony', in Dagmar Engels and Shula Marks (ed.), *Contesting Colonial Hegemony: State and Society in Africa and India* (1994). For a succinct summary, see Sunil Khilnani, *The Idea of India* (1997), 17–21.

[4] Kaviraj, 'On State, Society and Discourse in India', 77.

Muslim social organization in India was regarded in a similarly pitying fashion, being based on automatic belonging, unchangeable laws, and little scope for members to reinterpret either.

This pattern was believed to have important implications for India's capacity to sustain democratic politics. There was no lack of scope for collective action on the small scale of the *jati*, for at this level social obligations were both strongly felt and tightly regulated. However, the obligations concerned were also pre-ordained, involuntary, and non-negotiable. Moreover, they were interpreted and applied overwhelmingly by a single status group: the Brahmins. This reflected a heavily restricted conception of individual interests and rights. The development of civil society on Western lines required individuals who were capable of freely choosing their affiliations and projects. It rested on a notion of the self that was capable of reflection on its own choices and of revising them through an act of will; which was—in the modern language of civil society— 'unencumbered'. It also required an arena in which associations could be made, and interests discovered, deliberated, and expressed, for which the *jati*, characterized by felt duties—or social pressure—rather than rational persuasion, seemed an inadequate substitute. The notion of the free, individual citizen, choosing to unite for specific and temporary purposes with other such individuals in *Gesellschaft* organizations, and accepting obligations as a consequence of these choices, was the key mechanism of civil society. There seemed little space for it in Hindu society, where traditional commitments were complete and peremptory, and in which the compartmentalization of social groups made it difficult to conceive of action on a national scale.

It was also important that, in Hindu metaphysics, the inner core of culture was insulated from external political authority. This allowed much of the existing social order to continue relatively undisturbed by changes of ruler. Political demands were heard in an outer room, in which rulers and ruled negotiated within tight limits what the state might fairly demand, but from which the curtained, inner room of religion and social practice was always divided. The usual response of the 'circle of circles' to the challenge of a new group, whether the Moghuls in the sixteenth century or, initially, the British in the eighteenth, was merely to allow it to form a new circle of its own, creating slight alterations of position in the outer circle but little change in each of the existing, smaller circles of which it consisted. This too created a dilemma for those seeking to make Western conceptions of civil society function in India. The task of the ruler in Hindu India was little more than to uphold the customs and laws of self-regulating groups, periodically extracting revenue on the basis of accepted rules. The idea of a modern state, licensed through consent of the governed to intervene in many areas of social life, seemed alien. The authority exerted by existing groups occupied almost all the available space, leaving little room for a separate political domain. It was wondered whether such a system could ever produce sufficient consent to justify the far-reaching reforms to enable India to become a modern state.

The dominant question for the Progressive British observers who form the subject of this chapter was whether the emergence of Indian civil society was more likely under British rule or as a product of indigenous developments. India clearly did not have a functioning civil society. But had it perhaps, as orientalist scholars suggested, been lost, and, if so, might it be recreated, with or without Western encouragement, from indigenous traditions? Would such a civil society be sufficient to sustain democracy or a transition to modernity? If not, then what degree of assistance could be provided within colonialism? British rule had clearly assisted in 'calling forth' or provoking the emergence of something that at points resembled Western civil society. But was this a natural or healthy development? Imperialism had, it was assumed, provided the political stability, communications, and rule of law necessary for civil society to emerge. But was it now, as Indian nationalists argued, stifling it? Needless to say, these debates occurred not just as theoretical explorations in sociology but also within the perceived limits of imperial necessity, of which maintaining India's substantial contribution to imperial defence and in Britain's trading and financial networks were never forgotten.

III

The sheer power of the British irruption in India called for a different response from that hitherto made to foreign assertions of political authority. To simplify greatly, the responses had come in two very different political modes.[5] First, new forms of association had emerged to protect traditional ways of life, and to define the limits of the new and threatening form of state—sovereign, subcontinental, reforming, capitalist—that the British were engaged in constructing, and which increasingly stirred up society in depth. These organizations were primarily defensive, and based on social territory that was already held. Charismatic spiritual leaders were often the driving force behind them; religious and caste identities formed a necessary, if not sufficient, criterion of membership, and traditional methods were used to exert pressure on defaulters as a means of ensuring that the siren call of Westernization was not too audible. Examples of such groups are the cow-protection leagues and reconversion organizations of northern India in the 1890s, and the more martial youth groups of Bengal and Maharashtra.

In a second and different sense, however, civil society emerged on the new political terrain that the British had constructed. These initiatives engaged the British more directly, in the institutions that they had imported: assemblies, councils, law-courts, and the English-medium (rather than vernacular) schools and colleges. The methods employed were also imported ones, using, sometimes

---

[5] For a similar argument, see Sudipta Kaviraj, 'In Search of Civil Society', in Sudipta Kaviraj and Sunil Khilnani (eds.), *Civil Society: History and Possibilities* (Cambridge, 2001).

in novel ways, the procedures of the new judicial, bureaucratic, educational, and parliamentary institutions. While recruitment to such associations remained strongly correlated with existing religious and caste alignments, their methods showed a greater resemblance to the associational rules and routines of Western civil society, with greater freedom of entry and exit, negotiated rights and duties of membership, and deliberative decision-making rather than discipleship. By the late nineteenth century, this had led to the flowering of civil society on a very significant scale, concentrated around the main bridgeheads of British influence: the presidency cities of Madras, Calcutta, and Bombay, but also in smaller towns. Here was provided an intense, localized mix of professional association, civic debate, and political instruction, characterized by political meetings, petitions, editorials, reviews, and seemingly endless intense discussion.[6]

These two modes of organization, while clearly very different in shape, were in practice very often combined. Indeed, in many senses—ideological and political—they positively required each other. As Partha Chatterjee argues, there was much acceptance, even among nationalists, of the superiority of the West in science, technology, and government, and of the need for India to adopt its modern forms of progress. But since to do so would obliterate the distinctiveness of the Indian nation, and lead to a more or less permanent acceptance of secondary status, this was combined in nationalist thought with revival of traditional cultural forms. The first impulse found expression in the demand for constitutional advance and the modernization of traditional institutions and practices. The second emerged most strongly in the imaginative and literary recreation of a glorious Hindu past. Its political expression came in revivalist or fundamentalist cultural movements, drawing strongly on religious and communal allegiances.[7] Moreover, politicians increasingly found that they had to operate in both modes in order to succeed. Caste associations (*caste sabhas*), for example, often reasserted caste rules against Western-inspired criticism, whilst also lobbying the imperial state for higher status or a larger share of reserved posts and seats on the municipal councils.

Moreover, as the imperial state, anxious to acquire knowledge and control of its colony, undertook inquiries and censuses, and defined franchises and electorates, it hardened hitherto 'fuzzy' social boundaries, and forced a certain level of organization, even among groups that preferred to be left alone.[8] Competition between groups to establish claims of 'representativeness', which

---

[6] Anil Seal, *The Emergence of Indian Nationalism: Competition and Collaboration in the Later Nineteenth Century* (Cambridge, 1968).

[7] Partha Chatterjee, *Nationalist Thought and the Colonial World: A Derivative Discourse* (1986), 54–81.

[8] Bernard Cohn, 'The Census, Social Structure and Objectification in South Asia', in *An Anthropologist Among the Historians and Other Essays* (Delhi, 1987); Arjun Appadurai, 'Number in the Colonial Imagination', in Carol A. Breckenridge and Peter van der Veer (eds.), *Orientalism and the Postcolonial Predicament* (Philadelphia, 1993). The term 'fuzzy' is borrowed from Kaviraj, 'On the Construction of Colonial Power'.

might win them a better hearing from the British, had the same effect. Membership of the consultative and deliberative bodies established by the British was a valuable source of municipal contracts and jobs, and also an indispensable means of influencing regulations on matters of local, communal conflict. As election replaced appointment as the means of advancement, it became important to build support bases, which could be done most effectively out of existing materials. This forced politicians to find ways of linking operations in more than one mode. Since ascriptive loyalties were more deeply felt, and rallied groups more effectively, it was natural for even 'modern' politicians to employ them when hard pressed.

It was common, therefore, by the early twentieth century, to find that many of India's political leaders, operating in the recognizably Western associations of Congress politics, were simultaneously working in communal organizations dominated by quite different methods. It is important to be clear about the kind of balancing that this required. It was not primarily a case of weighing 'traditional' objectives against 'modern' ones. Concerns of both types were often fairly easily reconciled, with Congress, for the sake of unity, limiting itself to the shared territory of common interest, while the communal organizations pushed specific claims. Many of the communal groups were also 'modernising' ones, concerned with reforming such practices as widow remarriage, untouchability, or prohibitions on foreign travel, in the light of new thinking. Nor was it, as it sometimes seemed at first sight to British observers, just a matter of distinguishing between 'public' and 'private' life, for both types of organization were increasingly forced to operate in the public sphere. Rather, the balance lay in combining the very different political modes employed. An example came in the early 1890s in the famous clash between Tilak and Gokhale over the Pune Sarvajanik Sabha, the most prominent of the social reform associations in Maharashtra. For Tilak, the Sabha needed an injection of Hindu militancy and a greater willingness to confront the *raj*, a strategy that Gokhale opposed. When Tilak was defeated in the Sabha, he recaptured it by moving outside the organization to rally hitherto uninvolved parts of Pune Hindu society, organizing festivals with a strong Hindu bias, rallying opposition to British-backed reforms such as plague inoculation and the raising of the age of consent, and sending agents into the hinterland to rally rural cultivators.[9]

When it came to broadening the movement still further, this example proved instructive. Curzon's insistence on the partitioning of Bengal in October 1905 put moderate Congress leadership under pressure to adopt new methods of protest such as *swadeshi* boycotts, demonstrations, and civil disobedience.[10]

[9] Stanley Wolpert, *Tilak and Gokhale: Revolution and Reform in the Making of Modern India* (Berkeley, Calif., 1962); Richard Cashman, *The Myth of the Lokmanya* (Berkeley, Calif., 1975).
[10] Amales Tripathi, *The Extremist Challenge: India Between 1890 and 1910* (Bombay, 1967); Daniel Argov, *Moderates and Extremists in the Indian Nationalist Movement* (1967); Gordon Johnson, *Provincial Politics and Indian Nationalism: Bombay and the Indian National Congress, 1880–1915* (Cambridge, 1973); Sumit Sarkar, *The Swadeshi Movement in Bengal, 1903–08* (New

Partition was deeply unpalatable to the educated classes in eastern Bengal, who feared it would cut them off from career advancement in Calcutta, and that Bengali Hindus would be swamped among the larger numbers of Muslims and Assamese; and their counterparts in Calcutta who disliked the vivisection of the historical region, and the prospect of being lumped in with Bihar and Orissa. However, it was clear that campaigns based solely on the needs of the Western educated were simply too easily defeated unless they meshed with other, more popular, grievances. But the civil society of the towns was almost entirely disconnected from the values, concerns, and associative worlds of the rural masses. Rural politics was mainly concerned with land revenue, irrigation rights, and the availability and regulation of credit. The dominant relationships were those of caste and those between landlord and tenant, governed by traditional rules, money-power, and force. This was a world quite apart from—and largely untouched by—the concerns of urban civil society: access to the administration, legislative reform, Indian Civil Service (ICS) examinations, municipal funds, and posts.

With its own distinct traditions and history, the Indian peasantry could not be mobilized by appeals couched in the language of Western Progressives or, for that matter, by using the techniques favoured by European working-class movements. What was needed was to find a means of harnessing its pre-existing energies, expressed in an enormous variety of causes and campaigns, in opposition to rent rises, defence of customary rights and religious observances, and so forth. This could best be done by traditional, local methods: by exploiting caste taboos, resisting Western social reforms, and reviving Hindu ceremonies with an anti-Muslim cast. Hence, in Bengal, the methods employed were a mix of Western-style petition, demonstration and boycott, reinforced by the use of what Guha terms 'dharmic protest', that is, the attempt to enforce collective action through use of religious sanctions.[11] For example, failure to comply with the boycott was treated as a religious fault, and wearing foreign cloth as polluting. Caste sanctions, such as refusal to perform rituals of purification for offenders, were employed to coerce non-participants to join campaigns. The charismatic skills of religious leaders (*sadhus*, priests, etc.) were deployed to win support and religious events and locations (festivals and pilgrimage sites) were the occasions for rallies. These activities were unsettling for the Muslims, and, allied to the fear of their co-religionists in northern India that constitutional reforms would sideline them, played a significant part in the creation in 1906 of the All-India Muslim League. As well as using religious authority, Congress leaders also deployed their very considerable economic power to rally support.

Delhi, 1973); Rajat Kanta Ray, 'Moderates, Extremists, and Revolutionaries: Bengal, 1900–1908', in Richard Sisson and Stanley Wolpert (eds.), *Congress and Indian Nationalism: The Pre-Independence Phase* (Delhi, 1988); Ranajit Guha, 'Discipline and Mobilize', in *Subaltern Studies*, 7 (1992), 69–120.

[11] Ranajit Guha, *Dominance without Hegemony: History and Power in Colonial India* (Cambridge, Mass., 1997).

Sympathetic zemindars (large landowners) and their agents enforced the boycott on their tenants and other economic dependants.

This led critics of Congress to question the relationship between the educated, urban classes and the wider India. Civil society seemed to exist in a highly, perhaps excessively, developed form in the larger towns, but hardly at all beyond them. It was dominated by the higher castes, by the (English-) educated, by the professional classes and the affluent, and by men.[12] These social limitations were not necessarily problems in themselves. It was characteristic of civil society in most settings that groups formed on a more or less sectional basis. But it was not usually regarded as healthy if they *only* formed in some parts of society and not in others, or if there were few overlapping organizations, drawing people from different groups together. The critical question, therefore, was how the nationalist movement might be broadened and deepened to bring other sections of Indian society within its compass, while at the same time permitting them a sufficient degree of autonomy. The two perceived dangers were, first, that Congress might not trouble to engage in such broadening and deepening, relying on its existing social dominance to secure support; and, secondly that it might succeed too well, absorbing autonomous movements and countercurrents of dissidence.

To British observers, it was beyond dispute that these new and vital forms of civil society had emerged largely as a result of the colonial encounter, partly within the framework of the colonial state, and partly in opposition to it. What remained at issue, however, was whether imperialism was working to foster their further development or whether, as many Indian nationalists now argued, it had become an obstacle. The case for the latter view was highly plausible. The rule of law, though claimed as a British achievement, was in practice applied very unevenly, by a partial judiciary, and permitted very little effective control of government arbitrariness through the councils and boards. The development, after 1904, of criminal intelligence departments to monitor sedition gave provincial governments licence to attack civil liberties. The restrictive Press Acts, with their demands for forfeitable securities, fines, and confiscations, impeded the free expression of anti-imperial ideas. The unwillingness of the *raj* to share power, and its retention of official majorities and reserved legislation, made it hard for Indians to acquire real experience of government. The administration's own interests required it to show favouritism to 'loyal' groups, and its rigged electorates and fancy franchises distorted the natural interplay of ideas and interests. Above all, its inability to root itself in Indian civil society meant that

---

[12] For the social, religious, and regional composition of the early Congress, see the tables in P. C. Ghosh, *The Development of the Indian National Congress, 1892–1909* (Calcutta, 1960), 23–6. See also Seal, *Emergence of Indian Nationalism*; S. R. Mehotra, *The Emergence of the Indian National Congress* (Delhi, 1971), J. R. McLane, *Indian Nationalism and the Early Congress* (Princeton, NJ, 1977); 'The Early Congress, Hindu Populism, and the Wider Society', in Sisson and Wolpert, *Congress and Indian Nationalism*, 47–61; B. R. Nanda, *Gokhale, the Indian Moderates and the British Raj* (Delhi, 1977); Bipan Chandra, *Rise and Growth of Economic Nationalism in India: Economic Policies of National Leadership 1881–1915* (Delhi, 1966).

the *raj* lacked the capacity or authority to regenerate the Indian economy and society. Its finances were permanently squeezed by the demands of a military establishment, and of an expensive European-dominated administration and its pension funds. It pursued agricultural policies that merely created peasant indebtedness and famine, and industrial strategies that were haphazard and compromised by wider imperial interests. This left far too little money for extending educational provision, and thereby hampered the spread of modern ideas. The institutions of political liberalism were offered only in stunted form, and could not achieve anything without a supporting civil society, which in turn could only be achieved if the *raj* released its grip on Indian political life. In these ways, the arguments of civil society were neatly turned upon the British.

This created a puzzle for British sympathizers with Congress nationalism. Accustomed to Western notions of civil society, they had great difficulty in identifying the markers of authenticity in the Indian setting. Judged by the criteria of home, the emergence of a rich urban associational life, characterized by 'moderate' politicians speaking the familiar language of Western liberalism, seemed at first sight an authentic, if infant, development. Yet on closer inspection, it appeared somewhat artificial and imitative. The alternative forms of mobilization visible in so-called 'extremist' anti-partition politics initially offered different signs of authenticity: popular support, deep indigenous roots, and, most encouragingly, self-reliance. But they were quite unlike the forms favoured by Western exponents of civil society, relying as they did on pre-modern methods of mobilization and on the authority of caste and class. Moreover, appearances could be deceptive, for traditional organizations were often pushed into a superficial adoption of modern modes of organization. Registration with the authorities, for example, which involved supplying rules, reports, and accounts, gave them the right to hold property. Yet behind the Western façade, the older structures were still visible. To make matters worse, many Indian nationalists were employing more than one mode of politics simultaneously, or moved between them as circumstances dictated. There was therefore great variety in the types of movement that visitors to India encountered, reflecting not merely the greater or lesser distance from familiar Western forms but also the varied circumstances of locality and province, and the ebb and flow of factional competition, which could sometimes push groups into unexpected switches of strategy, such as a sudden appeal to tradition or a temporary alliance with modernizing British officials, in order to outflank a rival. Certain groups, moreover, anxious to impress British visitors whose endorsement might gain them local or metropolitan support, were not averse to describing the same movement in quite different ways to different audiences. Often naively believing before they embarked for India that they were about to witness a simple struggle between imperialists and nationalists, such visitors often found themselves, on arrival, somewhat out of their depth.

IV

It was into these dilemmas that Keir Hardie was plunged when, setting out on a world tour in 1907, he added India to his programme as 'an afterthought'.[13] At the time of Hardie's visit, both sides were engaged in rallying their supporters for the forthcoming Congress at Surat. In December 1906 at Calcutta, Tilak and his allies had managed to pass resolutions approving the use of boycott, *swadeshi*, and national education to fight partition in Bengal, and were now touring the country to consolidate their support in previously unsupportive provinces. The Moderates feared that these actions were likely to provoke the British into cancelling the reforms Morley had promised, and Gokhale was therefore also engaged in building his own base of support. Hardie's tour was deeply controversial. In his first speeches, he criticized the 'Russian methods' of the *raj*, and declared that India should have self-government on Canadian lines.[14] When this was reported home, Morley, addressing his constituents at Arbroath, accused Hardie of the 'grossest [and] . . . thoroughly dangerous fallacy' in supposing that India could borrow Canada's democratic apparel, which would be no more suitable than sporting a fur coat in the Deccan.[15]

Hardie seems fully to have accepted the nationalist fiction that India had, in its precolonial past, consisted of a mosaic of self-governing 'village republics', in which social relations were governed by common ownership and generally accepted conventions of mutual respect. These vital traditions, long-buried under the weight of imperial bureaucracy, might be disinterred, if only the *raj* would cease harassing local political activity. However, the Congress, as it had developed, seemed to him only the first step in ensuring popular representation. Given the lurid descriptions then in circulation, Hardie seems to have been surprised to find how tame it was. If treated correctly, he wrote, evidently with some disappointment, Congress was 'not only not seditious, [but] ultra-loyal'.[16]

[13] Hardie to Gokhale, 9 July 1907, Gokhale Papers, microfilm, India Office Library and Records, reel 11701. For brief accounts of his tour, see Kenneth O. Morgan, *Keir Hardie: Radical and Socialist* (1975), 190–5; Iain Maclean, *Keir Hardie* (1975), 128–30; H. V. Brasted and G. Douds, 'Passages to India: Peripatetic MPs on the Grand Indian Tour 1870–1940', *South Asia*, 2: 1–2, (1979), 97–8; W. H. Morris-Jones, ' "If it be Real, What Does It Mean?" Some British Perceptions of the Indian National Congress', in Sisson and Wolpert, *Congress and Indian Nationalism*, 90–118. For a full account, see my forthcoming *Labour and India*. This, and the account here, are drawn from the following sources: J. Keir Hardie, *India: Impressions and Suggestions* (1909); Morley Papers, MSS D 573, India Office Library and Records; Minto's Diary of Events, Minto Papers, Acc 2794, MS 12609 National Library of Scotland; Hardie's Notebook and Jottings on India, Hardie Papers dep. 176, Box 2, File 1, National Library of Scotland; India Office 'Public and Judicial' File, L/P&J/6/831, file 3476; the CID reports in Government of India 'Home-Political' files December 1907 File 23 (deposit) and February 1908 Files 50–63 (A), National Archives of India, New Delhi.

[14] Viceroy to Secretary of State, 7 Oct. 1907, India Office 'Public and Judicial' File, L/P&J/6/831, file 3476.

[15] 'To Constituents', Arbroath, 21 October 1907, in Lord Morley, *Indian Speeches, 1906–09* (1909), 29–47.

[16] Hardie, *India: Impressions*, 103

The Moderate faction was 'extreme in its moderation', while the Extremist group was 'moderate in its extremism'.[17] A way needed to be found to ground the aspirations of the educated, urban classes—currently the prey of 'wandering agitators'—in the hard earth of the peasant village. Hardie therefore proposed to make the village meeting—the *panchayat*—the basis of a system of indirect election by which popularly elected councils at district and municipal level would in turn elect provincial councils with enlarged powers. 'In this way', he argued, 'the whole superstructure of Indian administration would rest on popular election, and the people would be given a real control over their own affairs.'[18] Radical grass-roots democracy of this type was much more than Congress had asked for, and, one might suspect, much more than it wanted. In Hardie's vision, Congress would become merely one of many parties grubbing for the votes of peasants, a prospect far from the ambitions of its leaders for the opening up of opportunities in the administration and the legislatures. Congress leaders, however, were in no position to quarrel with an enthusiastic British visitor, who was also one of their few active supporters in the House of Commons.

Hardie did not spell out what he thought the enlarged powers of the provincial councils might be, and his plans were merely the outline suggestions of a passing visitor rather than a fully evolved policy. The main difficulty with empowering the *panchayat* was that, as the Hobhouse Commission on Decentralization found the following year, *panchayati*, far from idealized village moots, were very often factionalized along lines of caste. In many villages, more than one existed, and they did not command sufficient authority outside the caste to secure wider consent.[19] Hardie, however, believed that the solvent of caste antagonisms would be the extension of political participation, and, crucially, the growth of class-consciousness. He seems to have regarded castes as primordial social classes, or even, given the sheer number and variety of them, like demarcations in the working class. Just as the struggle for labour representation at home had involved bridging divisions of trade and occupation, so caste must coalesce into classes.[20]

The same experience was applied to Hindu–Muslim differences. 'He had some experience of religious feud and faction much nearer home', Hardie reminded an audience on his return from India.

[H]e refused to believe that there was in India more bitterness of feeling between Hindu and Mahomedan than there was until the advent of the Labour movement in Belfast between Catholic and Protestant . . . [H]owever much those good people might differ concerning their religious beliefs, they recognised that they had a common interest as citizens and peasants. He had . . . testimony . . . that the old spirit of strife and bitterness was dying out, if only officialdom would give it a chance to die out.[21]

---

[17] Ibid., 103.   [18] Ibid., 122.

[19] *Royal Commission upon Decentralization in India*, Cd 4360 (1908).

[20] Hardie, Speech at Caxton Hall, 19 April 1908, reported in *India*, 24 April 1908; Hardie, *India: Impressions*, 122; Speech at ILP Conference, 20 April 1908, reported in *India*, 24 April 1908.

[21] Hardie, Speech at Caxton Hall, 19 April 1908, reported in *India*, 24 April 1908.

This testimony came, as did most of Hardie's evidence, from the Congress leaders who had guided him around India. British officials were privately convinced that Congress had issued instructions to its local agitators to tell Hardie that the agitation was the result of the partition and the partiality of the *raj* towards an unrepresentative clique of Muslims anxious for government jobs; and that the poorer Muslim peasants supported the *swadeshi* campaign, which gave them greater employment.[22] This line of argument, though false, had the merit of appealing to Hardie's desire to see cross-religious campaigns based on shared economic interests. Hardie asked to meet some Muslims to verify Congress claims. However, it was claimed by the district magistrate, in a secret report to the provincial government, that the small group of Muslims produced for Hardie were bribed or placed under social pressure by their landlords, creditors, or potential customers:

The Muhammadans who met the party consisted of 11 men and 7 boys. Of the 11 men, 2 are tenants of Nibaran Babu [the Hindu landlord] and 3 take frequent loans from him. Out of the total number 2 only are petty cultivators, the rest are palky-bearers, punkah pullers and milk sellers . . . The 2 tenants of Nibaran Babu were the leaders and the boys shouted *Bande Mataram* because they were told that the schoolboys had done so on this side of the river and they would probably get a reward from the Saheb who was coming . . . Mr Hardie paid Rs 2 for the ovation which he received. A quarrel is now going on as to the distribution of the money, the biggest boy having got hold of it.[23]

Such claims, if true, might have given Hardie, had he known them, pause for thought about the mobilization of consent in a democratic India.

V

Hardie's view of the Moderates was initially shared by another visitor, the radical journalist H. W. Nevinson.[24] Nevinson visited India only a few weeks after Hardie. His speeches followed the same themes: the insensitivities of the *raj*, and the desirability of political concessions. However, he also made some 'rather sharp' criticisms of Hindu passivity and lack of organizational skills. He was told by British officials that Indians made good critics and talkers, but never took advantage of the powers that were there to make practical improvements, an impression he confirmed for himself on seeing filthy watertanks 'waiting for

[22] Le Mesurier to Risley, 12 Oct., 25 Oct., and 12 Nov. 1907; Risley to Lyall, 28 Nov. 1907, L/P&J/6/831, file 3476.

[23] Le Mesurier to Risley, 12 Nov. 1907, L/P&J/6/831, file 3476.

[24] For published accounts of Nevinson's tour, see H. W. Nevinson, *The New Spirit in India* (1908) and the second volume of his autobiography, *More Changes, More Chances* (1925), 226–83. Besides these sources, the following account is based on the hitherto unused, for these purposes, Nevinson Diary (MSS Eng.misc.e.614, Bodleian Library, Oxford). I am grateful to Professor Angela John for advice about using the diary, and for allowing me to read a draft chapter from her forthcoming biography of Nevinson.

the municipality' for repair.[25] 'I c[oul]d hardly get them to see my point in insisting on the swadeshi of self-help', he wrote in his diary, after his first discussions with Indian politicians.[26] Indians had failed to build civil institutions above the level of the locality for themselves, were now confronted by a powerful, efficient but foreign state, and had, as a result, got into the 'habit of looking to Gov[ernmen]t for every single thing and of expecting all from it'.[27] Hindu submissiveness also hampered political resistance to the *raj*. Nevinson was publicly critical of the 'weakness of Indians in over-politeness + taking things lying down'.[28] There was, he told one audience, 'no glory in ruling over a flock of sheep and there was no glory in being one of a flock of sheep'. What was needed were greater efforts to develop 'self-reliance and manliness'.[29] After his experiences in Russia, Nevinson found the scale of oppression in Barisal—the district Hardie had visited—'rather petty'. He told Aswini Kumar Dutt, a Bengali activist who had spent years building institutions for local arbitration and self-government, that he ought to have defied the orders of the notoriously diehard lieutenant-governor Bampfylde Fuller, and was surprised by the astonishment and hurt the comment caused. 'Yielding seemed so natural to him', he wrote in his diary.[30] Like other muscular radicals before him, such as H. M. Hyndman and W. S. Blunt, and still others later, such as H. N. Brailsford, Nevinson felt able, from a comfortable position of invulnerability to the *raj*, to urge defiance upon those in a much weaker position.

The Moderates told Nevinson that self-assertion would come from the growing confidence of Indians under British tutelage. Bhupendranath Basu argued that that the Moderates were 'strongly in favour of keeping [the] Brit[ish] Gov[ernmen]t because there is no other nation th[e]y w[oul]d rather be under, all the more because we go slow + give time for internal development.'[31] To Nevinson's even greater surprise, Gokhale defended Curzon's notion that 'inscrutable providence' had brought Britain to govern India, since 'England was supplying what most was lacking in the race—love of freedom and self-assertion ag[ain]st authority'.[32] As with Hardie, this did not seem sufficiently robust to Nevinson, and it was not until he met Aurobindo Ghose that he found a nationalist of whom he could wholeheartedly approve. Aurobindo, in contrast to the Moderates, had given up on the idea that India should acquire its political skills through apprenticeship under the British and was indifferent to such

[25] Nevinson Diary, 19 Dec. 1907, MSS Eng.misc.e.614, Bodleian Library, Oxford.

[26] Nevinson Diary, 2, 13, 15, and 20 Dec. 1907. According to a contemporary intelligence report, Nevinson also said that 'Indians often showed themselves too polite and submissive; they should assert themselves more', DCI report, 30 Nov. 1907, enclosed in Minto to Morley, 12 Dec. 1907, Morley Papers D 573 / 13, India Office Library and Records

[27] Nevinson Diary, 13 Dec. 1907.   [28] Nevinson Diary, 2 Dec. 1907.

[29] Director of Criminal Intelligence, report of 30 Nov. 1907, enclosed in Minto to Morley, 12 Dec. 1907, Morley Papers, D573/13; DCI report of 21 Dec. 1907, in Home-Political Proceedings A, No. 102, January 1908, microfilm IOR POS 5243.

[30] Nevinson Diary, 7 Dec. 1907.   [31] Nevinson Diary, 3 Nov. 1907.

[32] Nevinson Diary, 15 Nov. 1907.

tedious questions as distribution of seats in the legislature. Instead he concentrated on building national institutions based on Indian traditions, a 'renewal of national character + spirit, reduced since 1830 more + more in each generation to [the] condition of sheep or fatted calves'.[33] Within the Extremist camp, moreover, Aurobindo had set himself up against the 'peaceful ashrams and swadeshism and self-help' of which A. K. Dutt was a prominent advocate. In its place, he advocated boycott of British goods and institutions, and the creation of national educational institutions, national courts, and so forth in their place. He also favoured a social boycott of those who refused to join and ultimately armed struggle if necessary.[34] Nevinson was more naturally drawn to Aurobindo precisely because he seemed to have real influence with Indians, rather than relying on connections in London, as did Gokhale. Better still, the Congress 'volunteers' employed to enforce the boycott and fend off Muslim attacks were at least showing some manly virtues.[35] 'This is beyond doubt the true party', wrote Nevinson, 'the party with a future'.[36]

At the end of his tour, however, Nevinson attended Congress itself, and was horrified to find that the dispute between Moderates and Extremists came to a fist-fight almost immediately, in a spectacular display of political incivility. The Moderates expressed their willingness to see the Extremists depart rather than give any further encouragement to their programme of agitation. Nevinson recorded a 'sleepless night of perplexity and sick passion', followed by a '[l]istless morning listening to apprehensions of fighting'. As Gokhale had told him, the 'Indian character had far to go before fitted for self-gov[ernmen]t'.[37] The 'petulant irritation' of the Indians on both sides was 'very disquieting'. They were 'like helpless children'.[38] Aurobindo and the Extremists received noticeably worse press from Nevinson thereafter. Lajpat Rai, who had sided with the Moderates at Surat, now, in Nevinson's view, '[stood] highest of the Indians I have known'.[39] Nevinson now placed great stress on the need for education in India, to assist the proper growth of democracy. This would, of course, need to be liberal education, for the trouble with schools under indigenous influence, even such as those of Lajpat Rai's Arya Samaj, was that they were more interested in religious rote-learning—'as though the mind were a passive vessel to be filled through the passage of the ears', as Nevinson colourfully put it—rather than encouraging free thought.[40] On his return to Britain, and in his book *The New Spirit in India*, Nevinson expressed much greater faith in the Moderates and their programme of participation in local councils. Indians, he wrote, 'sh[ould] practise hard at their municipalities'.[41] What was needed in India was

---

[33] Nevinson Diary, 19 Dec. 1907.

[34] See H. Mukherji and U. Mukherji, *Sri Aurobindo and the New Thought in Indian Politics* (Calcutta, 1964).

[35] Nevinson, *New Spirit in India*, 185–6.   [36] Nevinson Diary, 19 Dec. 1907.

[37] Nevinson Diary, 28 Dec.1907.   [38] Nevinson Diary, 28 and 29 Dec. 1907.

[39] Nevinson Diary, 21 Jan. 1908

[40] Nevinson Diary, 20 Dec. 1907, 17 Jan. 1908; *More Changes, More Chances*, 278–9.

[41] Nevinson Diary, 14 Jan. 1908.

benevolent Western influence, not, or not yet, movements of self-reliance. For Nevinson, as for other British observers, Western liberalism, confronting the new 'extremist' spirit in India, had hit the buffers of its understanding. 'I have never approached any subject with more overwhelming distaste and uncertainty', he wrote gloomily in April 1908.[42]

VI

Two years later, Ramsay MacDonald published his own book on India, the result of a visit in 1909.[43] Efforts to reunite the Moderate and Extremist factions after Surat had proved unsuccessful. Violence against British officials and residents in the centres of Extremism (Bengal, Punjab, and Maharashtra) had also escalated, and had been met by arrests, deportations, including that of Lajpat Rai, and restrictions on political activity. Aurobindo Ghose had been tried for conspiracy with terrorism, and, although escaping the death and imprisonment sentences handed out to his co-defendants, had been forced by police harassment to leave nationalist politics for good. Tilak had also been tried for inciting violence and racial hatred and sentenced to six years transportation, while Bepin Chandra Pal fled India for Europe. The unresolved question at the time of MacDonald's visit was whether the departure of the Extremists had strengthened Congress by returning it to the path of mendicant constitutionalism, or weakened it by depriving it of the unexpectedly powerful impulses of Indian cultural renaissance.

MacDonald, unlike Hardie, believed that religion and caste were still absolutely central to Indian social life, and that they created problems that could not be readily brushed aside. Hinduism was 'the pivot round which the life of India turned', and its centrality gave Indian nationalism its peculiar, unsatisfactory qualities.[44] 'A ruling caste', MacDonald wrote, 'retaining power by force and fraud, holding authority over the masses without consulting them, oppressing them without compunction, and treating them at best as mere means to its own ends, appears to be the political system which alone corresponds to the religion of Hinduism.' The caste system seemed to MacDonald 'quite inconsistent' with the idea of a political community, or even of social progress.[45] With one eye on the infinite, the Hindu, in MacDonald's view, was prepared to put up with poverty and degradation as only things of this life.[46] Moreover, India's history was the product of sequential waves of invasion, and each race brooded darkly on the injuries inflicted by its successors. The greatest obstacle of all, therefore, was Hindu–Muslim tension. 'The whole of Indian culture',

---

[42] Quoted in John, 'Henry Nevinson', draft chapter, 17.

[43] For a brief discussion of MacDonald's tour, see David Marquand, *Ramsay MacDonald* (1977). MacDonald's own main writings on India are *The Awakening of India* (1910) and *The Government of India* (1919).

[44] MacDonald, *Awakening*, 182–3, 186.   [45] Ibid., 101.   [46] Ibid., 67.

MacDonald wrote, 'is pervaded with the assumption that India, the land, is sacred. To this extent Indian Nationalism is Hinduism. No Mohammedan can enter its Holy of Holies.'[47]

MacDonald therefore did not believe that the indigenous 'new spirit' initially identified by Nevinson in Aurobindo Ghose and the Extremists offered any real hope of advance. 'The extreme Nationalist has no programme except a demand for elementary rights, no ideas of what would follow upon a self-ruling India. He is a religious votary, not a politician'.[48] Bengali politics—which gave Extremism its vitality—was 'too volatile, too philosophical, too nervous' to be politically effective. Its positive contribution lay in its cultural revival of traditional Indian art-forms, which MacDonald believed was as vital to national growth as the synthesis of united political demands. It was 'creating India by song and worship'. By contrast, the political expressions of Indian nationhood, when contrasted with its cultural and artistic voices, were 'in some respects . . . its crudest and most ill-formed embodiments'.[49] Nationalism demanded heroic action, while politics necessarily involved gradualism and compromise.

Unlike Hardie, MacDonald had little time for the notion that India's past provided any basis for building democratic institutions. On the contrary, India before the British arrived was 'rent asunder by internal strife, crushed down by foreign armies'. Then the British came, and 'consolidation followed on our footsteps. Diversities of race and religion found liberty, and the spirit of a united India found rest to its harassed wings.'[50] Where Hardie held that the empire had merely impoverished India, MacDonald took a much more positive view of the imperial contribution. Whatever nationalists might say, 'the historical fact remains that England saved India'.[51] '[F]or many a long year', therefore, British sovereignty would be necessary.

[T]he warring elements in Indian life need a unifying and controlling power. Britain is the nurse of India. Deserted by her guardian, India would be the prey of disruptive elements within herself as well as victim of her own too enthusiastic worshippers, to say nothing of what would happen to her from incursions from the outside.[52]

However, while the *raj* had brought peace, and must stay, it could not without reform develop India further. 'This peace', MacDonald wrote, 'has been bought [by India] at the price of her own initiative.'[53] Indians did lack the skills of government. They lacked 'discipline, steady perseverance and courage'. But this was 'the result of generations of ancestors deprived of all responsibility for the ordering of their own lives'.[54] The solvent of communal and caste divisions would be council work, education, and greater employment of Indians in the imperial administration. Thus the early efforts of Congress Moderates to build

[47] MacDonald, *Awakening*, 184.   [48] Ibid., 186–7.
[49] J. Ramsay MacDonald, 'Introduction' to Radhakumud Mookerji, *The Fundamental Unity of India* (1913), x.
[50] MacDonald, *Awakening*, 211.   [51] Ibid.   [52] Ibid., 301–2.
[53] Ibid., 213.   [54] Ibid., 292.

an All-India movement seemed to MacDonald to deserve every encouragement. However, he was at pains to distinguish this project from one of simple Westernization. 'The East has got to develop upon its own lines', he later told parliament. 'For us to go and put a sort of western veneer upon the Eastern mind is to create something which is neither Oriental not Occidental. The system creates upon a racial basis the sort of man . . . who is neither at home in India nor in England.'[55] Where Hardie, believing that Indian society was coming increasingly to resemble that of Britain, had favoured Western political institutions built on a base of village *panchayati*, MacDonald instead argued for the slow development of institutions from within, matured under British influence. To borrow his own favoured botanical metaphor, indigenous plants were insufficiently robust, and the transplantation of a shoot from Britain would not take in the Indian soil. What was needed was not to nurse Indian shoots in English hothouses, but the grafting of a Western shoot on an Eastern root.[56] 'At the root of most of our mistakes', he wrote in *The Awakening of India*, 'is the assumption that India should copy us.'[57]

In a second book on India, written after his experiences on the Islington Commission on the Indian Civil Service, MacDonald dealt in more detail with the problem of Congress. Now that the Extremists had been driven out, the main problem with Congress was that it had failed to put down roots in Indian society, but '[a]nyone who professed to be a student of political conditions' knew that 'such a description could have been aptly applied to the earlier stages of every Liberal movement'. Congress—with all its faults—was 'the only proof that could ever be given that India was awake politically'.[58] The question of whether it was representative of Indian society at large seemed to MacDonald to be a red herring. In the first place, he believed that '[t]he true representative is not one who belongs to his constituency or who has personal interests similar to those of his constituency, but who understands it, and sympathises with it'.[59] It was quite inevitable that Congress should not be socially representative. In 'the nature of things', MacDonald believed, political agitation could only have been started by the educated and professional classes:

Self-government is demanded first of all by those in strong social or economic positions. It was so in Great Britain where the Liberal movement was middle class, rich and professional. The working classes come in later with their new causes of difference and tests of representation.[60]

MacDonald was setting down a plan of political evolution for Congress to follow, based on his observation of the processes of political change in Britain that had brought Labour to prominence. Nationalism was already spreading

[55] *Hansard*, 30 July 1912, vol. 41, cols. 1919–26.
[56] *Royal Commission on the Public Services in India: Report, Vol. 1*, Cd 8382 (1917). MacDonald's note is at pp. 391–3.
[57] MacDonald, *Awakening*, 214, 218.
[58] MacDonald, *Government of India*, 20–3.
[59] Ibid., 21.
[60] Ibid.

outwards into society, 'following the lines of our own Liberal, Radical and Labour evolution'.[61] After Congress gained power, MacDonald expected to see it break up under pressure of the irreconcilable social demands of its supporters. The Indian national movement, he wrote, was 'still in the first stage'. The solution was 'not to keep an adult India in tutelage, but to hasten on a more general awakening and to form a more representative Indian opinion and will', for Congress was 'not the last but the first word in how to make Indian public opinion politically effective'.[62] Indian nationalists should follow the same lines of evolution as the movement for labour representation had in Britain. Congress should carve out a broader based support among Indian workers and peasants, gradually reduce its dependence on middle-class activists, and campaign not merely for political independence but for social reform for India's underprivileged.

VII

A fourth and subtly different perspective was offered by the indefatigable Webb partnership. The Webbs visited India for four months in 1911–12 as part of a wider Asian tour.[63] Like MacDonald and Hardie, they were shocked at the incompetence of British officialdom. The ICS, wrote Sidney, carried out its own ideals well enough, but 'its ideals are still those of 1840'. Its members were 'intellectually 'individualists', vaguely remembering the political economy textbooks that they crammed up twenty years before!':

[Their] conception of government is to put down internal war, brigandage and violent crime; decide civil suits and maintain order, and for the rest to leave people alone.[64]

But the Webbs did not consider that leaving people alone was an adequate solution. Accordingly, they proposed 'a bold policy of Government exploitation'. Besides its outmoded ideals, the main problem for the government of India was the inelasticity of its revenue. The Hindu joint family stood in the way of death duties and income taxes, the consumption of luxuries was too low to make taxing them worth while, and home opinion precluded raising tariffs. This left the government dependent on good harvests, which, as Sidney Webb told Gokhale, was a 'real stumbling block when Government would like to be progressive'.[65] However, there remained 'the resource of profitable Government enterprise'.

[61] MacDonald, Government of India, 23.   [62] Ibid.

[63] The most useful account of the Webbs' tour is in Beatrice Webb's diary, Passfield Papers, LSE. Extracts from the Webbs' diaries, and a valuable introduction are to be found in Niraja Gopal Jayal (ed.), Sidney and Beatrice Webb: Indian Diary (Oxford, 1987). See also J. M. Winter, 'The Webbs and the Non-white World: A Case of Socialist Racialism', Journal of Contemporary History, 9: 1 (1974), 181–92.

[64] Beatrice Webb's Diary, 4 Feb. and 16–25 April 1912.

[65] Sidney Webb to Gokhale, 10 March 1912, Gokhale Papers, 11708.

We cannot help thinking that it would be well for the Government of India to turn over a new leaf—to go in for tobacco and spirit Government monopolies, take over the railways and work them on a unified system for public ends, to put capital—perhaps attracting it out of native hoards by a 'patriotic national loan'—into the more complete and more rapid development of its 240,000 square miles of forest, to start Government factories for matches, for paper, for rope and string and what not . . .[66]

To make grand schemes of this kind work in the vastness of India required the whole community to broaden its concepts of social purpose. The Webbs believed that, in principle, India might be '*more* adapted for collectivist enterprise by the Gov[ernmen]t (national, provincial or municipal) than for private capitalist enterprise on individualistic lines'.[67] The caste system, with all its faults, at least ensured that all members of the community readily accepted responsibilities. However, Hindus seemed peculiarly untroubled by poverty and inattentive to material well-being, and their caste hierarchies hampered collective action and active citizenship beyond the small scale of the village.[68] An Indian official told the Webbs that he did not believe that there was sufficient public spirit to run even local government satisfactorily.

At present every Indian is for himself and his family—he cares little for the Public Good; he does not even understand what you mean by it. He understands family obligation, and religious obligation. But the idea that he has any duty towards persons because they inhabit the same town or country is strange to him. Indians who have had an English education or who have mixed with Englishmen are getting this idea; but it is only limited to a few.[69]

'[T]he Hindu', wrote Beatrice, 'is an idealist, but alas! for his political efficiency, his ideals are "all over the place" and frequently he lacks the capacity to put them into practice—he can discover neither the means nor work at them with unswerving persistency'.[70] Associative life was restricted by traditional, religious alignments, and there was no real equivalent to the local bodies that gave expression to mutual obligations and civic identities in Britain. Without the framework of British rule, therefore, the modernizing aspirations of educated Indians would be swamped by the incompetence, laziness, and incorrigible religiosity of the mass of the population. India's leaders were, the Webbs wrote, too often 'dragged down by a multitude of lower castes—embedded in a population that seems strangely childish in intellect and undisciplined in conduct'.[71]

The Muslim community seemed no more promising. The Webbs thought the Muslims had a 'constitutional contempt for popular government', and merely wished to see the British remain in order to keep down the Hindus.[72] The Muslim teachers they met in the United Provinces and the North West Frontier Province were 'honest and pious men, no doubt, but obviously of the most

[66] Beatrice Webb's Diary, 4 Feb. 1912.
[67] Sidney Webb to Gokhale, 10 March 1912.
[68] Beatrice Webb's Diary, 10 Jan. 1912.
[69] Beatrice Webb's Diary, 24–6 Feb. 1912.
[70] Beatrice Webb's Diary, 16–25 April 1912.
[71] Ibid.
[72] Beatrice Webb to Lady Betty Balfour, 28 Jan. 1912, Passfield Papers, Box 2/4/F.

narrow-minded and feeble type', cramming their small pupils' heads with Urdu and theology rather than social science and Western medicine. 'These young citizens of the Oriental Empire', the Webbs wrote, 'were not learning anything that could be useful to them as independent members of a self governing State.'[73] As a result, even the educated Muslims were 'servile in dependence on the British Government, and horribly conscious (in spite of claiming to be a ruling race) of inability to organize or initiate or maintain anything without Government aid'.[74]

Moreover, the Hindu conception of the state as no more than the custodian of traditional ways of life was clearly highly unsuitable for the Webbs' purposes. Their schemes for modernizing the Indian economy required sympathetic politicians and a small army of experts and administrators. The Webbs attended the session of Congress that was to have been chaired by MacDonald, but found it rather a 'frost': poorly attended and listless.[75] Part of the problem was that the Westernizing of even the educated politicians was not deep enough. '[T]heir family, their caste, and their religion . . . are still the threefold centre of their life in spite of a perpetual striving to take their part in . . . European political life.'[76] Unlike the Japanese the Webbs had met earlier in the tour, Congress leaders were building their movement upon traditional loyalties rather than trying to educate on Western lines. Determining to raise a popular movement to oust the British, they had fostered an 'extraordinary recrudescence of religious Hinduism'. 'The only thing to counteract the disintegrating effect of caste exclusiveness', wrote Beatrice, 'is the sacredness of the cow + appeals to the amazing superstitious mysticism of simple-minded Hindu cultivators'.[77] Worse still, to Congress, government was 'a hostile force', whose role they were loath to see expand. The Congress leaders, the Webbs wrote, had 'almost a contempt for organization and a dislike for administration—no real interest in the problems of government apart from the sentiment of Home Rule'. They were 'all individualists at heart, and think our craving after governmental efficiency wholly disproportionate to its value'.[78] This 'cripples them in political programme [sic], because they are always urging retrenchment'.[79] In the Webbs' eyes, the nationalists were just as backward in their reading as the officials they sought to replace: 'two generations' behind contemporary English thinking. 'You will not get on far until you can induce the Government of India to become *more rich*', Sidney advised Gokhale. Far from trying to reduce the Home Charges and cut salaried posts and taxation, '[y]ou ought to be aiming at *doubling* the Gov[ernmen]t expenditure'.[80]

[73] Beatrice Webb's Diary, 11–16 Jan. and 9–12 March 1912.
[74] Beatrice Webb's Diary, 6–8 March and 9–12 March 1912.
[75] Beatrice Webb to Lady Courtney, 28 Dec. 1911, Passfield Papers Box 2/4/E.
[76] Beatrice Webb's Diary, 4 Jan. 1912.
[77] Beatrice Webb to Lady Betty Balfour, 28 Jan. 1912.
[78] Beatrice Webb's Diary, 4 Jan. 1912.
[79] Beatrice Webb's Diary, 16–25 April 1912.
[80] Sidney Webb to Gokhale, 10 March 1912.

It seemed inevitable, therefore, that the British would have to take the lead in creating the conditions of civil society. To work with them, the Webbs tried to identify groups sufficiently indigenous to appeal to a wide range of educated Indians, but sufficiently open to Western influence to develop the public spirit they believed necessary for democracy to work in Indian conditions. They found themselves drawn to the Arya Samaj, the movement that was the dominant force in Congress politics in the Punjab.[81] The Aryas had dedicated themselves to reforming the caste prejudices of Hinduism by insistence on the authority of a single text: the Vedas. As such it seemed to Sidney a kind of 'Vedic Protestantism', which would contest the ritual of Hinduism while preserving its spiritual content.[82] This was very much a first step, for India was still a long way off the 'Higher Criticism' of rationalism. In its main exposition, Swami Dayanand Saraswati's *The Light of Truth*, Sidney found 'the same combination of intellectual subtlety, wide culture, with an almost childish lack of sense of perspective or of scientific critical faculty, that is so common among the Hindu gentlemen whom we have met'.[83] But a first step in breaking down Hindu orthodoxy might best be made by something 'equally dogmatic and exclusive—faith in the absolute inspiration of the Vedas'.[84] In the fullness of time, dependence on the infallibility of even one book would repel the intellectual Hindu, and religion would decline.[85] The Webbs were also drawn to the Servants of India, established by Gokhale to train men for public service. The Webbs were much struck by his 'political sagacity and calm statesmanship' and his view that Indian nationalism had to be remade gradually through social and educational reform, self-education, and self-discipline.[86]

Thus while Hardie wished to anchor the Congress élite in the interests of peasant cultivators, the Webbs sought to find ways to *detach* the aristocracy of intellect from the uncivilized masses. It did not matter to the Webbs that the 'five hundred highly educated, widely cultured and usually travelled gentlemen' of Congress were 'not representative of the 250,000,000 of peasant cultivators, petty retailers, jobbing craftsmen, artisans and labourers of India', for 'they do not claim to represent them, any more than an elected Legislature of rich men and bourgeoisie resembles the millions of wage earning labourers in whose name it legislates'. They were to gain their authority not, as some increasingly chose to do, by appeals to religious communalism and caste prejudice, but through close alliance with sympathetic modernizing British officials. Reforms might thereby be 'made to appear essentially "Nationalist", and might even be made to seem to have been inspired and demanded by the Nationalists themselves'.[87] If the British would 'recognise this new governing class—and would

[81] On the Arya Samaj, see N. G. Barrier, 'The Arya Samaj and Congress Politics in the Punjab, 1894–1908', *Journal of Asian Studies*, 26: 3 (1967), 363–79; K. W. Jones, *Arya Dharm: Hindu Consciousness in 19th-Century Punjab* (New Delhi, 1976).

[82] Beatrice Webb's Diary, 29 Feb.–3 March 1912.   [83] Ibid.   [84] Ibid.   [85] Ibid.

[86] Beatrice Webb's Diary, 8–10 April 1912.

[87] Beatrice Webb's Diary, 4 Feb. 1912.

gradually take them into [their] confidence, with a view to making them party to the Government of India, then the British race might pride themselves on having been the finest race of school masters, as well as the most perfect builders of an Empire'.[88]

VIII

Although, in discussions of this kind, the political development of India was usually claimed to be decades, or centuries, behind that of the West, it is very evident that most of these Progressive prescriptions reflected very contemporary concerns about the extent of democratization in home politics. Despite the fact that Congress had been founded in 1885, some years before the Independent Labour Party (ILP) (1893) and the Labour Representation Committee (1900), Labour Progressivists saw it as a junior partner in need of education in the arts of civil society, seldom questioning whether tactics designed to advance the interests of uniquely class-conscious workers in an industrial society whose ruling classes generally eschewed repression were appropriate elsewhere. 'The working men of England had come through their own experience to believe whole-heartedly in representation', MacDonald had told the students of St Stephen's College, Delhi, in 1909. 'This was the true secret of political progress [for] today in India exactly the same condition existed as had been experienced by English working men before the advent of the Labour Party.'[89] For MacDonald, participation in the councils would be for Congress what parliamentary work was for the British Labour party, a necessary apprenticeship. It is unsurprising, therefore, to find that he favoured much the same long slog of institution-building and compromise in India that he advocated at home. In this, he was opposed by Hardie, who favoured in India, as he did in Britain, open confrontation of political opponents. The elements each disliked in Indian politics—Hardie the pusillanimous Moderates and MacDonald the flamboyant Bengali impossiblists—were in one guise surrogates for their respective domestic opponents: Lib–Labs and syndicalists. For Hardie, therefore, local councils were valued for a very different reason: because they would bring Congress leaders face-to-face with the problems of the village poor, and make the party thereby more responsive to local needs and democratically accountable. It was for this reason that he wished to build self-government on the foundation of the *panchayat*. For the Webbs, the purpose of reform was different again. For them, working with the British would enable India's natural leaders—the 'aristocracy of intellect'—to acquire the technical expertise to run a modern state. This was not dissimilar to the tactics of permeation of the élite that the Webbs had

---

[88] Beatrice Webb's Diary, 16–25 April 1912.
[89] MacDonald, Speech at St Stephen's College, Delhi, reported in *India*, 3 Dec. 1909; MacDonald, 'Some Indian Problems', *India*, 25 June 1915.

employed at home. Where Hardie insisted on grass-roots democracy, the Webbs saw little necessity for involving the peasantry. Sidney Webb told the students of the LSE that 'India was not, and could not possibly be governed by the democracy of India', which was seen, as the working classes were at home, as an ignorant drag on the energies of the élite.[90] These ideals, projected onto India, inevitably guided them to certain allies and projects.

At the heart of the problem, however, was confusion over the marks of authenticity. Indian civil society seemed to most Western observers too narrow, too shallow, and excessively derivative. Yet efforts to deepen and broaden it, or to 'Indianize' it, inevitably made it look even less familiar. Modernity seemed to be taking an unexpected turn in the Indian setting. Urbanization, which in Europe was believed to have precipitated civil society, had led in India to the growth of a similarly rich associative life, but also to an intensification of caste identities, as insecure migrants sought security in an alien environment. The spread of print journalism, another precondition of civil society, served in India not just to spread secular nationalism but also to sharpen communal identities and encourage readers to think of their religion in more dogmatic ways. The progressive introduction of representative politics had created arenas in which seemingly Western forms of political behaviour were practised in Western-designed institutions, but in which communal solidarities seemed to be hardening, not dissolving. Before the First World War, these signs troubled British sympathizers. However, they hoped that they were teething troubles. They expected to see the Indian movement follow the same lines as Progressive movements had at home. Ethnic and communal appeals were supposed to give way to the proper, modern divisions of class interest. Campaigners were supposed to learn the correct methods of politics through participation in British-led political reforms.

Judged against these expectations, the post-1920 Gandhian shift in Congress politics proved a huge disappointment.[91] Congress clearly now had a mass base, and it was no longer possible to argue that it was an unrepresentative clique of Westernized politicians. However, there were still worries about how this base had been acquired, and the relationship the Congress leaders had with it. Gandhi shared the belief of most British observers that institutions could not simply be transplanted from Britain to India. However, he was much more favourable towards the idea of revitalizing existing traditions in India than to a Western-led 'modernization' of Indian politics. His deployment of charismatic leadership, and the millennial promises of *ram-rayya* he made to peasant

[90] Sidney Webb, 'What are We To Do about India?', *India*, 6 Dec. 1912; 'Profession and Practice: Mr. and Mrs. Webb on British Policy in India', *India*, 22 Aug. 1913.

[91] For Gandhian ideas and politics at this time, see Ravinder Kumar, *Essays on Gandhian Politics: The Rowlatt Satyagraha of 1919* (Oxford, 1971); Judith M. Brown, *Gandhi's Rise to Power* (Cambridge, 1972); Bhikhu Parekh, *Colonialism, Traditionalism and Reform: An Analysis of Gandhi's Political Discourse* (New Delhi, 1989); Richard G. Fox, *Gandhian Utopia: Experiments with Culture* (Boston, Mass., 1989).

audiences, seemed retrogressive to those who believed that progress came through informed argument and reasoned debate. Gandhi himself linked the political project of *swaraj* (self-rule) to a religious movement of self-discipline and purification, and his techniques motivated and controlled supporters through a reworked conception of Hindu duties and celebration of an imagined past. Rather than bringing the rural masses closer to urban civil society, Gandhi favoured a partial return to the closed, hierarchical world of the Hindu village. Where Progressive observers had hoped to see Congress use education to teach villagers the lessons of modernity, Gandhi wished to see Congress leaders learn from Indian villagers. He recommended that Indian students, rather than embrace Western education, boycott the government schools. In sum, rather than attempt to deepen Indian civil society along Western lines through education and patient council work, Gandhian agitation gave expression to exactly those traditional forces that Progressive British observers believed precluded genuine democratic advance. While this mode of politics was disliked—and to some extent resisted—by those Indian politicians such as Nehru who shared Western assumptions about progress, they were nevertheless forced to rely on it as the only effective means of rapidly building a mass movement in Indian conditions.

Under Gandhi's influence, indeed, Congress itself grew to look less 'western'. Although it had, for official purposes, a democratic constitution, its procedures were not really democratic. Gandhi himself did not stand for election. His leadership was, it seemed, completely unaccountable to anything except his own divine inspiration. During periods of non-co-operation, he exercised the tightest personal control of Congress workers. Even when nationalists did participate in government, they seemed to stretch Western forms unacceptably wide. Where Progressive observers had hoped to see the development of political alternatives, and voter choice and party competition along lines of class interest, politics instead acquired a less voluntaristic, more communal, aspect. There were parties, but they were loose coalitions based around ambitious individuals, or communal factions, and seemed only to matter at election time. There were voters and supporters, but they had not been organized in a Western sense and continued to be recruited and rewarded in the old fashion. There were politicians, but they had not entirely settled to constitutional politics and remained too open to the possibility of reunifying their movement with traditional methods when the opportunity arose.

A further effect of the much deeper mobilization that Congress achieved under Gandhi was that it involved the capture—or even the creation—of other nascent organizations. Congress could only expel the British if it could show that it had attracted popular consent to a degree unmatched by the *raj*, and that it had created a single national will out of India's multiple identities. This required a much wider movement than Congress had hitherto mustered and one which had therefore to appropriate agitations which had very little to do with nationalist aspirations. The separate agendas of peasant agitators and industrial workers are now thoroughly well established by 'subaltern' and other schol-ars.[92] Yet for the wider purposes of Congress, every peasant agitation, every strike, had to be shown to be a manifestation of the desire to be free and as such a justification of its political demands. Nationalism could ill afford the clash of interests and ideas needed for the building of civil society. In practice, such movements often broke free of the settings in which the leaders had placed them. But the leaders could not easily disown the masses without also abandoning their claim to represent them. The emergent associations of the Indian peasantry (*kisan sabhas*) were created, or commandeered in their early stages of develop-ment, to be used as a resource for anti-British purposes.[93] Among India's indus-trial workers, too, much of the energy that created trade unionism was also anti-imperial in origin, and strikes were used not merely, as British trade unions believed they should be, in labour disputes, but as a means of putting pressure on British firms or those who failed to support Congress. Universities and schools were politicized by nationalist agitators and seemed incapable of developing the secular, liberal education necessary for a free-thinking, active citizenry.

This raised in an acute form the problem of the annexing of civil society for nationalist ends. It was not clear whether Congress nationalism had created the conditions in which associative institutions might flourish, or whether it was dragging them into an artificial alignment and stifling them in the name of unity. Parts of civil society seemed to have been created by the nationalist movement, a process that became immensely more powerful when the nationalist move-ment inherited state power.

However, what was missed by most contemporary observers were the important ways in which Indian civil society was strengthened not so much through participation in the representative politics of the *raj* as through organ-izing opposition to it. The Gandhian contribution here was very significant. Although Gandhi was opposed to imitation of Western modes of politics, he none the less identified the political arena as the one in which, in the present age, *moksha* (salvation) was to be sought. His revisions of the Congress constitution in 1920 reduced the membership fee to a mere 4 annas and restructured the organization on a linguistic basis to enable debates at the sub-national level to take place in local vernaculars rather than English. Gandhi was moreover an energetic creator of organizations: for handspinning, village hygiene, agricul-tural improvement, and the improvement of conditions for untouchables; and an untiring writer of weekly newspapers and public correspondence. These activities drew very large numbers of volunteers, especially from hitherto inac-tive groups, such as women and the middle and upper sections of the peasantry,

[92] The core of the enormous literature on this theme is to be found in Ranajit Guha *et al.*, *Subaltern Studies: Writings on South Asian History and Society*, (Delhi, 1982–). For discussion, see Vinayak Chaturvedi (ed.), *Mapping Subaltern Studies and the Postcolonial* (2000).

[93] Partha Chatterjee, *The Nation and Its Fragments: Colonial and Postcolonial Histories* (Princeton, NJ, 1993).

into associational activity. It was true that Ghandian organizations were often
funded by rich philantropists, rather than directly by the contributions of their
members; and that they did not empower weaker groups directly, but through
Gandhi's taking up of their cause. There continued to be questions about the
extent to which the reformed Congress really deepened involvement beyond the
professional classes and some business and commercial groups, and the degree
of control that was exercised from the top. Nevertheless, the example they set
has been very important since independence. Gandhi always insisted that
Congress focused too much on capture of state power and too little on grass-
roots activity in the villages. At the time of independence, he was to be found
arguing that Congress should disband as a party, and reform as a nationwide
organization of social service. Naturally, the temptations of state power were
much too great for this to be taken seriously. But in enshrining the moral duty
to campaign against the state when justice requires it, Gandhi provided a means
of widening participation and empowering society against the state which was
based much less in Western political theory than in his own reworking of India's
own socio-centric and religious traditions.[94]

From our own perspective, the most obvious flaw of these British perceptions
of Indian society is the narrowness of the concepts of 'civil society' they
employed. The assumption that there was a single path to democracy, defined
by the historical trajectories of Europe, was held in common not merely by
supporters and opponents of the *raj* in Britain, but also by a significant section
of Indian nationalists themselves. Furthermore, these historical assumptions
survived the transfer of power in India remarkably intact. Reworked to allow
for the effects of decolonization, they formed one of the major paradigms of
development theory in the 1950s and 1960s.[95] However, India's peculiar
combination of sustained democratic observances with persistent communal
identities, combined with the apparent lack of many of the features of civil society commonly argued to be essential to it, such as secularism, ethnic homo-
geneity, and 'unencumbered' or 'modular' selves, has proved to be quite
inexplicable within this paradigm without recourse to unsatisfactory notions of
'exceptionalism'. It is now increasingly argued that the problem lies in the inappropriate use of concepts, designed in the West as a tool of empire, and too
compromised to be of further use.[96] The lesson of these misdirected exports and

[94] For explorations of the roots of Indian democracy, see Rajni Kothari, *Politics in India*
(Hyderabad, 1970); Atul Kohli (ed.), *India's Democracy* (Princeton, NJ, 1990) and *The Success of
India's Democracy* (Cambridge: Cambridge University Press, 2001).
[95] Arturo Escobar, *Encountering Development: The Making and Unmaking of the Third World*
(Princeton, NJ, 1996).
[96] Among a vast literature, see especially Chris Hann and Elizabeth Dunn (eds.), *Civil Society:
Challenging Western Models* (1996); Gyan Prakash, 'Writing Post-Orientalist Histories of the Third
World: Perspectives from Indian Historiography', *Comparative Studies in Society and History*, 31:
2 (1990), 383–408; 'Postcolonial Criticism and Indian Historiography', *Social Text*, 31–2 (1992),
8–19; Gyan Prakash (ed.), *After Colonialism: Imperial Histories and Postcolonial Displacements*
(Princeton, NJ, 1994); Dipesh Chakrabarty, 'Postcoloniality and the Artifice of History: Who
Speaks for Indian Pasts?', *Representations*, 37 (1992), 1–26; *Provinicializing Europe: Postcolonial*

failed transplantations is perhaps that, just as democracy itself, though a European invention, can be successfully practised elsewhere in many different forms, so students of civil society need to stop regarding India as a deviant case, an imperfect copy, or, indeed, as an infirm patient in need of regular check-ups, and attempt to understand it in its own terms. Shaking concepts of democracy loose of these imperial accretions may provide new insights into the notion of civil society; or may show that there is considerably less explanatory value left in it, at least as applied to the formerly colonized world.

Thought and Historical Difference (Princeton, NJ, 2000); Kaviraj and Khilnani, *Civil Society: History and Possibilities*.

9

Military Service Tribunals: Civil Society in Action, 1916–1918

ADRIAN GREGORY

I

Much of the current discourse seems to make the tacit assumption that civil society is essentially a matter of associational life and voluntary action outside and distinct from the state. It is also presented in an almost universally positive light, as something warm and fuzzy that any decent person must obviously approve of.

Study of military service tribunals may add something useful to our thinking about this subject. To use these tribunals as exemplary of the operation of civil society is deliberately contrarian and provocative. While helping old ladies across the road is easy to approve of as a civic virtue, sending young men off to Passchendaele is rather more problematic. Even in terms of military service the tribunals may seem an odd case. After all, if current thinking about civil society were to be our guide, with its massive emphasis on voluntarism and associational life, then the logical focus of a study of civil society in wartime would be the Pals battalions of 1914–15. In most interpretations of military recruitment during the First World War, the Military Service Act of 1 January 1916 marks the crucial break, the moment when the responsibility for the provision of manpower passed out of the hands of civil society into the bureaucratic procedures of the military state; when the age-old historic distinctiveness of Great Britain disappeared, to be merged briefly with the more draconian controls over the lives of the population that typified the conscriptionist states of continental Europe.

In as far as they have been thought about at all, the military service tribunals have been seen through a distorting lens, as enemies of individual liberty, the essence of the tyrannical state. The stance before the tribunal is the central drama in the martyrology of the conscientious objector. The No Conscription Fellowship entitled its frequently suppressed newsletter *The Tribunal*; and this association of ideas is so pervasive that information about the handful of central records on the tribunals at the PRO is listed on an information sheet entitled 'conscientious objectors.' Some perspective on this image is required. A sample of cases that came came before the Banbury Local Tribunal in 1916 which were reported in the press demonstrates that conscientious objection was easily the *least* common ground for appeal against conscription: 40 per cent of appeals were based principally on domestic grounds; 40 per cent principally on occupational and business grounds; about 10 per cent on a combination of the two; and less than 10 per cent on conscientious scruples. Moreover, Banbury may have been untypical by national standards in having an unusually *high* proportion of conscientious objections. In 1917, the well-informed American journalist Arthur Gleason went much further and claimed that only 2 per cent of appeals were based on grounds of conscience.

It is also critically important to remember what tribunals were for. It was not their job to conscript people. Their job was to hear appeals against conscription. In this the military service tribunals of the war were close to their etymological roots. The original tribunes of the plebs had served as a check on the power of patrician magistrates, with the right to release citizens from arbitrary magisterial power and bring them before a tribunal for judgment. Moreover, far from being bureaucratic and anonymous, British conscription operated in an extremely complex, devolved, and flexible manner. A large number of men were exempted from consideration at the outset by virtue of belonging to 'badged' occupations. Local advisory committees helped to define those exempted in conjunction with trade unions and employers. If an unbadged man was called up he would then be subject to medical examination, which would rule as to whether he was fit to serve and in what capacity. Only after these two hurdles had been jumped would he actually be subject to conscription into the armed forces, at which point he might appeal to a tribunal or his employer could appeal on his behalf. Local tribunals would first hear the case and provide a ruling, which could be exemption, refusal of exemption, or temporary exemption. The appellant could then appeal this decision as could the military representative on the tribunal. In the event of an appeal the case could be taken to the county appeal tribunal. Finally, as a last court of appeal there was a central tribunal on the national level.

II

Tribunals are, to some extent, a great historical secret. One reason why they have not been taken as seriously as they should have been is an almost unprecedented degree of documentary attrition. There were roughly 1,800 local tribunals in Great Britain. But in 1921 the Ministry of Health ordered that the files of the tribunals should be destroyed, with the exception of two tribunals which were to be kept as samples: those of Peebles; and Middlesex (though a few more have in fact survived). The suspiciously minded will immediately point to this and interpret it as definite evidence that the overall records of the tribunals were a source of shame. The truth is more complex. Under the circumstances, it would be very surprising if these records did not include thousands of cases of arbitrariness, incompetence, and downright injustice. But it is doubtful that a full record would necessarily reflect unfavourably on the tribunals. The scale of tribunal activity was immense. Post-war civic histories give us a flavour of this. The Birmingham local tribunal, which had to divide into two parallel 'courts', sat 1,765 times over the course of 1916–18 and gave 90,721 decisions. Ultimately 34,760 men who appealed in Birmingham were sent into the army. The Croydon local tribunal sat 258 times and heard 10,425 cases in the same period. It is not absolutely clear how far numbers of cases relate to numbers of individuals, although we know that the Bristol local tribunal heard 41,000 cases relating to 22,000 men, of whom 17,000 were ultimately refused exemption. In Leeds the tribunal sat 435 times and held 55,101 hearings involving 27,000 individuals. Of these, 13,897 cases were dismissed outright and 41,204 claims were either withdrawn, or exemption—usually temporary—was granted. Together these four tribunal districts dealt with roughly 100,000 individuals claiming exemption. Even at the most conservative estimate, tribunals must have heard at least one and a quarter million individual cases. To put the issue of conscientious objectors into further perspective, it is worth noting that the Bristol Tribunal *alone* heard more cases than Philip Snowden's total estimate of the number of conscientious objectors for the whole country.

All of this sits uneasily with the received wisdom about conscription. In the first full-scale study of the conscript majority of the British Army in the First World War, Ilana Bet-El claims that conscription, unlike volunteering, was a bureaucratic process in which the individual was passive and events progressed automatically 'without his consent and without his knowledge'.[1] Doubtless true of most times and most places with compulsory military service, this was emphatically not the case in Britain between 1916 and 1918. The reason for this was the real possibility of appeal against conscription, an appeal that stood a decent chance of being successful at least as far as a temporary exemption was concerned. Success rates were wildly variable, but generally ranged between 20 per cent and 50 per cent, usually for a temporary exemption. A three-month exemption was well worth the effort. For the minority deemed fit for infantry service it radically improved survival chances. For the majority deemed fit for noncombatant service, it bought time to make personal arrangements. Furthermore it usually came with leave to resubmit the claim at the end of three months. Given that the right to appeal to a higher tribunal also existed, the tribunal procedure allowed many men to delay call-up by as much as a year.

It is quite clear that a perfectly normal response to conscription was not passive acceptance, but an appeal. This was certainly the contemporary impression. Michael Macdonagh in February 1916 described the tribunals in general as

---

[1] I. Bet-El, *Conscripts: The Lost Legions of the Great War* (1999), 29–30. Oddly enough the one example she gives of this 'passivity' undermines her argument, a man who appeared before tribunals not once, but twice, and did gain a postponement.

'clogged with work', the City tribunal sitting at Guildhall having to deal with 20,000 claims for exemption. One of the appellants, Harold Cousins, noted in his diary on 11 May 1916, that it was unlikely that the tribunals would be able to get through the immense number of appeals by attested men in that month. The odds of gaining at least a temporary exemption suggest that appeals were not purely formal, indeed the very numbers appealing clearly indicates that an appeal was felt to be worth trying. Cousins was able to gain complete exemption on the grounds of indispensability to his firm, the Alberta Land Company, on condition that he maintained his membership of a local volunteer unit. As a middle-aged man with a young son and an invalid wife, this was of great value to him. Unfortunately the exemption was lost when his firm went bankrupt in January 1917. Cousins then claimed that it was his domestic responsibilities that had prevented him volunteering. This was probably true: losing his job was a personal disaster to this middle-class man, but he accepted his eventual call up philosophically, primarily concerned about the loss of income involved in a private soldier's pay.[2]

Cousins had a strong case under the working of the act. Not everyone did. The audacity of some appeals almost defies belief, for example that of the man who appealed in Leeds for three months' delay in order to complete a course of hair restoration treatment; but such examples, which attracted much contemporary attention were untypical.[3] One young man who appealed was Frank Lockwood. Lockwood was a young and single lithographic artist working in the Colne Valley. Privately, he was clearly horrified by the war and its consequences. He did not attest under the Derby scheme and as a result was called up in early 1916. His experience with the local tribunal at Linthwaite was an unhappy one; they spent only a few seconds in dismissing his case. With the aid of legal representation he challenged the decision at the East Central appeal tribunal. On 3 April 1916 he turned up at the Huddersfield police court and secured exemption until the end of his apprenticeship. The Linthwaite tribunal had turned him down on the grounds that his trade was not of national importance, but Lockwood had appealed on educational grounds. The appeal tribunal accepted his argument that the relevant clause of the Military Service Act (MSA) was 'if a man is being trained or educated for any work . . . it is expedient that he should continue to be so trained'.[4] As a result, it was nearly a year before Lockwood found himself in uniform. Lockwood served in a support arm, but his appeal spared him a year of uniformed discomfort. Cousins appears to have had a genuine patriotic motivation to serve, Lockwood clearly did not. But this was not in theory the concern of the tribunals.

---

[2] H. Cousins, *Diary*, Imperial War Museum (IWM). M. Macdonagh, *London During the War* (1935), 98–9.
[3] W. H. Scott, *Leeds and the Great War* (Leeds, 1923), 47.
[4] F. T. Lockwood Diary, 15 March, 3 April 1916. IWM.

III

This system was anything but a model of bureaucratic anonymity. It was rooted in the localities and conducted in the full glare of publicity. The local press reported avidly on tribunal proceedings. One of the paradoxes of conscription in Britain was that the system could only be made to work by a massive volunteer effort. The canvass for National Service registration was entirely voluntary. In Leeds this involved 200,000 separate visits by thousands of volunteers. Who these canvassers were varied from area to area and sometimes within areas . The listing and photographs from Hyde in Cheshire shows them to be predominantly middle-aged men. Seventy-one of the canvassers named were male and nine were female, though most of the sub-districts had no female canvassers.[5] After the canvass was completed, the next stage was to constitute the tribunals.

Some sense of the complex process of recruiting and setting-up a tribunal can be found in the files of the Bedfordshire appeals tribunal. The process was initiated by a memorandum from the Local Government Board written by the board's president, Walter Long. It called on the chairmen of county councils to choose persons of 'judicial and unprejudiced mind', a phrase underlined in the Bedfordshire copy, who would 'command the confidence of the community'. A fair proportion were to be direct representatives of labour. The tribunals were not to include those eligible for military service or those who already sat on local tribunals unless they were willing to resign that post; and 'women may be placed on the tribunal with advantage'.

Informal soundings were then made across the county. A Luton businessman, Thomas Keen, was recruited and in turn was asked to suggest names to represent labour in the town. He suggested several names from the local Amalgamated Society of Engineers, but noted that they would be reluctant to serve unless mandated by a union vote. In the event the president of the local trades council agreed to serve and his employer granted him one day a week to participate. The council clerk was meanwhile looking for a suitable representative for agricultural labour. This proved difficult because such men were nervous about the expenses involved in travelling to serve on a tribunal. Furthermore there were legitimate doubts about appointing someone who would be thought susceptible to landowner influence. It was concluded that what was ideally wanted was 'a man who all his life had been a wage earner but was now independent of everyone'. Finding a representative of urban labour in Bedford proved equally difficult. The name of a Mr Seamark was forwarded, 'an advanced Trade Unionist and Socialist leader—the type of man who ought to be on an Appeal tribunal'. Barbara Prothero was approached to sit as a woman on the tribunal, and provisionally agreed: 'I should like to do all that I can in the present crisis.' The tribunal was finally able to begin sitting on

[5] Scott, *Leeds*, 35; R. Sidebotham, *Hyde in Wartime* (Hyde, 1916), 27.

22 March 1916. It was soon swamped with work and indeed in the first three months several members resigned including Mr Marks, the clerk who had kept the correspondence file.[6]

The Bedfordshire appeal tribunal was thus not directly elected, it was compiled through an extended version of the old-boy network. At the same time there was a scrupulous effort to correspond with the spirit of the original memorandum. When advanced left-wing views were being put forward as a positive recommendation for appeal tribunal service, it is hard to dismiss the tribunals as failing to secure balance. One weakness was the interpretation of what was meant by labour representation. Not unnaturally the tribunal recruiters looked to the ranks of organized labour. But this meant that workers without the protection of a trade union could be seen as peculiarly vulnerable.

The total numbers who served on tribunals nationally must have been very substantial. A minimum of 20,000 must have served and, allowing for turnover, a figure of 40,000 is much more likely. Many tribunals were sitting twice or more per week from early 1916 onwards. The men who served—for they were overwhelmingly men, although some women did sit on appeal tribunals—have been aptly described as the type of people who would be approached to verify a passport application, in other words the locally prominent and reliable. Thus in Hyde, the tribunal included the mayor, a justice of the peace, a councillor, a solicitor, the chairman of the board of the local cotton mill, and a businessman. It should be noted, however, that tribunals at both the local and appeal levels were actively encouraged to appoint representatives of labour, usually trade union officials, the secretary of the local Carders' Association in the case of Hyde.[7]

The work was hard. Whilst it might reasonably be objected that 10 or 15 minutes was woefully inadequate to sit in judgement on what could be a life or death decision, the sheer numbers made tribunal work time consuming. Neville Chamberlain, active in every voluntary activity, both locally and nationally, noted in a letter in January 1916 that the tribunal was his 'most tiring work', sitting for seven hours on three days of the week. Charles Repington, famous as the military correspondent of *The Times*, sat on the Hampstead tribunal. At the first sitting it took two and a half hours to hear ten cases, in May he abandoned plans to travel to Yorkshire 'owing to the pressure of tribunal work', and in August after a 'long sitting' he did not get home until 9 p.m.; 'the Hampstead Tribunal', he recorded, 'have worked like Niggers'.[8] In the context of 60-hour weeks in the factories, let alone the Western Front, sympathy for tribunal members might seem misplaced, but it should be remembered that for the vast

---

[6] Bedfordshire Record Office, AT/1.   [7] Sidebotham, *Hyde*, 29.

[8] R. C. Self (ed.), *The Neville Chamberlain Diary Letters Vol. 1: The Making of a Politician, 1915–20* (Aldershot, 2000), 110. Neville Chamberlain to Hilda Chamberlain (sister), 29 Jan, 1916. C. Repington, *The First World War, Vol. 1* (1920), cites diary for 12 Jan., 19 May, 3 Aug. 1916, 105, 203, 297.

majority this was only one of several volunteer tasks that many performed in addition to their regular occupations.

IV

One of the most complete archival records of a particular tribunal is for Calne in Wiltshire, which has been extensively analysed by the local historian Ivor Slocombe.[9] Whilst it might easily be objected that the records of any individual tribunal are by their nature unrepresentative, it is equally apparent that many of the basic features of the operation of a tribunal can be generalized. Standardized guidelines were sent out to each tribunal, and in fact every tribunal was a negotiation between a national pattern and local ways of doing things. In the course of three years, the Calne tribunal met sixty times to consider 683 appeals related to 317 individual applicants. The decisions of the Calne tribunal break down as follows: complete exemption 152, temporary exemption 404, refusal of exemption 52, exemption from 'combatant service' 4, withdrawn 42, no recorded decision 2, adjourned 20, incomplete record 7.

The first striking point to note is how heavily the odds in Calne favoured the applicants. Almost half of the applicants to the local tribunal received 'complete exemption' at some point. This did not mean that they automatically avoided military service; the military representative could and did appeal such decisions to the county tribunal, but equally some of those refused exemption or granted only temporary exemption could and did do the same. A total of 44 cases from Calne were appealed to the county tribunal either by the appellant or the military representative, the original decision was upheld in 15 cases, in 22 cases the decision was harsher, and in 7 cases more lenient. By far the most common decision taken by the tribunal was one of temporary exemption, usually for three or six months. Men temporarily exempted, were, by definition likely to come in front of the tribunal again. As these numbers indicate, the typical outcome of a second appearance was a further temporary exemption. Examination of the Calne records demonstrates that for the first eighteen months of the operation of the tribunal a temporary exemption was overwhelmingly the most likely outcome, but that as the war progressed a definite decision one way or another became more likely.

Were there any general correlations in Calne between the type of applicant and the outcome? Taking individual decisions, it is quite clear that the self-employed and those employed within the family were much more successful at getting complete exemptions than those employed by others. Taking the first two groups together, out of 106 cases heard there were 49 total exemption decisions, as opposed to only 9 refusals of exemption. By contrast the employees

---

[9] I. Slocombe, 'Recruitment into the Armed Forces during the First World War: The Work of the Military Tribunals in Wiltshire, 1915–1918', *The Local Historian*, 30: 2 (May 2000), 105–223.

received only 49 complete exemptions from a total of 211 applications; 27 of the employees were refused altogether, which was a higher proportion than among the self-employed, but a less conspicuous gap than that relating to total exemption. The typical decision for employees was temporary exemption and in fact the records show that this was generally what was being applied for by their employers. Employer support was absolutely critical for employees. Of the two main criteria for making an appeal, employment and personal circumstances, the former was more likely to succeed in Calne. In fact, the regulations regarding personal circumstances were notoriously vague. The Calne tribunal tended to operate a very strict construction, granting personal exemptions only when they were fairly convinced that conscription would result in the absolute destitution of a dependent relative (and, although this was rarely mentioned, presumably a resultant charge on the rates).

Regarding employment criteria, the Calne Tribunal did tend to be somewhat more generous towards agriculture than to those employed in other areas. Most of the self-employed and family-employed exempted came from farms, as did most of the employees. But whether this amounted to an outright 'bias' remains unproven. Certainly many agricultural labourers were presented to tribunals as having indispensable 'skills'; indeed very few applications were ever made for labourers as such, they were invariably presented as stockmen, dairymen, carters, and engine drivers. On the other hand, the increasing mechanization of farm work, and the fact that a significant number of general agricultural labourers would already have left for the army or industry before conscription had started, means that this is not automatically to be dismissed as special pleading.

Slocombe estimates that approximately 29 per cent of the pre-war population of military age made an appeal to the local tribunal in Calne district. It should immediately be noted that this percentage does not even begin to tell the whole story of appeals for exemption from military service, as the number of appeals relates only to the number of men actually called up. It therefore excludes those 'badged' as exempt on grounds of work of clear national importance (for example, most farm owners, railway workers, etc.) and those who had already been completely rejected from military service on health grounds. Of equal importance, it ignores those who had moved away since 1914 and those who had already volunteered. The latter number may have been very substantial, many appeals were couched precisely to indicate the indispensability of an individual applicant in a context where half or more of the pre-war workforce had already volunteered. In those circumstances it is fair to assume that a majority, and probably a substantial majority, of the men conscripted in the Calne rural district appealed the decision or had employers who would appeal for them. Conscientious objection was an exotic rarity, indeed in the whole county area for Wiltshire there appear to have been only 27 cases out of 1,500 appeals at county level (and these cases were much more likely than those relating to work or family circumstances to be appealed).

Overall the Calne tribunal was probably at the more generous end of the spectrum. The particular circumstances of agricultural needs and rural life made a systematic 'comb-out' particularly difficult by 1916–18 without immediate and obvious damage to the fabric of rural society and the all-important maintenance of food production. But were urban tribunals automatically more harsh in their operations?

The best description of an urban tribunal in operation, as seen from the 'bench', is by Harry Cartmell in Preston. Some of the cases before the Preston tribunal seemed to be drawn from the bumper book of Lancashire stereotypes. In all seriousness, boot repairers presented themselves as clog-makers and as such indispensable to local industry. An advocate argued the case for exemption of a tripe-dresser on the grounds that tripe, trotters, and cowheels were essential food. The mayor dryly responded that these were very delectable, but 'not perhaps essential'. Subsequently, in Cartmell's own words, 'from tripe to black pudding is an easy transit'. A black-pudding maker explained that his wares were very popular among the troops. Attempts to automate the process had failed and the job was unsuitable for women. Giving a lurid description of the processes involved, he had no difficulty in convincing the tribunal that his was not a profession open to dilution. Cartmell claimed that their only hesitation before exempting him was because, 'a man accustomed to this sanguinary business might find better scope for his skill in the army'.[10]

The Preston panel found themselves undergoing a rapid and thorough education in the ordinary working lives of Preston men. Impromptu demonstrations of skills were staged before the tribunal, products were displayed, and even on some occasions field trips were carried out to workplaces. Not everyone appealed in good faith; if the testimony of the many businessmen's sons who appealed on the basis that their father was too old to work at 50 were to be believed, Cartmell suggested, then 'senile decay sets in at a very early age in Preston'. Conversely many men in their early twenties were presented as surprisingly indispensable to their businesses, despite the fact that they were only receiving the salary of ordinary assistants. But the social investigation aspect of the tribunal revealed many cases of quiet virtue which Cartmell recorded with approval. There was a young man who revealed reluctantly under questioning that since his mother had died and his father was confined to bed by illness, he had become the household's sole wage earner, and also cared for his younger siblings and did all the domestic tasks. He was exempted temporarily. Even more striking to the tribunal was a widower who ran his business while bringing up five children 'without female assistance' and who displayed no awareness that he was doing anything remarkable. The tribunal exempted him unconditionally with praise for his devotion to duty. Referring to unmarried young men who had apparently made the decision to put their own interests second to caring for aged parents, Cartmell remarked, 'we met many heroes of that kind'.

---

[10] H. Cartmell, *For Remembrance* (Preston, 1919), 70–2.

Indeed Cartmell believed that young single men had been revealed to be admirable in their familial responsibility, more so than many of the married.[11] Most of those who appealed in Preston had legal representation. On the whole these local solicitors were conscientious in making a legitimate case for their clients, although in the case of a travelling fairground worker, the solicitor was largely pushed aside by the man's mother who conducted the appeal herself, to the amusement and exasperation of bench and brief alike. Neville Chamberlain appears to have been less sympathetic than Cartmell, but also saw humour in the situation:

One man begged to be postponed as unless he were there he did not know what would become of his troop of boy scouts! Another said he made Jews Harps for the export trade. I asked where he sent them to. 'To South Africa mostly, sir' 'Well' said I gravely, there are a great many jews there,' & the Committee all looked very solemn.[12]

Although such comments hardly accorded with the gravity of the decisions, it could be suggested that the long hours and serious responsibility involved in sitting on a tribunal made the occasional resort to bad attempts at humour almost inevitable. Nevertheless the civic dignitaries who sat on tribunals operated within powerful informal constraints. Arbitrary and tyrannical behaviour was not only against the spirit and purposes for which the tribunals had been set up in the first place, but, particularly for local politicians, likely to come back to haunt them. In fact, they found themselves performing a delicate balancing act: they needed to reflect popular opinion by not tolerating 'shirking' whilst at the same time providing adequate benefit of the doubt in dealing with 'genuine' cases. To understand how this balance might be struck it is necessary to turn to the appellants themselves.

V

The few remaining solicitors' briefs for tribunal hearings give a good feel for the nature of appeals. The firm of Brundrett, Whitmore, and Randall preserved a number of files on appeals which went before the City of London tribunal. An umbrella and walking-stick manufacturer appealed on behalf of two of his employees. One was his accountant and traveller, who was also his brother-in-law. His assistance was needed because the employer claimed defective eyesight. The other appeal was for a skilled worker. The firm had already lost ten out of fourteen men to the colours. There was no chance of substitution, 'even if I could obtain women sufficiently skilled, I could not employ them because the buildings could not be altered to comply with LCC regulations'. The employer needed these men to keep his business going, the profits of which kept himself,

[11] Cartmell, For Remembrance, 74–6.
[12] Self (ed.), Neville Chamberlain Diary Letters, Vol. 1:, letter to Ida Chamberlain (sister), 23 Jan. 1916, 109.

his wife, and three children. The solicitors in these cases charged the not inconsiderable sum of 3 guineas for their advice. Walking sticks and umbrellas were clearly not essential industry, but a claim by a family with an ironmongery business to maintain their son of military age centred on their production of 'trench barrows'. The firm had been reduced from twelve to five men and the unmarried 35-year-old man concerned was 'the only one left who knows anything of the business'. The most detailed claim, which came from a small businessman on his own behalf, affords both a snapshot of society in January 1917 and an example of the hundreds of thousands of detailed appeals being lodged. The appeal was supported by several other documents verifying details of the claim, which was both domestic and business related. It illustrates both the way that the conscription net was scooping up the owners of small businesses and one of the mechanisms they used to cope with this. Among the letters included is one from another businessman, who requests that he take over the business in order to keep it going, so that his family will receive support.[13]

Cartmell points out that a tribunal sat solely to hear appeals against conscription, that it had no power to initiate the process. This was not well understood. The tribunal would receive letters denouncing 'shirkers' and demanding that they be called up. The most extraordinary of these came from discontented wives. One woman wrote of her husband, 'I cannot understand him getting off every time . . . Come for him now, it will make a better man of him . . . he might be the missing link.' Another wrote that her husband, 'was impossible to live with through his drunkenness and temper . . . I have lost relatives in this War whilst he hides there to live a life of laziness.' In the latter case Cartmell wrote that the lady wanted a separation and felt that the tribunal would be just as effective as the magistrates, with the added advantage of a regularly paid allowance.[14]

Overall, regarding the real business of hearing appeals, Cartmell's description rings true. In many respects the tribunals were a safeguard against the tyranny of public opinion. The general public seem to have been much quicker to judge their neighbours as shirkers than the men on the bench. Cartmell had been convinced of the need for conscription precisely because he believed that the voluntary system was putting unbearable pressure on men whose responsibilities ought to keep them out of the army. He and his colleagues patiently investigated those responsibilities. In conclusion, Cartmell wrote, 'we were appointed to give effect to a pledge that the circumstances of men should be fully and carefully considered before they were called up to the Army. That pledge was carried out in Preston.'[15]

[13] Solicitors files: IWM, Misc. 133, 2051.   [14] Cartmell, *For Remembrance*, 84–5.
[15] Ibid., 86.

VI

Joking about cases, given the grave nature of tribunal activity, was to say the least in bad taste. Frank Lockwood was furious about his appeal tribunal hearing even though he was successful. He had been collecting examples of bizarre and perverse tribunal decisions in the form of press clippings.[16] Immediately after his own first unsuccessful appeal he had clipped an example from Market Bosworth where the men employed by the Atherstone Hunt were exempted on the grounds of their importance in maintaining the stock of horses: he commented, 'could farce go any further?' This did not stop him being hurt when he found himself pilloried in the local press as just such a phoney example. At his successful appeal, it was claimed in the press that his solicitor had argued for exemption on the grounds that as an apprentice map-maker he would be needed to 'alter the map of the world'. Lockwood was furious to read this, he was a lithographic artist and map-making was just a sideline, and it had not been his solicitor who had made the comment but a member of the tribunal. In his diary Lockwood vents his anger at such comments made at both his tribunal hearings. The joke continued to rankle; he copied a quotation from the popular weekly, *The Passing Show* which had coined a new definition; 'TRIBUNAL—Formerly a court of justice. Now a collection of local celebrities who send other men's sons into the army.' To which Lockwood added his own bitter coda, 'and make jokes about it'. Lockwood also cited a case of a woman whose seventh son and sole support was conscripted.[17]

But were the tribunals unfair? Lockwood might have paused to reflect that even though his pride had been offended, he had in fact been dealt with generously. The appeal tribunal in Huddersfield had used a very loose construction of the law to allow him to finish his apprenticeship and he had been extremely lucky. Repington's account records that he had initially been suspicious of his colleagues, but quickly concluded that they were 'careful, sympathetic and thorough' and that their decisions were very just. Repington was *parti pris*, but the image of the tribunals as tyrannical owes more to the martyrology of conscientious objectors than to social reality. While conscientious objection on socialist grounds was unlikely to get a fair hearing, conscientious objection on even the strangest religious grounds generally did. The real problem was less one of tyranny than of apparent whimsicality and the defence of local interests. A memorandum from Auckland Geddes to the War Cabinet in July 1917 complained that 'the present exemption system is based almost entirely on individual or local considerations'. The result was that one tribunal in a seaside town would exempt all of its bathing box keepers and boatmen on the grounds of vital interest to 'the national health', whilst another up the coast would indiscrim-

[16] Cartmell was critical of press coverage which tended to focus on 'amusing or abnormal' cases. Cartmell, *For Remembrance*, 86.
[17] F. T. Lockwood Diary, 16 April 1916, 28 Oct. 1916, 3 March 1917.

inately call up fishermen. Geddes was worried about the impression given: 'confusion breeds inequality of treatment; inequality of treatment, a sense of injustice; a sense of injustice, hatred; hatred of government, revolt and revolution'. Whilst this was overstating a bit, there can be little doubt that compulsion, introduced in the name of fairness, had thrown up its own contradictions.[18]

The vernacular Scots poet Charles Murray savagely satirized what he perceived as the corruption in rural tribunals where it was believed that local farmers co-operated to keep their own children and employees out of uniform. Murray probably had a point. Figures from several rural areas do seem to suggest that the families of tenant farmers were remarkably exempt from military service. This was to some extent deliberate, a means of ensuring essential food supplies, but caused anger none the less. Other forms of social pressure also existed. Letters to Geddes from South Wales suggest that local tribunals had more or less given up on ruling against miners, and the tribunals were almost in a state of mutiny. Small businesses, probably the hardest hit sector under the Military Service Acts, were beginning to organize local lobbying associations and were petitioning government. By January 1918 the tribunals had been rendered problematic more by their leniency than by their toughness.

VII

In April 1918 the discretion and independence of tribunals was limited by the introduction of tougher guidelines, as Geddes had long demanded. Nevertheless they continued to operate until the end of the war. Far from being anonymous and centralized, the British conscription law had been mediated through a tribunal system which was intimate, local, highly personal, and closely scrutinized. In practice, efficiency in the use of manpower had been traded for the manufacture of consent. A significant reason why conscription was not extended to Ireland was that the tribunal system was self-evidently unworkable in that context. Indeed one of the main reasons behind Geddes's support for Irish conscription was that it would serve as an opportunity to abolish the British tribunals. His cabinet colleagues baulked at this, but it meant that Irish conscription was never workable.

Do the tribunals help us with the idea of civil society? They certainly provide a classic case of how the British state operated in wartime. State power was strengthened by new statute law, and by a battery of emergency powers. But the operation of law occurred in a very local context. The tribunals constituted a site in which competing societal interests were weighed up. The rights of the individual were judged against the demands of the nation within a set of rules. These rules were generally accepted, but they required detailed negotiation. Interested groups were represented: organized labour, industrial employers,

---

[18] A. Geddes, 'The Theory and Practice of Recruiting', PRO, CAB 24, GT 1484, July 1917.

commerce and landowners, a few women; and the process was conducted with an eye to public perceptions of equity and justice. The volunteers who made the judgements, despite occasional and understandable lapses into inappropriate humour, generally did so with a full awareness of the desperate seriousness of their task. These voluntary bodies serving the state were absolutely typical. The most important wartime tasks were conducted in this fashion. Pensions committees dealt with the wounded and the bereaved, local food committees came to control rationing and distribution, land use committees made sweeping judgements about the competence or otherwise of farmers, eligibility for separation allowances was judged by the Soldiers and Sailors Families Association. Propaganda was carried out by local branches of the Parliamentary Recruiting Committees and later by the National War Aims Committee. The war itself massively extended the task of the volunteer magistracy who had to deal with the massive surge in workload caused by the enforcement of the provisions that were authorized by the Defence of the Realm Act. These 'state volunteers' mingled with and were sometimes almost indistinguishable from a huge 'private' volunteer effort. To draw a hard and fast line between voluntary association and the state in Britain in the context of the First World War is, or at least should be, self-evident nonsense.

10

The Countryside, Planning, and Civil Society in Britain, 1926–1947

JOHN STEVENSON

I

William Cobbett in 1829 had portrayed flourishing rural communities, but-tressed both by property rights and rights to public welfare, as an essential feature of what he called 'civil society'.[1] But, like many of Cobbett's viewpoints, this was an unusual perspective among users of the term. For much of the later eighteenth and the nineteenth centuries, rural life and agricultural interests were more often portrayed as the antithesis of the 'civil': as fatally imbricated in the gross inequalities of status, cultural torpor, and limitations on personal freedom associated (from a liberal and metropolitan vantage-point) with the residues of feudalism and protection. Echoes of this outlook—of rural interests and culture as being both excluded from, and antithetical to, wider civil society—can be heard on many sides in the 'countryside debate' of the early twenty-first century. Many recent theorists of civil society have likewise assumed that the associa-tional, participatory, and 'communicative' activities associated with civil soci-ety are quintessentially urban, and dependent upon the intimate geographical concentration of city life.

Nevertheless, the part played by rural affairs in the political culture of Britain during the earlier and mid-twentieth century belies this exclusively urban out-look. Between the two world wars concern for preservation and regeneration of the countryside, and of 'outdoor' activities associated with country life, became a major component of a wide public consensus that spanned both rural and urban dwellers. This development drew upon many different sources of inspir-ation, some of them 'public' but many of a voluntarist and 'private' character. At a largely imaginative level, in the visual arts and writing on 'country' themes, the rural landscape acquired a momentum as a symbol of national identity which was to find its apotheosis in many of the most pervasive images of Britain during the Second World War. This was not, however, a merely imaginative and

---

[1] William Cobbett, *The Poor Man's Friend or Essays on the Rights and Duties of the Poor* (1829), 9–29; *Cobbett's Cottage Economy* (1821); above pp. 26, 37.

cultural phenomenon, but one which found expression in a number of very weighty non-governmental organizations. Their concerns were to be increasingly reflected in the programmes of the various political parties, though moulded in each case by their distinctive ideologies. The Second World War witnessed, as in other spheres, a degree of compromise and co-operation on planning and the future of the countryside that was to last well beyond the war and decisively to shape the framework of policy for several decades to come. Legislation on key areas concerned with agriculture, conservation, access to the countryside, and planning control was realized in the years immediately following the war. In the transition from pre-war aspirations to a post-war legislative programme, a major role in shaping the outlook of central authorities was played by a group of fast-growing organizations and pressure groups concerned with a very wide spectrum of 'countryside' issues, that ranged from leisure access and preservation of 'natural beauty' through to economic regeneration and town and country planning. These groupings, often overlapping in personnel and issues, were crucial in shaping the wider consensus that found its opportunity in the collectivist mood of wartime and immediately post-war Britain.

II

Historians of British culture between the wars have become familiar with the concept of 'deep England'. As a cultural construct it has been seen as an often nostalgic reaffirmation of pastoral and ruralist themes in the face of industrialization and urbanization. Certainly from at least the 1880s there had been a gradually emerging exaltation of the rural way of life as the epitome of 'Englishness'. The Englishman was often portrayed as 'at heart a countryman', and national values as being based upon the timeless qualities of the landscape and village life. These ideas were carried forward into the 1920s by the Georgian poets and painters in a period when new challenges were being faced in the upheavals and uncertainties of 'modernity': the Great War, the Russian Revolution, the onset of the depression, and the rise of totalitarian governments of both left and right.[2] A more prosaic but potentially even more subversive challenge came from 'modernity' in a rather different guise, in the advance of a secular, cosmopolitan, consumerist mass culture, often American in origin. Against these threats to national identity could be pitted the unchanging values of the 'English' countryside. A striking feature of the years after the Great War was the popularization of writing about the rural landscape and way of life. There was an explosion of travelogue and guidebook literature on Britain's

[2] See J. Marsh, *Back to the Land: The Pastoral Impulse in England from 1880–1914* (1982); M. Wiener, *English Culture and the Decline of the Industrial Spirit* (Cambridge, 1981); A. Howkins, 'The Discovery of Rural England', in R. Colls and P. Dodd (eds.), *Englishness: Politics and Culture, 1880–1920* (1986).

countryside and heritage, and on 'country' related matters of every kind from gardening to ornithology. These areas became one of the most profitable and popular genres of English publishing between the wars, only rivalled in their appeal by detective stories (with many of the latter being typically located in idealized rural settings). The pace was set by H. V. Morten's *In Search of England* (1927), seeking the 'village that symbolises England'. Complemented by *In Search of Scotland* (1929) and *In Search of Wales* (1932), Morten's was soon only one of innumerable attempts to capitalize upon the growing market for books on the landscape and buildings of Britain.[3] The largest group were those produced by the publisher and writer Harry Batsford, particularly the two series entitled 'The Face of Britain' and 'British Heritage'. Characterized by their attractive, colourful dust-jackets, and liberally illustrated by prints, engravings, and photographs, they helped to weave the countryside, villages, country towns, and historic buildings into a tapestry of what was deemed to be peculiarly valuable in the nation's heritage. Urban landscapes and large towns were not excluded where they formed part of the 'historic' character of a region. In a theme that was to become increasingly insistent over the course of the 1930s, almost anything that was old was seen as requiring recognition and preservation. As Clive Rouse wrote in Batsford's *The Old Towns of England*, published in 1936:

It may be asked why one should write on the subject of towns at all, when every week-end sees an ever increasing rush away from them into the country. That in itself is a principal reason why more attention should be paid to them and to the preservation of the many treasures they contain. They are passing through a very critical stage, at the mercy of 'improvements', demolitions, and sickening modern standardization by a host of unsympathetic local authorities.[4]

Batsford's volumes in the 'British Heritage series' included almost everything that could be considered 'traditional', widening the remit of 'Heritage' to include London, 'Old English Customs and Ceremonies', 'Old Household Life', and 'The Old Public Schools of England'. These images of 'Olde England' were brought together in the multi-authored volumes of The Pilgrim's Library, published under such titles as *The Beauty of Britain*, *The Legacy of England*, *Nature in Britain*, and *The English Countryside*, with contributors who included H. J. Massingham, H. E. Bates, G. M. Young, J. B. Priestley, Edmund Blunden, Henry Williamson, and A. G. Street.

Arthur Mee's *The King's England*, one of the largest and most ambitious of the projects for the 'rediscovery' of Britain, styled itself as a 'A New Domesday Book of 10,000 Towns and Villages'. Its forty-one volumes, with an introductory volume entitled *Enchanted Land*, was organized on a county-by-county basis, but included large towns and a volume devoted solely to London. Highly illustrated by the standards of the time, the volumes were notable for their

---

[3] See V. Cunningham, *British Writers of the Thirties* (Oxford, 1988), ch. 6.
[4] C. Rouse, *The Old Towns of England* (1936), Preface.

close-textured survey of each county. The publicity for the series was in no doubt about their comprehensiveness:

Nothing like these books has ever been presented to the English people . . . The Compilers have travelled half-a-million miles and have prepared a unique picture of our countryside as it has come down through the ages, a census of all that is enduring and worthy of record.[5]

The King's England took on an almost reverential quality when it sought to depict the 'enduring' continuities of English life. Past battles between Saxon, Dane, and Norman, and the internecine wars of later centuries, fused imperceptibly with memorials of village churches and in particular with the very recent and poignant memorials to the Great War. Indeed the Arthur Mee guides could be seen as a principal target for the more austere virtues espoused by the *The Buildings of England* series, compiled by Nicholas Pevsner in the years after the war. Pevsner's series deliberately eschewed and parodied 'the three dictatorial qualities of our guidebook trade', 'quaintness, oldness or association'. But it was precisely these qualities which provided the staple fare for the guidebook industry between the wars.[6] Such books were also often extremely attractive. Travelogue and 'country' writing called for pictorial illustration, and it was fortunate for publishers that the collapse of print and picture sales during the depression drew many artists and engravers into commercial work for the burgeoning guidebook market. Artists such as Eric Ravilious, John and Paul Nash, John Piper, and Eric Bawden worked on the Shell Guides, whose first general editor was John Betjeman.[7] In some instances the quality of illustration turned the ventures into works of art in their own right, as with Clare Leighton's *Four Hedges: A Gardener's Chronicle*, published by Gollanz in 1935, which went through four impressions within the year and a cheap edition by autumn 1936. Such works doubtless responded to consumer taste and demand; but many of these artists were personally drawn to pastoral themes no less than the Georgian writers and poets, often deliberately eschewing any hint of modernity in their portrayal of an essential England:

The landscapes portrayed by many of these painters . . . lack suburban sprawl, home of Mr and Mrs Bungaloid. They lack telegraph poles, tractors and combine harvesters; corn is usually gathered in stooks and rabbits still scoot across the stubble. Although when used commercially, as in posters for railway corporations, these things could become a facile mannerism, they were also an affirmation of Britain which was under constant threat throughout the 1920s and 30s.[8]

   [5] The advertisement was placed before the frontispiece of each volume. The series employed an art editor for each volume; as an example, the Cornish volume of 317 pages contained 173 photographs and covered 250 locations.
   [6] Methuen's 'Companion' Books, covering most of the shire counties were another example. The comment from Pevsner's *Buildings of England* comes from the cover of the Penguin editions published from 1951. It was subsequently dropped from the hardback series.
   [7] I. Jeffrey, *The British Landscape, 1920–1950* (1984), 7–16; C. Hemming, *British Landscape Painters: A History and Gazeteer* (1989), 107–16.
   [8] Hemming, *British Landscape*, 25–6.

The 'country turn' also saw increasing interest in classic authors of an earlier era, such as Gilbert White and William Cobbett.[9] Where that rural order could be still recaptured in memoir, it was assured of ready success, as in Flora Thompson's trilogy, *Lark Rise to Candleford*, published between 1939 and 1944. Thompson's appeal lay in her depiction of a vanished era of village life in north Oxfordshire before the Great War. Henry Williamson's *The Village Book* (1930), Edmund Blunden's *English Villages* (1931), the Collins 'Britain in Pictures' series, and Francis Brett Young's *Portrait of a Village* (1936) were all part of a continuum of 'village' writing that flowed unabated into the period of the Second World War. Moreover, this was not a cultural trope which belonged to any one wing of the political spectrum. While G. D. H. Cole wrote a biography of Cobbett, Stanley Baldwin publicly espoused the evocation of Shropshire in the novels of Mary Webb, one of the most widely read 'rural' novelists of the period. Valentine Cunningham has identified the *Criterion* as 'a kind of house journal' for British ruralism in the aftermath of the Great War, but one which attracted a very politically diverse group of contributors that included Henry Williamson, H. J. Massingham, G. M. Trevelyan, John Betjeman, H. M. Tomlinson, T. F. Powys, and T. S. Eliot.[10]

The appeal of pastoral images and rural writing thus defies neat political categorization. While, for some, part of the appeal lay in anti-urbanism and a certain snobbish and élite distaste for mass urban society, for others it often accompanied a degree of demotic populism and an apolitical patriotism. Hence one of the most prominent characteristics of 'country' writing between the wars was its evocation of Englishness. For Batsford's *The Legacy of England* in 1935 England meant the English countryside, with essays on its principal features, including the landscape, the farm, the country house, the country inn, the country church, and the village. The landscape and the village were perhaps the most commonly evoked of the symbols of national identity. The landscape was the essential backdrop to many of the writings about the British character, few writers differentiating between 'Englishness' and 'Britishness' in this context. For many the landscape itself was endowed with unique qualities that were reflected in national character and institutions, as for Anthony Collett, writing (presumably with wholly unconscious irony) in the strike-torn year of 1926:

Thanks to long peace on our own soil, the development of English landscape has been rich and continuous. While the English have laid bare their bones in all lands, the villages that nursed them have been free to spread loosely afield, adding hedge to hedge and orchard to orchard, until they nestle in a landscape that has grown up with them. Nowhere else have man and Nature co-operated so intimately.[11]

---

[9] Cole's life of Cobbett was published in 1924, and was followed by a three-volume edition of Cobbett's *Rural Rides* in 1930. Cole also edited Cobbett's letters and other writings.

[10] Cunningham, *British Writers*, 230–1.

[11] A. Collett, *The Changing Face of England* (1926), x.

Virtually the same sentiments were articulated a decade later by W. S. Shears: 'No other land has a more glorious story of achievement, none a more entrancing countryside, where the works of generations of the people blend imperceptibly with those of nature. The splendour of our domestic architecture, and of our country gardens, is unsurpassed anywhere in the world.'[12]

The village, as we have seen, occupied a special place in country writing, not simply as a subject for nostalgic reflection but as the perceived core of the English way of life. It was a theme that became more insistent with the approach of war. C. Henry Warren's *England is a Village*, published in 1940 but written in the last months of peace, caught the transition exactly from a latent and relatively subdued sense of identity to one sharpened by the approach of danger. Warren wrote of his fictionally titled 'Larkfield':

Larkfield watches the approach of happenings which have no equal in terror or frightfulness. And meanwhile spring unfolds with a completeness only matched by the completeness of the winter that preceded it: the English countryside puts forth her loveliest and best to confront the enemy, like 'a kneeling angel holding faith's front line'.

Again, the village was not merely a nostalgic symbol, but something essential to survival and renewal:

it is a dream that must be kept before our waking eyes when the horrors that sought to blind us are past. For it is from the ashes (if such it be) of the Larkfields of England that our phoenix strength shall rise. England's might is still in her fields and villages, and though the whole weight of mechanized armies rolls over them, in the end they will triumph. The best of England is a village.[13]

At another level, representation of the English countryside took on a more transcendental dimension as an expression of national identity. In the introduction to a post-war edition of *The Natural History of Selborne*, James Fisher attempted to sum up Gilbert White's continued appeal, 'what makes him all things to all, so that he has a message for the sportsman and the scientist, the poet and the peasant, the nature-lover and the naturalist?' It was not, he suggested, merely love of nature, however universally understood:

I believe I know what it is: England. Not England as a material place so much as that England which lives in men's minds, and which many know and understand, but which can be described or crystallised only by the finest and truest and best. Indeed, to describe it, it is necessary not only to be simple and good and true, but to be intelligent, a quality which White had abundantly; and to be humorous, which he also was. Moreover, two further qualities are essential . . . and that they guide still, a great many English people is something to be thankful for. The qualities I mean are humanity and tolerance.[14]

Similarly, the 'Englishness of English Art' was seen as bound up in its nativist traditions of writing about and painting the landscape. In his chapter on

[12] W. S. Shears, *This England: A Book of the Shires and Counties* (1936), 7.
[13] C. Henry Warren, *England is a Village* (1940), ix.
[14] Introduction to Gilbert White, *The Natural History of Selborne*, ed. by J. Fisher (1947), xxi.

'Landscape' in *The Legacy of England*, Edmund Blunden drew upon, among others, the writings of Chaucer, Evelyn, Tusser, and Gilpin, concluding with the English school of watercolourists and 'Lake poets' of the romantic era.[15] Watercolour, lyric poetry, the flowing line of engraving, and the melancholy strains of English music were evoked as characteristic of a 'national' style. To Paul Nash's question in 1933: 'To what extent has contemporary art in England a national character?', Herbert Read answered in the affirmative:

One returns . . . to a certain nativeness, a quality representing the historic English tradition in English art . . . it is a quality which we find in the delicate stone tracery of an English cathedral, in the linear lightness and fantasy of English illuminated manuscripts, in the silvery radiance of our stained glass. The same quality is expressed, distinctly, in our poetry and our music. It is not a conscious tradition: it is perhaps an emanation of our soil and our climate, as inevitable and everlastingly vernal as an English meadow.[16]

III

Such sentiments among a cultured élite would have been less significant had they not infused a much broader spectrum of popular, urban, and even 'modernist' culture in inter-war Britain. The genres of 'travel' and 'country' writing were largely designed to interpret the countryside to suburban and city dwellers. Moreover, they also found a ready response in the 'substantive outdoor movement' of the inter-war years. Although the railways and cycling had opened up much of the countryside to urban recreation by the Edwardian era, it was after the Great War that urban irruption into the countryside began to generate a new kind of popular leisure economy. Several factors were at work here: greater affluence for those in regular employment; the spread of paid holidays; the enforced 'leisure' of the unemployed; and the cult of physical exercise and outdoor recreations. While seaside resorts and urban-based recreation grew apace, one of the most striking features of the period was the fashion for outdoor pursuits of every kind: hiking, rambling, cycling, mountaineering, camping, and youth hostelling. Combined with the growth of motoring (not at this time seen as posing a threat to pedestrian pursuits) and of coach and bus networks, the countryside was becoming increasingly popular as a playground for urban dwellers. Most significantly it ranged across the classes, Richard Hoggart noting in the west Yorkshire of the 1930s that

the craze was for 'hiking', and though that seemed to me to affect the lower middle-classes more than others, the working-classes went too, on to the dales and hills and moors, which luckily were not far from most of the large towns. If walking is not markedly typical of working-class people, then cycling is.[17]

---

[15] E. Blunden in *The Legacy of England* (1935), 1–35.
[16] Cited in A. Garrett, *A History of British Wood Engraving* (Tunbridge Wells, 1978), 202–3.
[17] R. Hoggart, *The Uses of Literacy* (1971), 278, cited in H. Taylor, *A Claim on the Countryside: A History of the British Outdoor Movement* (Edinburgh, 1997), 227, and *passim*, 226–41.

As Harvey Taylor has shown, such pursuits sustained a dense network of local clubs and societies, many of them with associational affiliations dating from before the First World War, such as the Workers' Education Association, the churches and political parties, and the numerous Clarion clubs. New rambling clubs sprouted, organized in local federations such as the Manchester Federation of Ramblers and the Sheffield and District Ramblers' Federation. When the Ramblers' Association was formed in 1935 it brought these local groupings into a national association with their own magazine.[18] But they were only the organized tip of the iceberg of thousands who poured out of the urban areas into the countryside at every opportunity. Cycling, like hiking, boomed, carrying individuals and organized bodies of cyclists into the countryside at weekends and holidays. The need for cheap accommodation other than camping, itself much encouraged by the burgeoning Scout and Guide movements, gave rise to the hugely popular Youth Hostel Association, founded in 1930. The YHA followed on from the hostels and basic accommodation already set up by bodies such as the Northumbrian Trampers' Guild, the Scottish Young Men's Holiday Fellowship, the Workers' Travel Association, and the Liverpool and District Ramblers' Federation, among others. It also attracted considerable backing from voluntary bodies who saw 'outdoor' recreations as offering a valuable alternative to urban life. The YHA received sympathetic assistance from the Forestry Commission and the National Trust, together with financial support from bodies such as the Cadbury and Carnegie Trusts. The YHA proved an enormous popular success: by 1939 there were 297 hostels, a membership of 83,000, and more than half a million 'nights' booked by youth hostellers.[19]

Motoring was also an increasingly pervasive factor in opening up the countryside. By 1939 there were 2 million private cars in Britain, and bank holiday traffic jams, Sunday afternoon outings, day trips, and excursions had become a commonplace. Although the first motor tour guides appeared before 1914, it was after the Great War that the motoring revolution really took off, exposing the small towns and villages of southern England and popular beauty spots in the countryside to an influx of tourism on a completely new scale. Guidebooks, like those of Shell and Dunlop, specifically catered for the motoring tourist, opening up the countryside with detailed maps and interesting things to see. The cover of the sixth edition of the Dunlop Guide showed a fashionable 'tourer' parked in the middle of a traditional English village. An introductory essay on 'Week-end Touring' offered the lure of escape to the countryside:

As every year brings increasing strain and effort and responsibility in the world of business, so every year the week-end respite becomes more precious to those who are in the thick of things, those to whom work and business mean something more than the

[18] See Taylor, A Claim on the Countryside, 231.
[19] Including the Ulster, Scottish, and Eire associations, the British Isles had 397 hostels and over 106,000 members by 1939. On the YHA and its antecedents, see Taylor, A Claim, 251–4.

jog-trot performance of an allotted task for eight hours a day. For those people, from the high financier down to the small but enterprising tradesman, the week-end break is the thing that makes the rest of the week endurable, and it goes without saying that the car and the freedom it brings are the essence of the weekend breaks so far as its recreative value goes . . . Here in Britain we have the most interesting old country in the world and an infinitely greater variety of landscape than can be found in any area of the same extent elsewhere. Then what a tragedy not to make the most of it . . .

The week-ender was also enjoined to appreciate not only the countryside and Britain's churches and castles, but also its country houses 'so often neglected' and to look out for 'the quaint and beautiful in old houses, including humble country cottages'.[20]

A further striking feature of inter-war years Britain was the way in which increasing interest in the countryside operated to produce simultaneously *both* a demand for greater access, particularly to moorland and mountain areas, *and* a growing concern for conservation and planning. Pressure was felt on every side. The very popularity of the outdoors brought threats to the unspoiled areas people sought to enjoy. 'Tripper-bashing' and a distaste for the large-scale invasion of the countryside and beauty spots, whether by 'mass rambles' or coach parties, became a stock-in-trade of some 'country' writers. For many the gimcrack development of caravan sites, filling stations, and cafés which sprang up to meet their needs were a disaster. 'Litter' was already being denounced as the 'grimy visiting card' of democracy;[21] while 'roadhouses' serving cocktails and exhibiting the chrome and plate glass of 1930s 'modernism' began to compete with 'picturesque' country pubs.

IV

Despite all its attractions, however, the visual beauty of the English countryside was a deceptive beauty of decay. Fears for the future of historic sites under the deluge of tourists and day-trippers only added to already existing concerns for the well-being of agriculture and the countryside as a whole. The long-running agricultural depression from the end of the nineteenth century through to the inter-war years—made worse by the artificial but temporary expansion of wartime—had left many parts of rural Britain in a parlous economic state. The 'great betrayal' of 1921, with the removal of the protection introduced for the duration of the Great War, exposed British agriculture to the full rigours of world competition at a time of falling prices. Whatever the beauties of the landscape and the virtues of village life, the depressing economic reality of British agriculture between the wars often took the form of landowners eager to sell-up

[20] *The Dunlop Guide to Great Britain*, 6th edn. (Cheltenham, 1930), xiv, xvii–xviii.
[21] *The Threat to the Peak* devoted a section to litter, pp. 44–7; bylaws existed against it from the 1888 Local Government Act.

and unwilling to invest in either land or buildings, over-burdened farmers who had bought out their tenancies with mortgages in the great land sales that followed the war, and a continued drift from the land of its traditional labour force. The break-up of the great estates and especially the decline of the middle-ranking landowners reinforced a sense of an old order crumbling. It was not simply the great houses, however, but many areas of the land itself that exhibited a derelict appearance. As the Scott Report noted in 1942:

Less arable land was to be seen in the landscape, the number of derelict fields, rank with coarse matted grass, thistle, weeds, and brambles, multiplied; ditches became choked and no longer served as effective drains; hedges became overgrown and straggled over the edges of fields; gates and fences fell into disrepair; farm roads were left unmade. Signs of decay were to be seen also in many of the buildings ... the landscape of 1938 had, in many districts, assumed a neglected and unkempt appearance.[22]

The harsher realities of rural life had been well known to social investigators for several generations. Incomes and living conditions were poorer in the country than in the towns and the squalor of urban slums was matched if not surpassed by the less visible, but more widely dispersed poverty of the countryside. The statistics of the rural economy told their own story. Agricultural wages, even for workers with scarce and specialist skills, were among the lowest in the country and remained so up to and after the Second World War, falling well below the average for unskilled labour in the towns. Investigation of living conditions in many rural areas revealed a situation in which the nineteenth-century revolution in sanitation had still to occur. Although some improvements had been made under inter-war housing acts, the Scott Report noted in 1942 that 'Thousands of cottages have no piped water supply, no gas or electric light, no third bedroom ... For the great majority of rural workers a bathroom is a "rare luxury" ...'. In 1938 less than one in ten agricultural holdings was served with electricity, while almost a third of the 11,186 parishes in England and Wales had no piped water supplies and almost half were entirely without sewerage systems. The flight of labour from the land continued apace, with a fall of a further 17 per cent in the rural working population between 1931 and 1938 alone. Although some measures to revive agriculture had been put in place during the 1930s with the introduction of marketing boards, there was a widespread recognition that a massive revival of rural life was required. A prosperous agriculture was increasingly seen as a key element in maintaining a well-managed countryside, as G. D. H. Cole (echoing the earlier views of Cobbett) noted for the Nuffield College Reconstruction survey in 1943: 'The well-being of rural communities depends primarily on what happens to agriculture and the agricultural population, and so to a great extent does the beauty of the countryside.'[23]

[22] See J. Stevenson, *British Society, 1914–45* (1984), 331–5.
[23] *Britain's Town and Country Pattern: A Summary of the Barlow, Scott and Uthwatt Reports*, Rebuilding Britain Series, No. 2, prepared by the Nuffield College Social Reconstruction Survey (1943), 86–7, 94–5.

If doing something to remedy the impoverished condition of British agriculture was essential to the well-being of the countryside, so too was the need to restrict or regulate rural development. Parallel to the depression of agriculture and the staple industries, the surge in new light-industrial development and speculative building in the Midlands and the South East was felt to be putting unprecedented pressure on the countryside environment, generating 'ribbon development' along the roads and the 'march of the pylons' for the electricity grid system. The huge housing boom of the inter-war years, with almost 2.5 million houses built for private sale, mainly on fresh sites on the edge of existing towns gobbled up great tracts of agricultural land. The mass slum clearance programmes of the 1930s also saw almost 0.75 million 'council' houses built, again mainly on the fringes of major cities or as satellite estates, such as Wythenshawe, south of Manchester, and the LCC's Becontree in Essex. Private house-buyers were wooed with proximity to the countryside, but at the price of an outward sprawl which increasingly affected so much of the rural landscape. The incorporation of hitherto unspoiled villages into London's suburbia, facilitated by extension of the tube network and electrification of overland railway lines, was replicated on a smaller scale around every major conurbation. In Manchester a great arterial route, Kingsway, soon to be lined with houses in a classic 'ribbon development', was thrown out southwards from the inner city in the mid-1930s towards Wilmslow and the commuter villages of north Cheshire. At the same time, the prevailing 'garden city' ethos of municipal planners and architects demanded low-density cottage-style houses for the rehoused slum-dwellers. The loss of productive and attractive agricultural land was being recognized with alarm during the inter-war years. With so much development concentrated in the South East, the almost unstoppable growth of London was recognized as a major problem. Between 1919 and 1939 the population of Greater London grew by about 0.75 million by natural increase, but by 1.25 million by inward migration. Over a quarter of the total population lived in London and the Home Counties by 1937. While the population of older industrial areas was declining, the insured population of the South East rose by 44 per cent in the ten years between 1923 and 1934.[24] Not only did it create an imbalance with other depressed industrial areas, but it also meant the almost unchecked expansion of London into the surrounding Home Counties and perpetuation of overcrowding and slum conditions in the capital itself.

The combined good of the capital, the countryside, and the whole nation were increasingly bundled together in an appeal for planning, conservation, and attention to the needs of agriculture. Access to the countryside and the preservation of remote areas, as well as the fabric of historic towns and cities, formed part of an agenda which attracted increasing support. Prior to the Second World War these concerns were almost entirely promoted by non-governmental bodies and voluntary associations. The National Trust was one of the oldest,

[24] Stevenson, *British Society*, 221–37; *Britain's Town and Country Pattern*, 22–3.

formed in 1895 specifically for the care of countryside and buildings of out-standing beauty. But as late as 1937 it only owned 60,000 acres, though these included such important pieces of landscape as the Buttermere Valley in the Lake District. Its acquisition of historic buildings and, in particular, of the country houses and their parks which later came to dominate its role, was restricted prior to the war. Ruined and uninhabited castles, abbeys, and other historic sites, fell within the remit of the Ancient Monuments section of the Ministry of Works, leaving the acquisition of inhabited buildings to the Trust. These could be gifted or purchased from donations, but the Trust insisted that it would not accept property unless it was self-supporting, by rent, gate-money, or endow-ment.[25]

These limits upon what the Trust would take on, and its relatively limited impact on rural conservation in general, led in 1926 to creation of the Council for the Preservation of Rural England. The CPRE aimed to co-ordinate the efforts of national and local societies interested 'in preserving rural scenery from some special danger or in protecting the artistic and historic features of country towns and villages'. By the late 1930s, it comprised some forty-two constituent bodies, twenty-eight country branches, a hundred and forty affiliated bodies, as well as an expanding individual associate membership. Its aim was propaganda and protest against specific threats. One of its sponsored publications highlighted the 'Need for Action': 'Combined action is urgently needed if the incessant and growing attacks upon the amenities of the countryside are to be overcome. Day by day the press records fresh act of disfigurement.' But as well as protesting against development, the CPRE also pursued constructive work. It was officially represented on the Minister of Health's Advisory Committee on Town and Country Planning and on the Minister's Housing Advisory Committee by its president, Lord Crawford, and by one of the country's lead-ing exponents of planning, Professor Patrick Abercrombie, later author of the wartime Greater London Plan and County of London Plan. By the outbreak of the Second World War the CPRE had a number of achievements to record, including the introduction of a rural amenities bill which acted as the precursor to the Town and Country Planning Act of 1932 and gave local authorities pow-ers for safeguarding areas of national and local beauty, as well as the preserva-tion of rural life. It also helped to secure the somewhat limited Restriction of Ribbon Development Act of 1935, working in collaboration with the Ministry of Transport, the Country Councils Association, and the various bodies rep-resenting road traffic interests. The CPRE was also attentive to the threat of roadside advertisements, in co-operation with the county surveyors and the Automobile Association. Liaison was also established with the Ministry of Agriculture, Forestry Commission, Central Electricity Generating Board, the engineering department of the GPO and the British Works Association. The Board of Education was lobbied about design of school buildings and the Air

[25] J. Lees-Milne, *The National Trust: A Record of Fifty Years' Achievement* (1945), x.

Ministry about airport buildings and layout. The CPRE also carried out surveys of sensitive rural areas, including by 1937, Devon, Cornwall, and the Thames Valley, and mounted exhibitions.[26] As well as lobbying, it also highlighted particular issues through its publications. In 1932 its Sheffield and Peak District Committee published *The Threat to the Peak*. With a foreword by G. M. Trevelyan, it detailed the threat to Peak District scenery and villages by incongruous buildings, advertisements, electricity supply lines, roads, and litter. 'By far the greater part of our finest scenery lies a prey, to indifference, or to Mammon', commented the epilogue, calling for the whole of the Peak District to be placed under effective town and country planning. It also called for stronger protection of its birdlife and wildflowers, offered a prototype 'Country Code', and pointed to the detailed prescriptions in the CPRE's own pamphlet series for carrying on building and repair which would harmonize with the environment.[27]

The CPRE was the most important co-ordinating body of rural preservation, but it operated within a much larger conservationist lobby. While the increasing diversity of the groups and individuals who campaigned on countryside issues tends to defy definition as a movement, there was little doubt that a powerful lobby was developing between the wars in which countryside groups, outdoor enthusiasts, and town and country planners made common cause on a range of issues. Harvey Taylor has noted the important development between the wars of a vigorous and expanding campaigning element and the affiliation of grass-roots associations into national bodies, like the CPRE, the Ramblers Association, and the YHA, which gave much of 'the muscle to lobbies for open access, national parks, long-distance footpaths, countryside conservation, and to a general urge to improve rural amenity . . .'.[28] As an example, the National Parks Committee, appointed by Ramsay MacDonald in 1931, brought together the CPRE, the Commons Open Spaces and Footpaths Preservation Society (COSFPS), the regional ramblers' federations, as well as influential individuals. The outdoor lobby and rural enthusiasts were often arguing along similar lines by the mid-1930s, a decade in which the threat to what remained of rural Britain seemed acute and in which the call for conservation and planning became almost the stock-in-trade of the 'country' writer. Shears's *This England* of 1936 contained the by now familiar warning that rural life was fast disappearing under the tide of modernity and urged the need to record and conserve it:

Cheap and popular means of transport, the cinema and broadcasting, mechanisation and migrations of industry, combine incessantly to introduce new ways and new ideas into the daily life of towns and villages throughout the shires. That this rush of new life is bringing undreamed-of comforts and opportunities is fully recognised, but to many it will seem a heavy price to pay unless by some means town and country are brought to desire the preservation of our really priceless possessions.

---

[26] See the account in C. Williams-Ellis (ed.), *Britain and the Beast* (1937), 315–21.
[27] *The Threat to the Peak*, 87–8.   [28] Taylor, *A Claim on the Countryside*, 244.

Shears noted with approbation the work of the National Trust, the CPRE, COSFPS, the Society for the Protection of Ancient Buildings, the Rural Community Councils, the Friends of the Lake District, the Men of the Trees, and bodies as esoteric as the Queen's Institute of District Nursing whose 'gardens scheme' had been instrumental in opening many private English gardens to public view.[29] Shears could have added scores of other local and regional bodies concerned with similar aims.

The political footprint of these bodies was wide ranging from the communitarian left to the ruralist right. The significant point during the 1930s and the subsequent war years was the fashioning of a set of proposals which satisfied a broad swathe of opinion, achieved a degree of political consensus, and were to be enshrined in post-war legislation. The range of support was well illustrated in *Britain and the Beast* (1937) edited by Clough Williams-Ellis. A searing 'indictment' of the destruction currently threatening the nation's countryside and townscapes, Williams-Ellis portrayed his contributors as 'a coroner's jury, conducting the inquest on a mutilated corpse'.[30] His 'jury' included well-known writers on country affairs, such as Massingham, Joad, Street, and Trevelyan, with town and country planners such as Thomas Sharp and Patrick Abercrombie. In addition there were contributions from J. M. Keynes on 'Art and the State' and E. M. Forster on 'Havoc', the latter a plea for sensitivity towards the still unspoiled 'small' places of England. The sea coasts, Scotland, and conservation lessons from Sweden, Switzerland, and Germany by Lord Howard of Penrith were also covered, along with end pieces on the work of the National Trust and the CPRE. *Beauty and the Beast* also contained 'Messages' of support from Lloyd George, Kingsley Wood, George Lansbury, Baden Powell, the Earl of Derby, Stafford Cripps, Julian Huxley, and J. B. Priestley.

As this list suggested, countryside conservation found favour across the political spectrum. The Conservative party had already planted its flag on many of the values of 'deep England' by association with the political hegemony exercised by Baldwin and the Conservative party between the wars. As a political culture, Baldwinian conservatism has been seen as appropriating various 'national' values to itself, including those centred on rural life and its quintessential 'Englishness'.[31] Baldwin had deliberately cultivated the image of himself as a countryman and in his speech 'On England' had famously stated that 'To me, England is the country, and the country is England'. Rural nostalgia and the evocation of a timeless, tranquil countryside have been seen as representing part of a constructed identity for inter-war conservatism and one which contributed to its appeal to an enlarged and increasingly diverse mass electorate. It was a theme taken up by Conservative-inclined writers in the 1930s who set out to rival the highly successful Left Book Club. Writers for the National Book Association and the Right Book Club, such as Arthur Bryant and Philip Gibbs,

[29] Shears, *This England*, 7.   [30] Williams-Ellis, *Britain and the Beast*, xiv.
[31] P. Williamson, 'The Doctrinal Politics of Stanley Baldwin', in M. Bentley (ed.), *Public and Private Doctrine* (Cambridge, 1993), and his *Stanley Baldwin* (Cambridge, 1999).

consciously evoked Britain's rural past and the traditional, stable, organic order it represented.[32] More directly, defence of landed interests within the limitations of national economic policy made much of the English shires the natural territory of the Conservative party. Under the Conservative-dominated National government, the plight of agriculture was given some acknowledgement in the creation of agricultural marketing boards and a recognition that some degree of intervention and protection was required; a claim later to be massively reinforced by war. Moreover, the issue of access to the countryside entered mainstream politics during the 1930s. While defending landlord interests, sections of the National government were sympathetic to popular outdoor rural pursuits. An increasingly powerful lobby introduced access bills in 1924, 1930, 1931, 1937, and 1938, with sufficient support in 1939, in a parliament still massively dominated by Conservatives, for the passage of a limited Access to the Mountains Act. Though to many on the left the act was far too favourable to landlord interests, its passage provides evidence before the outbreak of war of the degree to which such issues were successfully commanding public attention.

Traditionally the Liberal party had been the principal advocate of the agricultural labourer and opposition to landlordism. From the People's Budget to the *Green Book* of 1928 the Liberals sought to keep alive the flame of rural radicalism, with proposals for taxation and land reform designed to revitalize the countryside and rectify the undue concentration of economic and political power in the hands of the landlords.[33] After 1929 the Liberal party was largely reduced to political impotence, but some of its individuals remained important spokesmen on rural issues, such as L. F. Easterbrook. Ex-Liberals such as Christopher Addison also maintained an interest in rural issues, in his case eventually becoming Minister of Agriculture under the second Labour government. Although not always able to affect politics directly, Liberals and their allies had an important part to play in making the countryside and its well-being one of the constituent components of progressive politics.

Even more significant for the emergence of a significant consensus on conservation and rural planning was the evolution of Labour policy in the run-up to the Second World War. The Labour party had derived from its Ruskinite and Morrisite traditions a powerful rural nostalgia and a radical critique of landlordism since its early Lib–Lab days. Writers of the left, as well as Conservatives, laid claim to the values and beauties of the English countryside as a common inheritance. By 1931, earlier proposals for the taxation of land values had been abandoned by Labour in favour of a policy of land nationalization. This was outlined by Addison as the principal remedy for agricultural problems as late as 1939.[34] There were straws in the wind, however, that this policy

---

[32] E. H. H. Green, *Ideologies of Conservatism* (Oxford, 2002), 150–2.

[33] See I. Packer, *Lloyd George, Liberalism and the Land: The Land Issue and Party Politics in England, 1906–1914* (Woodbridge, 2001), see especially pp. 178 ff. 'The strange death of the land issue'.

[34] Lord Addison, *A Policy for British Agriculture* (1939). Left Book Club.

was softening. It was increasingly recognized, for example, that a significant proportion of the land was not in the hands of large landlords, but of hard-pressed former tenant farmers. The evident distress of much of the countryside undermined former perceptions of a wildly profiteering landlord class and pointed increasingly to the need for economic revival of the whole rural community.[35] Earlier socialist aspirations for a 'return to the land' were equally redundant by the 1930s. The party's interest in centralized physical planning and land-use control came increasingly to the fore, bringing Labour into the centre of the debate on town and country planning. By the late 1930s Labour's definition of planning encompassed physical controls to restrict the growth of London. Clement Attlee wrote for *Town and Country Planning* in 1937, urging the need for a national organization to determine the location of industry, of residential development, and of parks and open spaces. Taxation of land values was being replaced by questions of the compensation to be offered landowners if development rights were to be nationalized.

V

The appointment of the Barlow Commission on the Distribution of the Industrial Population in July 1937 by the National government has often been seen as the planners' breakthrough and a landmark in the history of planning policy in twentieth-century Britain.[36] It was prompted by a report of the Commissioner for the Special Areas in 1936, which drew attention 'to the danger involved in the continued haphazard growth of a vast industrial and commercial centre such as the Metropolis . . .'. Reporting just before the outbreak of the war, but only printed in December 1940, the Barlow Report, with its recommendations for a planned approach to the location of industry, opened the door to wider considerations affecting the countryside. The unchecked growth of London was recognized as consuming some of the best agricultural land in the country, especially in the traditional 'corn counties' and the valuable market-garden areas around London. The report explicitly noted that 'Providence has endowed Great Britain not only with wide tracts of fertile soil . . . but by no means least, with amenities and recreational opportunities, with hills and dales, with forests, moors, and headlands—precious possessions for fostering and enriching the nation's well-being and vitality.'[37] Whilst any detailed formulation of policy for agriculture or natural amenities lay outside its remit, it called for these 'wider issues' to be kept in mind as the national background against which 'solutions of the problems of the location of industry and of urbanisation must be formulated'. It was in part fulfilment of this agenda that

---

[35] See *Britain's Town and Country Pattern*, 88–9; Addison, *A Policy*, 30–1.
[36] J. B. Cullingworth, *Town and Country Planning in England and Wales* (1964), 23.
[37] *Royal Commission on the Distribution of the Industrial Population*, Cmd. 6153 (Barlow Report), 3, 14–15.

the Scott Committee on Land Utilization was set up by Lord Reith in October 1941.[38]

Reporting in August 1942, the Scott Committee reflected much of the 'countryside' agenda fashioned during the inter-war years. This was hardly surprising given the representations made to it by groups such as the National Trust, the CPRE, and the various outdoor lobbies. The majority report declared the countryside to be 'the heritage of the whole nation': the 'citizens of this country are the custodians of a heritage they share with all those of British descent, and it is a duty incumbent upon the nation to take proper care of that which it thus holds in trust'. The implications were that, while room should be found in the countryside for sympathetic industrial and residential development, including, where necessary new satellite towns and garden cities, the countryside should be revived and protected. Improved housing and amenities were required in rural areas and women were to be brought onto the Housing Committees of local authorities to advise on interior design. Farmhouses and other agricultural buildings were to be brought under full planning control, and villages provided with social centres and playing fields. Strict control was to be exercised over industry in rural areas, confined where possible to designated trading estates or garden cities, but rural craft industries to be encouraged. Footpaths were to be marked, 'hikers' highways' designated, and rights of way investigated and if necessary legislated for. National Parks should be delimited and a National Parks authority set up to control them.[39]

The Scott Report reaffirmed the pastoral image of Britain, whilst at the same time endorsing the modernizing influences of planning control, relocation of industry, and mass urban access to rural amenities. The need to conserve both agriculture and its countryside received fresh emphasis in wartime writing, film, and propaganda. To many the threat of aerial bombardment only re-emphasized the urgency of recording and preserving what was valuable in the national heritage. Parallel with the inauguration of the War Artists Scheme, Sir Hubert Llewellyan Smith, chairman of the Committee on the Employment of Artists in Wartime, approached the Pilgrim Trust to fund a project to record in topographical watercolour drawings 'places and buildings of characteristic national interest'. With advice from the CPRE and the Georgian Group, this project became the four-volume *Recording Britain* series, published by Oxford University Press.[40] Clive Rouse noted in 1943 from a wartime RAF Mess: 'One hopes that the loss of so much may make people all the more appreciative of what is left and more zealous of its preservation. The loss has been great. The opportunity is greater.'[41] 'Country writing' received a fresh boost from a combination of patriotic sentiment, the enhanced status of agriculture as a vital war industry, and increased acquaintance with the country through evacuation and

[38] Barlow Report, 15, para. 38.
[39] *Committee on Land Utilization in Rural Areas*, Cmd. 6378 (Scott Report).
[40] *Recording Britain*, 4. vols. (Oxford, 1946).
[41] C. Rouse, *The Old Towns*, 2nd edn. (1943–4), v.

wartime mobilization. Publishers such as Batsford utilized their scarce paper resources to reprint many of their heritage series.[42] In 1940 Harry Batsford produced *How to See the Country*, specifically meant for the large number of individuals and families of widely differing classes for whom wartime had forced 'first-hand acquaintance with the country for the first time in their lives'. In the course of 'the greatest shift of population the kingdom has ever known', many found country life exhilarating, but for others 'the change has spelt the direst depths of boredom and wretchedness', moving Batsford to offer his guide to the countryside, its vernacular architecture, and tips on tours and places to stay. The intention was not merely recreational:

It is pitiable that so many English folk—possibly, God help us, a large majority—should be so desperately out of touch with the real England. It is a state of affairs full of menace for the general welfare . . . No one is a true Englishman, or has lived a fully-balanced life, if the country has played no part in his development.[43]

This proved to be the first of a 'Home Front Library' series, in which Batsford offered books to people living in the country for the first time, so that they could 'use their leisure constructively for their own benefit and for the benefit of the nation in general': *How to Grow Food*, *How to See Nature*, and *How to Look at Old Buildings* were other titles in the series. Other new 'country' titles appeared, such as J. B. Priestley's edited collection, *This England*, first published in 1939, then reprinted in 1940; C. M. Joad's *An Old Countryside of a New People* in 1942; and H. J. Massingham's *The English Countryman: A Study of the English Tradition*, published in late 1942, and reprinted the following year. Lavishly illustrated in spite of wartime shortages, the last called for a regenerated agriculture as well as evoking the beauties of the English landscape. As Jeffrey Richards has shown, the evocation of the countryside was also an insistent theme in wartime films. In *The Way Ahead*, British Tommies gather around a wireless in North Africa to listen to a talk about the countryside at harvest.[44] Others, such as *Mrs Miniver* and *Went the Day Well*, placed the village at the centre of the British way of life that was being defended.

The centrality of the countryside in the Britain that was to be constructed after the war was established early. *Picture Post*'s 'Plan for Britain' in January 1941, contained an article by Easterbrook on 'The Land for All', calling for a land commission to apportion land between agriculture, housing, industry, and recreation; soil conservation together with scientific methods in agriculture; and a career structure for agricultural workers to halt the drift to the towns. Village life would be regenerated by building village colleges on the model pioneered in

[42] Paper was allocated pro rata on the basis of pre-war rates of use. Publishers therefore had a tendency to pursue successful pre-war items and genres. I am grateful to my research student Amy Flanders for information on this point.

[43] H. Batsford, *How to See the Country* (1940), Introductory Note.

[44] J. Richards, 'National Identity in British Wartime Films', in P. M. Taylor (ed.), *Britain and the Cinema in the Second World War* (1988), 42–61.

Cambridgeshire, catering for adult activities in the evening as well as school-children by day; while urban children were to be educated in the values and skills of rural life: 'The education of . . . children in the meaning of the land—in understanding the vital part the land must have in our national existence—should be a sacred trust'.[45]

Town and country planning enthusiasm reached new heights as the blitz stimulated thinking about the future, and plans for post-war reconstruction were fostered, albeit cautiously, by the Coalition government. Abercrombie's plans for London made stricter enforcement of the green belt the centrepiece of his prescription for reconciling London's growth with preservation of the country-side of the South East.[46] A green light seemed to be given to many pre-war planning enthusiasms, in which the countryside now played a significant part. Though largely devoted to *urban* reconstruction and with a foreword from Arthur Greenwood, chairman of the Ministerial Committee on Reconstruction, the McAllisters' *Town and Country Planning: A Study of Physical Environment: The Prelude to Post-War Reconstruction* (1941) had as its frontis-piece a photograph of a harvest field 'typical of the heart of the English scene, a fitting background for the noble towns of tomorrow'. Its largely technical sur-vey of current thinking on planning concluded with the sentiment: 'Out of death and destruction, out of ugliness and despair, a new spirit is born . . . bringing with it . . . a vision of noble towns planned against a background of green, unspoiled countryside'.[47]

The countryside and its conservation moved decisively out of the realm of the merely visionary and into real politics during the war. The critical importance of agriculture to national survival raised its profile as an essential national industry. It was agreed by the Coalition government that agricultural prices would be maintained after the war—the eventual victors of the 1945 election, the Labour party, having accepted that a prosperous and protected agriculture would be essential to meet the nation's economic and nutritional requirements in straitened post-war circumstances. By 1945, both Attlee and Bevin were on record as having accepted the need for guaranteed agricultural prices, an effi-cient mechanized agriculture, and continuation of a degree of wartime control via the Ministry of Agriculture. In the same year land nationalization, which threatened co-operation with the farming interests, was dropped from the Labour manifesto.[48] In addition, Labour lined itself up with the town and coun-try planning agenda and the desire to protect the countryside. The wartime coalition had given its broad approval to the Scott Report in 1943, and Labour

[45] *Picture Post*, 4 January 1941, 24–6.
[46] P. Abercrombie, *Greater London Plan* (1944) and *County of London Plan* (1945); see also Cullingworth, *Town and Country Planning*, 189–92 on the London Green Belt.
[47] G. McAllister and E. G. McAllister, *Town and Country Planning* (1941), frontispiece, 189.
[48] For Labour policy in the Second World War, see M. Tichelar, 'The Labour Party's Policy Towards Land Reform, 1900–45', unpublished D.Phil. thesis, University of the West of England, 2000, 186–255. I am grateful to Dr Tichelar for permission to cite some of his conclusions.

welcomed the Dower Report of 1945 proposing National Parks, already fore-shadowed by the coalition White Paper on Land Utilization. Moreover Labour was enthusiastic about bodies such as the National Trust, which doubled the acreage of its holdings during the war, greatly increasing its stock of country houses. Attlee, Dalton, and Cole were all supportive of its work in securing private properties for public amenity.[49]

Although, as with other aspects of wartime 'consensus', there remained important divisions between the political parties, a factor brought out in the often bitter debates over the Town and Country Planning Bill of 1944, a certain convergence had occurred by 1945. Whatever government came to power, agricultural production would be promoted and the structure of ownership left largely untouched. Some form of centralized planning machinery with provision for protection of the countryside and national parks was ensured. So too, was strengthening of existing green belt legislation and restriction on the unrestrained growth of London into the Home Counties. As it happened, it was a Labour government which came to power in 1945, one sympathetic to planning of land use and many of the nostrums of the inter-war planners. But it was a Labour party that had now abandoned land nationalization and was encouraging bodies such as the National Trust in maintaining the national heritage. Thus, in common with other spheres of public policy, the countryside had become a part of consensus which spanned the political spectrum and drew heavily upon a group of national voluntary associations, which were themselves representative of a wider network of local voluntary effort.

VI

By the end of the Second World War, countryside issues had entered the political mainstream in Britain. Countryside conservation through enforcement of the green belt was to become the crucial weapon in the war against the developer. The need to balance development across the nation meant that control of land use around major conurbations, especially London and the South East, was seen as necessary for the nation as a whole. Access had long been hotly debated, but many saw provision of national parks as one means to achieve a compromise between the need for conservation and the demand for an economically regenerated countryside. Crucially, the focus had increasingly shifted from the traditional battle of radicals and socialists against landlordism, towards a conservationist and planning agenda. The post-war Labour party framed its policies towards town and country planning not primarily on redistributive grounds but on the economic and social benefits of an adequate system of planning and land use. 'To plan, not to tax', as a Labour discussion document put it, became

---

[49] Tichelar, 'The Labour Party's Policy', 92, 215–16.

the keynote of measures such as the Town and Country Planning Act of 1947.[50] An efficient, prosperous, and protected agriculture was now viewed as an economic necessity, with agricultural subsidies initially retained for the first phase of post-war reconstruction, but then permanently continued into the post-war era. Britain became used to a prosperous, mechanized, and subsidized agriculture which contrasted sharply with the memories of pre-war years. This prosperity chimed in well with the powerful tide of sentiment about the countryside which the war had reinforced. Wartime propaganda had raised the profile of agriculture, as well as stressing the values of the 'English' countryside; while the possibility that the new 'industrialized' agriculture might itself become a major threat to rural conservation occurred to no one in the political climate of the 1940s. Within limits national parks and the work of the National Trust offered reasonable access 'for all' to the countryside, even though much of the national heritage remained in private hands. There was ample evidence after 1945 that urban dwellers responded to this compromise, making bodies such as the National Trust, the YHA, and the Royal Society for the Protection of Birds some of Britain's largest voluntary organizations. The countryside had become an integral component of the post-war consensus and one that was regulated by central government, but mediated in large part by non-governmental and advisory bodies. Civil society in several of its many forms had moved into the countryside.

[50] Labour Discussion Series, *Town and Country Planning*, No. 12 (1946), 13. This was despite the fact that the act imposed a levy on development values, a measure portrayed not as 'taxation' but as the recovery of value created by the granting of planning permission by the community.

11

Women and Civil Society: Feminist Responses to the Irish Constitution of 1937

SENIA PASETA

I

Much discussion of 'civil society' presupposes the possibility of simultaneously maintaining free democratic institutions, a powerful grass-roots associational culture, and the transcendence of status-differences based on ethnicity, gender, vocation, religion, and class. As we have seen in earlier chapters, many continental observers in the eighteenth and nineteenth centuries had seen the society of Great Britain as, if not literally embodying those goals, nevertheless moving incrementally in that direction. Much Irish commentary on British rule, by contrast, had focused not on Britain's successes but on its prolonged failures in many of these respects. Yet the attainment of such goals was to prove no less elusive in an independent Ireland, and in some ways even more so, as may be seen in the tensions and controversies that arose over gender relations and the constitutional definition of women's rights.

During early years of the twentieth century, a highly politicized context nurtured a lively and vigorous Irish women's movement which, like its British counterpart, maintained within its ranks a diversity of political opinion and social aspirations. The main political question of the period was Home Rule, and its corollary, Ulster unionism. The animosity between these creeds threatened the country with civil war, a catastrophe only narrowly averted by the intervention of the First World War. The deep divisions between Protestants and Catholics were replicated in the women's movement, not so much on the grounds of religious conviction, but on the political stands so deeply ingrained in each community. While some attempts were made to bridge these divisions in the interests of pan-suffragism, such organizations as the Irish Women's Franchise League and the Conservative and Unionist Women's Suffrage Association could not be budged. The objective of winning equal citizenship rights through the franchise was therefore undermined by sharply contrasting notions of citizenship itself. While some activists professed their loyalty to a

Home Rule Ireland, others staunchly defended their British nationality. The rise of republicanism complicated this still further. While nationalists and unionists might have found common cause within a devolved United Kingdom or even within the empire, the 1916 Proclamation of Independence promised women equal citizenship rights within an idealized Irish republic. This was, of course, anathema to the many women for whom the very notion of an Irish republic was as objectionable as it was foreign. Irish women, north and south, were enfranchised under the 1918 Representation of the People Act, and this right was carried over into the new Irish Free State and Northern Ireland.

Such divisions were almost inevitable, appended as they were to already deep chasms in Irish society. It would, in fact, be absurd to imagine that women from diverse backgrounds, of different ages, and with varying aspirations could come together in a national movement when so much else separated them. Irish women were increasingly politicized in this period and exclusive emphasis on the suffrage issue obscures the myriad activities in which they were involved. The two most important issues were socialism and educational reform, the latter probably producing the most tangible improvements to the lives of Irish women. Most of the women who were to become the leading lights in Ireland's feminist movement, and often in other political campaigns including socialism, pacifism, and republicanism, cut their political teeth on educational politics.

The University Question, as it came to be known, was one of the most pressing and loaded questions of the second half of the nineteenth and early twentieth century. The main disagreement turned on the question of how far successive British governments were willing to accommodate an increasingly vocal Catholic hierarchy which insisted on sectarian education. 'Mixed education' was ruled out; the co-education of Catholics and Protestants was apparently an invitation to a waning of faith and exposure to liberalism, secularism, and anti-clericalism. For women, however, mixed education was much more a matter of co-education between the sexes than the creeds. Organizations including the National University Women Graduates' Association led a largely successful campaign to equalize educational opportunities.

It was mainly women who had benefited from educational reform, who became the most prominent activists in the early twentieth century, and who were to remain so after independence. Though a number of women served in the Dáil, mainly as republicans, most in the early years appeared to be there by virtue of their relationship with a dead 'martyr', rather than through any independent political conviction. Very little interest was expressed in feminist politics, as a multitude of problems experienced by the early Free State took precedence. Even some of the women who had earlier been active in politics and advocates of pluralism, appeared to retreat into the divisions which had been reinforced by the civil war and the subsequent nationalist split over the Anglo-Irish Treaty.

The groundswell of radical politics after 1912 had allowed individual women to become involved in political activity in unprecedented ways, but as Ireland settled into normality and became increasingly conservative, the women's movement lost both momentum and support. This is not an uncommon pattern in post-revolutionary societies. Crisis stimulates alliances and demands which would be unthinkable in ordinary times and odd partnerships certainly had been struck in revolutionary Ireland. Expectations had been raised by such temporary alliances, but they were shattered after independence. As this realization increasingly dawned on Irish women in the 1920s, feminist activity began to revive. Yet this was largely led by the same women who had headed the movement before the end of British rule. Younger women joined campaigns, of course, but the prominence of such well-known activists as Hanna Sheehy Skeffington, Mary Hayden, and Louie Bennett is striking. The campaigns they pursued were less glamorous and the reaction they provoked was less sympathetic than hitherto. This was most clearly seen in the 1930s when women's citizenship rights became the focus for a new feminist campaign.

II

A well-known columnist summarized the apprehension felt by many Irish feminists when she declared in 1937 that 'the death knell of the working woman is sounded in the new Constitution which Mr de Valera is shortly to put before the country'.[1] Like a number of other prominent feminists, 'G.G.' (Gertrude Gaffney), believed that the new constitution was an exercise in definition; it attempted both to identify and prescribe Irish national identity. The 1937 constitution was framed entirely by men,[2] and replaced its 1922 predecessor which had been formulated during a period of social and political unrest. The years following the unveiling of the Free State's constitution witnessed the evolution of an expressly Catholic and conservative discourse on a number of social and sexual questions, and a consequent series of legislative measures to enshrine such views in law. Debates on issues including fashion, divorce, birth control, and censorship reflected deeper questions about intellectual and sexual liberty, and about public and private morality.

The 1937 constitution dealt explicitly with many of these issues as well as introducing specific clauses about gender roles, thus becoming the latest in a series of legislative measures which affected the working and political lives of Irish women. The constitution consequently provoked a vocal feminist campaign which looked to both the recent Irish past and the political climate of the 1930s to justify its claim that the document threatened women's citizenship rights. Gaffney's opposition to the constitution was based on two broad arguments which reflected general feminist sentiment. The language of citizenship was employed to advocate equal political rights for men and women; while at

[1] *Irish Independent*, 7 May 1937.
[2] Y. Scannell, 'The Constitution and the Role of Women', in B. Farrell (ed.), *De Valera's Constitution and Ours* (Dublin, 1988), 123.

the same time women's 'special interest' in social questions was emphasized in an attempt to justify their involvement in the political life of the country.

Feminist advocacy of citizenship rights was based firmly within the discourse of nation building. Irish women had 'proved' that they were deserving of political rights by virtue of their role in the revolutionary events of 1916–22 which had propelled Ireland towards independence. As Gaffney argued:

But for the women of Ireland Mr. de Valera would not be in the position he holds today. He was glad enough to make use of them to transport guns and munitions, to carry secret dispatches, and to harbour himself and his colleagues when it was risking life and liberty to do so. If the women had not stood loyally *behind* the men we might be to-day no further than we were before 1916. It is harsh treatment this in return for all they have done for their country.   (my emphasis)[3]

But she also advised de Valera to remember that women were largely responsible for the availability of social services including school meals, free milk, school medical inspection, and organized welfare help for mothers and children. 'Women pioneers' had initiated such services, which would be in 'a sorry state' had they been left to men to organize.

Such arguments had found expression when de Valera abolished the Irish senate in 1936 and the composition of a new upper house began to be discussed. The Irish Women Workers' Union (IWWU) and the Joint Committee of Women's Societies and Social Workers (JC) wrote to de Valera, urging him both to consider their concerns about the composition of a new second chamber and to agree to a meeting with representatives of their organizations. The JC maintained that 'women should have equal representation with men on the Seanad— that in Seanad of 50 there should be 25 women', that women should be chosen on a vocational rather than a party basis, and that women should be deemed to be the 'best judges of who should represent their interests'.[4] The IWWU similarly claimed that as it was virtually impossible for women, 'however distinguished', to 'secure a responsible position in the direction of public affairs', provision should be made to secure the inclusion of women in the new senate. They too favoured the election of women on a vocational basis.[5]

The JC acted on behalf of a number of women's groups, including the IWWU,[6] and although the IWWU sent its own proposals to de Valera, the organization's demands were similarly based on the notion that women were uniquely suited to co-ordinating social legislation. The IWWU thus urged de

---

[3] Ibid.   [4] *Irish Independent*, 19 November 1936.
[5] IWWU to de Valera, 4 January 1937, Department of An Taoiseach (D/T), S.9278, National Archives of Ireland (NAI).
[6] The other groups represented by the JC were: Irish Women's Citizens' and Local Government Association; Cumann chun na bPaisti; the National Council of Women in Ireland; the Central Association of Schoolmistresses; the National University Women Graduates Association; the Girls' Friendly Society; the Girl Guides; the Irish Countrywomen's Association; the Irish Matrons' Association; the Mothers' Union; the Women Graduates Association, TCD; the Women's National Health Association; the Holy Child Association; and the Society for the Prevention of Cruelty to Children.

Valera to establish a 'panel representative of Public Health and Social Services', which would deal with 'issues whose vital importance to the nation becomes increasingly appreciated, and to which women have always devoted special care'.[7] This panel, they believed, should become one of five from which members of the senate would be elected on a vocational basis. The JC likewise argued that women must be included in the new senate because there were a number of questions 'of vital importance to women with which women are especially fitted to deal'; these issues included: the care and feeding of children, 'matters connected with the home', and 'social problems'.[8]

De Valera at first refused to meet representatives of the women's organizations, claiming on a number of occasions to be too busy to do so, but promising to see them when 'it was practicable'.[9] He had asked the JC to send him a memorandum outlining their concerns, but he continued to put off setting up a meeting with them. The JC responded by publishing their correspondence with the president, arguing that 'the ignoring of women and their interests would seem to be a concerted policy of the Government', and calling for an emergency meeting in order to discuss de Valera's refusal to receive their deputation.[10] The president's office responded by suggesting that the JC supply de Valera with a further memorandum which summarized their views and rebuked the organization for publishing only selective correspondence.[11]

De Valera finally agreed to meet representatives of organizations including the JC, the IWWU, the Mothers' Union, the National Council of Women (NCW), and the Women Graduates Association (WGA); they met de Valera on 29 January 1937. The main topics of conversation were the role of women in the new upper chamber, although other issues including women and the civil service, the establishment of a women's police force, and the Criminal Law Amendment Act were also discussed. De Valera agreed to consider carefully their suggestions, but argued that he doubted that the establishment of a panel representing social services 'would fit in with the general scheme', and he further noted that

any inadequacy in the representation of women in the legislature and in public bodies was attributable to public opinion. It would be difficult to do anything to give women a larger place in public life while public opinion remains as it is.[12]

The notion that feminist demands contravened 'public opinion' (or Catholic opinion) was to become a central plank in subsequent anti-feminist rhetoric.

[7] IWWU to de Valera, 4 January 1937, D/T, S.9278, NAI.
[8] JC to Irish Independent, 19 November 1936.
[9] De Valera's representative to JCGSG, 5 January 1937 D/T, S. 9287, NAI and Irish Independent, 19 November, 1936.
[10] JC to de Valera, 11 November, 1936, D/T, S.9278, NAI and Irish Independent, 19 November 1936.
[11] De Valera's private secretary to JC, 26 November 1936, D/T, S. 9278, NAI.
[12] Memorandum on de Valera's meeting with the JC, 30 January 1937, D/T, S.9278, NAI.

Press coverage of the meeting was largely neutral, although the patronizing tone which was to characterize much reporting of feminist concerns about the new constitution was anticipated by one journalist who described de Valera's interview with 'a number of singularly persuasive members of the sweet-spoken sex':

They merely ask that a certain number of places should be reserved, in advance, for members of 'the sex'. The male members of the new Chamber are, it appears, to be elected, or selected, by vocational bodies. The ladies do not want, it is stated, to be subjected to that hazard; they want their cards placed on the backs of the seats at Leinster House as soon as the Bill constituting the new Chamber is enacted. It that does not spell 'equality' it, at least, spells 'enterprise'.[13]

De Valera asked the representatives to refrain from publicizing details of the meeting; the spokeswomen accordingly told reporters that they had been received 'courteously and sympathetically' and claimed that they were 'hoping for good results'.[14] In private, however, they were far less optimistic. The IWWU representatives explained to their members that 'the President has not much use for women out of their homes, but said he would consider the social service aspect of the case put. Not very hopeful.'[15] Prominent writer and feminist Rosamund Jacob condemned de Valera, claiming that he was 'not willing to do anything to secure representation for them, said they had no public opinion behind them and made difficulties to everything they suggested'. She maintained that 'he badly needs to be taught a lesson, if there were only enough women with the guts to do it'.[16]

The JC sent de Valera a further memorandum, reiterating their claims and outlining the historical justification for their demands for equal citizenship. In their opinion, this right had been guaranteed by the involvement of women in the state's most important institutions such as the Dáil and political parties including Sinn Fein and Fianna Fail.[17] Acknowledging that they could not rely on any established political party for support, feminist critics of the constitution based their objections on two major claims: their 'historical right' to citizenship; and the notion that women could play a unique role in the political life of the country by virtue of their special interest in social issues. These claims seemed to make odd bedfellows: how could women advocate the politics of difference and at the same time claim that because they had taken up guns, entered the male bastion of high politics, and served as ambassadors they had a right to citizenship rights?

This seemingly incongruous position proved to be a thorn in the side of feminist opposition to the constitution, a thorn which threatened at times to tear the movement apart. The Representation of the People Act and the enfranchisement

---

[13] *Sunday Independent*, 7 February 1937.   [14] *Irish Press*, 30 January 1937.
[15] IWWU Executive Committee Minutes, 4 February 1937, 16609, Irish Labour Archives (ILA).
[16] Rosamund Jacob Papers, 25 February 1937, MS 32582(81), National Library of Ireland.
[17] JC to de Valera, 3 February 1937, D/T, S.9278, NAI.

of women aged between 19 and 29 in the Irish Free State in 1923 had largely satisfied most early twentieth-century Irish feminists, but at the same time these major concessions had ensured the disintegration of the loose alliance of women's groups which had co-operated on the issue of women's suffrage. Feminist co-operation and indeed the relevance of feminist politics had been further eroded by the revolutionary events of 1916–22 and the consequent radicalization of Irish politics during the 1920s. Like their male counterparts, feminists split over the Anglo-Irish Treaty and although many old allies together opposed legislation on women's working conditions, divorce, and birth control, the campaign against the 1937 constitution exposed the fragility of feminist alliances and highlighted the increasingly polarized agendas espoused by disparate women's groups.

III

The issue of women's representation in the senate was pushed to the background by the publication of a draft version of the new constitution. Its publication on 1 May 1937 was accompanied by a new wave of feminist agitation led by the JC, the IWWU, the WGA, and the NCW, whose worst fears seemed to have been confirmed. Many of the features of the 1937 constitution are well known and controversial aspects of the document have been discussed elsewhere.[18] Irish feminists were particularly concerned with articles 9, 16, 40.1, 41.2, and 45.4. Article 40.1 read: 'All citizens shall, as human persons, be held equal before the law. This shall not mean that the State shall not in its enactments have due regard to differences of capacity, physical and moral, and of social function.' Feminists urged de Valera to remove the second paragraph on the grounds that 'it would give the State dangerous power of passing enactments on sex or class lines'.[19] This article remained unchanged. Article 45.4 2° stated that

The State shall endeavour to ensure that the inadequate strength of women and the tender age of children shall not be abused, and that women and children shall not be forced by economic necessity to enter avocations unsuited to their sex, age or strength.

Many feminist campaigners were especially concerned about the implications of article 41.2, which read

1° In particular the State recognises that by her life within the home, woman gives to the State a support without which the common good cannot be achieved.
2° The State shall, therefore, endeavour to ensure that mothers shall not be obliged by economic necessity to engage in labour to the neglect of their duties in the home.

---

[18] See, for example: T. Brown, *Ireland: A Social and Cultural History, 1922–1985* (1985), 164–5; J. J. Lee, *Ireland, 1912–1985: Politics and Society* (Cambridge, 1989), 206–7; J. H. Whyte, *Church and State in Ireland, 1923–1970* (Dublin, 1971), 50–6.

[19] JC to de Valera, 24 May 1937, D/T, S.9880, NAI.

The JC, the IWWU, and the National Council of Women in Ireland's Standing Committee on Legislation Affecting Women requested a meeting with de Valera in order to discuss their grievances. Their request was duly granted and the president received two deputations representing women's organizations on 14 May 1937. De Valera assured the women that 'whist he did not at all share their apprehension', he would consider carefully their objections. To the satisfaction of some campaigners, he also agreed to consider inserting in article 9 a provision which would 'set up a constitutional barrier against the possibility of an Act being passed discriminating against women in the matter of citizenship'.[20]

Some feminist groups accepted the president's assurance that articles 9 and 16 would be 'amended in such a way as to guarantee no interference with women's political rights or status', but calls for the deletion or modification of articles 40.1, 41.2, and 45.4 continued.[21] A separate IWWU delegation met with de Valera on 27 May and it was after this meeting with de Valera that different priorities began to emerge, and the ideological and political differences within Irish feminist groups became clearer. Although the IWWU continued to oppose the second paragraph of article 40.1, it felt that it had won a major concession in persuading de Valera to amend article 45.4 by adding the word 'men' to the clause in order to emphasize that it was not aimed explicitly at women and by removing the phrase 'the inadequate strength of women'.[22] It would be very easy to argue that the article provided increased constitutional protection for men rather than upholding rights for women, and room for the abuse of women's rights clearly remained. Yet the IWWU described the amendment as 'rather a victory' and, apparently appeased, largely withdrew from the broader feminist campaign.[23]

The IWWU had earlier agreed to co-operate with other women's groups and agreed that it should continue to do so even after withdrawing from the public meetings organized to publicize feminist opposition to the draft constitution. Their withdrawal from the public arena had, however, weakened the wider campaign and disappointed the other women's groups. The IWWU acknowledged this situation: 'The other women's societies were rather disappointed that we did not go on with public meetings, but after our interview with the President, we thought it wiser to hold our hand.'[24] The IWWU was censured by the NUWGA, but decided that the matter should be 'allowed to drop'.[25]

Louie Bennett had echoed some of the opinions expressed by Gertrude Gaffney, who had claimed that only exceptional women preferred work to marriage. In common with Gaffney—who also emphasized the impact of the

[20] Government memo, 14 May 1937, D/T, S.9880, NAI.
[21] JC to de Valera, 24 May 1937, D/T, S.9880, NAI.
[22] The new version of the article read: 'The State shall endeavour to ensure that the health and strength of workers, men and women, and the tender age of children shall not be abused, and that citizens shall not be forced by economic necessity to enter avocations unsuited to their age, sex or strength.'
[23] IWWU Executive Committee Minutes, 10 June 1937, 10609, ILA.   [24] Ibid.
[25] Ibid., 8 July 1937.

new constitution on the rights of working-class women and claimed that 'ninety per cent of the women who work for their living in this country do so because they must'[26]—Bennett also highlighted the impact of certain articles on working-class women. This is hardly surprising, given Bennett's trade-union background, but what is striking is her defence of the sanctity of the family, the home, and traditional parental roles. She argued, for example, that

In our humble opinion Sections 43 and 45 of the Constitution indicate the right and natural road towards protection of the family and the mother. But if greater emphasis on this point is desirable, it would be preferable to gain it through emphasising the father's needs as the natural guardian of the family.[27]

The IWWU's conduct must be understood in the context of Bennett's belief—and that of many of her fellow trade unionists—that the need for women to work outside the home was a 'social evil' which could only be remedied by the achievement of higher wages for working men and a consequent rise in the living standards of working-class families.[28] An IWWU statement insisted that 'A Constitution is hardly the place for the expression of vague and chivalrous statements. Mothers would prefer concrete proposals, which would release them from the pressure of economic necessity to work outside the home.'[29] Although Bennett and her colleagues undoubtedly endorsed equal pay for equal work and the right of women to enter the paid workforce, the IWWU was primarily committed to wider political issues. According to the IWWU's annual report of 1937: 'there are other articles in the Constitution which carry more serious menace to the interests of workers, both men and women, and your committee preferred to take the more general stand-point of the Labour Movement as a whole in connection with the subject'.[30]

Such sentiments were not endorsed by prominent members of organizations including the JC, the NUWGA, and the NCWI, which consisted overwhelmingly of professional women. The political and ideological views of individual members of these organizations often differed; this was inevitable given that the organizations claimed no affiliation to political parties or religious creeds. Common, however, to most members was a profound belief in the right of women to engage in paid work under the same conditions as their male counterparts. The argument that some women chose to work, and that this did not necessarily imply that they were forced to because they had remained unmarried or had been widowed, was central to their campaign; this campaign became increasingly heated as it became apparent that de Valera was not going to bow to their demands.

---

[26] *Irish Independent*, 7 May 1937.   [27] *Irish Press*, 15 May 1937.
[28] M. Daly, *Women and Work in Ireland* (Dundalgan, 1997), 48.
[29] M. Jones, *These Obstreperous Lassies: The Story of the Irish Women's Workers' Union* (Dublin, 1988), 142.
[30] Ibid.

Mary Kettle, chair of the JC, informed de Valera that her organization maintained its belief in 'the principles of equal opportunities for both sexes, and equal pay for equal work'. She further objected to article 45.4 2° because it might be used to 'limit women's legitimate choice of occupation, on the ground that their strength is inadequate'. She also predicted that 'sex antagonism' might arise 'out of legislation restricting women's right to work'.[31] The NUWGA pursued similar arguments in its 'Memorandum on the Status of Women', claiming that certain articles in the proposed constitution appeared to 'menace the citizen's right to work in whatever legitimate sphere he or she may deem suitable'. Members agreed that 'mothers should not be forced to engage in labour to the neglect of their duties in the home', but believed the state should keep out of the private affairs of the family, affairs best left to the husband *and* wife to consider. They reiterated their belief in 'equal pay for equal work', the sort of system they had benefited from as members of a university in which 'perfect equality' had been enjoyed by men and women since its foundation in 1908.[32] Mary Hayden, a leading NUWGA member and prominent academic, asked: 'is women's sphere to be limited to the home?' She answered her own question in the negative, claiming forcefully: 'we women don't want flattery—what we want is liberty to work'.[33]

Such views found little bureaucratic or media support. The women's campaign received some sympathetic coverage from the *Irish Times*,[34] but press opinion seemed largely to concur with the views of the president. De Valera defended his stand on women's rights, claiming 'I seem to have got a bad reputation. I do not think I deserve it.'[35] He received some support for this view,[36] but Gertrude Gaffney—who claimed to have chastised a woman for referring to de Valera as 'a darling'—was more representative of feminist opinion on the matter of the president's alleged tolerance. 'He might', she argued, 'be a darling, but I [have] no use for his attitude to women.'[37] Louie Bennett's views were savaged by the editor of the *Irish Press*, who claimed that women should 'wholeheartedly and unreservedly' support the constitution as it sought to guard the home and the central role of the mother in the Irish home; this, he argued, 'is the noblest and most humane principle applicable to women ever enshrined in a Constitution'.[38] Mary Kettle faced similar treatment after she published a letter in the same newspaper. Describing her position as chairman of the JC as 'evidently a very important position', the editor accused her of trying to 'poison the minds of the women of the country against the Government'.[39] Media criticism of the feminist campaign led to the condemnation of feminists themselves

---

[31] JC to de Valera, 24 May 1937. D/T, S. 9880, NAI.
[32] NUWGA, Memorandum on the Status of Women, 23 May 1937, D/T, S. 9880, NAI.
[33] *Irish Press*, 22 June 1937.
[34] Margaret Ward, *Hanna Sheehy Skeffington: A Life* (Cork, 1997), 326.
[35] Dail Eireann: Parliamentary Debates, vols. 67–8, 64 (1937).
[36] See, for example, *Irish Press*, 15 May 1937.   [37] *Irish Independent*, 7 May 1937.
[38] *Irish Press*, 15 May 1937.   [39] Ibid., 13 May 1937.

and the line between personal insult and objective analysis became increasingly blurred.

The political tone of feminist rhetoric changed markedly during the campaign and the variety of political opinions held by participants did not prevent feminist leaders from framing their objections to the constitution in ideological terms. The new constitution and de Valera himself were condemned as traitors to both the 'national cause' and the 'nation's history' as citizenship rights were increasingly discussed within a historical context. The 1916 Proclamation of Independence was lauded as both an exemplary assurance of equal citizenship rights and as a genuine expression of Irish nationhood. Article 3 of the 1922 constitution, which guaranteed citizenship rights without distinction of sex, was thus considered to be a bona fide reading of the 1916 proclamation. As the Irish Women's Citizens' Association explained:

The I.W.C.A. feel that the position of women in Saorstat Eireann has deteriorated in recent years from the ideal implicit in the Proclamation of 1916 and the Constitution of 1922, and that therefore it is necessary to retain Article 3 explicitly.[40]

In a similar vein, the Association of Old Cumann na mBan argued that 'the Proclamation of Easter Week 1916 gave to us women equal rights and equal opportunities in simple language that no legislation could change or tamper with, and on the Declaration of Independence did Cumann na mBan base its Constitution'.[41] Tampering with the rights explicitly awarded to women in 1916 was tantamount, in the opinion of many feminist campaigners, to tampering with the ideological basis of Irish independence. According to the NUWGA, the 'omission of the principle of equal rights and equal opportunities enunciated in the Proclamation of Independence' and confirmed in article 3 of the 1922 constitution was 'sinister and retrogressive'.[42]

The fact that the new constitution was introduced by a Fianna Fail government which contained both survivors and supporters of the republican struggle further disappointed many feminists. Republican Irish women, especially in the Dáil and in organizations including Sinn Fein, had been among the most adamant anti-treatyites in the 1920s, and the new constitution was seen as a betrayal to those women who had supported the republican cause. Hanna Sheehy Skeffington claimed that the 'best' had been lost in 1916 and 1922–3, allowing power to fall 'into the hands of lesser men who no longer really care[d] for the ideals inspiring Easter week'.[43] She further explicitly linked de Valera's alleged mistrust of women with his refusal to accept the assistance of women during Easter week, 1916, and his subsequent framing of the 1937 constitution; she vowed to never again vote for Fianna Fail.[44] Having known him for years,

[40] IWCA to de Valera, 20 May 1937, D/T, S.9880, NAI.
[41] Association of Old Cumann na mBan to de Valera, 18 May 1937, D/T, S.9880, NAI.
[42] *Irish Press*, 11 May 1937.   [43] *Irish Independent*, 11 May 1937.
[44] Ward, *Hanna Sheehy Skeffington*, 326–7.

she claimed she could 'testify' to his anti-feminism: 'his ideal is the strictly domestic type of woman who eschews "politics" as male concerns'.[45]

The involvement in the feminist campaign of prominent female republicans including Dorothy Macardle, Maud Gonne MacBride, and Kathleen Clarke was advertised, as was their espousal of the 1916 Proclamation, but female members of the Dáil expressed little or no concern about the position of women under the new constitution or its relationship to the country's republican struggle.[46] The notion that the Proclamation of Independence guaranteed women's citizenship rights was, however, adopted by prominent feminists who had actually opposed both the Easter rebellion and Irish republicanism itself. Mary Hayden and Mary Kettle had been members of the Irish Dominion League, which had opposed Sinn Fein and supported the Anglo-Irish Treaty of 1921. They none the less played prominent roles in the feminist campaign and embraced what Kettle described as 'the classic simplicity of the language of the Proclamation of the Republic'.[47]

De Valera was quick to claim that there was 'nothing in [the] Constitution which in any way detracts from the rights which women have possessed here'.[48] He added a party-political slant to the issue by suggesting that women's groups were being led by the former attorney-general, John A. Costello.[49] Costello had claimed that 'under the draft women, have not, as of constitutional right, any claim to the exercise of the franchise with men',[50] but while feminists might well have agreed with Costello's assessment of the draft constitution, there is no evidence to suggest that Costello or any other prominent member of Fine Gael co-operated with the women's groups.

Despite the efforts of several women's groups, the Dáil passed the constitution in June and it was accepted by the country at a referendum held in July. Aware that they could not hope to change de Valera's mind, the JC agreed to form an all female political party which would represent their opinions. By November 1937, the Women's Social and Political League (WSPL) had been established.[51] Many of the women who were drawn to this new organization had been Fianna Fail voters but found they could no longer support what they deemed to be an anti-woman party. The WSPL followed in a long line of Irish feminist groups which had refused to organize along sectarian lines, and although the WSPL was an explicitly political organization, its *raison d'être*— women's rights—ensured that women professing various political beliefs were able to join.

---

[45] *Irish Independent*, 11 May 1937.

[46] Mary Clancy, 'Aspects of Women's Contribution to the Oireachtas Debate in the Irish Free State, 1922–1937', in Maria Luddy and Cliona Murphy (eds.), *Women Surviving: Studies in Irish Women's History in the Nineteenth and Twentieth Centuries* (Dublin, 1990), 224–5.

[47] *Irish Press*, 11 May 1937.   [48] Dail Eireann: Parliamentary Debates, vols. 67–8, 64 (1937).

[49] Ibid.   [50] *Irish Independent*, 6 May 1937.   [51] Ward, *Hanna Sheehy Skeffington*, 327.

IV

The feminist campaign against certain sections of the constitution was domi-nated from the outset by middle-class, educated women, many of whom were well-known veterans of numerous political campaigns stretching back to women's suffrage in the early years of the twentieth century. Despite deep polit-ical differences, women including Mary Hayden, Hanna Sheehy Skeffington, Louie Bennett, Mary Kettle, and Rosamund Jacob played leading roles in the debate about the constitution. Their notoriety was not lost on their critics, many of whom stressed the fundamental differences between these women and 'ordin-ary Irish women'. The idea that most Irish women had more pressing issues with which to concern themselves was also used by critics to highlight the differences between feminists, who were often unmarried professionals, and 'the majority of Irish women', who were variously classed by one writer as 'mothers and nuns and widows and flappers and teachers and the wives of butchers, of publicans, of doctors, and of merchants, and nursery maids and priests' housekeepers', who cared little for the debate about the constitution because they had 'too much common sense and too much else to bother or interest or amuse them'.[52] Claiming that 'not one of them, outside the little coteries of Dublin' had any interest in the matter, he further argued that feminists had 'nothing but contempt for the average woman, simply because she has had a truer sense of values than they have'.[53]

The alleged unrepresentativeness of the feminist campaign and of feminists themselves became a common feature of much public debate on the issue. De Valera employed this kind of rhetoric in the Dáil, arguing that '99 per cent of the women of this country will agree with every line of [the constitution]'.[54] He was supported by most national newspapers including the *Irish Press*, whose editor claimed variously that no article deprived working women of protection under the law,[55] and that 'every right thinking person' would support clause 45.4 2° of the constitution, which sought to ensure that women were not forced by eco-nomic necessity to engage in paid work.[56] One of de Valera's supporters—who regretted that the president was 'disposed to take the clamour of those suffer-agettes [sic] so seriously'—even urged him to make clearer that his 'desire was to send women back to the home where they belong'.[57]

Critics of the articles relating to Irish women largely avoided condemning the influence of Catholic social thought on the constitution. Analysis of the religious aspect of the document was, in fact, almost entirely absent from feminist dis-course on the issue, featuring only in protests aired by independent commenta-tors such as Edna Fitz Henry, who objected to the constitutional ban on divorce which she claimed would involve 'injustice to a section of citizens'. Her claim

[52] Louis J. Walsh, 'Our Most Distressful Women', *Irish Rosary*, 41 (1937), 570.   [53] Ibid.
[54] Dail Eireann: Parliamentary Debates, vols. 67–8, 64 (1937).   [55] *Irish Press*, 11 May 1937.
[56] Ibid., 13 May 1937.   [57] Walsh to de Valera, 13 May 1937, D/T, S.9880, NAI.

that many Catholics and non-Catholics disapproved of the ban but were reluctant to speak publicly on the issue because to do so was to 'lay oneself open to misinterpretation'[58] helps to explain why an explicit link was not made by feminists between the articles relating to women and Catholic social teaching. Supporters of the constitution showed no such reluctance; the expressly Catholic tone of sections of the constitution was in fact applauded by many commentators.[59] In a piece entitled 'Women Graduates Again', the editor of the *Irish Press* went so far as to accuse women who denounced the constitution of opposing the Pope and the teaching of the Catholic church: 'they are in reality assaulting the weighty and deeply pondered words of the Sovereign Pontiff'.[60]

The reluctance of usually outspoken women to comment on the religious complexion of the constitution reflected the widespread disapproval with which any criticism of the Catholic church and its role in Irish society was routinely met. The prominent feminists and educationists, Mary Hayden and Agnes O'Farrelly had experienced such censure in 1930. They condemned as 'anti-Trinity' a motion passed by fellow members of the University College, Dublin, congregation, who advocated that a closer watch be kept on Trinity College's medical faculty 'at once in the interest of the University and of Catholic medical practice in Ireland'. A writer for the *Catholic Mind* conceded that the two women were 'notable', but claimed that 'their work for Catholic action has not been notable. In fact, we dare to say that possibly they have not given Catholic needs as much thought as the circumstances of the time warrant.'[61]

The 'circumstances of the time' played a crucial role in both the framing of the constitution and the opposition to aspects of it. The constitution was clearly a product of its time. As J. J. Lee has argued, 'the social clauses of the constitution blended prevailing Catholic social concepts with particular attitudes rooted in social structure'.[62] The Catholic social movement had expanded rapidly in Ireland in the 1920s and 1930s, and a plethora of organizations and periodicals had emerged to co-ordinate the diffusion of Catholic ideas about personal and corporate morality.[63] The role of the family was central to much Catholic discourse during this period and the role of women—especially as mothers—was a frequent topic of discussion. Although it was acknowledged that some women were destined to live 'the single life in the world',[64] there was no doubt that either marriage and motherhood or the religious life were considered to be preferable occupations for women. Marriage was deemed by one commentator to be more important to women than men because if the marriage failed men had recourse to other distractions such as business, while women had 'little

---

58 *Irish Independent*, 13 May 1937.
59 See, for example, letter of B. B. Walters, *Irish Times*, 22 May 1937.
60 *Irish Press*, 17 December 1937.   61 *Catholic Mind*, April 1930, 90.
62 Lee, *Ireland, 1912–1985*, 206.
63 M. Adams, *Censorship: The Irish Experience* (Alabama, 1968), 62–95.
64 *The Catholic Laity*, I: 1 (May 1931), 3.

opportunity of distraction as our ethical code permits her almost no social life independent of her husband'.[65] Some women did not marry, however, and one Catholic commentator encouraged the 'independent' girl to 'be modern, whoever you are'. This 'modern girl' engaged in paid work but, before setting off for 'business' each morning, she would attend 7.30 mass and prepare breakfast for herself and her invalid mother. Paid work was, in her case, acceptable and marriage clearly impossible or at least delayed while she cared for her incapacitated mother. But going out into the world did not corrupt this modern girl who did not 'smoke or swear' and kept 'to the fashions as long as the fashion keeps within the bounds of *good taste* and *refinement*, but she [drew] the line at extremes. In fact her frock-line [was] about three inches below the knees.'[66]

Much of the pastoral guidance aimed at Irish women during the 1920s and 1930s warned them to beware of the corrupting influence of such modern evils as fashion, dancing, and cinema. Condemnation of these dangerous temptations was largely articulated through explicitly religious and political language. Editorials and articles warned Irish women to guard against the secular press, and the 'excessive cult of pleasure, the passion for a "good time" which prevails among young people of both sexes, the dancing craze, the readiness to submit to foreign dictation in the matter of fashion, even when modesty is offended'.[67] These vices were deemed to be a product of 'English domination' as Ireland's declining social system was based on an 'English Protestant model'.[68] The antidote to these alarming trends was modesty, chastity, marriage, and motherhood. According to Fr Gallagher, large families were 'natural', 'national, in the best sense', and 'most pleasing to the Divine Majesty'.[69] He also advised that women should 'praise at every moment the idea of a large family', and that 'no girl over 19 [was] too young to marry.'[70]

Single women, particularly professional women, were consequently deemed unfortunate at best, unnatural at worst, and seemed to require protection and guidance. In an advice book for young women, Fr Gallagher advised his 'niece' that he took no pleasure from her news that she had a job because 'I look upon jobs for girls as a necessary evil, but an *evil*.'[71] He warned her that although some working women 'imagined' themselves to be satisfied for a while ('too often, until it is too late'), 'deep down' they craved their own home and the 'God-ordained privilege of motherhood'.[72] Another commentator, Dr J. C. Flood, conceded that some women had succeeded in hitherto masculine occupations, but he none the less claimed that 'such women are often abnormal

[65] M. J. Scott (SJ), *Courtship and Marriage: Practical Talks to Men and Women* (Dublin, 1935), 12.
[66] B. Wyse, 'Womanly Whispers', *Little Flower Monthly* (organ of the Little Flower Guild), 12 (1928), 19.
[67] *The Irish Messenger of the Sacred Heart* (organ of the Apostleship of Prayer), 43 (1930), 96.
[68] E. Cahill (SJ), *Ireland's Peril* (Dublin, 1930), 2.
[69] L. Gallagher (SJ), *Specially for Men* (Dublin, 1942), 23.
[70] L. Gallagher, *What a Girl Should Know: Being the Letters of an Uncle to a Niece* (Dublin, 1941), 17–18.
[71] Ibid., 10.   [72] Ibid., 11.

either physically or mentally; we all recognise the "mannish" woman and the effeminate man, and these persons gravitate quite naturally into occupations more suited to the opposite sex'.[73] This view might have been extreme, but it reflected prescriptive ideas about gender roles. 'How puny', argued another commentator, 'is the stature of the play girl beside the woman who labours in the business of maintaining the sanctities of the home?'[74] The notion that the church oppressed women was, in the opinion of another writer, 'perhaps the most extraordinary of all the popular falsehoods in circulation'. He added, however, that the church recognized that 'her happiness is bound up with the inviolability of the family'.[75] The constitution formalized the fundamental importance of the family in Irish society and of the role of women within the family. De Valera himself viewed the articles relating to women's position within the family as 'a tribute to the work that is done by women in the homes as mothers', and he asked:

I would like to know from any women's organisation or from any woman what is wrong in saying that we should strive for a social system which will be such as will not compel women to go out and work to supplement either the wages of their husbands or otherwise maintain the household?[76]

It might reasonably be argued that articles 40.1, 41.2, and 45.4 of the Irish constitution of 1937 both represented and endorsed contemporary opinion and that de Valera's own views on women's rights 'reflected those of most people in Irish society at the time'.[77] 'Popular opinion' is notoriously difficult to quantify, but it was certainly the case that no widespread opposition arose to challenge the president's interpretation of appropriate roles for Irish women. It would, moreover, be incorrect to assume that 'the problems confronting Irish women [were] somehow unique',[78] and that restrictive employment legislation and conservative ideas about women's biological functions were particular to Ireland. As Mary Daly has pointed out, similar restrictive legislation was applied in the US and in other parts of Europe (including the 'marriage bar' imposed on women in teaching and public employment in Great Britain).[79] However, recognizing that Irish women laboured under restrictive legislation which was common to a number of other countries should not obscure the important point that feminist activists themselves internationalized their predicament in explicitly political terms, condemning in particular the fascist overtones of the

---

[73] J. C. Flood, 'The Modern Girl and Her Work', *The Modern Girl*, 1 (1935), 22.

[74] *Catholic Truth Quarterly*, 1 (1937), 15.

[75] *Up and Doing* (organ of the Lay Apostolate; published by the Catholic Truth Society of Ireland), 1 (1935), 11–12.

[76] Dail Eireann: Parliamentary Debates, vols. 67–8, 64, 1937.

[77] Scannell, 'Constitution and Role of Women', 123.

[78] Mary Daly, ' "Oh, Kathleen Ni Houlihan, Your Way's a Thorny Way": The Condition of Women in Twentieth Century Ireland', in A. Bradley and M. Gialanella Valiulis (eds.), *Gender and Sexuality in Modern Ireland* (Amherst, 1998), 103.

[79] Daly, *Women and Work in Ireland*, 50.

document. Hanna Sheehy Skeffington, for example, objected to the replacement of the 1916 'model of equal citizenship' by 'a fascist model',[80] while the IWWU warned that the constitution should be protected against 'fascist intrusions'.[81] The most strident commentary was offered by Betty Archdale, the chairman of the Six Point Group, who argued that the offending clauses were

based on a fascist and slave conception of woman being a non-adult person who is weak and whose place is in the home. Ireland's fight for freedom would not have been so successful if Irish women had obeyed these clauses. You who have fought all your life for the freedom of your country can surely not wish to deprive Irish women of the freedom for which they have also fought.[82]

The experience of Irish women *was* unique in many ways and their particular circumstances should not be dismissed as unimportant. The rights and expectations of Irish women were, after all, formalized in a document which carried enormous legal and symbolic importance. Coming as it did after decades of political turmoil and various attempts to identify and formalize Irish sovereignty, it served as an exposition of nationhood. Although the constitution guaranteed a woman's right to vote and to become a TD, it watered down the explicitly egalitarian language of the 1922 constitution which guaranteed citizenship rights regardless of sex. More importantly, it effectively outlined the state's model of the ideal female citizen, a model which reflected both the conservative turn in Irish politics and the increasing marginalization of the Irish women's movement.

[80] *Irish Independent*, 7 May 1937.   [81] IWWU to de Valera, 24 May 1937, D/T, S.9880, NAI.
[82] B. Archdale to de Valera, 14 June 1937, D/T, S.9880, NAI.

12

Civil Society and the Clerisy: Christian Élites and National Culture, c.1930–1950

MATTHEW GRIMLEY

In August 1939, just before Britain declared war, the Anglican missionary and author J. H. Oldham wrote a letter proposing the formation of 'an order of Christian laymen'. 'If there is to be a new Christendom', he argued, 'the Christian cause must have its storm-troops.'[1] Among the recipients of this letter were T. S. Eliot, the critic John Middleton Murry, and the Hungarian-born sociologist Karl Mannheim. They were all members of the Moot, a discussion group which Oldham, a prominent Anglican missionary and pioneer of ecumenism, had convened after the 1937 ecumenical Oxford Conference on Church, Community and State, and which ran from 1938 to 1947.[2] Oldham's suggestion for the creation of a sort of Christian élite started a debate among the Moot members, which rumbled on throughout the early part of the war. Various names were suggested for this élite, including 'koinonia', 'the brotherhood of the common mind', and 'the Christian conspiracy'. It was envisaged that it would include around sixty influential figures in public life.[3] Mannheim added his support in a paper in December 1940, in which he wrote that this order 'should have the function of revitalising the existing leadership of the country'.[4] But from some members of the Moot there was scepticism. The Moot's minutes for 10–13 January 1941 record that 'T. S. Eliot said that a group of literary folk with Christian propensities presented peculiar difficulties; it would be a long time before they got anywhere.'[5]

---

[1] Letter of J. H. Oldham, 23 August 1939, University of London, Institute of Education, Fred Clarke Moot Papers, file 1. I am very grateful to the Institute of Education and New College, Edinburgh, for permission to quote from the Moot records in the Fred Clarke, J. H. Oldham, and John Baillie Papers, and to Professor Jose Harris and Dr Marjorie Reeves for their invaluable insights on the Moot.

[2] For Oldham's career, see K. W. Clements, *Faith on the Frontier: A Life of J. H. Oldham* (Edinburgh, 1999).

[3] Minutes of 4th Meeting of Moot, 14–17 April 1939, New College, Edinburgh, J. H. Oldham Papers, file 13.

[4] Mannheim, 'Notes on the Proposed Order', Moot Paper, December 1940, Clarke Papers, file 6.

[5] Minutes of 10th Meeting, 10–13 January 1941, Clarke Papers, file 6.

Oldham's plan never got anywhere either, and the order was never formed. Looking back on the debates now, there does seem something rather unreal about them. They are strongly reminiscent of H. G. Wells's 1905 novel, *A Modern Utopia*, which described a parallel world where an order of 'samurai', bound by a rule, provided cultural and spiritual leadership.[6] But in suggesting a Christian fraternity, Oldham was reflecting a broader preoccupation among Christian intellectuals in wartime with the need for an 'élite', or 'order', or 'intellectual aristocracy', or 'clerisy'—all these phrases were frequently used— to govern or educate modern democracy. T. S. Eliot may have been sceptical about the particular programme espoused by Oldham, but along with Mannheim and Middleton Murry, he wrote extensively during and after the Second World War about the need to create an élite. With other intellectuals, he repeatedly urged that the new, democratic society which would emerge after the war would only succeed if it was led by a cultured, and Christian, intellectual class. Several proponents of such an élite—Walter Oakeshott, high master of St Paul's; Walter Moberly, chairman of the University Grants Committee; and Fred Clarke, director of the Institute of Education—were prominent figures in education policy-making, and their élitism fed into the broader discussion about educational reforms which preceded and succeeded the 1944 Butler Act.

The Moot is an interesting case-study for students of civil society in Britain because it shows the resurgence in twentieth-century political thought of a medieval concept of civil society. Most writing on civil society has tended to assume that it is an Enlightenment concept, which marked out a secular, morally neutral sphere for activities such as economics.[7] But civil society had a much older provenance, and in the middle ages the concept had been used to describe a hierarchical, divine order of society, all of the activities of which were governed by Christian principles. The older strain of civil society shared with some modern readings an emphasis on the autonomy of groups against the state, though it had asserted this autonomy on theological rather than economic grounds. It was this concept of a Christian civil society which was revived by continental Roman Catholic theorists in the 1920s and 1930s, and which passed into non-Catholic political thought in Britain during the Second World War through the Moot. For writers like T. S. Eliot, it offered a middle way between the cultural disintegration of liberal democracy and the totalitarianism of the dictators.

A striking fact about the large amount of writing on élites in the Second World War is that it occurred in the context of the debate about the formation of the welfare state. It would be natural to assume that those who extolled élites would be hostile to the welfare state but, though they often attacked the shape which it was taking, they almost all assumed that it was inevitable and broadly

    [6] Wells, *A Modern Utopia* (1905; 1994 edn.), ch. 9. I am grateful to Philip Waller for pointing out this connection.
    [7] See, e.g., J. Hall (ed.), *Civil Society: Theory, History, Comparison* (Cambridge, 1995); J. Keane, *Civil Society: Old Images, New Visions* (Cambridge, 1998).

desirable. Élitism did not equate with anti-statism. That élitism was seen as essential to the welfare state might seem surprising to us because we have come to associate the welfare state with universalism and egalitarianism but, of course, as the 1944 Education Act showed, selection was always implicit in the welfare state. Many welfare-state theorists envisaged a technocratic cadre of expert planners.[8] The Moot circle shared this preoccupation with leadership, but conceived their élite more broadly and culturally; they did not want specialists, but generalists, cultural leaders with the breadth of vision to direct society.

Historians and literary critics have written much about élite and popular culture during the 1930s and 1940s. But those writers, exemplified by John Carey in *The Intellectuals and the Masses*, and D. L. LeMahieu in *Culture for Democracy*, have concentrated on *artistic* élitists—on the Bloomsbury Group, on Harold Nicolson, on F. R. Leavis—whose élitism largely consisted in decrying suburbia and being rude about Arnold Bennett.[9] That vein of élitism was not constructive; it did not offer an alternative political project to reform or direct mass culture. The élitism of Middleton Murry, or Mannheim, or Eliot was different. First of all, it was Christian, and saw its responsibility as the upholding of Christian standards in mass society. Secondly, this élitism *was* constructive. The élite was to be engaged and permeative; it was not going to retreat to Charleston or Sissinghurst, and pull up the drawbridge. In this respect the Moot was the heir of Coleridge's clerisy and Matthew Arnold's Hellenistic bearers of sweetness and light.

The Moot met two or three times a year, usually in the Home Counties or Oxford, and had between thirty and forty members. Wartime exigencies meant that they were often unable to attend its meetings, but they participated in debate through the circulation of papers, and through the columns of the weekly *Christian News-letter*, which was established in 1939. An extraordinarily disparate array of individuals also attended Moot meetings on an *ad hoc* basis as invited guests. They included Frank Pakenham, Reinhold Niebuhr, Oliver Franks, Michael Polanyi, Richard Southern, and R. H. Tawney.[10] Oldham (who had himself never been ordained) deliberately drew the Moot's members from lay people rather than from the clergy, though a few clergy such as Alec Vidler and V. A. Demant did attend. This was a conscious effort to eschew the institutional churches, though Archbishop William Temple corresponded with the Moot, sometimes using it as a sounding board.

---

[8] See, e.g., H. Laski, 'Choosing the Planners', in G. D. H. Cole *et al.*, *A Plan For Britain* (1943), 101–27; H. Morrison *et al.*, *Can Planning be Democratic?* (1944).

[9] J. Carey, *The Intellectuals and the Masses: Pride and Prejudice Among the Literary Intelligentsia* (1992); D. H. LeMahieu, *A Culture for Democracy: Mass Communication and the Cultivated Mind in Britain between the Wars* (Oxford, 1988). See also, F. R. Leavis, *Education and the University* (1943); H. Nicolson, *The War Years: Diaries and Letters* (1967).

[10] For an attempt (albeit incomplete) at collating attendance at the Moot, see R. Kojecky, *T. S. Eliot's Social Criticism* (1971), 237–9.

As with the ideas of any group, we have to be careful about ascribing too much of a common outlook to the members of the Moot. It was after all deliberately eclectic. Though its standpoint was avowedly Christian, it did not restrict itself to any denomination, and one of its most assiduous attendees, Karl Mannheim, was a Jew. Among other members were the liberal Anglo-Catholic Alec Vidler, the Scots Presbyterian John Baillie, and the Roman Catholic historian and sage Christopher Dawson. Nor, despite its preoccupation with élites, was the Moot even loosely Conservative. One prominent member, John Middleton Murry, was a pacifist and former Communist who had been experimenting with an agrarian community in East Anglia. Philip Mairet, a frequent attendee (though not actually a member), had been associated with guild socialism and social credit. Even T. S. Eliot was not a straightforward Tory; as Maurice Cowling has pointed out, those who have rifled carelessly through his essays to find evidence of tweedy obscurantism (or worse, anti-semitism) have missed the revolutionary nature of his proposals for social reordering.[11] Eliot and Mannheim were the two dominant figures in the Moot, and among its most assiduous contributors, and most of the writing on the Moot has concentrated on them, eclipsing the contributions of other thinkers.[12] This chapter tries to set their ideas in the broader ideological context of the Moot. It draws on the Moot Papers and the *Christian News-letter*, as well as on the books and articles which Moot members published before, during, and after the war.

Three books written in 1939 by prominent members of the Moot each called for the establishment of some sort of élite. John Middleton Murry's *The Price of Leadership* was a plea for the establishment of a new ruling class. This was to be 'a really dynamic class, the class of men educated to rule—to rule politically, to take conscious decisions that determine the lives of the people of the country, and decide the future of society'.[13] The Roman Catholic convert Christopher Dawson's *Beyond Politics* contained a similar plea. 'What is necessary', wrote Dawson, 'is some organisation which is neither political nor economic and which will devote itself to the service of national life and the organisation of national culture.'[14] Eliot quoted this passage in his 1939 lectures on *The Idea of a Christian Society*, in which he also acknowledged a debt to Middleton Murry. He called for a 'Community of Christians', which would 'contain both clergy and laity of superior intellectual and/or spiritual gifts'.[15]

---

[11] M. Cowling, *Religion and Public Doctrine* (Cambridge, 1980), i. 95–127.

[12] For a recent example, see S. Collini, 'The European Modernist as Anglican Moralist: The Later Social Criticism of T. S. Eliot', in M. S. Micale and R. L. Dietle (eds.), *Enlightenment, Passion, Modernity: Historical Essays in European Thought and Culture* (Stanford, 2000), 207–29. For exceptions, see M. Reeves (ed.), *Christian Thinking and Social Order: Conviction Politics from the 1930s to the Present Day* (1999), and W. Taylor, 'Education and the Moot', in R. Aldrich (ed.), *In History and in Education: Essays Presented to Peter Gordon* (1996), 159–86; and K. W. Clements, 'John Baillie and the Moot', in D. Fergusson (ed.), *Christ, Church and Society: Essays on John Baillie and Donald Baillie* (Edinburgh, 1993), 119–219.

[13] J. Middleton Murry, *The Price of Leadership* (1939), 45.

[14] C. Dawson, *Beyond Politics* (1939), 28.

[15] T. S. Eliot, *The Idea of a Christian Society* (1939), 37.

What prompted this desire for an élite? In part it was a reaction to the cults of leadership being seen on the continent. It is significant that Oldham had borrowed Nazi language to describe his order as 'spiritual storm troops'. Middleton Murry's *The Price of Leadership* analysed the way the Nazis and Soviets had created new ruling classes, arguing that if democracy was going to succeed against them, it would need leadership of its own.[16] Despite being a refugee from Nazism, Mannheim was particularly keen to borrow from the Nazi élite's manipulation of mass emotion, complaining to the Moot in January 1941 that, in comparison with Germany, 'so far democracy had failed to see the importance of the élites guiding and leading emotional trends'.[17]

The writers also believed that traditional liberal democracy had failed because it ceased to provide common values, in particular religious values. Dawson spoke for them all when he proclaimed that 'liberalism is a dying power'.[18] It had gone wrong because it had become neutral and value-free. It is significant what a dirty word 'neutral' was in and around wartime, when neutrality had very different connotations (of compliance, treachery, or amorality) from those benign ones which it has since acquired. Eliot's critique of contemporary Britain in *The Idea of a Christian Society* was not that it was pagan—it was not—but that it was 'neutral'.[19] In an essay on 'The Crisis in Valuation', circulated to the Moot in 1942, and printed in the *Christian News-letter*, Karl Mannheim used the example of Weimar Germany (from which he had come) as a 'neutralized' democracy whose lack of common values had laid it open to totalitarianism. Only a democracy based on common values could survive.[20] Dawson likewise wrote in 1939 that 'if western democracy is to be saved it is necessary to find some way of removing the divided aims, the lack of social discipline and the absence of national unity that are the weaknesses of democracy, without falling under the tyrannies of dictatorship, and the fanatical intolerance of a totalitarian party.'[21] Dawson and Mannheim both believed that the source of these common values in a democracy should be a cultural élite. The educationist Fred Clarke agreed, telling the Moot in 1942 that 'the only security for democracy was that it should create its own aristocracy'.[22]

Moot writers were particularly critical of *academic neutrality*. Academics and teachers, they argued, were retreating into subject specializations, and using academic neutrality as a shield, because they did not want to address controversial philosophical and religious questions. The result was that children were receiving a neutral, and hence secular, education. In his 1945 book *What is Christian Civilisation?* the Scottish theologian John Baillie expressed his fears of

---

[16] Middleton Murry, *The Price of Leadership*, 56.

[17] Minutes of 10th meeting, 10–13 January 1941, Clarke Papers, file 6.

[18] Dawson, *Beyond Politics*, 102.   [19] Eliot, *The Idea of a Christian Society*, 9.

[20] Reprinted in K. Mannheim, *Diagnosis of Our Time: Wartime Essays of a Sociologist* (1943), 25.

[21] Dawson, *Beyond Politics*, 12.

[22] Minutes of 14th meeting, 27–30 March 1942, Oldham Papers, file 13.

what would happen to Christian children, subjected to neutral culture as they grew up. 'If these, though born into a spiritual home, are to be educated in spiritually neutral schools and then launched into a spiritually neutral society fed by neutral newspapers and a neutral BBC, how many of them will be strong enough to swim against the tide?' he asked.[23] Sir Walter Moberly, first chairman of the University Grants Committee, continued the attack on neutrality in his book *The Crisis in the University*, which was published in 1949 but which had begun life as a Moot paper in 1940. Moberly's book attacked the secularization of university education, the fragmentation of academic disciplines, and the 'sham' of academic neutrality.[24] Moot members took different views of the type of religious education syllabus which should be taught in schools and universities, but they all agreed that all education must be fundamentally religious.

What were the origins of the Moot's ideas on elites? There were three main sources: the liberal Anglican tradition; the sociological writings of Karl Mannheim; and the medieval idea of civil society. The most obvious source lay in the liberal Anglican tradition. As Julia Stapleton has recently pointed out, that tradition—the tradition of Arnold and the British Idealists—had been ambivalent about élites. On the one hand, particularly in the nineteenth century, they were needed to act as Platonic guardians of national culture. On the other hand, and particularly in the twentieth century, Idealism proclaimed equality and education for citizenship, through adult education and the Workers' Education Association (WEA).[25] In the late 1930s and 1940s, disaffection with democracy led some Anglican writers to go back to nineteenth-century authorities, and in particular to three archetypes—Samuel Taylor Coleridge, Thomas Arnold, and his son Matthew Arnold. In *On the Constitution of Church and State* in 1830, Coleridge had addressed the question of what the job of a national church should be in a denominationally pluralist society. He concluded that it must act as a cultural educator, and developed the concept of the national clerisy, a learned Christian order consisting of clergy and schoolteachers, whose job it was to educate the public. For Coleridge, this clerisy was coterminous with the national church, though it included laymen. Its job lay 'in producing and re-producing, in preserving, continuing and perfecting, the necessary sources and conditions of national civilisation'. 'A permanent nationalized, learned order, a national clerisy or church', wrote Coleridge, 'is an essential element of a rightly constituted nation, without which it wants the best security alike for its permanence and progression.'[26]

T. S. Eliot drew heavily on Coleridge in *The Idea of a Christian Society*. He explained that he derived his use of the term the *Idea* of a Christian society from Coleridge, and also explicitly drew on Coleridge's idea of a clerisy as the basis

[23] J. Baillie, *What is Christian Civilisation?* (1945), 40.
[24] W. H. Moberly, *The Crisis in the University* (1949), 53–4.
[25] J. Stapleton, 'Political Thought, Elites and the State in Modern Britain', *Historical Journal*, 42 (1999), 251–68.
[26] S. T. Coleridge, *On the Constitution of Church and State* (1976), 53, 69.

for his own concept of the 'community of Christians'.[27] Eliot's community of Christians was a bit different from Coleridge's clerisy—it was wider, in that it was to include non-Christians, but also narrower, in that it was to be more restricted to those of particular intellectual gifts, and was not to include the whole of the teaching body.[28] Middleton Murry also used the term 'clerisy', and frequently invoked Coleridge and the Arnolds for their ideas of the Christian nation. Unless England could understand itself, he wrote in *The Price of Leadership*, 'I believe, it is doomed; and I believe that the only way it can understand itself is as Coleridge and the Arnolds understood it, as a Christian national society' (p. 171). Middleton Murry's theories about the education of the ruling class were derived from the Arnolds. Eliot, though, was critical both of Thomas Arnold, whose theology he thought defective, and of Matthew Arnold, whom he accused of wanting a politically disengaged form of culture, 'culture in a vacuum'.[29]

Coleridge and the Arnolds particularly appealed to writers at the start of the Second World War because they had addressed questions about the moral role of the state and the dangers of democracy to cultural unity. All three nineteenth-century writers had expounded doctrines of an organic state, with moral responsibilities, and these doctrines acted as inspiration for those who were trying to safeguard the moral unity and Christian character of the welfare state. For Coleridge, the state was 'a moral unit, an organic whole', while for Matthew Arnold it represented 'our best self'.[30] Middleton Murry was especially attracted to the Arnolds' idea of the state, and in *The Price of Leadership* he even went as far as Thomas Arnold in envisaging the eventual convergence of church and state in a single body. Hostile critics of reconstruction recognized the affinity between the welfare state and the Coleridgean tradition. Writing in the *Christian News-letter* in 1944, the editor of the Roman Catholic *Tablet*, Douglas Woodruff, branded apostles of the welfare state as the 'new clerisy'.[31]

A second source for the Moot's ideas on élites was Karl Mannheim himself. It is worth separating him from other members of the Moot because he was a more systematic thinker than the rest, and because, as a Hungarian who taught at Frankfurt until 1933, he had been subjected to different intellectual influences. Mannheim's book *Man and Society in an Age of Reconstruction* had originally been published in 1935, but was translated into English in 1940, and was very influential in Britain. In it, Mannheim argued that the greater functional rationalization of modern industrial life—the fact that people only performed a particular task—meant that most of the population were too engrossed in that task to take a long view of society. An élite was therefore required to do the thinking for them. 'A few people can see things more and

---

[27] Eliot, *The Idea of a Christian Society*, 67.   [28] Ibid., 35–8.
[29] Murry, *Price of Leadership*, 171; Eliot, *The Idea of a Christian Society*, 79; 'Cultural Forces in the Human Order', in M. Reckitt (ed.), *Prospect for Christendom* (1945), 58.
[30] M. Arnold, *Culture and Anarchy* (Cambridge, 1993), 181.
[31] *Christian News-letter*, Supplement to No. 207 (3 May 1944).

more clearly', he argued, 'while the average man's capacity for rational judgement steadily declines once he has turned over to the organiser the responsibility for making decisions'.[32] But, Mannheim argued, just when an élite was
becoming so crucial, its quality was deteriorating; élites had become cut off
from Europe's traditions (including the Christian tradition), and they were no
longer being chosen on grounds of achievement—in Nazi Germany, for example, they were absurdly being chosen on grounds of race. This decline in the
quality of élites, said Mannheim, represented a process of 'negative democratisation'.[33] Mannheim's influence on the Moot was considerable, but not over-
weaning. As Colin Loader has argued in his study of Mannheim's thought, he
took as much from it intellectually as he gave.[34] He used the Moot as a test-bed
for his ideas, and his 1943 book, *Diagnosis of Our Time*, was heavily based on
his contributions to Moot meetings.

Mannheim came closer than anyone else to providing the Moot with a clearly
articulated theory of the state, something which was glaringly absent from most
of its contributions.[35] He advocated a 'third way' between Communism and
Fascism, 'planning for freedom', by which he meant a democratic, planned society, with considerable power to direct the individual.[36] Mannheim's state was
organic, and he argued that its organs, such as youth, could be forced to act
towards the greater good, hence his advocacy of compulsory youth service. He
does not seem to have differentiated between the interests of the state and those
of the community. 'Planning for Freedom' became something of a mantra for
members of the Moot, who seem to have been rather in awe of the copious and
ponderous papers which Mannheim set before them at their meetings.
Middleton Murry resented the uncritical attitude of the other members towards
'Planning for Freedom', complaining in a letter to Oldham in 1942 that 'we have
accepted the idea of Planning for Freedom as a kind of orthodoxy, without ever
having submitted it to radical criticism'. This left the Moot open to accusations
of 'dilettantism'.[37] Middleton Murry's disaffection with Mannheim was such
that he ceased to attend Moot meetings after 1942.

The third source for the Moot's idea of élites was what we might term the
medieval-pluralist tradition. As the Anglo-Saxon echoes of its name suggested,
the Moot was receptive to medievalism, and among its attendees and correspondents were the medieval scholars Walter Oakeshott and Richard Southern.
The medieval concept which drove much Moot discussion was that of a civil
society of orders, divided according to function. The Moot received it via two
recent intellectual sources. First of all, guild socialist writers like G. D. H. Cole
had argued that the different orders of modern industrial society should each be

[32] K. Mannheim, *Man and Society in an Age of Reconstruction* (1940), 59.   [33] Ibid., 88.
[34] C. Loader, *The Intellectual Development of Karl Mannheim: Culture, Politics and Planning*
(Cambridge, 1985).
[35] For an exception, see A. Vidler, 'Has the State a Conscience?' Moot Paper, 8 May 1944, in New
College, Edinburgh, Baillie Papers, vol. 10.
[36] Minutes of 11th Meeting, 4–7 April 1941, Oldham Papers, file 13.
[37] Middleton Murry to Oldham, 14 September 1942, Clarke Papers, file 15.

corporately represented in a democracy. This idea of functional democracy suffered an eclipse in the mid-1920s, and was discredited by Mussolini's corporativism, but some of its proponents like Maurice Reckitt continued to propagate the idea of a society of functions through Christian think-tanks like the Christendom Group. From the guild socialist insistence upon a society of occupational groups distinguished by function, it was but a short step to arguing that one of these groups should be an intellectual or administrative order which should direct the rest of society. In a book on *Aristocracy and the Meaning of Class Rule*, published in 1931, Philip Mairet, a Swiss-born associate of the guild socialist A. R. Orage, argued the need for a new aristocracy.[38] Democracy, said Mairet, had failed because it had not recognized that social orders were necessary. Only a society of orders, regulated by a new aristocracy, or 'axiocracy', would survive. A former member of C. R. Ashbee's arts and crafts community at Chipping Campden, Mairet later joined the Church of England, becoming an attendee at the Moot during the war.[39] Two other Moot contributors, V. A. Demant and Christopher Dawson, had been supporters of guild socialism in their youth, and retained a pluralist suspicion of state power.[40] Both men had written for Eliot's *Criterion* in the 1930s, and Eliot had been influenced by their pluralist ideas. Stefan Collini has recently argued that Eliot's later political thought is best understood as belonging in the pluralist tradition.[41]

The other guise in which neo-medievalist ideas on élites reached the Moot was through the Roman Catholic revival of Thomism, and principally through the French philosopher Jacques Maritain. Here a short digression is required on medieval ideas of civil society. The Canadian philosopher Charles Taylor has recently argued that the crucial legacy of medieval political thought is 'in a sense a negative fact; that society is not defined in terms of its political organisation'. For Taylor, this fact is 'one of the origins of the later notion of civil society and one of the roots of western liberalism'.[42] The popularity of civil society in recent years has led some historians to look at its medieval antecedence, and how it was conveyed into the modern period.[43] Although medieval authors used a bewildering array of terms to describe civil society, their ideas shared a number of characteristics—principally, a belief in a God-given hierarchy, in which different orders fulfilled different functions, and an insistence that parts of that society (among them the church) were beyond the state's control. The autonomy of civil society was sometimes unclear; in Aquinas's writings, for example, there was an

---

[38] P. Mairet, *Aristocracy and the Meaning of Class Rule: An Essay upon Aristocracy Past and Future* (1931).

[39] For Mairet, see C. H. Sisson, *English Perspectives* (Manchester, 1992), 96–108.

[40] For Dawson's early guild socialism, see 'The Passing of Industrialism' (1920), in *Enquiries into Religion and Culture* (1933), 55.

[41] Collini, 'The Later Social Criticism of T. S. Eliot', 210.

[42] C. Taylor, 'Invoking Civil Society', *Philosophical Arguments* (Harvard, 1995), 210–11.

[43] A. Black, *Guilds and Civil Society in European Political Thought from the Twelfth Century to the Present* (1984); J. Ehrenberg, *Civil Society: The Critical History of an Idea* (New York and London, 1999), ch. 2.

unresolved tension between an Aristotelian belief in the unity of the political community, and a countervailing insistence that man was not completely absorbed by that community.[44] But this apparent ambivalence in Thomist thought nevertheless enabled later interpreters to cite Aquinas in support of the rights of individuals and groups against the state.

This pluralist interpretation of civil society was especially attractive to mid-twentieth-century Roman Catholic writers looking for an alternative to state socialism. In his 1931 encyclical *Quadragesimo Anno*, Pius XI drew on Aquinas to propose a pluralist body politic in which power was handed down the social hierarchy to vocational groups organized by function. This was the principle of subsidiarity:

> It is an injustice and at the same time a grave evil and disturbance of right order to assign to a greater and higher association what lesser and subordinate associations can do . . . The supreme authority if the state ought, therefore, to let subordinate groups handle matters and concerns of lesser importance . . . those in power should be sure that the more perfectly a graduated order is kept among the various associations, in observance of the principle of 'subsidiarity of function', the stronger social authority and effectiveness will be and the happier and more prosperous the condition of the state.[45]

During the 1930s, Jacques Maritain drew on this encyclical and on his own reading of Aquinas to develop the idea of a functionally organized civil society.[46] A former supporter of Charles Maurras's Action Française (to which Eliot had also been attracted), Maritain had publicly repudiated the movement and become a trenchant critic of Catholic fascism, condemning the bombing of Guernica. He was well known in British Catholic circles, and his book *Religion and Culture* had been published in Dawson's 'Essays in Order' series in 1931.[47] He had also written for Eliot's *Criterion*. Rather like the East European civil society theorists of the 1980s and 1990s, Maritain found it instructive to counterpoise the diversity of medieval civil society to the uniformity of the contemporary totalitarian state. But, like Dawson, he was also critical of liberal democracy, which his 1935 book *Freedom in the Modern World* proclaimed was 'finished . . . bankrupt by the turn of events'. Instead, Maritain proposed a pluralist vision of civil society, in which 'the economic and political order of civil society would embody distinct and compact social groups, be they called corporations or guilds or what you will. But each of these lesser entities in the social order would have its own spontaneous life, not derived from the state.'[48]

---

[44] A. Black, 'The Individual and Society', in J. H. Burns (ed.), *Cambridge History of Political Thought I, c.350–1450* (Cambridge, 1988), 588–606. See also above, Ch. 1.

[45] *Quadragesimo Anno* (1931), 79–80.

[46] For Maritain's debt to Aquinas, see J. P. Hittinger, 'Reasons for a Civil Society', in T. Fuller and J. P. Hittinger (eds.), *Reassessing the Liberal State: Reading Maritain's Man and the State* (Washington, 2001), 11–23.

[47] J. Maritain, *Religion and Culture* (1931).

[48] J. Maritain, *Freedom in the Modern World* (1935), trans. by R. O'Sullivan, 55, 63. In the French edition of this book, *Du régime temporel et de la liberté* (1933) and in *Humanisme intégrale*, Maritain used the French phrase 'société civile', which his English translators rendered as 'civil society'.

In his 1936 book *Humanisme intégral*, published in Britain in 1938 as *True Humanism*, Maritain gave a full account of what this pluralist society would be like. Maritain was adamant that it was not possible to return to the unity of medieval Christendom, and that modern civil society would have to be more diverse, and so proposed 'une cité pluraliste' (a 'pluralist commonweal'). There would be 'une hétérogénie organique dans la structure même de la société civile' (an 'organic heterogeneity in the structure of civil society').[49] Such a society would be Christian in its orientation, standards, and values, but tolerant of other religions, and would embody only a 'minimal unity'.[50] The Christian values of society would be guaranteed by lay orders of intellectuals, which he variously described as 'civic fraternities' and 'cives praeclari', 'the most politically evolved and most devoted section of the Christian laity'. These orders would play an 'animating and formative' part in the life of civil society.[51] Maritain's society would be a new form of 'personalist democracy', which upheld human dignity in a way that liberal democracy had not done. It would defend the right of groups and individuals against the state, but it would also be more 'authoritarian' than a liberal democracy.[52]

The influence of *True Humanism* on the Moot circle when it was published in Britain in 1938 was enormous, and it was the subject of discussion in January 1939.[53] John Baillie acclaimed the work in a Moot paper, pointing out how close Maritain's idea of 'cives praeclari' was to Middleton Murry's clerisy. Maritain had shown 'how to transcend the weakness of liberal democracy without surrendering to the totalitarian principle'.[54] The book became a constant point of reference for later discussions, and was a key source for Eliot's *Idea of a Christian Society*. Maritain, who spent most of the war in North America, met with Moot members at Eliot's club during a visit to Britain to discuss the creation of an order.[55] That Anglicans and Presbyterians were so heavily influenced by a French Roman Catholic was an important reflection of the increasing ecumenism of the 1930s and 1940s, and of a new receptiveness on the part of British Protestants to Roman Catholic natural law theories (though some, like Alec Vidler, were sceptical).[56]

Several aspects of the society described in *True Humanism* had a particular appeal for Moot members. The idea of a society which combined Christian values with freedom for non-Christians appealed to Oldham, who wrote in a 1940 pamphlet on *The Resurrection of Christendom*, that Christendom could no longer be 'a society in which all men are Christians', but that it should be 'a society leavened by Christian insights and standards'.[57] Eliot's *Idea of a Christian*

---

[49] Maritain, *Humanisme intégrale* (Paris, 1936), 177, trans. by M. Adamson as *True Humanism* (1938), 157.
[50] Maritain, *True Humanism*, 165.   [51] Ibid., 162–6.   [52] Ibid., 176.
[53] R. Kojecky, *T. S. Eliot's Social Criticism*, 168.
[54] Undated paper by Baillie, Oldham Papers, file 14.
[55] Anonymous undated note, Oldham Papers, file 13.
[56] Vidler, Moot Minutes, 27–30 March 1942, Clarke Papers, file 12.
[57] J. H. Oldham, *The Resurrection of Christendom* (1940), 52.

Society was based, like Maritain's, on a 'minimal unity', and he was even pre-pared to see non-Christians in his elite.[58] In redefining a Christian society, Maritain thus helped the Moot to address the objection that such a society was no longer realistic or desirable. Moot members recognized that the new welfare state was not going to be a confessional state, but they did not accept that it therefore had to be a neutral state.

The term 'civil society' was largely eschewed by members of the Moot. (Significantly, one of those who did use it, John Baillie, was a Scot.[59]) Nevertheless, although they did not use the term, we can discern aspects of Maritain's idea of civil society in the ideas of national culture articulated by V. A. Demant and T. S. Eliot before, during, and after the Second World War. At William Temple's Malvern Conference in 1941, Demant argued that England had a clearly marked-out sphere of society, free of state control, which was pluralistic, but also united by a common purpose. 'Her political life . . . reflected a plurality of social functions, such as culture, knowledge, economic occupation and law, each with its own vitality drawn from a common sense of human purpose and therefore an independence of the central executive.'[60] Later in the war, Demant developed his ideas on the Christian character of this sphere of society, which he now called 'culture.' In a collection of lectures given in 1944 on *Our Culture* (to which Dawson and Dorothy L. Sayers also contributed) he wrote that a nation's culture included 'its politics, economic life and the natur-ally given forms of community like the family, as well as the free associations of those who are bound by social allegiances such as religion', but did not include the authority of the state.[61] Demant's culture, then, was close to Maritain's 'civil society'—a sphere of diverse associational life which was free of state control.

Eliot's own ideas on culture were strongly influenced by Demant, and his 1948 book, *Notes Towards the Definition of Culture*, had originated as a Moot Paper on 'Cultural Forces in the Human Order'. A striking and rather baffling aspect of the book was its very diverse and permissive definition of culture, in which Eliot famously included Wensleydale cheese, beetroot in vinegar, the cup final, and dog racing.[62] But this incongruously plebeian list is more comprehen-sible if Eliot's definition of culture is seen in the light of Maritain's idea of soci-ety. Like medieval civil society as described by Maritain, Eliot's 'culture' was a single, holistic organism, which included a hierarchy of diverse activities but which also pursued a common good. Eliot was happy to see culture separating into different levels—this was a natural process—but he strongly resisted cul-tural disintegration.[63] This was why he was so insistent on the need for the élite

---

[58] Eliot, *The Idea of a Christian Society*, ch. 2.
[59] Baillie, 'Comments on Murray's Paper', undated Moot Paper, Oldham Papers, file 14.
[60] V. A. Demant, 'Christian Strategy', in *Malvern 1941: The Life of the Church and the Order of Society, Being the Proceedings of the Archbishop of York's Conference* (1941), 128.
[61] V. A. Demant (ed.), *Our Culture: Its Christian Roots and the Present Crisis* (1947), 2.
[62] Eliot, *Notes Towards the Definition of Culture* (1948), 31.   [63] Ibid., 48.

to remain engaged and outward-looking. While Mannheim and Michael Polanyi envisaged multiple élites of specialists, Eliot insisted that there must be a single clerisy, otherwise culture would disintegrate.[64] There were other sources for Eliot's and Demant's ideas on national culture, not least Christopher Dawson's own broad, anthropological definition of culture. But in Maritain's pluralist hierarchy they found a clue to the problem of how to maintain a common (and loosely Christian) national culture without forfeiting the diversity and freedom of associational life.

This pluralist-medievalist perspective sometimes brought Eliot, Dawson, and Demant into conflict with the liberal Anglican and Mannheim traditions, both of which saw civil society (including culture and religion) as open to direction by the state. This led to rows in the Moot. At the second meeting of the Moot in 1938, John Middleton Murry wrote an article calling for 'the Christianisation of the state', on the grounds that it was 'an instrument for realising the kingdom of God'.[65] This drew objections from Eliot and Dawson, who accused him of failing to distinguish between state and society, and of subjecting the church to the needs of the state. Middleton Murry was also criticized for basing his argument on such dubious statists as Rousseau, and Thomas and Matthew Arnold, and Eliot later accused him of being 'ready to go a long way towards totalitarianism'.[66] In a 1941 paper, 'Planning and Culture' Dawson took issue with Mannheim's belief in cultural planning, insisting that that 'the planning of culture cannot be undertaken in a dictatorial spirit, like a rearmament plan'. He challenged Mannheim's assertion that the state could remould human nature. 'If the state is entrusted with this task it will inevitably destroy human freedom in a more fundamental way than even the totalitarian states have yet attempted to do.'[67] V. A. Demant also complained of the 'artificiality' of attempts to propagate culture, insisting that 'neither education, nor politics, nor planning can create a culture, they can only grow out of one'.[68]

There were a number of other points of conflict within the Moot, one of which was how the élite was to be educated. There was general agreement among the Moot that it must be drawn from all different social classes. T. S. Eliot stated that 'I should not like the community of Christians . . . to be thought of as merely the nicest, most intelligent and public spirited of the upper middle class', though, as Raymond Williams pointed out, he sometimes seemed to want *exactly* that.[69] Not surprisingly, given events in Germany when they were writing, none of the Moot attempted to argue that the élite should be selectively

[64] Ibid., 37–41; Eliot to Moot, 22 November 1944, Baillie Papers, vol. 10.

[65] Middleton Murry, 'Towards a Christian Theory of Society', Oldham Papers, file 14.

[66] Dawson and Eliot, undated comments on Middleton Murry Paper, Oldham Papers, file 14; Eliot, *The Idea of a Christian Society*, 81.

[67] Dawson, 'Planning and Culture', n.d., Oldham Papers, file 14.

[68] Demant, 'The Incompetence of Unaided Virtue', Moot Paper, 7 February 1946, Baillie Papers, vol. 10.

[69] Eliot, *The Idea of a Christian Society*, 60–1; R. Williams, *Culture and Society 1780–1850* (1958), 227–43.

bred through eugenics, as Dean Inge, for example, had done in the 1920s and 1930s. Instead, it was agreed that élites should be chosen from *all* social classes by rigorous academic selection. The Moot members' belief in a society in which people were classed by their social *function* meant that they were attracted to the theories of selection by aptitude being pioneered by educationists like Cyril Burt.[70]

The education of élites was to involve civic training. Mannheim was a vociferous advocate of a national youth movement, drawing (albeit critically) on the example of the Hitler Youth.[71] As Jose Harris has shown, compulsory youth service was among the proposals of the sub-committee on education of the Conservative Reconstruction Committee, in which Eliot and Oakeshott were involved.[72] The sub-committee's 1942 report, 'A Plan for Youth' (largely drafted by Walter Oakeshott), was rejected as unacceptably authoritarian by the Conservative Central Committee and the press, because it advocated a compulsory youth service. The role which a youth service could play in the education of an élite was described in a 1943 book by F. C. Happold, *Towards a New Aristocracy*.[73] Happold, the headmaster of Bishop Wordsworth School in Salisbury, described his own experiment with creating a Company of Honour of Service in his school. He saw such a feudal order as inculcating élite values in his boys. Though not a member of the Moot, Happold drew heavily on Fred Clarke, Mannheim, Oldham, and Eliot in making a case for the education of a Christian élite.

But there were differences among Moot members about the curriculum for teaching élites. Professor Fred Clarke, director of the London University Institute of Education, for example, saw the education of the élite in inclusive terms, as about 'democratising the aristocracy'.[74] For Clarke, élite education was part of a much wider programme of educational reform. Eliot, by contrast, opposed expansion of educational opportunity, believing that the main job of educators was 'the training of the superior few to superior reason and even to holiness'.[75] Fred Clarke felt that the old classical curriculum favoured by the public schools was too narrow, and should be modernized. Eliot warned luridly against the abandonment of classics in *Notes Towards the Definition of Culture*, declaiming that educationists were 'destroying our ancient edifices to

[70] See, e.g., C. Burt, 'Ability and Income', *British Journal of Educational Psychology* (1943), 83–98.

[71] See, e.g., Mannheim, 'The Problem of Youth in Modern Society', reprinted in *Diagnosis of Our Time: Wartime Essays of a Sociologist*, 31–53.

[72] J. Harris, 'Political Ideas and the Debate on State Welfare, 1940–45', in Harold Smith (ed.), *War and Social Change* (Manchester, 1986), 241–6. See also J. Harris, 'Enterprise and Welfare States', *Transactions of the Royal Historical Society* (1990), 192.

[73] F. C. Happold, *Towards a New Aristocracy: A Contribution to Educational Planning* (1943).

[74] F. Clarke, 'Some Notes on English Educational Institutions in the Light of the Necessities of "Planning for Freedom" in the Coming Collectivised Regime', 1939, Clarke Papers, file 2.

[75] Eliot in *Christian News-letter*, 8 July 1942.

make ready the ground upon which the barbarian nomads of the future will encamp in their mechanised caravans'.[76]

Another, rather fundamental, cause of confusion in the Moot was what exactly the élite was supposed to do. Middleton Murry called it a ruling class, and held that it should govern. For most of the others, though, the élite was about cultural leadership, not government, and during the crisis of 1940 there was no serious discussion of the possibility of taking power in the event of invasion. Walter Moberly saw the élite's job in idealist terms. 'They represent our own real, but hitherto unconscious and ineffective wills', he said; this was not very far from Matthew Arnold's idea of the 'better self'. It is significant that Moberly used Reith's BBC as an example of the sort of cultural leadership which the élite should offer. Unlike Hollywood, the BBC had not given the public what it thought it wanted, but 'the best it would put up with', and had thus educated public taste.[77]

Not all Christian writers in the Second World War shared the Moot's élitism. It is strikingly absent from the writings of prominent churchmen like William Temple and A. D. Lindsay, Master of Balliol, both Christian Socialists who belonged to a more democratic, egalitarian tradition of writing about community. Lindsay is a particularly interesting point of comparison because he was himself involved in the Moot. Although he did not attend its main meetings, Lindsay received and commented on Moot papers. He shared many of the preoccupations of the Moot's organizers. Like them, he was concerned by the compartmentalization of culture, and of the university syllabus. His educational experiment at the University College of North Staffordshire at Keele (in which he was strongly supported by Walter Moberly as chairman of the University Grants Committee) aimed to create a university like the one which Moberly advocated, in which specious divisions between academic disciplines were removed, and a broad curriculum was pursued. Lindsay also shared with other members of the Moot circle a belief in the indispensability of Christian education, which he tried to make compulsory for all students at Keele. Lindsay also sometimes appealed to the values of an idealized, public-spirited aristocracy. In his valedictory letter to his college on leaving Balliol for Keele in 1949, he wrote that 'the things we are proud of here, intense care for distinction and values, a life of the kind of leisure and free conversation among equals which helps to cultivate the things of the spirit, and a wide and generous toleration, are on the whole aristocratic virtues'.[78] But Lindsay's letter went on to praise the way that these aristocratic values coexisted with democratic ones, and it was his insistence on democracy, as well as revulsion against authoritarianism, which led him to reject Mannheim's idea of an élite. Writing to his daughter in 1942, Lindsay described a meeting with Mannheim and Oldham at which 'Mannheim . . . was

[76] Eliot, *Notes Towards the Definition of Culture*, 108.
[77] Moberly, *The Crisis in the University*, 141–2.
[78] Quoted in W. B. Gallie, *A New University: A. D. Lindsay and the Keele Experiment* (1960), 72.

in great form, putting extremely well the difference between dictatorial and democratic planning'. But, he went on to lament, 'I still feel that he doesn't get across the democratic side of it though.'[79] In a radio broadcast on Mannheim's death, Lindsay recalled that 'I, while welcoming and interested in almost all he said, thought him too systematic, too elaborate, too much of a planner.'[80] In a 1952 review of Mannheim's posthumously published *Freedom Power and Democratic Planning*, he complained that Mannheim's idea of 'planning for freedom' was undemocratic and 'too like Plato's Republic'. He particularly criticized Mannheim's idea of forming an order, saying 'there seems to be no sense behind this proposal at all'.[81]

Lindsay conceded that there must be expert leadership in society, but insisted that it should be subject to democratic control. In his most famous book, *The Modern Democratic State* (1943), he displayed his Presbyterian background when he remarked that he preferred the idea of an *elect*, who were chosen by God, to that of an *élite* chosen by men. He conceded that élites were necessary, but said that they needed to be tempered by the practical good sense of ordinary people. And he drew an implicit distinction between his own position and that of some of the Moot when he said 'the real issue between the democrats and the anti-democrats is that democrats think of a society where men can and do act as responsible persons. The anti-democrats talk of the mob, or the herd or the crowd.'[82]

The Moot had been predicated on the need for cultural leadership in conditions of crisis. When that crisis passed, its élitism lost much of its allure, and the Moot lost its momentum. When Karl Mannheim died, in January 1947, Oldham decided to wind it up, and it met for the last time in December 1947. In so far as the Moot had failed to reach agreement on any significant question, it had been a failure. As T. S. Eliot pointed out, in a letter in 1943, its very constitution had always made agreement impossible. 'It seems to me very doubtful whether the Moot, by nature of its composition, is fitted to frame any sort of "programme" to which all the members would spontaneously and whole-heartedly adhere with no qualifications to blunt its force', Eliot wrote. But, as Eliot hastened to add, this very disparateness was what had given the Moot its 'zest'.[83] The mark of the Moot's success was in its influence upon the thought of its members: Mannheim, Moberly, and Eliot all published influential books which had begun as Moot papers. Of course, the aspirations expressed in these books were almost all disappointed by social developments after the war. The welfare state which emerged at the end of the 1940s—centralized, morally neutral, and avowedly egalitarian—was very far from what the Moot had envisaged. The multicultural society which was developing at the time of Eliot's death in 1965 was, it is true,

---

[79] Lindsay to Drusilla Scott, 15 June 1942, Lindsay Papers, Keele University, vol. 152.
[80] Talk to BBC European Service, Lindsay Papers, Keele University, vol. 204.
[81] A. D. Lindsay in *British Journal of Sociology*, 3 (1952), 85–6.
[82] Lindsay, *The Modern Democratic State* (1943), 278–80.
[83] Eliot, letter to Moot, 9 August 1943, Baillie Papers, vol. 10.

diverse and pluralistic, but also far more secular and fragmented than he had envisaged. The Moot had lost the argument, but that loss should not blind us to the significance of its endeavour. By marrying nineteenth-century ideas of common culture with medieval ideas of Christian civil society, the Moot's thinkers had made an intriguing, if doomed, attempt to preserve religion, hierarchy, and common culture in the context of a modern mass society.

13

'Simple Solutions to Complex Problems': The Greater London Council and the Greater London Development Plan, 1965–1973

JOHN DAVIS

I

Historical writing on town planning stands out of all proportion to the actual achievements of town planners. Always a marginal component of the welfare state historiography of the 1960s and 1970s, with a strong emphasis on the idiosyncratic phenomena of the new towns, planning history survived the historiographical onslaught on the welfare consensus by transmuting itself into a branch of intellectual history. We have a fulsome knowledge of the ideas of Ebenezer Howard, Patrick Geddes, Thomas Sharp, and Patrick Abercrombie, even if one of the things we know is that few of their designs bore fruit.

This has produced a paradox. While planning historians continue to interest themselves in 'grand designs' for towns, the idea of top-down planning has been largely rejected by analysts of the contemporary planning process. As long ago as the 1960s, planning theorists in the United States, prompted by popular rejection of grandiose urban renewal programmes, began to question the concept of the planner as god. Galvanized by the example of the civil rights movement, the profession's radicals devised the concept of 'advocacy planning', by which planners offered aid to the urban voiceless, particularly those affected by road programmes, gentrification, and other threats to neighbourhood and community. On their own, these planning heretics and the underprivileged that they represented might have made little impact, but the general rejection of big government—including big local government—throughout the Western world from the mid-1970s reinforced doubts about large-scale town planning.[1] For

---

[1] A. J. Scott, 'Global City Regions: Planning and Policy Dilemmas in a Neo-Liberal World', in R. Freestone (ed.), *Urban Planning in a Changing World: The Twentieth Century Experience* (2000), 252–4.

this reason radical theorists during the last twenty years, responding to the new right's market-based assault on planning, have not sought a return to the Olympian ideals of planning pioneers. Modernist planning has been rejected as offering 'a plan without contradiction', which 'fails to include as *constituent* elements of planning the conflict, ambiguity and indeterminacy characteristic of actual social life'.[2] Radical planning theorists have called instead for a closer engagement of the planning profession with civil society.[3] For those at the cutting edge of this movement, even advocacy planning appeared too élitist, as theorists wrestled with the problem of whether white male professionals could or should speak for the ethnic minorities, the single mothers, the gays, and the disabled of the metropolis. The ideal of community 'empowerment' has brought an unfamiliar humility to the profession, reinforced by post-modern ideas of the metropolis as *unübersichtlich*—unknowable and therefore unplannable. The leading intellectual architect of this conversion sees 'urban planners being passionately engaged in a transformative politics for inclusion, opportunity for self-development and social justice. It is a politics driven by a civil society that is beginning to reassert itself in all of its diversity.'[4]

Historians' preoccupation with planning as intellectual history therefore threatens to obscure the process by which planners came into contact with 'real' societies, and the kind of negotiation entailed when planning departments sought to apply their projects to communities other than those in new towns or blitzed cities. This chapter seeks to capture this moment of engagement with civil society, through a case-study of a critical moment in the social rejection of top-down planning in Britain: the defeat of the Greater London Development Plan in the 1960s and 1970s.

II

To understand the conflicts of the 1970s we must understand the planning ethos of the 1940s. During the Second World War town planners benefited from public eagerness to build a better post-war world. The rejection of inter-war sprawl encouraged rational urban planning, and in many towns and cities aerial bombing provided the opportunity. The work of the leading planners—of Sharp, of Holford, and above all of Patrick Abercrombie—gained widespread attention and respect, and the post-war Labour government passed the 1947 Town and Country Planning Act—the foundation of the modern planning system.

---

[2] J. Holston, 'Spaces of Insurgent Citizenship', in L. Sandercock (ed.), *Making the Invisible Visible. A Multicultural Planning History* (Berkeley, 1998), 46.

[3] M. Carley, 'Top-down and Bottom-up: The Challenge of Cities in the New Century', in M. Carley, P. Jenkins, and H. Smith (eds.), *Urban Development and Civil Society* (2001), 3–15.

[4] J. Friedmann, 'The New Political Economy of Planning. The Rise of Civil Society', in M. Douglass and J. Friedmann (eds.), *Cities for Citizens. Planning and the Rise of Civil Society* (Chichester, 1998), 34–5.

The 1940s planners aspired to harness urban social dynamics. Abercrombie envisaged the plan not merely as a design exercise but as 'a social organism and a work of art.'[5] His two *magna opera*, the *County of London Plan*, produced with the London County Council's architect J. H. Forshaw in 1943, and the *Greater London Plan of 1944*, actually published in 1945, sketched a framework for urban life. This was, though, beyond the aspirations of the Attlee government: the 1947 act largely limited itself to the regulatory side of planning—the curbing of random and anti-social development. A national planning system emerged, with local authorities producing quinquennial development plans, but the emphasis was placed upon land use planning and development control. By the time this modern Domesday was completed, in 1961, a new generation of professional planners questioned the limited vision of the 1947 system.

Two principal criticisms emerged. The first was that a catalogue of land use could not reflect changing social habits, particularly the increase in personal mobility facilitated by the private car. The second was that the 1947 system embodied the *dirigisme* of its time, in its inflexibility, its emphasis upon control, and its failure to provide for consultation of the communities affected. Two landmark reports signalled the change of mood. The Buchanan Committee's *Traffic in Towns* (1963) argued that planners' anxiety to accommodate the growth in private transport had allowed traffic to choke city centres and damage urban life. It advocated rational design principles to canalize traffic and safeguard the realm of the pedestrian: purpose-built highways, elevated walkways, pedestrian precincts. Two years later, the Ministry of Housing's Planning Advisory Group asked 'how the planning system can be made a better vehicle for planning policies'. Arguing that development plans were often clogged by detail, it called for a separation of strategic and local planning. For larger urban areas it advocated

a new type of urban plan which concentrates on the broad pattern of future development and redevelopment and deals with the land use/transport relationships in an integrated way, but which excludes the detailed land use allocations of the present town maps[6]

Details could be left to the local planning process, leavened in future by more extensive public consultation and participation.[7]

Thus was born the concept of 'structure planning', which found its apogee in the Greater London Development Plan (GLDP). The preparation of a new strategic plan for London was the principal statutory duty assigned to the Greater London Council on its creation in 1965. The GLDP, published in 1969, was the most ambitious exercise in British urban planning since Abercrombie's 1944 plan. In attempting to shape demography, economy, mobility, housing, recreation, and the environment in the London of the future, it aspired to

[5] P. Abercrombie, *Planning in Town and Country* (1937), quoted in D. A. Hart, *Strategic Planning in London, the Rise and Fall of the Primary Road Network* (Oxford, 1976), 56.

[6] Planning Advisory Group, *The Future of the Development Plans* (1965), 1, 9.

[7] Ibid., 11, 39, 53.

Abercrombie's holism. One of its architects, Peter Stott, the GLC's director of highways and transportation, had been a member of the Planning Advisory Group, and the GLDP reflected the group's concern for strategy and flexibility. It sought 'an equilibrium between houses-work-movement', based upon empirical study of London life, in a plan flexible enough to be amended on the strength of current knowledge and future trends, rather than devoted to fixed objectives: 'housing + work + movement = the way that Londoners live'.[8]

To the officials of the Ministry of Housing and Local Government, steeped in the routine of development plans, the GLDP promised 'almost a revolution in planning techniques'.[9] To apply revolutionary techniques to a conurbation as large as Greater London was to invite trouble, and the eventual downfall of the GLDP doubtless owed much to the incautious ambition of its promoters, but the purpose of this chapter is not to stigmatize yet again the hubris of 1960s planners. It is rather to use the material generated by the GLDP to depict both the planners' aims and the public reaction to those aims. There has, of course, been no shortage of studies in the 'failure of planning' since the 1960s, but these are, in the main, treatments of small-scale popular—usually working-class—resistance to local redevelopment or slum-clearance projects. The recent release of the copious papers of the GLC's Planning and Transportation Department has made possible, though, a fuller understanding of the planners' objectives, while the inclusion in that collection of the 30,000 or so objections to the GLDP, along with the transcripts of the public inquiry into the plan, illustrates a public reaction more sophisticated than simple 'nimbyism'. In fact, no previous planning episode in Britain had entailed such a severe collision between planners and public.

III

Public reaction to the GLDP was, overwhelmingly, reaction to its most prominent feature—the proposal for three new[10] orbital motorways or 'Ringways'. Failure to respond to the challenge posed by the automobile had been the principal charge against traditional planning. The problem was most acute in London, given the capital's size and its higher levels of car-ownership. Abercrombie had pointed out that the radial bias of the existing metropolitan road system drew traffic into the centre, where an ancient street pattern could not cope with it, a problem which would be accentuated by the construction of

---

[8] Quotations from GLDP Preliminary Report, Autumn 1966, p. 2, and GLC/London Borough Councils, Joint Working Party on Town Planning, 'The Purpose and Nature of the Greater London Development Plan', 31 January 1966, p. 3, both in Stott Papers, London Metropolitan Archives, GLC/TD/CTD/02/020 (1).

[9] V. D. Lipman, Assistant Secretary, Planning, MHLG, in 'Meeting of Officers from Government Departments and Officers of the Greater London Council, . . . County Hall . . . 7th June 1966', GLC/TD/LU/01/096, p. 2.

[10] In fact the northern section of R2 was to be an upgrade of the existing North Circular Road.

a national motorway network centred on London. The Herbert Commission of 1963, which had recommended the creation of a Greater London Council, had seen strategic road planning as the council's principal purpose. By 1965, when the GLC came into being, London's traffic problems were a regular feature of press complaint,[11] and occasioned an emergency debate in parliament.

It was, therefore, inevitable that transport would be central to any London structure plan. Its prominence in the published support material, and in particular in the 1969 *Report of Studies*, was none the less disproportionate, giving rise to the charge that the GLDP was less a structure plan than 'a motorway plan, which makes transport the master, rather than the servant, of mankind'.[12] More than a quarter of the council's *Report of Studies*, the statutory document accompanying and explaining the plan, was devoted to transport.[13] What this demonstrates is a feature inherent in the professionalization of planning. Abercrombie's 1944 plan, though drawing upon expert advice, had been the product of one man's mind. Aware that 'town planning is in danger of becoming road planning',[14] Abercrombie had sought to keep the components of the plan in balance. Once planning became a local government duty, however, it became vulnerable to departmental rivalries and imbalances within planning authorities. The GLC's predecessor, the London County Council, had begun to shift its policy emphasis from housing to transport in the 1950s,[15] and with transport planning seen as the GLC's *raison d'être*, the Planning and Transportation Department became the council's favoured section.[16] In contrast, the downgrading of housing was reinforced in 1967 with the return of a Conservative majority which sought to diminish the council's housing role, selling houses to their occupiers and transferring GLC estates to the London boroughs.

Critically, this disparity became embedded in the empirical work on which the planning process rested. Abercrombie had worked by personal consultation with borough engineers and other specialists and was in no position to commission research. By the 1960s, though, it was a commonplace that, as J. R. Fitzpatrick, the GLC's assistant director of planning and transportation put it, 'the prerequisite of planning is information',[17] and the information gathered by the GLC and its predecessor was extensive. It was also lop-sided. The new priority given to transport in the early 1960s had prompted the compilation of the three-volume London Traffic Survey from 1962, which became the basis

[11] See, e.g., the editorial 'Road Sense', in *Evening Standard*, 10 September 1965; and Judy Hillman's article 'One Evening When London Nearly Died', *Evening Standard*, 4 November 1965.

[12] GLDP Inquiry, Objection 1641 (R. H. H. Taylor, SW17), GLC/TD/GLDP/09/017.

[13] Greater London Council, *Greater London Development Plan. Report of Studies* (1969), 139–222.

[14] P. Abercrombie, *Planning in Town and Country* (1937), quoted by D. A. Hart, *Strategic Planning*, 66.

[15] D. A. Hart, *Strategic Planning*, 110.

[16] P. Hall, *Great Planning Disasters* (1980), 62–3, 82–3.

[17] J. R. Fitzpatrick, Memorandum 'The GLC in the Field of Highways and Transportation. The Situation in April 1967', in Fitzpatrick Papers, GLC/TD/DPT/02/009.

of the GLC's traffic projections. The council's London Housing Survey, in contrast, was far less ambitious and was only completed in 1968, too late significantly to influence the GLDP.

The consequence was the intellectual poverty of the housing section of the GLDP, which the report of the public inquiry thought 'did not, in effect, constitute a strategic plan for housing in London'.[18] Yet London was, in these years, in the throes of a severe housing shortage: after the 'Rachman' and 'Cathy Come Home' scandals, most Londoners identified housing and homelessness as the capital's most pressing problems. The Ringway proposals threatened the demolition of up to 30,000 houses. This was a tiny proportion of London's housing stock: the annual rehousing rate over the motorways' thirty-year schedule would be no greater than that necessitated by schools and open spaces, council spokesmen often pointed out, 'and no one thinks it is wrong to rehouse people for these purposes'.[19] None the less, any diminution of the housing stock at a time of housing shortage was hard to defend: the 100,000 votes won by the single-issue Homes Before Roads party in the 1969 borough council elections[20] provided an early indication that the GLC had misjudged London's appetite for motorways.

Its failure reflected the difficulty of inferring public opinion from public behaviour. The GLC planners, like planners everywhere, based their proposals upon extensive empirical foundations. If the prerequisite of planning was information, the council had plenty of it: in addition to the London Traffic Survey, the council planners collated the central area land use survey of 1962, workplace tabulations from the 1961 census, surveys of office floor space in new buildings, Factory Inspectorate statistics on central area industries, 1948 and 1959 surveys of canal and riverside premises, London Transport's annual journey-to-work surveys, a 1962 central area car parking survey, a sample survey of business trip generation from 666 central area firms, work on housing stress areas, a 1964 survey of department stores in the centre and the west end, a 1964 analysis of central hotel accommodation, information on the seating capacity of cinemas and theatres, and even interviews with the users of Lincoln's Inn Fields and the Victoria Embankment.[21]

Except for the last, though, these were surveys of outcomes rather than attitudes. 'HOW DO THE GLC KNOW WHAT THE PEOPLE OF LONDON WANT? HAVE THEY EVER ASKED THEM?' demanded one of the objectors.[22] The GLC planners remained cautious about attitude surveys: market

---

[18] *Greater London Development Plan. Report of the Panel of Inquiry* (1973), Vol. I, Report, p. 185.

[19] Robert Vigars at the Lewisham Concert Hall meeting, *Lewisham Borough News*, 13 February 1969.

[20] P. Hall, *Great Planning Disasters* (1980), 79.

[21] From the summary of research material in 'Toward Policies for Central London—Appendix IV', Stott Papers, GLC/TD/CTD/02/020(1).

[22] S. Dermen, NW5, Obj.17921, in GLC/TD/GLDP/09/175, original capitals.

research techniques might be appropriate when 'a range of simple questions can be asked upon a particular topic', but 'would not be suitable for complicated major issues of strategy or policy'.[23] If market research confirmed behavioural surveys it would be redundant; if it conflicted with them it would be dubious. The reasoning was comprehensible, but it would none the less prove dangerous to infer public preferences from the council's voluminous survey material. This was demonstrated by the use made of the London Traffic Survey (LTS).

The reason for measuring traffic movements had been the problem of rush-hour congestion, but analysis of the LTS had produced a shift in emphasis by the time the motorway plans were published. In February 1965, presenting the conclusions drawn from the first two LTS volumes, Stott accepted that 90 per cent of journeys to work were made by public transport, but argued that the real problem lay in the clogging of the existing road network by intra-urban journeys not easily made by public transport—'journeys of the type Dagenham to Putney, Greenwich to Hampstead'. Orbital motorways facilitating such journeys offered, in plannerspeak, 'the only real opportunity available to secure adequate amenity provision in a modern pattern of living'.[24] The Traffic Survey had not only shown rising levels of car-ownership, but also suggested that future growth in car use would occur less for work than for pleasure. 'People's preferences are fairly clear at all income levels', Stott asserted 'We know that public transport and prohibition represent a lower standard of living than that we have arrived at . . . We must provide more road capacity.'[25] The motorways were recreational: the Conservative chairman of the Highways Committee after 1967, Robert Vigars, called the Ringways 'social roads'.[26]

This belief in a bottled-up public demand for high-grade urban roads may have encouraged the over-provision of motorways in the GLDP and the GLC's initial confidence that the motorways would be popular. It presumably explains the decision to present the roads as a social attraction rather than an economic necessity. In the preparation of the *Report of Studies* volume, it was decided that 'the material should state very early on that transport was a major element in determining the development of London, particularly in respect of general amenity—that is, the facility for movement and the quality of the environment'.[27] Anticipating a doubling of car-ownership between 1962 and 1981, Stott argued that 'the contribution that this personal mobility makes to efficiency and enjoyment is tempered by congestion and environmental deterioration'.[28] The

[23] Brief for meeting with members of the Skeffington Committee, 19 December 1968, in GLC/TD/PM/PC/01/016.

[24] P. F. Stott, 'Memorandum on the Future of London Communications, with Particular Reference to the Safeguarding of a Motorway Ring' (February 1965), Stott Papers, GLC/TD/CTD/02/028(1), p. 3.

[25] Stott, 'Presenting the Case for the GLDP: A Personal View', 30 July 1969, J. R. Fitzpatrick papers, GLC/TD/DPT/02/002.

[26] J. M. Thompson, *Motorways in London* (1969), 51.

[27] Memorandum by T. J. Widaker and B. V. Martin on the projected *GLDP Studies* Volume (22 March 1968), 1, Stott Papers, GLC/TD/CTD/02/020(1).

[28] GLDP Preliminary Report, Autumn 1966, p. 4, Stott Papers, GLC/TD/CTD/02/020(1).

argument that urban motorways are environmental assets appears puzzling now. It would, indeed, come under fire during the public inquiry, but it is clear that it was held with confidence by the GLDP's architects. It was, though, dangerously conjectural. There is no doubt that car-ownership levels were rising, or that the environmental blight caused by congestion was a nuisance, but these facts could not guarantee public support for the Ringways at all costs. Above all, in making one feature of 1960s' affluence—car-ownership—the basis for policy, the GLC neglected the implications of another—rising owner-occupation.

IV

'It really is ridiculous', complained one objector, 'People are encouraged to become "property owning democrats." They put a large part of their savings effort throughout their lives into buying a house. Then you come along and make it virtually worthless.'[29] 'I do not wish to live in Council accommodation—', protested another, 'all we want is our own home & to leave it at my convenience & not to be pushed out of it by the GLC & other bodies that limit our freedom to live where we choose'.[30] 'Our house is not only to be considered as a property but it is above all a home which took great sacrifices and considerable time to find and to adapt for our families [sic] purposes', wrote an objector in Camden.[31] The files of objections to the GLDP bristle with submissions from owner-occupiers who knew or feared that their houses lay in the path of the motorways. Those attending two of the local meetings held to discuss the GLDP in 1969 were disproportionately owner-occupiers.[32] So were the suburban opponents of Ringways 2 and 3: the Bromley-based Ringway 2 Resistance Group, for instance, found that of 349 people canvassed along the road's proposed route 80 per cent were owner-occupiers and all but three of them opposed the road.[33] 'Why have the GLC said it must be privately owned property that is blighted and not their own?', asked a Bromley woman.[34] The answer was, as the Planning Committee imprudently admitted,[35] that paying an owner sufficient

[29] GLDP Inquiry, Objection 17 (M. Geare, W4), GLC/TD/GLDP/09/001.

[30] GLDP Inquiry, Objection 18225 (P. Sherlock, NW6), GLC/TD/GLDP/09/178.

[31] GLDP Inquiry, Objection 2247 (A. Hedin, NW3), GLC/TD/GLDP/09/023.

[32] At the Camden meeting 54% of Camden, 35% of Islington, and 35% of Westminster respondents were owner-occupiers, against 1966 census figures of 12%, 14%, and 7% owner-occupiers for those boroughs as a whole. At the Croydon meeting the figures were 82% against 55% for Croydon and 80% against 63% for Sutton. M. Harris and M. Myers, 'The Public Meeting as a Means of Participation', GLC, *Quarterly Bulletin of the Research and Intelligence Unit*, 9 (December 1969), 5.

[33] GLDP Inquiry, Inquiry Support S27/92 (Ringway 2 Resistance Group), GLC/TD/GLDP/08/595.

[34] GLDP Inquiry, Inquiry Support S27/159 (M. Bayly, Bromley, Kent), GLC/TD/GLDP/08/595.

[35] Joint Report of Planning and Transportation Committee and Strategic Planning Committee, 14–15 July 1969, in GLC Minutes, 22 July 1969. This indiscretion was noticed by Mrs M. Grosvenor, GLDP Inquiry, Inquiry Support S27/94, GLC/TD/GLDP/08/595.

compensation to buy a new house was cheaper than rehousing council tenants, but the political cost was high indeed.

This was a middle-class resistance movement.[36] It is self-evident, though, that only a small proportion of the 30,000 objectors to the GLDP (mostly private individuals) were directly threatened by the road plans. The motorway protest was not simply a revolt of householders protecting their gardens. The significance of growing owner-occupation lies rather in its effect upon civic politics, in its encouragement of what David Donnison called the micro-politics of the city.[37] Analysis of those attending the Camden and Croydon public meetings showed that around a third of those present belonged to civic or amenity groups.[38] The marked expansion of owner-occupation in 1960s Britain had been accompanied by the rapid growth of the Civic Trust—the principal umbrella organization for amenity groups.[39] Owner-occupation perhaps conferred enhanced concern for the urban fabric; this was certainly the view of one Ministry of Housing official surveying the amenity group phenomenon in 1969: 'with rising wealth and aspirations, some of the wealth, and more importantly, some of the aspirations, will be turned to the physical environment'.[40] The growth of amenity groups typified an emergent conservation movement concerned less with the preservation of individual buildings than with the defence of familiar locales. 'There are no specific buildings that one can say attract people', explained one objector, of riverside Chiswick, 'there is no specific grassy patch or anything like that, but yet the whole build-up of that area, the way that it has been built up, appeals.'[41] The representative of the Grove Park Group in Chiswick challenged the plan's unadventurous approach to conservation, which largely confined itself to predictable national treasures:

the Plan merely states the obvious and nobody wishes to destroy St Paul's Cathedral and that is specifically mentioned but Oxford Street where it is mentioned is mentioned only as a problem area and yet Londoners who live in Dalston and Sunbury and Kingston make weekly expeditions to Oxford Street, not just St Paul's Cathedral, important though it is.[42]

---

[36] By extension, one of the very few instances of positive support for the road proposals came from working-class tenants along the West Cross Route (now the M41) who hoped that the motorway would get them rehoused. N. Raynsford, 'Motorway Madness', Community Action, 2 (April–May 1972), re: the Townmead Road area meeting.

[37] D. Donnison, 'The Micro-Politics of the City', in D. Donnison and D. Eversley (eds.), London. Urban Patterns, Problems and Policies (1973), 383–404.

[38] Harris and Myers, 'Public Meeting', 5.

[39] While the number of the Trust's affiliates had risen by 10 a year or fewer in the 1940s and 1950s, it had increased by 40–60 a year in the 1960s: W. Solesbury, 'The Needs of Environmental Planning', Background Paper, Symposium on Environmental Planning, Churchill College, Cambridge, January 1969, 4, Public Record Office, HLG 136/278.

[40] Solesbury, 'Needs of Environmental Planning', 5.

[41] Mr Ward, Chiswick Motorway Liaison Group, GLDP Inquiry, Notes of Proceedings, 91st Day, 22 April 1971, GLC/TD/GLDP/08/093, p. 46.

[42] GLDP Inquiry, Notes of Proceedings, 41st Day, 1 January 1971 (Mrs Jackson, Grove Park Group), GLC/TD/GLDP/08/043, p. 31.

The growth of these groups in London was rapid: by 1973 the 700 or so active community groups necessitated the publication of a separate *London Community Planning Directory*.[43] They varied in kind. Some had been formed in the early 1970s in order to defend working-class communities against the wave of redevelopment associated with the property boom; these groups played little part in the opposition to the GLDP. But the GLC calculated that 83 per cent of the first 21,000 objections either came from, or were supported by, local groups of some kind.[44] Many of the suburban groups were traditional ratepayers' associations.[45] Others had clearly been called into existence by the GLDP itself: the London Motorway Action Group, which spearheaded the resistance to the GLDP, included eighteen local anti-motorway groups among its corporate members. In inner London a number of well-established local societies, such as the Islington Society or the St John's Wood Preservation Society, essentially antiquarian local history groups, became active in the guerrilla campaign against the Ringways. They were joined by newer associations reflecting inner-city gentrification. The Barnsbury Association, formed in 1964, is exemplary. During the 1960s the proportion of professional and managerial families among Barnsbury residents had risen from 4 per cent to just over half.[46] The association was formed in August 1964 when news leaked that the area was to be redeveloped. From the summer of 1965 it had advocated an 'environmental plan with local citizen participation', lobbying government and running candidates in local elections.[47]

Such organizations mattered particularly because they embodied the resistance to Ringway 1—the 'motorway box'—the most fiercely contested of the three roads. The route plan of Ringway 1 amounts to a gazetteer of gentrification, encompassing Hampstead, Highgate, Islington, riverside Greenwich, Blackheath, Battersea, and other parts of the nineteenth-century urban rim, where middle-class colonists were renovating 'characterful' property. The GLC consistently underestimated this phenomenon. It stressed the dereliction of much inner area property as a selling point for Ringway 1,[48] without any apparent comprehension either of the amount of capital invested in gentrification or of the articulacy and determination of the gentrifiers.

The Barnsbury Association acknowledged its reliance upon 'an influx of professional people, many of whom are architects, traffic experts, town-planners and so on'.[49] The eventual public inquiry into the GLDP witnessed a debate on

[43] Advertisement in *Community Action*, 5 (November–December 1972); D. Eversley, *The Planner in Society. The Changing Role of a Profession* (1973), 210.

[44] 'Objections—Situation at 10 a.m., 10 March 1970', in GLC/TD/LU/01/103.

[45] e.g. the Federation of Ravensbourne Residents' Associations, a collection of 24 local groups brought together by the creation of the London Borough of Bromley in 1965: GLDP Inquiry, Notes of Proceedings, 88th Day, 19 April 1971 (G. C. Jenkins, Bromley Residents' Association), GLC/TD/GLDP/08/090, p. 2.

[46] A. Power, *A Battle Lost—Barnsbury 1972* (1972).

[47] 'Brief History of the Barnsbury Association', with the association's submission to the Skeffington Committee, PRO HLG 136/267.

[48] e.g. GLC, *Greater London Development Plan Statement* (1969), 11.

[49] 'Brief History of the Barnsbury Association', PRO HLG 136/267.

planning technique precisely because the opposition included so many people *au fait* both with current planning theory and with the case against it. But this was not just a planners' dispute: it involved a wider circle of informed white-collar laymen—teachers, lawyers, academics, and local government officers—who ensured that the case against road-building was elevated above the mere defence of property.

There is greater uniformity than might be expected in the 30,000 or so objections to the GLDP. In part this reflects effective organization by the opposition: many individual objections followed pro forma prescriptions devised by particular groups (GLC analysis identified 26 standard forms of objection in multiple use.)[50] Many of the arguments advanced in the opposition 'Bible', *Motorways in London*, written by the LSE economist J. M. Thompson for the London Amenity and Transport Association, became common objector currency. The GLC privately acknowledged the force of Thompson's book and urged their inquiry counsel to familiarize themselves with it.[51] Thompson provided a damaging critique of the LTS and its methodology. He demonstrated the poor return on capital provided by Ringway 1, provided the clearest exposition of the argument that new roads actually generated traffic, and called for a powerful Planning Inquiry Commission along the lines of the Roskill Inquiry into London's third airport.[52]

Beyond these influences, the objections display several themes illustrating middle-class sentiment on urban life in the early 1970s. Two seminal works had clearly entered the metropolitan bloodstream, by Steen Ellen Rasmussen and Jane Jacobs. Rasmussen's *London, The Unique City* (1934), a paean to the diversity and individuality of London villages, became received opinion among the GLDP's opponents.[53] 'London is, you know, a number of villages', the inquiry was told, 'each village with its group of suburbs which link together.'[54] Not only nominal villages like Blackheath and Highgate, but Chiswick and Barnes, even Lewisham and the Isle of Dogs were so depicted.[55] Chiswick, for example, was 'one of the few remaining village centres in London where they still play cricket on the Green on Saturdays in summer.'[56] The Ratepayers'

[50] 'Objections—Situation at 10 a.m., 10 March 1970', in GLC/TD/LU/01/103.

[51] 'Notes on Objections to the GLDP. Section 2: Transport', summary of Thompson by A. M. Voorhees, 23 July 1970, in GLC/TD/LU/01/103.

[52] J. M. Thompson, *Motorways in London* (1969).

[53] S. E. Rasmussen, *London, the Unique City*, 1st English edn. (1936). Rasmussen was specifically cited by N. Jackson, Grove Park Group, GLDP Inquiry, Notes of Proceedings, 41st Day, 1 January 1971, GLC/TD/GLDP/08/043, p. 32.

[54] R. F. Marsh, St Pancras Civic Society, GLDP Inquiry, Notes of Proceedings, 41st Day, 1 January 1971, GLC/TD/GLDP/08/043, p. 27.

[55] GLDP Inquiry, Inquiry Support S27/103 (Barnes Motorway Action Group), GLC/TD/GLDP/08/595; Inquiry Proofs E27/57 (Lewisham Society), GLC/TD/GLDP/08/548; E27/93 (Cllr. J. Daly, L. B. Hounslow), GLC/TD/GLDP/08/551; Objection 9163 (Harry Brack, for Tower Hamlets Society), GLC/TD/GLDP/09/087 for Isle of Dogs.

[56] GLDP Inquiry, Inquiry Support S27/25 (W. T. Newtold, Highgate), GLC/TD/GLDP/08/592, Inquiry Proof E27/45 (Grove Park Group) GLC/TD/GLDP/08/548.

Association in Beddington, known to many as the site of the Croydon sewage farm, recited their village's history since the Conquest.[57] 'Villages' nurtured 'community', which the Ringways would destroy. Purpose-built oases like Bedford Park emphasized their community spirit, but the Lewisham Society argued that even 'the quiet red-brick suburb of Hither Green has a much more deep-rooted community than the more dramatic environment of Blackheath'.[58] Community was 'a very delicate thing'; a motorway through Chiswick would drive out 'those people who would plant their oak seeds there', turning it into a second Earls Court:

and it is no reflection on the people of Earl's Court that they do not care very much for the environment, and you do not have amenity societies and others in Earl's Court; the people are only there for a couple of years and they cannot care.[59]

The modern American city was a terrifying spectre. In its determination to impose an expressway network upon London, the GLC would Americanize the capital. Some of the objectors were influenced by Jane Jacobs's *The Death and Life of Great American Cities*, an influential product of American urbanism, first published in 1961.[60] Jacobs asked what sustained and what threatened community life in the modern city. She did not attack American cities so much as conventional planning theory (her sub-title was *The Failure of Town Planning*), but the fear was implanted in British minds that American cities 'show how a community can be destroyed through planning which is not concerned with human values'.[61] The USA, a land of 'choked cities and dead lakes',[62] offered a warning for British planners; indeed, 'the Americans come and see us because we have not spoilt London yet'.[63] If the roads were built, 'the noise, the fumes and the accidents will multiply and the smog now found over cities like Los Angeles, Washington and New York will hang heavily over a bleak, nerve-racking London'; 'tourists will not want to come here if it is simply the Los Angeles of Europe'.[64]

---

[57] 'The Domesday Book shows that Baddintone manor was then occupied by one Robert de Wateville . . .', GLDP Inquiry, Inquiry Support S27/111 (Beddington and Wallington Ratepayers' and Residents' Association), GLC/TD/GLDP/08/595, p. 5.

[58] GLDP Inquiry, Inquiry Proofs E27/96 (A. Best, Bedford Park), GLC/TD/GLDP/08/551, E27/57 (Lewisham Society), GLC/TD/GLDP/08/595, p. 3, though see the submission of the Blackheath Society, ibid., E27/56, p. 12.

[59] GLDP Inquiry, Notes of Proceedings, 91st Day, 22 April 1971 (G. Foley, Chiswick Group), GLC/TD/GLDP/08/093, p. 10.

[60] e.g. Neil Jackson, Grove Park Group, GLDP Inquiry, Notes of Proceedings, 41st Day, 1 January 1971, GLC/TD/GLDP/08/043, p. 33, Cleveland Ward, Ealing, Residents' Association, Objection 58, in GLC/TD/GLDP/09/058.

[61] GLDP Inquiry, Objection 2247 (A. Hedin, NW3), in GLC/TD/GLDP/09/023.

[62] GLDP Inquiry Support, S27/169 (Mrs E. Dalton), in GLC/TD/GLDP/08/596.

[63] D. Beecham, GLDP Inquiry, Notes of Proceedings, 2nd Day, 8 July 1970, GLC/TD/GLDP/08/004, p. 13.

[64] GLDP Inquiry, Objection 16923 (D. Wiggins, SW7), Obj. 16900 (P. F. Strawson, Oxford), both in GLC/TD/GLDP/09/165.

When objectors spoke of 'the American city', they generally meant Los Angeles, a city believed to be cribbed by expressways and smothered by smog. Jacobs had described Los Angeles as 'an extreme example of a metropolis with little public life'.[65] Expressways had not been especially prominent in her argument, but her emphasis upon the way in which maladroit physical planning could accentuate social polarization became the principal component of the opposition case. 'Forced segregation . . . is the antithesis of proper urban life', wrote a Hampstead civil engineer.[66] Urban roads destroyed the inner city while simultaneously providing an escape route for the rich. Blight would destroy the areas immediately surrounding the motorways themselves, though 'they may however be useful to meths drinkers and those who wish to chop up their professional rivals'.[67] As 'no community spirit can exist between people living on opposite sides of a motorway', the motorway box would 'emphasise the difference between rich and poor as is seen in America'.[68] An American priest who had moved to Chiswick urged the GLDP's proponents 'to give America a try first. A year in an American city without an automobile or twenty years with one, either experience will certainly convince them that the present course is inadvisable'.[69]

V

The sheer volume of opposition to the GLDP, and in particular to its road proposals, showed the GLC planners that they faced a political battle. Few of them were political animals. The members of the Planning and Transportation Department were generally technocrats. Stott himself was a civil engineer who had joined the LCC from private industry in 1963.[70] They took the principles of planning to be beyond argument, much as health service professionals thought socialized medicine uncontentious. They had not anticipated the political implications of the shift from development planning to the new structure planning. In 1970 A. F. Dunning, the council's director of public information, noted that where town planning had once been characterized by 'a bi-partisan approach', now 'with strategic planning so much involved with economic planning and overall policies this has become another matter'.[71] In fact, party politicization

---

[65] J. Jacobs, *The Death and Life of Great American Cities. The Failure of Town Planning*, Pelican edn. (Harmondsworth, 1964), 83.

[66] GLDP Inquiry, Inquiry Support S27/318 (D. E. Hennessy), GLC/TD/GLDP/08/577.

[67] GLDP Inquiry, Objection 2693 (G. M. Howell, NW3), GLC/TD/GLDP/09/027. The reference is to the widespread belief that the concrete of the Bow Flyover contained the remains of the Krays' henchman Frank Mitchell, axe-murderer and Dartmoor escapee. See W. G. Ramsey, *The East End Then and Now* (1997), 508.

[68] GLDP Inquiry, Objection 16841 (A. N. Dalton, Reigate), GLC/TD/GLDP/09/164; Obj. 18081 (P. and R. Facey, Westbourne Park Road), GLC/TD/GLDP/09/176.

[69] GLDP Inquiry, Inquiry Proof E27/94 (Revd J. McCarthy, Chiswick), GLC/TD/GLDP/08/551.

[70] C.v. in his papers, GLC/TD/CTD/02/062 (11).

[71] Note by Dunning, 3 April 1970, in the file on Public Participation in Planning, GLC/TD/PM/PC/01/017.

did not occur until the early 1970s, when several Labour borough councils came out against the plan.[72] Labour would oppose the Ringways in the 1973 GLC elections, but the Labour-controlled LCC had conceived the motorway box and the Labour majority on the first GLC had pressed it forward until 1967. A fear that opposition was hard to rouse either on the GLC or in the boroughs was, indeed, one reason why *ad hoc* local pressure groups dominated the resistance to the motorways.[73] Their emergence, though, intensified the problems which the GLC faced over the issue of public participation.

Greater public involvement in the planning process had been advocated by the 1965 Planning Advisory Group report. It had been embedded in the 1967 White Paper on Town and Country Planning and in the 1968 Town and Country Planning Act. The 1969 Skeffington Committee on Public Participation in Planning had investigated ways of encouraging participation. The GLC was aware of these proposals and wished to accommodate to them. When the GLDP was being devised in the mid-1960s, it hoped to encourage 'public interest in the Council's proposals and planning activity',[74] assuming broad public support for its work. In publicizing the GLDP, it went beyond the current requirements of the law.

There was, though, a difference between publicity and participation, and the form of any meaningful public participation in the creation of structure plans remained unclear. Abercrombie had consulted instrumentally: he sought out traffic experts, drainage specialists, or demographers, but even when his informants were local authority officers, they were consulted as specialists rather than as representatives of their communities. Interest in participation in the 1960s really related to small-scale improvements: its main proponent was Wilfred Burns, City Planning Officer of Newcastle upon Tyne and a member of the Planning Advisory Group. Burns was familiar with American participation initiatives, and he described to the Skeffington Committee the results of Newcastle Corporation's experiments at co-operation with community groups.[75] Such local-level consultation had been the limit of the Planning Advisory Group's ambition, but once the 1968 act generalized the obligation, it became necessary to ask how it could be applied to structure plans. The two principal problems were the difficulty of inducing the public to 'think strategically', and the near impossibility of identifying representative public groups with which to consult

[72] e.g. in west London in 1971–2, N. Raynsford, 'Motorway Madness'.

[73] See, e.g., the claim of H. Gilmore (Ealing Residents (Cleveland Ward) Association), himself an Ealing councillor for nine years, that the borough councils 'may be so full up with day-to-day business that they haven't got time to consider points of principle . . . and that residents' associations such as ours can look at the thing rather more as a matter of principle, consider the background', GLDP Inquiry, Notes of Proceedings, 68th Day, 12 March 1971, GLC/TD/GLDP/08/070, p. 19.

[74] 'GLDP, Progress and Publicity, Joint Report by the Clerk to the Council and the Director of Planning, 7 July 1966', in Stott Papers, GLC/TD/CTD/02/020 (2).

[75] 'Co-operation and the Public', note by Mr Burns, July 1967, in Town and Country Planning Bill, 1968, Bill Papers, PRO HLG 29/774.

at a level above the local. Each problem was acute in London, given the size of the metropolis and the number of its *ad hoc* community groups.

Burns acknowledged that at the structural level planning was 'a complicated and difficult process, and to understand it means hard work and real intellectual effort'.[76] The GLC planners agreed, and doubted if 'any but the professional and other informed sections of the public would positively criticise strategic policies or make alternative suggestions'.[77] The general public, argued Fitzpatrick, 'just do not understand the nature and purpose of a structure plan. By and large they are concerned with their own back yard.'[78] The council could negotiate with the London boroughs, but it balked at parlaying with innumerable amenity societies, let alone Motorway Action Groups who existed purely to oppose the GLDP. Such consultation in Camden, for instance, would entail dealing with fifteen different, unconnected, societies.[79] 'I never know quite how responsible or representative one of these groups is', Vigars argued. 'It may really represent public opinion or—for all I know—it may just be a man and his wife.'[80] 'Why should one group of residents get preferential treatment just because they band themselves into a pressure group to shift the line of a road to someone else's road?', asked Betty Turner, of the GLC's Public Information Branch.[81] The council was probably over-eager to ascribe 'nimbyism' to its opponents, but when a group could guilelessly call itself the South Orbital Road Diversion Committee the suspicion remained.[82] The ideas mooted before the Skeffington Committee—and eventually endorsed by them—for *ad hoc* community fora conflicted with established principles of representative local democracy. The committee assumed that one reason for the apparent distance between the public and the planners was lack of faith in local government: the GLC unsurprisingly denied that, and fell back upon a robust defence of the role of the elected member.[83] Betty Turner called for 'the inclusion of civics in the school curricula' to draw the public back to constitutional orthodoxy.[84]

The advocates of participation before Skeffington argued simply that 'local democracy should have the right to produce a bad plan';[85] the GLC was unwilling to risk planning badly on a metropolitan scale. Vigars put the matter

[76] 'Participation and All That', Conference Report of the Standing Conference of Councils of Social Service, Durham, September 1969, p. 33, in London Council of Social Service papers, LMA Acc.1888/246/6.

[77] Memorandum from J. G. S. Wallace to Mr Bourne, 28 May 1968, GLC/TD/PM/PC/01/016.

[78] Note by J. R. Fitzpatrick to B. Collins, 'The Form of Inquiry for Structure Plans', 12 December 1971, in Stott papers, GLC/TD/CTD/02/062 (2).

[79] Notes on meeting with Skeffington Committee, December 1968, GLC/TD/PM/PC/01/016.

[80] *The Times*, 24 July 1968.

[81] Memorandum 'Public Relations', 4 April 1970, GLC/TD/PM/PC/01/017.

[82] GLDP Inquiry, Objection 2625, GLC/TD/GLDP/09/027.

[83] 'We pray in aid of the role of the elected member in opposition to the idea of community forums, community development officers, etc.', note by Dunning, 3 April 1970, GLC/TD/PM/PC/01/017.

[84] 'Public Participation in Planning. Observations on the Draft prepared by Mr Lewis', 24 March 1970, GLC/TD/PM/PC/01/017.

[85] 'Notes on Views of County and County Borough Planning Officers in Wales', p. 20, Skeffington Committee, Digest of Evidence to 27 June 1968, PRO HLG 136/269.

characteristically bluntly: 'on major matters such as the planning of the strategic highways network, the GLC had to take policy decisions and then consult'.[86]
This was less Orwellian than it sounds: one proposal to facilitate participation
at the strategic level was to devise alternative options and then put them to the
public. In principle the GLC supported this approach,[87] but it carried the insu-
perable drawback of exacerbating planning blight. Blight was the debasement
of the value of property threatened by a proposed road or other construction,
making it impossible for owners to sell until the scheme was approved and compulsory purchase could take place. The GLC understood the corrosive effects of
blight and pressed without success for more generous compensation powers.[88]
Announcing a multitude of possible routes for the sake of consultation would
worsen blight and delay the final choice of route.[89] Skeffington had considered
an increase in blight to be an acceptable price for greater public involvement;
besieged by irate property-owners, the council could not.[90]

For these reasons, the GLC's engagement with the public never ranged
beyond didactic and promotional exercises. The Public Information Branch,
formed soon after the council's creation, spent much of its time promoting
transport policy. Early efforts to sell the transport management strategy
employed the black arts of advertising, with dubious results. The GLC paid an
agency £200,000 to teach it to preach that anti-social parking was 'the act of a
stupid child rather than of a reasoning adult' ('a few interpolated words of one
or other of the current popular [television] police inspectors . . . would have real
significance').[91] By the time the campaign for the GLDP proper was launched,
the techniques were more sophisticated, but the danger of patronizing the public remained. An introductory public meeting in the Queen Elizabeth Hall in
November 1968 was followed by nine shamelessly promotional local meetings.
The Ealing meeting, 'arranged by the slick and efficient operators of the GLC's
press and public relations office' in January 1969 'had the air of a well run television show. There were even girls in mini-skirts to welcome people at the
door.'[92] What Abercrombie would have thought of this we can only guess; what
the council's sceptical audiences thought is clear. In reality few of those who
attended the meetings were sufficiently open-minded on the roads question to be
swayed by such methods: 'the vast majority of those attending tend to be

[86] 'Notes of a Meeting with the London Borough Councils . . . 4 July 1968', in
GLC/TD/PM/PO/022.
[87] 'Planning and the Public', Draft Report by the Director General and the Director of Planning,
n.d. (?1968), in GLC/TD/PM/PC/01/016.
[88] 'Building New Roads: Compensation and Blight', Paper read by Kenneth Blessley, Valuer,
Greater London Council, Roads Campaign Council, House of Commons, 18 February 1969, 6–7,
GLC/TD/CTD/02/004 (3).
[89] Sir Desmond Plummer, 'Homes Versus Roads', *Evening Standard*, 20 January 1969.
[90] Memorandum from Dunning to Joint Directors of Planning and Transportation, 2 January
1970, GLC/TD/PM/PC/01/016.
[91] Adgroup Organization, 'The Use of Public Relations and Advertising Techniques in Easing
London's Traffic Problems', n.d. (but 1966), p. 7, in GLC/TD/PM/PO/2/021.
[92] *Acton Gazette and Post*, 16 January 1969.

activists of one sort of another', Gerard Vaughan, chairman of the Strategic Planning Committee, told Skeffington.[93] With hindsight, the GLC accepted that 'public presentations by a large organisation will always result in a high proportion of aggressive criticism rather than praise for proposals'.[94]

In a hostile climate promotional sophistication became in itself sinister, re-inforcing the impression that the council was more interested in selling its proposals than in consultation.[95] 'The glib advertising language that is used to sell the plan to the unsuspecting public: improved environment and all that crap',[96] did little good. In any case, whatever educative advantages the promotional campaign brought were soon offset by the public relations disaster of Westway, which prompted the most heated anti-road protests that London has ever seen. Westway, the motorway-standard extension of Western Avenue to join the projected Ringway 1, was an uncouth intrusion into the Ladbroke Grove area, carrying eastbound traffic within feet of inhabited houses at roof level. Even the British Road Federation considered Westway one of 'the insensitive and socially unacceptable examples of motorways'.[97] 'You only have to look at Westway,' claimed one of the few council tenants to appear before the public inquiry: 'people who live on that can shake hands with a motorist on the thing. But they expect people to live on it.'[98] Even the GLC's counsel acknowledged 'the failure or the inability . . . to resolve properly the local environmental effects' of Westway.[99] Westway scarred London's fabric in the 1960s much as the construction of the Metropolitan Railway had done a century earlier. While the council mounted its glossy campaign for the plan, Westway showed the reality of urban road-building. As one objector told the inquiry, 'one bases one's experience on the Westway, because we have not got another urban motorway'.[100]

All of this strengthened the objectors' demand that the GLDP should be subjected to proper scrutiny, by 'a full Government Commission of Inquiry into the GLC Development Plan as a whole and not a series of local inquiries'.[101] They got their way in December 1969 when the Labour government announced the

[93] Vaughan to Skeffington, 11 February 1969, in Skeffington Committee, correspondence with local authorities, PRO HLG 136/285.

[94] J. G. S. Wallace, Draft Report of Strategic Planning, General Purposes and Planning and Transportation Committees on Public Participation in Planning, 11 April 1969, GLC/TD/PM/PC/01/016.

[95] e.g. at the St Pancras meeting, J. Hillman, 'Will the New London Put People First?', Hampstead and Highgate Express, 21 February 1969.

[96] GLDP Inquiry, Objection 9880 (P. Ayrton, N5), GLC/TD/GLDP/09/094.

[97] GLDP Inquiry, Notes of Proceedings, 94th Day, 27 April 1971 (W. Bor and P. Ahm, BRF), GLC/TD/GLDP/08/096, p. 35.

[98] W. J. Piggin, Woodberry Down Tenants' Association, GLDP Inquiry, Notes of Proceedings, 91st Day, 22 April 1971, GLC/TD/GLDP/08/093, p. 39.

[99] D. Christy, GLDP Inquiry, Notes of Proceedings, 85th Day, 14 April 1971, GLC/TD/GLDP/08/087, p. 83.

[100] M. Armitage, GLDP Inquiry, Notes of Proceedings, 89th Day, 20 April 1971, GLC/TD/GLDP/08/091, p. 55.

[101] GLDP Inquiry, Objection 106 (R. W. Russell, W4), GLC/TD/GLDP/09/002. This was the first of 102 identically worded objections.

intention to mount such an inquiry. It was eventually constituted under Sir Frank Layfield, who, with a panel of experts to advise him, was charged with investigating every aspect of the plan. The inquiry held its first session in July 1970. It would sit for 237 working days, until May 1972, making it at that time Britain's longest planning inquiry.

Though the council claimed to welcome the inquiry, it must, in reality, have viewed it as an unsolicited intrusion. It was already reassessing the philosophy behind the plan. Where initially the case for the Ringways had been based upon mobility and personal freedom, by 1969 the GLC's emphasis was shifting to ameliorating the problems created by congestion. The statutory written statement accompanying the plan argued that unchecked congestion would disable business, paralyse vital services, and 'lead to more families leaving London'.[102] Writing to *The Times* in November 1969, Stott borrowed the objectors' image of American cities to warn of social polarization if congestion continued: London would become 'a place where there is no intermediate between the very rich and the rather poor. It is not my idea of a city.'[103] This change of emphasis was doubtless primarily tactical, but one major change behind the scenes indicated that it was more than cosmetic. Once it had become clear that the GLDP would be scrutinized by some kind of major public inquiry, a new Strategy Branch had been created within the Planning and Transportation Department, and a new chief planner (Strategy) appointed in David Eversley.

Eversley was a historical demographer and the only non-planner among over 200 applicants for the post. He was also something of a sceptic towards the GLDP, questioning the 'belief in the possibility of physical (land use) planning solving almost every urban problem'.[104] He saw the planner as 'a listener, a researcher, as well as a decision-maker'.[105] His view of 'strategy' included 'a consideration of direct action, pressure, advocacy, community involvement, new legislation, collaboration with neighbouring authorities . . . as a means of achieving a total planning process', which led him to take an interest in Skeffington's community fora, to the alarm of his colleagues.[106] Standing 'well to the left of the Labour Party', Eversley saw planning as political—felt, indeed, that 'planning . . . was essentially redistribution'.[107] He had arrived too late to play any part in shaping the GLDP, and had the plan proceeded smoothly to its anticipated approval by the secretary of state his heresies would doubtless have been smothered, but the approach of Layfield laid every aspect of the GLDP open for reconsideration.

---

[102] GLC, *Greater London Development Plan Statement* (1969), 22.

[103] *The Times*, 1 November 1969.

[104] D. Eversley, 'Three Years at the GLC. 1. Changes in Planning', *Built Environment*, February 1973.

[105] GLC, *Tomorrow's London. A Background to the Greater London Development Plan* (1970), 44.

[106] Eversley, 'Three Years at the GLC. 1'; note from Betty Turner, 21 September 1971, in GLC/TD/PM/PC/01/017.

[107] Eversley, 'Three Years at the GLC. 1'.

As Eversley put it, 'the Inquiry became the Plan'.[108] It inevitably produced much crankiness, but two years of probing revealed the GLDP's weaknesses. The council was criticized for replicating Abercrombie's transport proposals while neglecting his concern for social dynamics.[109] One manifest flaw, actually the reason for Colin Buchanan's hesitancy about endorsing the GLDP, was rapidly brought to light: while claiming flexibility as an advantage of the new system of structure planning, the GLC was boxing London into an inflexible infrastructural cage—as counsel for the London borough of Greenwich put it, 'there can be few things more immutable than a motorway'.[110] The existence of a demand for orbital journeys was challenged on the basis of the under-use of the Broad Street to Richmond railway.[111] The council's dismissive view of public transport (it had no power over British Rail and only acquired responsibility for London Transport in 1969) attracted much criticism. Its relaxed attitude towards the problem of pollution was attacked, as vehicle exhaust threatened to undo the work of the Clean Air Act.[112] The panel experts demonstrated the GLC's unclear demographic priorities, its limited comprehension of the London economy, and its flimsy housing strategy.[113]

Though the plan's opponents thought themselves disadvantaged by the forensic nature of the public inquiry—'the difficulties of individual objection against a mountain of Background papers . . . and in the face of massed professional expertise'[114]—this was a battle within the planning profession as much as between planners and public, and the opposition could invoke much technical expertise. The author of the above statement was, in fact, a Master of City Planning from Harvard, an Associate of the RIBA, a member of the Royal Town Planning Institute, and the chairman of the Haringey Planning and Development Committee. If anything, the debate with the council over planning theory was conducted more effectively by such specialist witnesses than by the panel. So was broader discussion of the nature of the city. The Town and

[108] Ibid.

[109] GLDP Inquiry, Notes of Proceedings, 91st Day, 22 April 1971 (Mr Ward, Chiswick Motorway Liaison Committee), GLC/TD/GLDP/08/093, p. 2.

[110] Graham Eyre, GLDP Inquiry, Notes of Proceedings, 61st Day, 3 March 1971, GLC/TD/GLDP/08/063, p. 47; for Buchanan, see his letter to B. Collins, 6 January 1971, GLC/TD/CTD/020/3 ('In a nutshell we are concerned that, in spite of all the protestations in the Consultation Text about flexibility, the GLDP . . . will in fact impose a considerable degree of rigidity on the future development of London').

[111] GLDP Inquiry, Notes of Proceedings, 89th Day, 20 April 1971 (Mrs M. Armitage, Strand on the Green Association), GLC/TD/GLDP/08/091, p. 48.

[112] 'Who are the GLC trying to kid? You know as well as I do, every stinking rotten motorcar and van that comes through, every time it stops, is belching out—even your GLC ambulances—are belching out smoke and filth', W. J. Piggin, Woodberry Down Tenants' Association, GLDP Inquiry, Notes of Proceedings, 91st Day, 22 April 1971, GLC/TD/GLDP/08/093, p. 39.

[113] The Layfield Panel found that the GLC's population estimates were 'out of date, based on a dubious methodology', the employment section of the Revised Written Statement contained 'unnecessary descriptive matter, unproductive generalisation and dubious rationalisation of past events' and the housing content of the original Written Statement was 'thin and unconvincing': *Greater London Development Plan. Report of the Panel of Inquiry* (1973), Vol. I, Report, 627, 127, 633.

[114] GLDP Inquiry, Inquiry Proof E111/3 (Cllr B. G. Falk), GLC/TD/GLDP/08/541.

Country Planning Association's evidence about the relationship of city and region, Chris Holmes's analysis of gentrification in Islington, the account from the spokesman of the St Pancras Civic Society of the social and ethnic mix in modern Camden, even the *aperçu* from the Grove Park Group representative that Carnaby Street was a 'place that gained momentum until it was not possible for a local authority to overplan it'—all showed an understanding of urban evolution not evident in the GLDP. The objectors could assault the plan from all angles without any need to ensure overall coherence, while GLC witnesses had to keep their testimony consistent with the plan as a whole, which became increasingly difficult. By day 100, after 70 hours' examination of GLC witnesses, Fitzpatrick was rightly worried that 'it is not possible for witnesses to be certain as to Council policy' as panel questioning became ever more stringent.[115]

This was all the more true because council policy continued to evolve during the inquiry, as Eversley found his feet. His background paper on the aims of the plan, stressing that the planner was 'deeply involved with the efficient functioning of the economy, the growth of communities, the correct use of scarce resources' and other things that the Planning and Transportation Department was not, in fact, very deeply involved with, was published after internal censorship in 1970.[116] In the uncertain economic climate of the early 1970s, Eversley formed apocalyptic views of London's future, believing 'not simply that London Bridge was falling down but that London was dying',[117] as depopulation robbed the centre of its most productive elements. He had no time for conservation groups,[118] whose conservatism would create 'a London composed of only five million people, of whom a high proportion are pensioners, out of a job, [or] too poor to buy much'.[119] Consequently, his scepticism towards physical planning did not lead him to disown the Ringways: Eversley saw the car as 'the redundant worker's passport to a new and better job'. Once the talisman of prosperity, the Ringways now became a defence against decline.

Eversley's unorthodoxy made enemies within the council, particularly among those involved with the plan from the start. The Planning and Transportation staff did not understand Eversley's preoccupation with economic and demographic movements, and did not think that such things lay in the province of the planner. They could not substantiate his concerns about social polarization and were concerned at the prospect of 'a complete somersault on the definition of London's problems'.[120] Less predictable was the implosion of Eversley's own section. The new Strategy Branch was staffed, in Eversley's account, by 'not-so-good geography graduates' whose 'desks were littered, according to sex, with

---

[115] Fitzpatrick to Vigars, 14 May 1971, Stott papers, GLC/TD/CTD/02/062.

[116] GLC, *Tomorrow's London*, 44; for authorship and censorship see Eversley, 'Three Years at the GLC. 1'.

[117] Letter from Graham Lomas, London Council of Social Service, *Built Environment*, April 1973.

[118] Eversley, *Planner in Society*, 186–7, 207, 270.

[119] D. Eversley, note, 'GLC. Who Loses?', *Built Environment* (May 1973).

[120] Lomas, in *Built Environment* (April 1973).

copies of knitting patterns and recipes for low-calorie meals, or motor sports journals and racing papers'. It became the preserve of the public sector left, devoted to 'bureaucratic guerrilla warfare' against capitalism.[121] It was probably inevitable that Eversley's approach to the planning process would let the political genie out of the bottle. The young planners in the Strategy Branch voiced a critique of redevelopment—public and private—fuelled by the property boom that peaked in the early 1970s. They had more in common with the Westway protestors than the conservationists and amenity group stalwarts so visible at the inquiry. A new journal, *Community Action*, appeared in 1972, largely written by members of the Strategy Branch. It provided a steady critique of redevelopment and gentrification, and offered support to 'action groups in low-income areas'.[122] It advocated 'new kinds of political action that will combine argument with pressure, lobbying with sanction and direct action': 'remember Watts got burned because the blacks got tired of waiting—then the money trickled in'.[123] It blamed Eversley himself for 'perpetuating policies that have the interests of industrialists and developers, rather than London's workers, at heart'.[124] Caught between the unsympathetic traditionalists of Planning and Transportation and the 'immature pseudo-revolutionaries' in his own section, Eversley suffered a nervous breakdown and left the council in July 1972.[125]

By then Stott had concluded that 'the value of the whole system is becoming very questionable', and that 'nobody is likely to suggest another GLDP . . . for a long time'.[126] Though Layfield had still to report,

we remain afeared of attempts to cobble up an approval of some GLDP at all costs, because we consider that everybody ought to do a sufficiency of thinking about improving the system of planning, or non-system, which London appears to be saddled with under present arrangements.[127]

In this context the Layfield Inquiry's perverse recommendation to build only Ringway 1—the most expensive and unpopular of the three roads—was academic: few at the GLC now expected any of the roads to materialize.[128] Labour's victory in the GLC election of the following month ensured the Ringways' demise, but it did not cause it. Though the campaign was dominated by motorways, Labour won because a Conservative government at Westminster was beset by growing economic problems. Had Labour been in government, the

[121] Eversley, *Planner in Society*, 3; D. Eversley, 'Three Years at the GLC. 2. Inadequate for the Task', *Built Environment* (March 1973).

[122] Editorial, *Community Action*, 2 (April–May 1972).

[123] *Community Action*, 3, (July–August 1972)—P. Marris at Editorial/Advisory Group meeting; ibid., 6 (January–February 1973).

[124] I. Binns, 'What are we Trying to Achieve through Community Action?', *Community Action*, 6 (January–February 1973).

[125] Eversley, 'Three Years at the GLC. 2'.

[126] 'Structure Plans. Note for Discussion', 4 October 1972, GLC/TD/CTD/02/062.

[127] Bernard Collins, Joint Director of Planning and Transportation, to W. R. Cotton, 14 March 1973, Stott papers, GLC/TD/CTD/02/062 (10).

[128] D. Wilcox, *Evening Standard*, 4 April 1973.

270   John Davis

Conservatives would doubtless have retained control of the GLC, but the roads would still not have been built. The GLDP died[129] because its over-ambition had been exposed during the public scrutiny process, and because the bureaucracy behind it collapsed in the attempt to respond to criticism.

In the early 1970s London thus decided not to follow the path taken by the Victorians—not to sacrifice substantial parts of the urban fabric to the needs of transport. Londoners resolved not to acquire a road system comparable to the local railway network built in the nineteenth century. This was not acknowledged by all involved—most of the objectors to the motorways persuaded themselves that the solution to London's traffic problem lay in greater investment in public transport—but some understood that they were really arguing for 'restraint by congestion'.[130] The concept is familiar to Londoners today.

VI

'Once upon a time we were all seeking simple solutions to simple problems—now I think we seek simple solutions to complex problems!', wrote Stott wistfully, as he watched ten years' work crumble.[131] In effect, the social topography of London had become too complex by the 1960s for the simple solutions—or even the complex solutions—of Abercrombeian planning to succeed. It had proved relatively easy, in Glasgow or in Birmingham, to drive a road through derelict inner-urban areas and passive working-class communities by executive *force majeure*. But even in the 1960s, gentrification already meant that inner London no longer consisted exclusively of a mute and malleable working class. Planning objectives could no longer be achieved without consultation. Though the planning profession acknowledged the consequent need for greater accountability and explored systems of participation, it proved impossible to build meaningful consultation into the strategic planning process. Instead the issues were contested in gladiatorial manner in a mammoth public inquiry. This proved fatal to the planners. In the first place, the inquiry magnified every flaw in the plan. Worse, the need to produce a multifaceted defence of the plan brought to the surface policy disputes within the planning authority which had been largely suppressed when planning strategy had been left to the road-builders. The resultant internal tensions, at a time when the plan was coming under constant attack at the inquiry, sapped the will of the planners to proceed. The social dynamics of the city proved too complex for the machinery of planning.

[129] Strictly, the remnants of the plan, without the motorways, received ministerial approval in 1976 and survived as the basis of London's development planning until the abolition of the GLC.
[130] Mr Sherlock, Islington Society, GLDP Inquiry, Notes of Proceedings, 89th Day, 20 April 1971, GLC/TD/GLDP/08/091, p. 26. See also the evidence of Douglas Jay, 82nd Day, 5 April 1971, GLC/TD/GLDP/08/084, p. 79.
[131] Stott to A. Driver, 14 March 1973, Stott papers, GLC/TD/CTD/02/062 (10).

The consequences for London were substantial. The GLC had already been largely thwarted in its attempts to play a strategic role in housing by the resistance of suburban boroughs to its attempts to relocate inner-city tenants,[132] and the very Conservative administration that pressed ahead with the road programme had begun to devolve the council's housing powers to the boroughs. The demonstration of its impotence in strategic transport planning raised the question of the GLC's *raison d'être*. Attempts on the London Tory right to question the council's purpose were contained by the party's GLC leadership in the late 1970s, but when the cause was taken up by the national Conservative government in the 1980s, the case against abolition proved hard to sustain. The immediate motive for the abolition of the council in 1986 was the wish to eradicate Ken Livingstone's new left régime, but this political coup would have been impossible had the GLC been administratively indispensable. It was not, and nor were the other metropolitan counties abolished with it. The concept of the strategic metropolitan authority, questioned even when extended to the provinces in 1974, was anachronistic by the mid-1980s. In London the attempt to do away with any central elected authority proved unsustainable, but the Greater London Authority, Assembly, and elected mayor created in 2000 have more limited aims and powers than the GLC, and real power today lies with the London boroughs and the City Corporation.[133] The period since 1986 has also seen a more tentative extension of community planning,[134] exemplified by projects like the renewal of the Coin Street area. Major road building has stayed off the agenda.

VII

This chapter has sought to recapture a critical moment in the post-war history of British planning, at which the cream of the profession first encountered large-scale resistance from the community for which it was planning. The appeal of such episodes to the apostles of civil society thinking is easily understood. Most of Britain's welfare state was dismembered by the neo-liberal right in the 1970s and 1980s, aided by market failure and inflationary pressure, but in general this was not true of the town and country planning régime. The GLDP example is telling: the motorway proposals were said to cost as much as the Channel Tunnel, the third London airport, and Britain's share of Concorde combined, and they could hardly have survived the expenditure cuts of the mid-1970s, but cost was not the reason for their abandonment. The GLDP was abandoned because of wide-scale opposition within metropolitan society. Admittedly we

[132] K. Young and J. Kramer, *Strategy and Conflict in Metropolitan Housing* (1978).

[133] M. Hebbert, 'Governing the Capital', in A. Thornley (ed.), *The Crisis of London* (1992), 134–48.

[134] G. Nicholson, 'The Rebirth of Community Planning', in Thornley (ed.), *The Crisis of London*, 119–33.

cannot know whether it could have been forced through had central government been more committed to it: Whitehall's lack of interest in the structural remodelling of the capital—striking in itself—was compounded by its subsequent enthusiasm for participation, so that the GLC became a beleaguered fraction of authority. It is also true that the planners' defeat owed something to internal debates within the council, epitomized first by Eversley's appointment and then by the dissent of the young radicals in the Strategy Branch. But both Whitehall's misgivings and internal dissent in the GLC were stimulated by the scale of public resistance to the plan. Before all else, the GLDP was defeated by the resistance of metropolitan society.

This was an early victory for the principle of public participation in planning. The sledgehammer of the Layfield Inquiry was, of course, very different from the range of participatory devices characteristic of 1990s local government—neighbourhood fora, citizens' juries, 'community governance'[135]—but it was in these years that the principle took root that a directly elected authority could not claim simply from its election a mandate to interfere with the property and environment of a substantial section of the community. A more direct form of consultation was required.

The Ringways were jettisoned as a result, and nobody has since proposed the resurrection of this grandiose scheme, but it should also be pointed out that the GLC planners accurately anticipated some of the problems associated with public participation. Their concerns about establishing the representative credentials of 'the public' had some force. The opponents of the Ringways, though numerous, displayed a narrow social base. Not only were the capital's economic élites largely silent, but the inquiry heard very little indeed from the London working class. The inquiry generated at least one radical ginger group, Women on the Move, but in general the objectors came overwhelmingly from the ranks of owner-occupiers and public-sector professionals. The comprehensive nature of strategic planning allowed this group to appear to speak for metropolitan society as a whole, but the kind of middle-class resistance which they embodied is usually more localized, particularistic, and above all defensive than it appeared in this case. Other episodes, such as the efforts of the Barnsbury Association to canalize traffic away from an upwardly mobile area of Islington and into neighbouring streets,[136] exemplify more familiar amenity group action, and the kind of conflict that would become familiar in the gentrifying London of the 1970s.

Radical planning theorists have long been aware that participation might entail the empowerment not of civil society as a whole but of well-organized fractions of it, who might be militiamen, white supremacists, or other groups

[135] H. Atkinson and S. Wilks-Heeg, *Local Government from Thatcher to Blair. The Politics of Creative Autonomy* (Cambridge, 2000), 171–2, 178–81; J. Stewart, 'Innovation in Democratic Practice in Local Government', *Policy and Politics*, 24: 1 (1997), 29–40.

[136] J. Ferris, *Participation in Urban Planning. The Barnsbury Case. A Study of Environmental Planning in London* (1972).

with inappropriate political credentials.[137] The risk that participatory planning will be 'captured' by axe-grinders is inescapable: in Britain the most frequent concern has been that community institutions will be controlled by the dominant group in mixed-race communities. The experiment with neighbourhood councils in Tower Hamlets after 1986 has been shown largely to have excluded the large Asian community, and racism has been alleged in housing nomination policy both there and in the Coin Street Community Builders project, the epitome of community planning in modern London.[138]

For these and other reasons, more fundamentalist forms of direct democracy have not become widespread in British local government: the emphasis has been on decentralization rather than democracy.[139] But even decentralization is hard to reconcile with strategic thinking. Community-oriented planning has gained much momentum in recent years, but its achievements remain small-scale, and it would be a mistake to see it as a solution to the metropolitan problems which defeated earlier generations of strategic planners. To imagine that these problems could be solved by greater involvement with the community seems no less utopian than to imagine that they can be solved by the top-down prescriptions of a Geddes or an Abercrombie. Modern Britain now displays a model of metropolitan governance in which municipal boosterism confines itself to museums, sports stadia, shopping centres, and similar *grands projets*, while community action produces small-scale housing schemes and playgroups, and the traffic grinds to a halt. The questions faced by Abercrombie and the other heroic planners were real problems of social aggregation. Urban society still needs to solve them.

[137] J. Abu-Lughod, 'Civil/Uncivil Society: Confusing Form with Content', in Douglass and Friedmann (eds.), *Cities for Citizens*, 233–4, etc.

[138] V. Lowndes and G. Stoker, 'An Evaluation of Neighbourhood Decentralisation. Part 1: Customer and Citizen Perspectives', *Policy and Politics*, 20: 1 (1993), 55–6, 59; Atkinson and Wilks-Heeg, *Local Government from Thatcher to Blair*, 172; and for Coin Street, T. Brindley, Y. Rydin, and G. Stoker, *Remaking Planning. The Politics of Urban Change*, 2nd edn. (1996), 94.

[139] B. Jeffrey, 'Creating Participatory Structures in Local Government', *Local Government Policy-Making*, 23: 4 (1997), 25.

14

Civil Society and the Good Citizen: Competing Conceptions of Citizenship in Twentieth-century Britain

MICHAEL FREEDEN

I

In the Hegelian tradition, civil society was pitted dialectically against the state, while concurrently recognizing that civil society contained some of the trappings and the potential from which the state could draw. The state was the substantive and ethical realization of many of the formal features of civil society, in particular of the universally acknowledged status of a largely voluntarist and commercialized association of self-interested individuals. When the philosophical school of Idealism struck root in late nineteenth-century Britain, it attached these insights to an Aristotelian reading of the ethical role of the state, a view according to which being a good citizen was a supreme civic virtue.[1] However, the British liberal tradition redefined and amplified that view of virtue by insisting on its development through private activity as well as through the public sphere. Illumination came from J. S. Mill's ideal of a harmony among individual abilities that valued differences between individual persons, not from Hegel's method of resolving conflict by transcending it. Being a citizen involved drawing upon many of the skills imparted through individual self-development and voluntary interaction from within the sphere of civil society. The state was not superimposed on civil society, but in some spheres was conjoined to it and in others clearly separated from it. Conduct in civil society offered models of behaviour that could also be put to the service of the state.

II

In 1901, those self-appointed guardians of workers' interests, the Fabians, published the fourth edition of a tract or, if you wish, a directive, entitled *What to*

[1] See S. den Otter, *British Idealism and Social Explanation* (Oxford, 1996), 47–51.

Read.[2] Among the alphabetically ordered themes, ten books appear under the heading 'citizenship'. Intriguingly, half of those were written by Idealists—hardly the motive force behind the Fabian brand of socialism—including works by Bosanquet, McCunn, and Bradley. But a range of Idealist understandings of citizenship formed a dominant idiom at the beginning of the twentieth century, providing the inspiration for a number of popular books on citizenship some time after Idealism itself as an intellectual movement had all but evaporated. Books such as Henry Jones's *The Principles of Citizenship* (1919), W. H. Hadow's *Citizenship* (1923), and even H. J. Laski's *The Grammar of Politics* (1925), with its ostensibly different social-liberal provenance, achieved a wide circulation.

The first two books were heavily didactic in nature. Jones's slim tome, replete with long-winded purple prose verging on a religious sermon, while plainly off-putting to the present-day reader, is nevertheless historically very revealing. It imparted a dual message. First, citizenship is above all a state of moral grace; second, citizenship is an acquired skill, or set of virtues, the paternalist consequence of regarding 'the function of the state' as being 'to educate [its citizens] for their own sakes'[3] which, on an Idealist understanding, will coincide with the good of the community or the state. That there is a skill to be imparted to the members of a society was quaintly expressed in Jones's post-war obligatory diatribe against Germany, whose greatest crime was against its own citizens (here presumably referred to in a legal, not ethical, sense), in failing to value 'research in the domain of morals as it has valued it in that of industry and militarism'[4]—an argument far more reminiscent of the French positivism of Saint-Simon than of the German Idealism of Hegel.

A somewhat different approach to citizenship was reflected in the plethora of quasi-technical primers on what was required to become a citizen. In this genre Hadow, as befitted a vice-chancellor of the University of Sheffield (1919–30), regarded a citizen as the product of an imparted body of knowledge—an education or training in what already existed institutionally—rather than the unfolding of a moral potential. Citizenship consisted of a cognitive understanding of the facts of municipal and local government, the workings of parliamentary government, and their relationship to voluntarism. Schools, universities, and adult education, through libraries and discussion groups, would provide maps of public life and enhance the awareness of rights and duties, all necessary for the development of humanity in a citizen. Though indebted to Jones's spiritual vision of the citizen and his state, Hadow's approach was more matter of fact. His was not the citizenship of dynamic participation, but one that entailed the fitting of skills—acquired through the institutions of civil society—into an established and given political structure, thus enabling individuals to play a part in the economic and social life of the

[2] The Fabian Society, *What to Read*, 4th edn. (1901). Fabian Tract No. 29.
[3] H. Jones, *The Principles of Citizenship* (1919), 136.   [4] Ibid., 135.

country. 'Education in citizenship', he wrote, 'has these two principal aims in view, to present the truth and to fit the minds of men to its reception.'[5] Hence, citizenship was defined in terms of loyalty and faithfulness[6]—the latter term injecting a hint of religiosity into political obligation, whereas the former appealed to affective values of trust and friendship, while retaining a hint of feudal fidelity and service.

By contrast, in a book entitled *The Making of Character*, reprinted nine times between 1900 and 1931, John McCunn—a professor of philosophy at the University of Liverpool and a graduate of Balliol College—attached citizenship to traditional conceptions of character: 'the manly and man-making duties of local and imperial citizenship'. Dismissing mere knowledge about political and economic systems as inadequate, he attempted to channel understandings of the public good into a democratically underpinned patriotic love of country. Citizenship was to include historical teaching, and that importantly covered 'national examples of heroism and devotion, and of the moving struggles and victories of war and peace that are a country's heritage'. And while the hurly-burly of politics was not the obvious sphere in which moral character was improved, 'the exceeding cunning of the national Destiny', by some process equivalent to Smith's invisible hand, ensured that participants in political life 'gain far more than they consciously seek'.[7] Citizenship was hence a central feature of a communal moral project through which individuals subscribed to a vision of shared combative and rousing masculinist virtues.

III

In stark contradistinction to these approaches, another conception of citizenship was emerging, and it proved to be the most powerful, certainly the most eloquent, of the views in circulation. It split into two variants, the one approaching the issue from a social, and the other from an individual, angle, though the two eventually coalesced. The first version recoiled from employing virtue and a dutiful and spiritual harmony as central features of citizenship, appealing instead to the idea of a flourishing society. The liberal weekly *The Nation* expressed this in simple terms: 'it is a demand for life, for more abundant life'.[8] Not the good life of the ancient Greeks, distilled through generations of students on an Oxford diet of Aristotle, but the good life of well-being, drawing upon the powerful and recent discourse of social utilitarianism. One—though not the only—motivation for this emphasis was the prevailing obsession with national efficiency—with enabling currently excluded sections of the population to live 'a sound human life' and to rear 'a family to do good service to the commonwealth as workers

---

[5] W. H. Hadow, *Citizenship* (1923), 204.   [6] Ibid., 3.
[7] J. McCunn, *The Making of Character* (1931), 124, 125, 127.
[8] 'The Claim for a Share in Life', *Nation*, 28 September 1912.

and citizens'. The language of individual rights was consequently rejected in favour of that of social efficiency and social security.

In more extreme forms, indeed, paternalism and state-direction—the Fabian version of socialism—accompanied the various discourses on citizenship. When George Bernard Shaw briefly discussed the question of citizenship, in his *Everybody's Political What's What*, it was to declare—with his usual mischievous contrariness of insight—that in the advanced civilization of citizenship there would be both more freedom and less. 'The State will proselytize as ruthlessly as parents are able to do at present, and far more powerfully; for citizenship, like all forms of corporate life, is impossible without a common fundamental religion; and this had better be inculcated by a democratic state with a strong interest in tolerance and free-thought than by parents divided into hundreds of sects . . .'.[9] A plea, perhaps, for a strong secular ideology? There certainly is a curious resonance here, in one strand of early twentieth-century political thinking, with current emphases on the responsibilities rather than the rights of citizenship. Even among those who argued persuasively in favour of the correlativity of duties and rights, the right to minimal social goods—a right designed to raise the marginalized to the status of full social members—was frequently interpreted as serving not the cause of individual flourishing but as enabling individuals to respond to the 'call of the state', as H. A. L. Fisher put it in 1924. In other words, citizenship entailed above all good social behaviour, a predominantly one-way flow of making 'a contribution to the well-being of the community of which we are members'.[10]

L. T. Hobhouse's handling of citizenship issues reflects the opposite angle of the reconciliation between individual and state. For him, it implied that government was the servant of the people, but it was to be differentiated from 'the link of language or nationality'. Reciprocity was again perceived in quasi-legal terms as an expression of the will of those who obey the state. The novelty in the context of the above arguments was the insertion of equality as an ingredient of citizenship, conjoined with the liberal insistence on an individual who can 'shape his own life and whose rights and responsibilities are determined principally by his own actions and agreements'.[11] Here participatory citizenship involved not merely activity in an already given political sphere, but crucially the drawing up of the constitutional ground rules that identify and delineate that sphere, as well a clear recognition of the font and origin of citizenship in the private domain. Atypically in the citizenship debate of the pre-1914 era, Hobhouse showed awareness of the problems of minorities and multiple nationalities within the boundaries of the polity. The modern state had 'not only to generalize the common rights of citizenship as applied to individuals, but to make room for diversity and give scope for collective sentiments which in a

[9] G. B. Shaw, *Everybody's Political What's What* (1944), 82.
[10] H. A. L. Fisher, *The Common Weal* (Oxford, 1924), 22.
[11] L. T. Hobhouse, *Social Evolution and Political Theory* (New York, 1911), 140–1.

measure conflict with one another'.[12] This qualification constraining the statist organic tendency, distinguishing realms of public yet non-state conduct that were incompatible with a unitary notion of citizenship, was to be notably lost in later treatments, such as T. H. Marshall's.

IV

Hobhouse subscribed to the pervasive liberal model of movement through space and time, one that conceived of the spread of citizenship in simple zero-sum spatial terms, namely, the 'development of the principle of citizenship at the expense of the principle of authority, until ideally it is extended to all permanent residents in the territory'. The main forms of social space progressed through kinship, clan, and tribe to kingships, states, empire, towards a world state. Within the modern state there was a further movement from individuals through localities to nationalities. And there was also a qualitative progression: kinship was the lower stage, the system of authority was an advance towards civilization (echoes of Max Weber), and citizenship characterized the higher civilization. Concurrently, the expansion occurred over time—Athens, Rome, and Europe.[13]

This is worth considering for a moment. The dominant liberal narrative, in which the concept of citizenship was caught up, was heavily evolutionary. But it embodied a confident and exclusive evolutionism. It was less a liberal view of history, such as the Whig interpretation, and more a historical view of liberalism, in which liberalism was itself understood as a body of ideas subject to movement in time and in space. Hobhouse and other new liberals bestowed on liberalism an ontology in which the releasing of biological and spiritual energy was the motive force: 'a movement of liberation, a clearance of obstructions ... for the flow of free, vital, spontaneous activity', for what might be called the flourishing of civil society (though this was not a term prominent in new liberal discourse). The movement at the heart of liberalism was threefold: first, an 'active mission' towards the attainment of political objectives. Second, it was a carrier of truth, which moved in 'an expanding circle of ideas'—a theme also found in Hobson's writings, when he wrote that 'Liberalism will come more definitely to concern itself with the liberation and utilisation of the faculties and potencies of a nation and a municipality, as well as with those of individuals and voluntary groups of citizens.'[14] Here the human resources in civil society were interpreted as the foundation and the bedrock of citizenship. Third, it represented a life-force, the march of civilization itself. Truer citizenship was correlated with a better civilization.[15] Hobhouse contended that 'The Liberal

[12] Ibid., 147.   [13] Ibid., 142, 148.
[14] J. A. Hobson, *The Crisis of Liberalism* (1909), 95.
[15] H. J. W. Hetherington and J. H. Muirhead, *Social Purpose* (1918), 24.

movement . . . is coextensive with life'; 'Liberalism is an all-penetrating element of the life-structure of the modern world.'[16] This was the conceptual backdrop to notions of citizenship. These notions were Anglo- and Eurocentric, nourished also on the Anglicized reworking of Greek political theory. Citizenship was the goal of a contagious and contiguous view of progress, a historically and spatially contingent universalism, multidimensional in its relationships between individual and institution, but also called forth 'by the special circumstances of Western Europe'.[17] If not quite the teleological view of citizenship called up by Idealist thinking, and if lacking the imperative ethical tone through which Idealist citizenship was promoted, it was none the less a cautiously optimistic assertion of the correct path that the nexus of political relationships would take.[18]

The quotation from Hobson also importantly indicated that the British voluntarist tradition should be accommodated within the purview of citizenship. As he wrote elsewhere, one of the advantages of increasing personal liberty and nourishing the private personality was in that

some of the finest and most profitable uses of leisure will consist of the voluntary rendering of social services of a non-economic order. I allude in particular to a fuller participation in the active functions of citizenship, a more intelligent interest in local and national politics, in local administration and in the numerous forms of voluntary association which are generally social in the services they render. More leisure is a prime essential of democratic government.[19]

This was no mere resurrection of the significance accorded to leisure in public life in the Greco-Roman world. Rather, using biological and psychological insights, citizenship advanced beyond the world of duties and entered that of the pleasurable expenditure of energy, a pastime that contributed to social needs. Clearly, citizenship focused on the *public* status of members of a polity, but that public status was also one they held as members of civil society in their relations with the state. Membership of civil society was not a refuge from the public domain, as Hegel had already realized. It was the point at which the public domain effected interaction between individuals, their wants and needs, and the relationship of these to public policy and conduct. It was a public that could involve the state, the locality, or the duties of other individuals. The public skills acquired in civil society had direct political significance.

---

[16] Hetherington and Muirhead, *Social Purpose*, 46–7.

[17] L. T. Hobhouse, *Liberalism* (1911), 19.

[18] This paragraph draws on M. Freeden, 'Twentieth Century Liberal Thought: Development or Transformation?', in M. Evans (ed.), *The Edinburgh Companion to Contemporary Liberalism* (Edinburgh, 2001), 21–32.

[19] J. A. Hobson, *Work and Wealth* (1914), 248.

V

One striking, and frustrating, feature of most of the early twentieth-century books *directly* engaged in the subject of citizenship is their lack of analytical discussion concerning what it means to be a citizen, as distinct from how a citizen is supposed to behave. Citizenship was often held to be synonymous with being a member, or subject, of a state, and its obvious anchorage in the norms of civil society often went unnoticed. The term itself was broadly unproblematic for its users. The main exception to this mode was the study by H. J. W. Hetherington and J. H. Muirhead, *Social Purpose*. The two post-Idealists[20] offered an exceptionally nuanced and subtle treatment of citizenship, and its relationship to what they termed 'civic society'. While their views overlapped with those of many other progressives, their conceptual configurations adopted a slightly different emphasis. Hetherington and Muirhead endeavoured to unpack the 'ambiguity' of the word 'civic'. Acknowledging its local, as against national, implications, they preferred nevertheless to move away from that conventional spatial distinction, as well as from Hegel's individualistic interpretation, and to contend that 'the word denotes rather a stage in the development of society than an element in its constitution'.[21] Put differently, civic society was for these two thinkers 'more than a fact'; it was 'a moral claim upon the allegiance of its members'. Rather than being positioned—institutionally or ethically—between the family and the state, it transcended concrete social institutions. In asserting this, Hetherington and Muirhead introduced a new spatiality. Unlike patriotism, which constituted devotion to the 'near and the present', the civic theory of citizenship indicated 'devotion to the remoter interests of humanity'. Those interests—'the intelligent conception of the nature of civic society'—included its relationship to the individual, to other societies within and outside itself, and to the future human race.[22]

Tellingly, the object of civic loyalty was no longer a specific government or state, but the civic structure itself.[23] The state ceased to occupy the role of the sole Hegelian actualization of the ethical idea; rather, its highest function was in 'the extension of [citizens'] interests to what lies beyond itself'—an understandable view even among post-Idealists, following the perceived wartime betrayal of the intellectuals by the very state they had so enthusiastically promoted before 1914. The organicist perspective, according to which 'to be a citizen is to merge one's being in that of others' was preserved, the nation-state was even the preferred vehicle of civic society, but the state was reduced to being but an enabling agent for civic virtue and for the emergence of a civic consciousness, the latter tantamount to a consciousness of the commonality of human life.[24]

---

[20] By which I mean scholars trained in the Idealist tradition who had abandoned some of the key Idealist postulates while maintaining a broadly sympathetic attitude to its general arguments.
[21] Hetherington and Muirhead, *Social Purpose*, 19.   [22] Ibid., 47, 26, 29.   [23] Ibid., 39.
[24] Ibid., 95, 98, 291.

VI

All the while, a radically different notion of citizenship was on the ascendant, one in which the analogy with social health, the health of the body-politic, so frequently deployed by organicist theorists, began to be construed as a central component of the politics of individual human nature. The shift occurred mainly thus: throughout much of the nineteenth century participation and contribution as properties of the good citizen related to the individual as energetic and active, in full, rational, command of his or her powers, which were to a considerable extent put at the disposal of society. That focus continued as a core feature of Western liberal and socialist positions. Recall the ending of Mill's *On Liberty*: 'The worth of a State, in the long run, is the worth of the individuals composing it, and a State which postpones the interests of their mental expansion and elevation . . . will find that with small men no great thing can really be accomplished . . . for want of the vital power which . . . it has preferred to banish.'[25] But alongside that view another perspective was emerging: an understanding of human nature as vulnerable and fragile, and of the status of a citizen as one that protected human beings from the more unseemly consequences of this endemic condition. That theme had been far more evident in French welfare thinking, but in the French context had become associated with the sheer normality of risk.[26] British social thinkers of the left adopted a slightly different line. Rather than relinquishing the pathological status of fragility and weakness, namely as a character defect, and converting it instead into a natural or 'normal' attribute which society would recognize in its practices as a matter of course, they adopted a different tactic. They simply broadened the range of human attributes to be protected or promoted through social arrangements to include psychological as well as physical, mental, and moral properties. This unremitting growth in human complexity—from a static to a dynamic being, from an isolated to a socially anchored person, from a rational to a rational *and* emotional entity—began to replace the philosophical purism and teleological thinking of Idealism as well as the atomistic and timeless contractarianism of the free market and the intellectualist developmentalism of Victorian liberalism. A more concrete and, ostensibly, scientific, engagement with human conduct was offered, and the idea of human flourishing was considerably extended.

---

[25] J. S. Mill, *On Liberty* (1910), 170.

[26] See M. Freeden, 'The Coming of the Welfare State', in T. Ball and R. Bellamy (eds.), *The Cambridge History of Twentieth-Century Political Thought* (Cambridge, 2003), 7–44.

VII

Cecil Delisle Burns, who held the telling title of Stevenson Lecturer in Citizenship at the University of Glasgow, wove these two strands together in introducing one of his books, entitled *Democracy: Its Defects and Advantages*:

Two points only are intended to be emphasized in this book—first, that a positive contribution of thought and action from every member of the Community is needed, if government, industry, and social culture are to develop, and secondly, that the common man has many abilities, hitherto unused, from which such contribution could be made. The fundamental issues of contemporary life involve psychological factors . . .[27]

For Burns, the main psychological factor was the group mind and its impact on public affairs. Collective behaviour was a deep-seated drive evident in all walks of life, and citizenship was a formal recognition of the importance of harnessing this innate property to communal ends. In addition, individual impulses had to be directed to socially innovative uses: 'The kind of community we actually inhabit is dependent upon the kind of impulses represented or given play, in the normal intercourse of its members; and if we desire to change any social situation, we should first study the sort of impulses which we may release or repress.'[28]

Such a holistic view of the social and political value of human attributes had been some time in the making. Being a citizen had become a more intricate and layered set of practices and statuses, though one that reinterpreted rather than ditched the legal and participatory aspects of citizenship. Membership of the polity was interpreted in terms that avoided the standard language of rights and duties, which stood accused of depersonalizing the social relationship in its very attempt to protect the parties to this unsigned contract. A different language was now invoked: human beings were beneficiaries of the social goods society put at their disposal, and—here the influence of Burns's colleague Hobson was apparent—enjoyers of the social condition, with the means it provided for human expression and development. The full drawing out of human potential necessitated a continuous revision of what constituted a human being, not a revision of participatory duties. A re-synthesizing of scientific (and pseudo-scientific) arguments with political prescription generated a new excitement. It held out the promise of tapping into unknown quantities and qualities of human potential.

Citizenship thus required society to enable the release of that potential, through granting its members access to the raw material without which they would remain in animated suspension. But the rewards for that distribution of a range of need-satisfying resources—for investing directly in the quality of civil society—were immediate, in the form of the major improvement of communal

[27] C. Delisle Burns, *Democracy: Its Defects and Advantages* (1929), 7.
[28] C. Delisle Burns, *Civilisation: The Next Step* (1938), 29.

life. Citizenship had become an enterprise of optimization, and its etymological relation, civilization, became tantamount to political and social thriving, not merely to the realization of superior standards of educated and reasonable conduct. Moreover, instead of the authoritative unlocking, by those in the know, of individual capacities most conducive to their good and to the good of the state—as advocated by the older, and less radical, generation of citizenship theorists—democratic participation had become essential to defining the qualities of citizenship. One example was afforded by Burns's recognition of irreconcilable psychological attitudes: selfishness in industry versus co-operation in the social sphere, which greater democratization, he believed, would swing in the latter direction.[29]

The democratization of notions of citizenship meant that, when rights were still the primary focus of discussion, citizens' duties became increasingly defined not in obligation to an ideal, perfectly behaved, state, but in relation to the blemishes of existing ones. Progressive thought, by postulating a fusion between public and private wills, had naively thought to eliminate the disjuncture between government and governed that had been a staple of older theories in their honoured evocation of the right to resist tyranny. That rosy progressivism had all but evaporated after 1918. In his celebrated *Grammar of Politics* Laski noted that a citizen, just because he is one, 'has the duty of scrutinising both the motive and the character of governmental acts'. This seemed to move beyond principles of civil disobedience that applied only when fundamental constitutional arrangements had been infringed. Though Laski would have balked at the suggestion, we have here an early version of what later in the twentieth century became the consumer view of citizenship. If government provided a product, it had to do so following good practice—once again, a utilitarian perspective of optimizing opportunities, but one that in a feedback loop then put the instructed judgement of the citizen at the disposal of the public good.[30] The values embedded in practices of civil society remained the yardsticks for assessing good government.

Interestingly, there was no hint of all these early twentieth-century developments in the 1933 edition of the *Oxford English Dictionary*, though dictionaries tend to be conservative and slow to react to new thinking. A citizen was minimalistically defined as 'one possessing civic rights and privileges, an enfranchised inhabitant of a country, as opposed to an alien; in U.S., a person, native or naturalized, who has the privilege of voting for public offices, and is entitled to full protection in the exercise of private rights.' The guardians of the language sheltered behind a wholly legalistic approach to citizenship, emphasizing the term as a constructor of the boundaries of political favour, both internal and external to a state.

---

[29] Burns, *Democracy*, 164.
[30] H. J. Laski, *A Grammar of Politics* (1925), 89, 113, 117.

VIII

The most famous essay by a British twentieth-century century theorist on citizenship was unquestionably that by T. H. Marshall. It is a somewhat overrated piece, partly because it was the culmination of many predecessors' inputs, and partly because Marshall's endlessly re-echoed account of developmental progression from civil through political to social rights was simplistic and misleading (though he did concede that each of these three strands travelled at its own speed and went its separate way). Marshall's essay 'Citizenship and Social Class' was initially delivered as a lecture at Cambridge in 1949, honouring his namesake Alfred Marshall. At least, though, it offered a serious analysis of the concept and institution of citizenship. It proceeded, Marshall claimed, from the rights necessary to individual freedom, to the rights necessary to participate in the exercise of political power, and finally—the language should by now be familiar—to the 'whole range from the right to a modicum of economic welfare and security to the right to share to the full in the social heritage and to live the life of a civilized being according to the standards prevailing in a society'. The latter proviso consciously recognized the space- and time-bound limits of welfare, and reinforced the ripple-effect theory of the spread of civilization at the heart of liberal thought. Interestingly, citizenship was for Marshall, too, 'by definition, national'. That unity of national structure and interest was to prove one of the major shortcomings of his approach.[31]

One could expound at length on Marshall' theory, but some features of interest, not all of which are compatible with each other, invite particular scrutiny. One is the abandonment of the symmetry of rights and duties, so important both in Idealist and in organicist thinking. The rise of ideas of equality, he maintained, has resulted in a shift of emphasis from duties to rights. Citizenship was, for Marshall, a system of 'claims', in the language of the 1912 *Nation* article. A second is the satisfaction of citizenship claims not only through the state but through institutions of civil society. In particular, Marshall argued that trade unions created a secondary system of industrial citizenship through the collective bargaining that was, in fact, a symptom of a free market, although the rights gained through this process were universal, rather than proportionate to the market value of the claimants.[32] A third is the retention of central themes of citizenship that preceded Marshall. Thus—in Idealist, or even socialist, fashion but removed from Mill's more permissive formulations—the citizen 'has a duty to himself, as well as a right, to develop all that is in him'.[33] That duty is not, however, claimed by society.

Fourth, Marshall's conception of equality (despite frequent misreadings of his views on this point) was a liberal minimalist one, and involved no notion of discouraging difference. To the contrary, 'the right of the citizen in this process

---

[31] T. H. Marshall, *Class, Citizenship and Social Development* (New York, 1965), 78, 79, 80.
[32] Ibid., 103–4.   [33] Ibid., 117.

of selection and mobility is the right to equality of opportunity . . . In essence it is the equal right to display and develop differences, or inequalities; the equal right to be recognized as unequal.'[34] Although this was little different from the social-democratic ideas promoted by revisionist socialism, Marshall's language and choice of words in this respect were significantly non-socialist. Fifth, Marshall's assertion that there now was a movement from contract to status— an inversion of the movement from status to contract detected by Maine—needs to be clarified and refined. Status often implies 'stasis', but citizenship was not just a question of the recognition of one's formal standing in a community, though it was that too. It was also the expression of an active, demand-generating, and socially constructive populace, embodying a dynamic cluster of social interactions within the domain of both state and civil society. Nor were contractarian elements ever removed from understandings of citizenship, as we can learn from both Beveridge and Blair. But Marshall curiously and contro-versially identified the 'duty to work' ethic as implying the negation of contract, because contract implies the liberty not to work, a liberty absent from the work ethic.[35] Even more confusingly still, Marshall continued to regard the duty to work as the route to full citizenship, understood as access to the means of flour-ishing. But if, as Marshall put it, 'the personal obligation to work . . . is attached to the status of citizenship' what would happen, one might ask, were that obligation not to be discharged? Arguably there would still be a tacit contract, which would be contravened. In political theory, contract has never been lim-ited to the realm of economic markets alone; indeed, it long preceded the full development of market institutions. So obligations creep back into an argument in which rights-claims have been defined as predominant, and Marshall's con-sistency falters.

IX

If Marshall is the most famous of the British twentieth-century theorists of citi-zenship, Richard Titmuss is one of the most thought-provoking. While most theorists of the left in mid-century based citizenship on universal rights grounded on a commonality of needs, Titmuss advanced a theory of citizenship as altruism, as entitlement to best available practice, and as the exercise of choice. Titmuss was not a professional political thinker, nor did he offer a general social theory of welfare, as his writings pertained mainly to the health services. Yet interspersed among his specialized texts are some of the most mem-orable phrases of twentieth-century welfare theory, with a central bearing on citizenship. Referring specifically to the National Health Service, but applicable more widely to the welfare state as the main vehicle of post-war applied

---

[34] Marshall, *Class, Citizenship and Social Development*, 120.
[35] Ibid., 122, 129.

citizenship, he wrote: 'The most unsordid act of British social policy in the twentieth century has allowed and encouraged sentiments of altruism, reciprocity and social duty to express themselves.'[36] Titmuss was located in a tradition to which the progressive Idealist philosopher David George Ritchie had significantly contributed over half a century previously. In Ritchie's famous book, *Natural Rights*, a convergence between a simple individualistic utilitarianism and a social utility perspective was cemented: 'Happy citizens—and that in the long run means healthy citizens, healthy in mind, body, and estate—will prove the most useful citizens.'[37]

One of the most interesting facets of Titmuss's notion of the relationship between state and individual was derived from the change of emphasis referred to earlier: the legitimation of views of human nature that saw it as inherently fragile. A crucial shift had occurred from a world of individual responsibility, with its concomitants of foresight and planning, to a world in which uncertainty and unpredictability were rampant. Conceptions of citizenship were trapped between the idea of a rational, scientifically planned society and the indeterminate fortunes of individuals vulnerable to illness, accidents, or unemployment. Individuals had been expected to plan their own lives and to stick to such plans, and they were socially, often legally, penalized when they lacked that prudence. But once the attributes of health were brought *into* the core of human nature, unpredictability became a constituent component of human life, not of fate, divine will, personal recklessness, institutional negligence, or even misfortune. Vulnerability had become a human attribute, not a human pathology. 'Abnormalities' under the older way of thinking had been marginalized and addressed through private or semi-private mutual settlements. But 'normal' implied a factual attribute aspiring to universality, and hence a shared feature of social existence, not even a characteristic of particular professions and life-styles in the manner adopted by the tentative national insurance schemes in Britain. Both health and illness came to be viewed as 'natural' in a much more significant sense than hitherto, namely, that social arrangements had to be constructed around these new insights or be doomed to irrelevance. Titmuss seized upon the identification of a new relationship between private and public, between state and citizen, based not just on personal security, economic interest, or the expression of human agency-cum-autonomy, but on the universal fact of human need and of the emergence of practices designed to meet such needs. The politicization of need was an important consequence of the shift of 'health' from its earlier marginal and largely metaphorical status, to that of being an important defining element in what constituted an 'individual' and thus in his or her demands upon the public.

Titmuss was far more of an intellectual successor to new liberal thought than 1950s social democrats—whether through historical ignorance or political

---

[36] R. Titmuss, *The Gift Relationship* (Harmondsworth, 1973), 254.
[37] D. G. Ritchie, *Natural Rights* (1895), 99.

obduracy—were ever willing to acknowledge. Indeed, before becoming a Fabian, he had supported the Liberal party, by then in a state of decline. Those historians who contend that the organic analogy disappeared after the First World War might take note of his remarks on the following:

All collectively provided services are deliberately designed to meet certain socially recognized 'needs'; they are manifestations, first, of society's will to survive as an organic whole and, secondly, of the expressed wish of all the people to assist the survival of some people. 'Needs' may therefore be thought of as 'social' and 'individual'; as interdependent, mutually related essentials for the continued existence of the parts and the whole.[38]

In marked contrast to current propensities to transform all citizens into consumers, Titmuss insisted on reversing the process. For him consumers were beneficiaries, contributors, members—that is, citizens.[39] If civil society had become regulated by the state, it was not in order to destroy voluntarism and individualism but precisely the reverse: in order to encourage and develop the private, or interpersonal, values of altruism and care.

One of Titmuss's intellectual heroes was Durkheim, with the latter's emphasis, first, on the division of labour as a fundamental social attribute; and, second, on the rise of professional groups with solidarities based on 'likenesses in skills, functions, and prestige'.[40] Here Titmuss's implicit theory of citizenship becomes particularly interesting. He contended that the dual specializations of medicine and administrative organization had combined to create a double dependence of doctors on the natural sciences and on society and fellow doctors. But, summarizing Durkheim, Titmuss noted that increased social dependence was a function of the growth of individualization itself.[41] Here, then, was the other side of the coin. 'Science, by enlarging the potential field of choice and action, simultaneously enlarges the potential for individual freedom.' Science had the dual capacity for beneficence and for authoritarianism—the parallel hazard of syndicalist professional solidarities. Medicine ought not to be reduced to a technology. Intriguingly, this argument was intended not only, or even mainly, to protect the consumers of medical services but to protect the providers. It was crucial that doctors were free agents who could *as a consequence* exercise responsibility. Responsibility meant choice rather than compliance with public norms; it meant in particular the freedom of doctors to serve their patients according to the latter's needs. Needs thus signalled the recognition of diversity, assessed by professional, socially reinforced but nevertheless subjective, judgements, rather than the search for uniform objectivity. Citizenship therefore also required the provision of the best expertise, in an optimally ethical manner, to the members of a society, but the sphere of its expression was firmly located in the professional organizations of civil society. Citizenship was conceived not

[38] R. Titmuss, *Essays on 'the Welfare State'* (1963), 39.
[39] R. Titmuss, *Commitment to Welfare* (1976), 62.   [40] Titmuss, *Essays*, 189.
[41] Ibid., 44, 183, 187–8.

only as status and need recognition, but also as the professionalization of services and expectations and the provision of optimal social goods combined with good practice. On this level, however, some facets of citizenship had to be optional. Titmuss emphasized unequivocally 'the social rights of all citizens to use or not to use as responsible people the services made available by the community in respect of certain needs which the private market and the family were unable or unwilling to provide universally'.[42] This libertarian aspect of Titmuss's creed gave priority to individual choice over the social insistence on the scrupulous discharge of a duty to be healthy, the latter a legacy of the authoritarian, élitist, or paternalist conceptions of welfare often identified with the Webbs. But it also made an important concession to the market, in that the regulation of experts was at least partly shifted away from the ballot box to direct control by, or feedback from, the consumers of essential social and personal goods. The civil society ethos of voluntarism was permitted, in an intriguing way, to penetrate the norms of state citizenship.

Possibly the most remarkable of Titmuss's formulations was the employment of the extraordinary phrase 'the right to give' as central to his ideology of welfare. This totally circumvented the more traditional question of the rights of individuals to receive health benefits. It implied, rather, that social arrangements have to enable the individual to flourish in acts of (largely anonymous) altruism, a significant aspect of working out his or her nature as human being and as citizen. Titmuss was moving towards identifying a new virtue of citizenship encapsulated in the blood donor relationship: the love of strangers, the empathy of individuals not only for their kith and kin. Mutual responsibility encompassed the personalization of the impersonal: the attachment of emotional proximity to all vulnerable human beings. True, this could already be found in that other love of strangers already linked to patriotism, which mystically and mythologically transforms them into brethren. However, Titmuss was not concerned with the interests of the collective as a group (except in so far as the latter might make provision of services more efficient). Instead, he 'privatized' altruism by affixing it to each and every individual, and to their care for each other. Once again, the emotive vitalism so central to the early twentieth-century liberal tradition, rather than its alternative persona expressed through market rationalism, was at the heart of the public domain. Distinctly, it entailed 'no contract of custom, no legal bond, no functional determinism'.[43] Instead, the codes of optimal private conduct sited in civil society were appealed to. Titmuss thus rejected the narrow constitutionalism of liberalism, which liberals themselves had, of course, in large measure superseded. But he also rejected an exaggeratedly communitarian view of human relationships, namely, that the core of individual identity is merely a function of group membership. Ultimately, the right to give was a right of citizenship that individuals could waive—for mandatory altruism is no altruism at all—but at considerable cost

---

[42] Titmuss, *Commitment to Welfare*, 129.   [43] Titmuss, *The Gift Relationship*, 269.

to themselves, just as for Mill individuals could choose not to develop, but both they and society would be much the poorer for that. Through detaching the right of the donor to give from any corresponding duty of the recipient to reciprocate, the de-marketization of these dimensions of citizenship was underlined. The donor's right was to the natural and noble satisfaction attained through giving; by implication, societies that hindered such acts of altruism dehumanized the donor rather than the recipient.

X

Contrast all this with the recent citizenship theories of New Labour, with its American-inspired nexus of rights and responsibilities. Ostensibly we return to the mutual balancing of rights and responsibilities as two sides of the same coin, as Idealist theory would have it. That would, however, be a false conclusion. In rights theory, the right of one individual is usually paired with the correlative duty of another individual, or agency, to protect that right. In Blairite newspeak, among others under the influence of the American communitarian sociologist Amitai Etzioni, a right is paired with a responsibility located in the same individual.[44] The refusal to grant rights without responsibilities suggests that an individual right is *purchased* by the good social behaviour of that individual. Not only are rights once again reduced to a conditional status, but their attainment is to all effects and purposes commercialized. They are embedded in an exchange transaction in which the defence of the social fabric is the prism through which respect for the individual is viewed, and in which communities shed any significant value-pluralism they might have and become repositories of a shared but rather inflexible moral language, with its corresponding shared practices. This bleak view of citizenship has drifted away from the currents of the British progressive tradition, but it is couched in terminology entirely suitable for its intended consumers in a post-Thatcherite age.[45]

Liberal theory in particular regards citizenship as a set of attributes nourished in civil society, and a set of practices that does not necessarily—certainly not wholly—engage the state. From some ideological viewpoints, the state is the regulator of standards of good public conduct, and that conduct is oriented towards a universal ethical perspective which only the state is thought able to provide. Twentieth-century British liberalism, however, has allowed for an identification of public spheres that involve the state only tangentially or not at all, but which nevertheless serve as the prime arenas of good citizenship, or prime recruiting grounds for desirable political practices. Rather than being a reserved space away from the public eye, civil society on that view constitutes

---

[44] A. Etzioni, *The Spirit of Community: Rights, Responsibilities and the Communitarian Agenda* (1995).
[45] See M. Freeden, 'The Ideology of New Labour', *Political Quarterly*, 70 (1999), 42–51.

the most important sphere of socially responsible activity. British thinking on citizenship has vacillated between these two poles of seeing one (state-dominated) public domain or *two* (state-plus-civil society) public domains throughout the twentieth century. The various attempts to combine the two, or to make one of them decisively trump the other, merely serve to emphasize that they still coexist in an unresolved but arguably healthy tension.

15

Britons, Settlers, and Aborigines: Civil Society and its Colonized 'Other' in Colonial, Post-colonial, and Present-day Australia

TIM ROWSE

I

It is precisely in civil society's conceptual irresolution that I find a connection with my own work on Australia, and particularly in the many variants of the term by which the colonizing British understood their difference from the colonized Indigenous Australians. For example, Jose Harris, in the first chapter of this book, draws attention to the well-established contrast between relations of 'contract, choice, "civility" and self-interest' and relations that are 'familial, tribal, sacramental'.[1] That contrast not only defines 'civil society', it also pinpoints a hierarchical duality in the colonists' conceptions of what constituted social order—between 'civil' colonists, on the one hand and 'uncivil' Indigenous Australians, on the other.

However, in settler colonialism the colonists had to account for themselves not only in terms that held the colonized 'other' at a distance, but also in terms that brought him/her up close as a fellow-subject of a legitimate political order. This duality in colonial self-conception resonates with a duality that we find in many of the uses of 'civil society' in its British and European constructions. Not only do civil society theorists contrast 'civil' with 'uncivil', they also value the 'integrative' and 'universalizing' dynamic that is thought to be characteristic of the 'civil'. Contributions to this volume by Harris and Goldman suggest that German intellectuals over several centuries have admired Britain's 'civil society' for its containment of violence, its moderation of ethnic and class antagonism, its ability to hold privilege accountable to the rule of law, and to substitute internalized disciplines for harsh despotisms.[2] Such perceptions have also played an

Grateful thanks to Ann McGrath and Frances Peters-Little for their comments on a draft version of this chapter.
[1] Above, pp. 2–3, 6–10.   [2] Above, pp. 2–3, 24–5, 98–113.

important part in British national identity and self-awareness. 'Civil society' in its many different forms is seen as referring to a social solidarity that is effected through characteristically modern institutions, conventions, and modes of subjectivity.

Yet these many meanings of 'civil society' seem to include, rather paradoxically, two very different societal logics: a logic of dichotomy, bifurcation, separation, and contrast; and a logic of integration, of inclusion of that which is potentially heterogeneous and different. That double logic in civil society is mirrored by Australia's settler-colonial liberalism. The characteristic challenge for settler-colonial liberalism has been to reconcile two very different statuses that the colonist cannot help but attribute to those whom they have colonized: the colonized are different from us, but they are also the same as us, because they co-habit in the same territorial space.

The resolution of this paradox, I shall argue in this chapter, has been sought in the tutelary relationship. That is, civil society can be defined in terms of its exclusions while being simultaneously praised for its inclusiveness, only so long as we are able to imagine a process of tuition or rehabilitation by which the excluded become the included. In Australia, the imagining of this tutelary process has been one of the most active and difficult strands of our settler-colonial liberalism.

I shall argue that liberal rule in Australia has had to ponder whether the Australian social order was made up of two 'societies'—the colonial and the Indigenous—or of one single society—a unified British realm in which the Indigenous/non-Indigenous difference was of dwindling significance. Neither the one-society nor the two-society model of 'Australia' has ever been securely acknowledged as the sociological premiss of liberal rule in Australia. The pressure of the unresolved persistence of both models has produced a continuing concern for the relationships and processes of tuition.

II

The British colonists of Australia generally did not see the Aboriginal people as constituting a social order with its own processes of self-government. The British Admiralty had instructed James Cook in 1768 'to take possession of convenient parts of the country in the name of the King of Great Britain'. He was to do so 'with the consent of the natives', unless he found the country 'uninhabited'.[3] In August 1770 Cook's act of possession of the eastern half of the continent proceeded without 'the consent of the natives'. Note that I said 'without the consent' rather than 'against the wishes' of the native Australians. The native wishes were not overridden; they were simply unknown in 1770 and were

---

[3] 'Additional Instructions for Lieutenant James Cook', in J. M. Bennett and Alex C. Castles (eds.), *A Sourcebook of Australian Legal History* (Sydney, 1979), 254.

thus treated as of no consequence by the British. The reason why this disregard for the native presence did not scandalize British conceptions of responsibility under international law was that the Aborigines had no apparent government and they were not an agricultural people. Only a people with some kind of political system could cede sovereignty through a negotiated agreement. Only a native people who tilled the soil could be deemed 'owners' of it. To assert British sovereignty over the land that Aborigines roamed was not to dispossess them by conquest but to include them within the British realm as among its subjects. The land of the Aborigines was thus neither ceded nor conquered—it was 'settled'.[4]

Had the Australian colonies been either ceded by treaty or 'conquered', it would have been necessary, according to then accepted notions of international law, for the British colonists to have some regard for the indigenous system of law that had preceded their imposed sovereignty. The doctrine that Australia was 'settled' cleared the way for all Indigenous Australians to be treated simply as subjects of the British Crown. But dealing with Aborigines simply as British subjects was not always easy. There are moments in the history of colonial law and administration when we can see the authorities struggling to apply the fiction that Indigenous Australians had no laws and customs of their own. In the abstract, we can distinguish two ways of conceiving the problem. One of them postulated Aborigines as lacking any capacity to regulate their own conduct; the other attributed to them a system of self-regulation that was so different from the British law that it incapacitated them for subjection to it.

In practical terms it did not necessarily matter which of these two models of Aborigines' non-subjection operated in the colonists' minds. Authorities could qualify the liberties of Aborigines, on the ground that they were not responsible enough to exercise a particular liberty. Thus colonial officials pondered whether to dispense with the usual trial procedures, a dispensation that could work for or against the Aborigines concerned. In 1826, an Aboriginal man charged with attempted murder in New South Wales was discharged as being beyond the jurisdiction of colonial law. Likewise in 1829 an Aborigine charged with murdering another Aborigine went untried because two justices of the Supreme Court thought that it would be unjust to try him.[5] When a group of Aborigines in South Australia killed survivors of the shipwrecked *Maria* in 1840, Judge Cooper of that colony's Supreme Court advised that the group's leaders should be subject to the summary justice of the police, since the Aborigines concerned lived beyond the limits of British settlement and had thus 'never submitted themselves to our dominion'. After two men were sentenced at a 'rudimentary trial' and hanged, London officials expressed dismay that South Australian

    [4] J. Hookey, 'Settlement and Sovereignty', in P. Hanks and B. Keon-Cohen (eds.), *Aborigines and the Law* (Sydney, 1984), 16–18.
    [5] On this and other instances of the difficulty of framing and applying colonial law, see Barry Bridges, 'The Aborigines and the Law: NSW 1788–1855', *Teaching History*, 4: 3, December (1970), 40–70.

authority could behave so unlawfully.[6] In each of these cases we see tension between London's idealized and locals' pragmatic conceptions of the effective spatial domain of British law.

If it was the extent of settlement that effectively defined the 'dominion' of British law for authorities in the colonies, then it was possible to imagine that beyond the limits of settlement there remained an indigenous dominion with its own customary law and processes of government. However, this was a difficult thought for the colonists to accommodate. To imagine such a native jurisdiction would place a question mark over, for example, the legality of the sale of Crown land. For it had not taken long for observant and open-minded colonists to realize that Aborigines had a conception of themselves as landowners. As David Collins, the first Deputy Judge Advocate of New South Wales, reported in his *An Account of the English Colony of New South Wales* (1798), Aboriginal families understood themselves to be owners of heritable estates.[7] It would be awkward for colonial rule if such customary ownership were to exercise a legal restraint on the Crown. A judicial ruling of 1825 confirmed that lands could be held privately only with the Crown's permission. In 1835, when one settler attempted to acquire land by his own treaty with Aborigines in the Port Phillip area, the Crown quickly asserted that the deal had no legal standing.

While not doubting the sovereignty of the Crown, some colonial officials became so concerned to protect Aborigines on the pastoral frontier that from 1852 they imposed a measure of 'land rights' (as it would later be called) as a reservation on the rights allowed in pastoral leases. Colonial Secretary Earl Grey's dispatch to New South Wales Governor FitzRoy on 11 February 1848 urged that it was 'incumbent on Government to prevent ["the Aboriginal Tribes"] from being altogether excluded from the land under pastoral occupation'. He wrote that 'leases are not intended to deprive the natives of their former right to hunt over these Districts, or to wander over them in search of subsistence, in the manner in which they have been heretofore accustomed, from the spontaneous produce of the soil except over land actually cultivated or fenced in for that purpose.' The New South Wales governor in April 1850 proclaimed (after Queen Victoria's consent) that pastoral leases could include any conditions and limitations on the pastoralists' rights which a government considered to be in the public's interest. Although the wording of this 'Order in Council' did not explicitly recognize Aboriginal rights in land under pastoral lease, such recognition has recently been inferred by some historians and by some High Court judges in the Wik judgment of December 1996.[8]

---

[6] A. Castles, *An Australian Legal History* (Sydney, 1982), 524–6.

[7] D. Collins, quoted in H. Reynolds, *Aboriginal Sovereignty* (St Leonards, 1996), 112.

[8] H. Reynolds and J. Dalziel, 'Aborigines and Pastoral Leases—Imperial and Colonial Policy 1846–55', *University of New South Wales Law Journal*, 19: 2 (1996), 315–77, see p. 357 for Grey; see also H. Goodall, *Invasion to Embassy: Land in Aboriginal Politics in New South Wales, 1770–1972* (Sydney, 1996), 44–56.

Nineteenth-century ameliorative measures which might nowadays be interpreted as recognition by the colonists of authentic Aboriginal law were almost invariably no more than *ad hoc* devices. Two nineteenth-century cases became authoritative on the question of whether or not Aboriginal people had a recognizable law. In 1836, in what is known as Murrell's case, three judges of the New South Wales Supreme Court heard murder charges against two Aboriginal men. The defendants' lawyer argued that the accused were not Her Majesty's subjects, but were subject to Aboriginal laws, and that it was by those laws that the accused should be punished. The judges rejected this plea, saying that British law extended to all offences, even those in which Aborigines were both perpetrators and victims. As one judge argued, Aborigines 'had not attained . . . to such a position in point of numbers and Civilization, and to such form of Government and Laws, as to be entitled to be recognized, as so many *sovereign states, governed by laws of their own*'.[9] In 1889, Britain's Privy Council, hearing an appeal from the New South Wales Supreme Court on a matter that had nothing to do with the interests of Aborigines, reviewed the legal status of British law. The Council's decision included a remark that was to become authoritative in Australian law—that 'there was no land law or tenure existing in the colony at the time of its annexation to the Crown'.[10]

Recent jurisprudence, however, has combined with revisionist history to make us aware of the gap between the legal fiction propounded in the Murrell and the Cooper cases, on the one hand, and the colonists' practical experiences of governing, employing, and otherwise dealing with the Aboriginal people, on the other. Henry Reynolds argued in 1996 that between the Murrell case of 1836 and the Cooper judgment of 1889, a series of credible settlers and respected ethnologists had substantiated and elaborated the colonists' early intuitions of an Indigenous system of law and government. Moreover, this was not merely an 'academic' concern. In 1859 a Victorian parliamentary inquiry into the conditions of Aborigines posed sixty-nine questions on the nature of Aboriginal law and custom to a panel of experts. Those interested in such matters debated the shape of Indigenous government, particularly whether powers were concentrated in tribal chiefs or dispersed in a network of relationships. 'While most observers believed that authority was exercised the mechanism was difficult to detect.'[11] One respected writer, publishing in 1904 the results of many years' observations, distinguished between the impression gained by 'an ordinary observer'—the apparent absence of 'a recognized form of government'—and the actual state of affairs that only 'intimate acquaintance' with the natives could reveal. 'There must be some authority and restraint behind this seeming freedom', argued A. W. Howitt, 'for it is found that there are well-understood customs, or tribal laws, which are binding on the individual, and which control

---

[9] Cited by R. H. W. Reece, *Aborigines and Colonists* (Sydney, 1974), 119.
[10] *Cooper v. Stuart* (1889), extract from judgment in Bennett and Castles (eds.), *Sourcebook of Australian Legal History*, 288.
[11] Reynolds, *Aboriginal Sovereignty*, 30.

him, and which regulate his actions towards others'.[12] Citing many such attributions of 'government' to Aborigines from the late 1830s onwards, Reynolds concludes that the Privy Council *obiter dicta* in 1889 were inconsistent with an existing body of credible knowledge of Aboriginal ways. The assertion that Aborigines had no law governing their occupation and use of land did not merit becoming the legal doctrine that it became.

To credit Aborigines with their own system of government and law was one thing; to devise practices of colonial government that treated Aborigines as subjects of customary law was quite another. There were at least three reasons why even the most humanitarian colonists could not see Aboriginal subjection to an Indigenous system of law as a basis for continuing to treat them differently.

The first of these was that humanitarian critics of colonial practice perceived the Aboriginal people themselves as being better off in circumstances where authorities took seriously their status as British subjects. As the pastoral frontier expanded and consolidated in New South Wales and Tasmania in the 1820s, public opinion among settlers was deeply divided about frontier violence. Humanitarians insisted that Aborigines, no less than the richest colonist, were subjects of the British Crown, entitled to all its liabilities and protections. In an intensely controversial case in 1838, seven settlers were hanged for killing an Aboriginal child. In 1839, 1840, and 1844, colonists in New South Wales, Western Australia, and South Australia moved (in New South Wales against considerable opposition) to make Aboriginal evidence admissible in court.

Secondly, although a growing scholarly literature attested that Aborigines *were* a people with their own law and government, it was clear to settlers that this did not stop Aborigines from behaving in often violent and frightening ways. In the middle decades of the nineteenth century, a series of massacres of colonists outraged public opinion. To name but three of the more notorious occasions, when Aborigines killed the survivors of the shipwreck *Maria* in 1840; the residents of Hornet Bank homestead in 1857; and those at Cullin-La-Ringo homestead in 1861, they reinforced in the popular mind an image of sub-human savagery. It was difficult in those times to present such incidents as instances of the workings of some effective Aboriginal social order. To the vast majority of settlers these and similar incidents became meaningful in only one way, as proof that the Aboriginal mind was unfathomable and that Aboriginal behaviour was dangerously unpredictable, even to those of long acquaintance.[13]

Thirdly, among most of those who acknowledged the humanity of Aborigines and who looked for something to respect in their ways, the religious dimension of life was of supreme importance. Humanitarian critics of colonial

---

[12] Howitt, cited in Reynolds, *Aboriginal Sovereignty*, 31.

[13] R. Foster, R. Hosking, and A. Nettlebeck, *Fatal Collisions: The South Australian Frontier and the Violence of Memory* (Kent Town, 2001), 13–28; G. Reid, *A Nest of Hornets: The Massacre of the Fraser Family at Hornet Bank Station, Central Queensland 1857 and Related Events* (Melbourne, 1982); R. Evans, 'Across the Queensland Frontier', in B. Attwood and S. G. Foster (eds.), *Frontier Conflict: The Australian Experience* (Canberra, 2003), 63–75.

brutality commonly believed that conversion to Christianity was a prerequisite for Aborigines to acquire civilization.[14] The spiritual depth of the Aborigines' own social order did not become a theme of popular understanding until the second half of the twentieth century, when it came to be celebrated as perhaps the most positive feature of Aboriginal civilization. However, in the nineteenth century Indigenous spirituality was not acknowledged.[15] Missionaries began to evangelize Aborigines in the early 1820s, beginning in New South Wales. They were dismayed by Aborigines' nomadism, which prevented the development of the system, familiar to many missionaries, of instructing large numbers frequently and regularly in one settled place. By 1848 all of the first generation of missions to New South Wales had been abandoned.[16] When they found Aborigines resistant to conversion, missionaries did not infer that a stronger, deeply rooted, native religious system might be thwarting them. Rather they concluded that 'Aborigines who had absorbed undesirable aspects of European civilization were . . . incapable of absorbing Christianity'; they particularly regretted the sexual (mis)behaviour of ungodly colonists and native heathen.[17] Here we find the beginnings of an important theme. Aborigines were thought to be morally and physically vulnerable to unsupervised contact with many aspects of European civilization. If they were to benefit from that contact, they required careful tuition in its demands and temptations.

III

How to govern Aborigines' interaction with European civilization continued to provoke anxiety as more of the continent became colonized. In the early 1920s, the Aboriginal author David Unaipon voiced the widespread opinion that contact with civilization was as likely to corrupt Aborigines as to uplift them. He wrote that 'my race, living under native and tribal conditions, has a very strict and efficacious code of laws that keeps the race pure. It is only when the Aborigines come in contact with white civilisation that they leave their tribal laws, and take nothing in place of these old and well-established customs. It is then that disease and deterioration set in.'[18] This view prompted Aborigines and their supporters among the colonists to advocate that large areas of land not yet settled by Europeans should be proclaimed by governments to be reserves for Aboriginal people. Victoria's 1859 inquiry, with its concern to know more of

[14] J. Woolmington, 'The Civilisation/Christianisation Debate and the Australian Aborigines', *Aboriginal History*, 10: 2 (1986), 90–8.
[15] W. E. H. Stanner, 'Religion, Totemism and Symbolism', in M. Charlesworth *et al.* (eds.), *Religion in Aboriginal Australia* (St Lucia, Qld., 1984), 137–44.
[16] J. Woolmington, ' "Writing on the Sand": The First Missions to Aborigines in Eastern Australia', in T. Swain and D. B. Rose (eds.), *Aboriginal Australians and Christian Missions* (Bedford Park, 1988), 88.
[17] Ibid., 81.
[18] D. Unaipon, *Legendary Tales of the Australian Aborigines* (Carlton South, Vic., 2001), 7.

Aborigines' customary governance, was one of the earliest statements in favour of the 'reserve' as a device of colonial governance.

By the 1920s, large portions of land far from the cities had been declared to be reserves in Queensland, the Northern Territory, South Australia, and Western Australia (and there were smaller portions in Tasmania, Victoria, and New South Wales). Although Christian missionaries were allowed to evangelize in these lands, the reserves implied an official view that there survived an Aboriginal social order whose territorial base should be secured. In 1927 over 7,000 Australians signed a petition urging the Australian government to take this recognition a further step: 'a model Aboriginal State' that would 'be ultimately managed by a native tribunal as far as possible according to their own laws and customs but prohibiting cannibalism and cruel rites'. The Aboriginal state would be closed to 'any persons, other than aborigines, except Federal Government officials and duly authorised missionaries, teachers and agricultural instructors'. The governing tribunal—eventually to be composed of 'natives'—would decide 'the extent to which control shall be exercised over such natives still in their wild conditions as are within the State'. Aborigines were to be granted autonomy, and they would grow into that autonomy through guided reform. The petition mentioned David Unaipon as an example of a 'full-blooded aboriginal' who would be 'competent to assist in founding the proposed State'.[19]

Nevertheless, when the Commonwealth asked Queensland's Chief Protector of Aborigines, J. W. Bleakley, to review its Aboriginal welfare policies in the Northern Territory in 1928, he advised against the model Aboriginal state. He reported that

They have no conception of democracy as understood by civilised nations. Their native laws and customs seem to utterly fail to conceive any idea of combination or federation of tribes for mutual government or protection. Each tribe is a separate and distinct group, with its own language, customs, and laws environing its peculiar totem, and has interest in nothing outside of those associations.[20]

The governing elected tribunal proposed by the petitioners, Bleakley predicted, would never find legitimate foundations in this tribalized polity. These comments ended the Commonwealth's brief flirtation with the proposed 'model Aboriginal State'. Bleakley did not deny that Aborigines had a system of government. His objection was that it was an inappropriate system—tribal and inward-looking rather than democratic and outward-looking. Cherishing democracy and federation as essential features of Australian government, Bleakley assumed that a model Aboriginal state would require a radical reconstruction of Aborigines' 'tribal' political culture—a transition quite beyond Aborigines' capabilities as he estimated them.

[19] M. Roe, 'A Model Aboriginal State', *Aboriginal History*, 10: 1 (1986), 40–4.
[20] Bleakley, quoted in Roe, *Aboriginal History*, 10: 1 (1986), 44.

While the 'model Aboriginal State' was under discussion, Fred Maynard, leader of the Australian Aborigines Progressive Association, was reported to be suggesting that its residents 'be provided with their own communities, with schools and other public buildings, and *should be supervised generally by educated and capable aborigines*'.[21] Such distinctions between 'educated and capable' Aborigines and others who required education were commonly made by the articulate Indigenous critics of Australian colonial rule who emerged in the 1920s. They evoked the possibility of Aboriginal people progressing, under the impact of colonization, from a pre-modern to a modern condition, as long as civilization were competently mediated to those who did not yet have it. These Aboriginal critics complained that the harsh paternalism of the various state governments (including policies that amounted to theft of land and of children) neither acknowledged the existence of this progressive Indigenous movement nor respected those who had benefited from it.

In presenting Aborigines as a distinct people with a capacity for self-government, this emergent Indigenous intelligentsia evoked the strengths and weaknesses of their heritage. Maynard told the Labor premier of New South Wales in 1927 that Aboriginal custom had prefigured the Australian welfare state:

Your present scheme of Old Age Pensions was obtained from our ancient code, as likewise your Child Endowment Scheme and Widow's Pensions. Our divorce laws may yet find a place on the Statute Book. The members of this Board [of the Australian Aboriginal Progressive Association] have also noticed the strenuous efforts of the Trade Union leaders to attain the conditions which existed in our country at the time of invasion by Europeans—the men only worked when necessary—we called no man 'Master' and we had no king.[22]

Maynard's egalitarian version of Aboriginal heritage, in particular his remark on the absence of kings, contrasts with the statement by a man known as Burraga in 1933, when petitioning for Aboriginal representation in federal parliament. 'Before the white man set foot in Australia, my ancestors were as Kings in their own right. And I, Aboriginal chief Burraga, am a direct descendant of the royal line.'[23]

However different their accounts of customary government, these Indigenous critics were united in condemning the Europeans' callous, degrading, and authoritarian practices of government, and their refusal to respect Aborigines who had become modern:

Our people have, however, accepted the modern system of government which has taken the place of our prehistoric methods and have conformed to same reasonably well when the treatment accorded them is fully considered. We are, therefore, striving to obtain full

---

[21] *Sydney Morning Herald*, 15 Nov. 1927, in B. Attwood and A. Markus (eds.), *The Struggle for Aboriginal Rights: A Documentary History* (St Leonards, 1999), 70, emphasis added.

[22] Fred Maynard to J. T. Lang, 3 Oct. 1927, ibid., 68.

[23] Transcript of *Cinesound Review*, 100, 29 Sept. 1933, ibid., 73.

recognition of our citizen rights on terms of absolute equality with all other people in our own land.[24]

Maynard and others suggested that any residual Aboriginal 'backwardness' shamed not Aborigines but the governments who denied them education.

These demands for equality of citizenship, on the basis of Aborigines' achieved or incipient modernity, did not imply an end to all difference. Indigenous political discourse of the 1930s touched frequently on the issue of how to give institutional recognition to the distinct perspectives and needs of Indigenous Australians. Some thought that they should have their own representatives in the federal parliament; others did not.[25] Not all of them thought that Aborigines benefited from living on reserves.[26] Some who appreciated the land security that reserves provided questioned the quality of the officials that administered them. David Unaipon, for example, called for South Australia's reserves to be handed over to humanitarian organizations whose members were 'longer-experienced and more sympathetic than public servants, who have merely had a clerk's training'.[27] Pearl Gibbs called for 'an equal number of Aborigines as whites on the Welfare Board' and for such boards to include personnel from the humanitarian advocacy groups.[28]

This emergent Indigenous intelligentsia demanded not only equal citizenship but also, in some cases, a role within the government of their own people, sometimes in alliance with non-Indigenous humanitarians. Thus, in April 1938 a deputation of twenty Aboriginal people presented the prime minister (Joseph Lyons) with a ten-point 'long range policy for Aborigines'. Its third point requested that a new Department of Aboriginal Affairs be advised by a 'Board, consisting of six persons, three of whom at least should be of Aboriginal blood, to be nominated by the Aborigines Progressive Association'. The policy's eighth point addressed the problem of 'uncivilised and semi-civilised Aborigines':

We suggest that patrol officers, nurses, and teachers, both men and women, of *Aboriginal blood*, should be specially trained by the Commonwealth Government as Aboriginal Officers, to bring the wild people in to contact with civilisation.[29]

Outspoken Aborigines of the 1930s were putting themselves forward as mediators between colonial authority and those 'wild' Indigenous people who were its still problematic subjects.

---

[24] Maynard to Lang, 3 Oct. 1927, Attwood and Markus, *The Struggle for Aboriginal Rights*, 68.
[25] William Ferguson, quoted in *Australian Abo Call*, 1 (April 1938), ibid., 88.   [26] Ibid., 89.
[27] *News* (Adelaide), 3 Nov. 1936, ibid., 114.
[28] Pearl Gibbs, radio broadcast, 8 June 1941, ibid., 97.
[29] *Australian Abo Call*, 1 (April 1938), 'Our Ten Points', ibid., 91, emphasis in original.

IV

In 1925 a Western Australian Aboriginal man, William Harris, rebuked the Opposition leader, Sir James Mitchell, in a letter to the *West Australian*, for making 'misleading and bitter' observations about people of mixed Aboriginal and European descent ('half-castes' in official jargon), such as himself. He protested that his people were

living exactly the same as whites, when possible—by hard work. There is no other way in which they can live. Most of them do contract work: some have farms and are educated, and in that respect they compare more favourably with the class of Indian that come here. Moreover, the aborigines and half-castes are not aliens; they are in their own land and some scientists hold that the aborigines are of the same root stock of the Aryan branch of the human family, and, that given an equal chance, they are mentally, morally, and physically the equals of any other kind of human being.[30]

Like other articulate Indigenous Australians who defended themselves against the intrusive legislation of the 1920s and 1930s, Harris pointed to the distance that the articulate had travelled, from their pre-colonial condition to 'civilization'. His demand to be respected and to be free of government supervision called attention to the economic and social capacities that such people had cultivated on that journey.

  After the Second World War, Australian governments put forward a new philosophy in Aboriginal affairs— namely, assimilation. Whereas the old 'protection' policies of the period 1890s to 1930s had segregated Aborigines and denied their citizenship rights, the new 'assimilation' policy was inclusive: governments would end discrimination against Aboriginal people as they showed themselves to be capable of living as other Australians lived. The most influential promoter of assimilation was Paul Hasluck, a journalist turned public servant who became Minister for Territories in 1951. Hasluck, a Western Australian, had known the Harris family in the 1930s and sympathized with what he understood to be their aspirations. But what was that understanding? In his 1988 memoir, Hasluck has given us a splendid example of how a reforming liberal could construe a protesting Aboriginal voice. Hasluck recalled William Harris as

stirred to protest mainly because some of his own relations, who had a similar capacity to look after themselves and attend the schools as white children, were under risk or had suffered the experience of being grouped with Aborigines on native settlements or of being excluded from the same rights and privileges as the whites. It is an odd turn in historical studies that fifty years later he has been hailed as an early spokesman for Aborigines whereas his main concern was that he and his family should be regarded as fully assimilated members of Australian society and not treated as though they were 'blacks'.[31]

[30] William Harris, letter to the editor, *West Australian*, 25 Sept. 1925, ibid.,118.
[31] P. Hasluck, *Shades of Darkness* (Melbourne, 1988), 19. Readers wishing to assess Hasluck's representation of Harris's views should read documents by Harris, reprinted in Attwood and Markus, *The Struggle for Aboriginal Rights*, 118–27

Harris's critique of the legislative persecution of his people was thus represented by Hasluck as a plea that selected families be exempt from that legislation.

Hasluck's assimilation policy promoted Indigenous Australians' exit from the stigmatized milieu of legally defined Aboriginality—a world of custodial institutions and supervised lives. He postulated the Aborigines' desire, and if not desire then long-term need, to escape, to 'pass over' to the white side, in way of life, outlook, and legal status. Those who displayed solidarity with their Aboriginal milieu dismayed him and sometimes provoked his accusations. For what was there to cling to? In 1988 Hasluck reiterated his 1950s view of what had remained of Aboriginal society and culture when he became minister. 'Here and there throughout the continent there were crumbling groups of Aboriginal people bound together by ancient tradition and kinship living under a fading discipline.'[32] Referring to 'tattered threads of kinship', he affirmed that 'none of these groups could be identified as a society in the same way as the rest of the people of Australia could be identified as a society.' The breakdown of Aboriginal society had been so rapid that it had left individuals 'stranded'.[33] The individual unsupported by custom was, in his opinion, the state's reason to act and also defined the nature of that action: 'the sheltering, protecting, guiding, teaching and helping and eventually, as the final and perhaps most difficult act of native welfare, quietly withdrawing without any proud fuss when the Aboriginal entered the Australian community'.[34] If the state did not offer such unobtrusive nurturance, Hasluck feared, the stranded individual 'might seek his own shelter and protection within a group composed of persons like himself and these groups had a tendency to harden and become less penetrable than the individual'.[35] Hasluck worried that settlements and missions might abet this 'hardening' of the group, thereby becoming ghettos where stranded individuals would shelter, instead of stepping out into the promise of the wider Australian society. In Hasluck's scenario, the most intimate associations among Aboriginal people, the persistence of custom and language, the obligations to relatives, even the bond between mother and child in many cases, were constraints on individuals' development.

Within the mire of custom and circumstance, Hasluck could discern the raw material on which the state's rehabilitative work could rest. 'More and more we will have to think in our native welfare administration of individual persons of Aboriginal descent. The behaviour of the individual, the response of the individual, the aspiration or the effort of the individual, the heart and mind of the individual person are at the core of our problem.'[36] The tenacity of the bonds between Aboriginal people thus perplexed him. In 1988, he recalled, self-critically, that 'we did not see clearly the ways in which the individual is bound by membership of a family or a group.'[37] He had found it difficult, he later admitted, to evaluate the basis of the attachment of individuals to their

---

[32] Hasluck, *Shades of Darkness*, 131.   [33] Ibid., 131.   [34] Ibid., 131.
[35] Ibid., 131–2.   [36] Ibid., 133.   [37] Ibid., 130.

Aboriginal associates. 'We see some odd things happening', he once remarked, 'and it may be hard to disentangle the real from the spurious.'[38] He described his policy's ethical dilemma: 'Just as an individual should not be forcibly held inside a group, so a group should not be broken up into a number of individuals while it still has cohesion as a group.'[39]

Hasluck's public discussions of assimilation thus evoked cultural change in contrasting ways. On the one hand, the evident decay of Aboriginal social life warranted 'welfare' intervention, by state and church, in order to facilitate the changes in Aboriginal individuals and families; on the other hand, the survival of certain forms of Indigenous communality made such interventions difficult and ethically questionable. Decay/survival, malleability/autonomy—these were the inescapable dichotomies of Hasluck's evocations of Indigenous sociality in the post-war era.

By 1970, policy-oriented intellectuals—influenced by anthropological and Aboriginal critics of government practices—were beginning to agree that the communal traditions of Aborigines were more resilient and more constructive than Hasluck had at first thought. One of the architects of a new approach was Charles Rowley, whose views on Aboriginal affairs were shaped by his long association with Australian policy in Papua New Guinea. There the Commonwealth government saw native society as resilient and adaptive, not fragile and inhibiting. Australian policy idealized the Melanesian village and feared the detachment of individuals from its communal life. The government had encouraged Melanesians to form village-based commercial co-operatives and councils with delegated powers. Rowley drew on this policy tradition when he argued against the insistent individualism of policy towards Aborigines:

The aim of 'assimilation' has been to winkle out the deviant individual from the group, to persuade him to cut the ties which bind him and his family to it, and to set him up as a householder in the street of the country town. But policies which aim to change social habit by educating individuals, while ignoring the social context which has made him what he is, can have only limited success. A program involving social change must deal with the social group.[40]

Rowley suggested that governments encourage Aboriginal people to form local councils and corporations. Taking up this idea in 1971, the Council for Aboriginal Affairs (a panel of non-Indigenous advisers) pointed to the possible *continuity* between Indigenous traditions of communality and emergent formal modes of indigenous association. 'Often when corporate action has been successful the element of traditional continuity has been important. To regard such continuity as always working against adaptation is mistaken. Often the breach of this continuity has led to demoralisation and disintegration'.[41]

---

[38] Ibid., 132.   [39] Ibid., 120.
[40] C. D. Rowley, *Outcast in White Australia* (Canberra, 1971), 417.
[41] Council for Aboriginal Affairs, cited in T. Rowse, *Obliged to be Difficult: Nugget Coombs' Legacy in Indigenous Affairs* (Melbourne, 2000), 132.

Such thinking bore fruit in the Fraser government's Aboriginal Councils and Associations Act of 1976. Minister Ian Viner argued that

What is so important about this measure is that it will recognise cultural differences between Aboriginal and non-Aboriginal societies and enable Aboriginal communities to develop legally recognisable bodies which reflect their own culture and do not require them to subjugate this culture to overriding Western legal concepts.[42]

The High Court's decisions in the Mabo (1992) and Wik (1996) cases marked the climax of the Australian state's post-1970 trend towards recognizing and affirming the customary communality of Indigenous Australia. In those decisions, the High Court recognized Indigenous Australian customary law as a source of Australian law. The court postulated the common law notion of 'native title', declaring that native title rights continued to run in Australia except where they had been lawfully extinguished by a Crown grant of title.

Both the Australian Commonwealth and its constituent states have codified 'native title' in their own statutes in order to regulate the rights of native title holders and others, in respect to any land on which native title survives. Critical legal theorists, such as Canadian Jeremy Webber, have protested against the narrowing of 'native title' to a mere property right. 'Native title', they argue, implies that the British proclamation of sovereignty did not extinguish totally 'the autonomous legal orders from which indigenous title derives'; it should thus provoke governments 'to structure the indigenous/non-indigenous boundary'.[43] Webber also seeks 'recognition of the intersocietal and constitutional dimensions inherent in that title'.[44] Legislation and its interpretation should take up the Mabo judgment's challenge to respect Indigenous Australians 'not merely as individual or familial proprietors, but as members of societies with their own law, their own cultures and institutions, their own patterns of social order, and their own conceptions of land use and landholding'.[45]

So far, Australian political and legal institutions have shown little interest in such a paradigm change. Frank Brennan has pointed to the liberal bases of their continuity with pre-Mabo conceptions of law. In Brennan's view 'from 1788 to 1986, there has been a gradual change to the font of sovereignty from the Crown to the people'. Accordingly,

Aboriginal attempts to expand the effect of the Mabo decisions such that the common law as declared by the High Court would include recognition of Aboriginal law other than the law relating to land are not likely to succeed. The obstacle will be the court's regard for the sovereign power of governments and parliaments.

---

[42] R. L. Viner, *Commonwealth Parliamentary Debates*, vol. 99, 2946–7.

[43] Jeremy Webber, 'Beyond Regret: Mabo's Implications for Australian Constitutionalism', in D. Ivison, P. Patton, and W. Sanders (eds.), *Political Theory and the Rights of Indigenous Peoples* (Melbourne, 2000), 60–88, 73.

[44] Ibid., 83.   [45] Ibid.

In addition,

> The principle of non-discrimination will necessitate a recognition that laws affecting citizens' activities and which make no reference to Aborigines apply to them as to any other citizens. In every instance the statutory law would cover the field and extinguish any previously operative customary law. Customary law in the fields of criminal law, family law and contract law will require statutory recognition or at least some legislative directive to the judiciary to accommodate such law or its underlying principles.[46]

If the discretion exercised by law-makers and judges is to favour the course urged by Webber, then their opinions about the persistence and content of Indigenous custom will matter.

V

It has greatly affected the recent politics of representing the Indigenous social order that Indigenous intellectuals of the 1990s, like those of the 1930s, have been prepared to acknowledge that Indigenous custom includes at least some beliefs and behaviours that Indigenous Australians should be pleased to leave behind them. The 1930s Indigenous leaders confidently contrasted their modern selves with those Aborigines in some regions who were still less than modern; there was now an opportunity for more civilized Aborigines to guide the less civilized Aborigines to modernity. In the late 1990s, there emerged a new language for making distinctions among Indigenous Australians, a language drawing less on evolutionary historicism (primitive/modern) and more on a sociology of individual well-being and social pathology.

Since the 1970s, because of changes in the ways that the Australian Census and other administrative data have been collected and presented, it has been possible to compare systematically the well-being of Indigenous Australians with 'all Australians' (the latter registering very high on international comparisons of well-being). By all conventional indices—such as employment status, income, education, mortality and morbidity rates—Indigenous Australians are less well off than other Australians. In 1991 the report of a Royal Commission (into Aboriginal deaths in custody) added to the currency and authority of this story of persistent Indigenous disadvantage; it also suggested that mechanisms within the Indigenous domain (and within Indigenous individuals) were exacerbating Indigenous hardship. Many studies show that the proximate causes of some Aboriginal deaths and hospital admissions were actions of Aborigines themselves: family violence, self-mutilation, suicide. No one disputed that alcohol abuse was a massive contributing factor, not only to violence but also to poor school attendance and to absence from the labour force. The complex

---

[46] F. Brennan, '*Mabo* and its Ramifications for the Future of Indigenous Australians', in E. Johnston, M. Hinton, and D. Rigney (eds.), *Indigenous Australians and the Law* (Sydney, 1997), 167–82, 171.

business of explaining and attributing responsibility thus began to include a reconsideration of what was required of Indigenous Australians if they were to live up to the promise of 'self-determination'.

In 1997 one Indigenous champion of his people's rights, the young Indigenous historian and lawyer Noel Pearson, commented on the Howard government's substitution of Indigenous 'self-empowerment' for Indigenous 'self-determination'. The government 'cannot deny our right to self-determination. But the concept of empowerment gives a refreshing emphasis to the fact that as bad as our situation is and as poverty-stricken and disadvantaged as the great majority of our people are, we have to engage in the solutions. We cannot just be passengers. We cannot just sit back.' Adding that 'self-determination is hard work', Pearson regretted that it was the government, not Aboriginal people, who had put forward 'self-empowerment' as a new theme for action. 'We should be the ones realising that we have to do it ourselves, and promoting this idea among our peoples.'[47] In a series of widely reported addresses, Pearson soon began to elaborate his theme that Aborigines should become more willing and able to 'do it ourselves'. His book *Our Right to Take Responsibility* (2000) offers a historical and sociological account of his people's degenerating capacity for collective action.

'Aboriginal society in Cape York Peninsula today is not a successful society', Pearson declares.[48] He argues that his people, particularly those in Cape York, have been 'poisoned' since about 1970 by their access to cash welfare benefits and to welfare programmes in kind. He insists that 'we have . . . *a right to an economy*'.[49] His concept of 'economy' is moral, flowing from his judgement about what is good in human relationships. The 'real economy' is defined by institutionalizing 'reciprocity'. Reciprocity, a traditional Aboriginal value, has been undermined by too easy access to welfare benefits. People who receive welfare are not required to do anything in return; they thus get used to being passive and without power. Indeed, they become self-righteous about what they see as their entitlement to receive without reciprocity. Those who administer Aborigines' welfare arrangements tend to support this conception of the recipients' rights. They also assume that the recipients lack the capacity to act. Thus donors and receivers are locked in a shared self-perpetuating mentality. The ethical shortcomings of the new welfare-based economy—not just the longer standing phenomena of racism and associated psychological trauma—make Cape York people what they are now. 'Children who have grown up in this passive welfare economy have little understanding of and have never experienced life in the real economy. Values, expectations and aspirations are limited in this artificial context.'[50]

In his emphasis on widespread Indigenous social pathology and on individual responsibility to recover from it, Pearson might seem to be recapitulating

[47] *Courier Mail*, 6 Feb. 1997.
[48] N. Pearson, *Our Right to Take Responsibility* (Cairns, 2000), 15.
[49] Ibid., 94, emphasis in original.   [50] Ibid., 30.

Hasluck's individualist liberalism. However, there is an important difference between Hasluck and Pearson. Pearson seeks an institutional framework in which Indigenous and non-Indigenous social orders will coexist, for Indigenous Australia (in Cape York at least) remains in his view a viable enclave. This raises the issue of the quality of Indigenous leaders, the mediators between state support and its Indigenous recipients. Pearson lists fundamental values—'unity, co-operation, respecting rights, sharing power, taking responsibility, encouraging others, supporting each other'—and he asserts that 'the promotion of these values throughout the community is the particular responsibility of leaders'.[51] 'We need a leadership that fosters the social support of individuals and which underlines the importance of individual engagement for success', he writes.[52] People will resist taking more responsibility, he anticipates, but good leaders can overcome this resistance (which he calls 'going against the instincts of many members of our community') without 'dictating' to people that they must change.[53] He remarks that 'there has to be a healthy tension between leadership (by community leaders and by family leaders) and individuals in working out what acts of reciprocity will be expected in return for these programmes'.[54] For some recipients of welfare, the first step towards recovery will simply be to take responsibility for those aspects of their health that lie within their control, such as ceasing substance and alcohol abuse. Another step will be to engage in 'education and self-improvement'. Yet another requirement is to be more considerate of the welfare of family members, especially the old and the young. Finally, people will be asked, in ways Pearson does not specify, 'to contribute to the community at large'.[55] In Pearson's view, it would be difficult for governments to oblige Indigenous Australians to take such improving actions as official bodies are not recognized by these welfare recipients as having moral authority. They are too remote, they are not transparent, and the memory of unjust treatment at the hands of government is too fresh in Indigenous Australians' minds. For reciprocity to enter into the welfare recipients' moral framework, '*it must be defined and imposed by the Aboriginal people of Cape York Peninsula and their leaders, possibly in partnership with government*'.[56]

Thus Pearson's position harks back not to Hasluck's liberalism but to those Indigenous leaders of the 1930s who put themselves forward as mediators between imposed European civilization and the as yet untutored 'wild' Aborigines of the Australian hinterlands. The Indigenous hinterland that Pearson would mediate, as a regional leader promoting the recovery of Aborigines' 'reciprocity', is defined, however, in different terms. The language of 'civilized' and 'primitive' has been replaced by the terms of the communitarian critique of the welfare state.

[51] Ibid., 59. [52] Ibid., 58. [53] Ibid. [54] Ibid., 84. [55] Ibid., 86.
[56] Ibid., 87, emphasis added.

Bibliography and Further Reading

Because the range of historical themes and contexts addressed in this book is very broad, a full-scale bibliography would be impracticable. Readers are referred to footnotes where source materials, both printed and archival, are cited in detail. The following highly selective list relates only to works that specifically address the history of civil society or its conceptual meaning, and have been found useful, suggestive, or contentious by the authors of this collection of studies.

Bermeo, N., and Nord, P., *Civil Society before Democracy: Lessons from Nineteenth-century Europe* (Lanham, Md: Rowman and Littlefield, 2000).

Black, A., *Guilds and Civil Society in European Political Thought from the Twelfth Century to the Present* (London: Methuen, 1984).

Cohen, J. L., and Arato, A., *Civil Society and Political Theory* (Cambridge, Mass.: MIT Press, 1992).

Dahrendorf, R., *Society and Democracy in Germany* (Munich, 1965, English trans. by the author, London: Weidenfeld and Nicolson, 1968).

—— *After 1989: Morals, Revolution and Civil Society* (Basingstoke: Macmillan, 1997).

Ehrenberg, J., *Civil Society: The Critical History of an Idea* (New York: New York University Press, 1999).

Figgis, J. N., *Studies of Political Thought from Gerson to Grotius* (Cambridge: Cambridge University Press, 1907).

—— *Churches in the Modern State* (London: Longmans, Green, 1914 edn.).

Garrard, J., *Democratisation in Britain. Elites, Civil Society, and Reform in Britain Since 1800* (Basingstoke: Palgrave, 2002).

Gellner, E., *Conditions of Liberty: Civil Society and its Rivals* (London: Hamish Hamilton, 1994).

—— 'Civil Society in Historical Context', *International Social Science Journal*, 43: 3 (1991).

Gierke, O., *Political Theories of the Middle Age* , trans. F. W. Maitland (Cambridge: Cambridge University Press, 1900).

Glasius, M., Kaldor, M., and Anheier, H. (eds.), *Global Civil Society* (Oxford: Oxford University Press, 2002).

Green, D. G., *Civil Society. The Guiding Philosophy and Research Agenda of the Institute for the Study of Civil Society* (London: Institute for the Study of Civil Society, 2000).

Habermas, J., *The Structural Transformation of the Public Sphere* (Berlin, 1962), trans. T. Burger and F. Lawrence (Cambridge: Polity, 1989).

Hall, J. A. (ed.), *Civil Society. Theory, History, Comparison* (Cambridge: Polity, 1995).

Janoski, T., *Citizenship and Civil Society: A Framework of Rights and Obligations in Liberal, Traditional, and Social Democratic Regimes* (Cambridge: Cambridge University Press, 1998).

Joyce, P., *The Social in Question: New Bearings in History and the Social Sciences* (London: Routledge, 2002).

Kaviraj, S., and Khilnani, S., *Civil Society: History and Possibilities* (Cambridge: Cambridge University Press, 2001).

Keane, J. (ed.), *Civil Society and the State: New European Perspectives* (London: Verso, 1998).

Kumar, K., 'Civil Society: An Inquiry into the Usefulness of an Historical Term', *British Journal of Sociology*, 44: 3 (1993).

MacCarthy, K., *Women, Philanthropy and Civil Society* (Bloomington, Ind., 2001).

Morris, S., *Defining the Non-profit Sector: Some Lessons from History*. Working paper, 3 (London: Centre for Civil Society, London School of Economics, 2000).

Trentmann, F. (ed.), *Paradoxes of Civil Society: New Perspectives on Modern German and British History* (Oxford: Bergahn, 2000).

Urban History, 23: 3 (1998), special issue 'Civil Society in Britain'.

Walzer, M. (ed.), *Towards a Global Civil Society* (Oxford: Bergahn, 1995).

Index